Consumer Reports

ELECTRONICS

BUYING GUIDE 2007

Today's
Best Buys in...

▶▶ **LAPTOP COMPUTERS**

▶▶ **DIGITAL CAMERAS & CAMCORDERS**

▶▶ **VIDEO & AUDIO GEAR**

▶▶ **CELL PHONES & MORE**

THE EDITORS OF CONSUMER REPORTS

PUBLISHED BY CONSUMER REPORTS ▶ A DIVISION OF CONSUMERS UNION ▶ YONKERS, NY

ELECTRONICS
BUYING GUIDE

CONSUMER REPORTS PUBLICATIONS DEVELOPMENT

Editor-in Chief, Print Publications	Margot Slade
Editor	David Schiff
Contributing Editor	Steve Ditlea
Contributing Writers	John Blackford, Steven Schwartz
Manager, Content Resource Scheduling	Nancy Crowfoot
Coordinating Editor	Robin Melén
Coordinating Editor, Master Content	Merideth Mergel
Design Manager	Rosemary Simmons
Art Director	Joseph Ulatowski
Contributing Art Director	Virginia Rubel
Technology Specialist	Jennifer Dixon
Production Associate	William Breglio
Editorial Assistant	Joan Daviet
Retail Sales and Marketing Director	Tracy Bowen
Product Manager, CR Publications Development	Carolyn Cicale
Manufacturing/Distribution	Mark Yatarola

CR ELECTRONICS STAFF

EDITORIAL DIVISION

Editor	Paul Reynolds
Deputy Editor	Eileen McCooey
Technology Editor	Jeff Fox
Associate Editors	Michael Gikas, Donna Tapellini
Editor-at-Large	Greg Daugherty
Web Senior Editor	Paul Eng

TECHNICAL DIVISION

Senior Director of Testing	Evon Beckford
Managers	Gerard Catapano, James Langehennig
Program Leaders	Dean Gallea, Richard Sulin
Senior Project Leaders	Christopher Bucsko, Richard Fisco, Joseph Lazzaro, Maurice Wynn
Project Leaders	Kerry Allen, Claudio Ciacci, Charles Davidman, Aaron Fournier, Ernst St. Louis
Assistant Project Leaders	Susan Daino, Chris Lam, Thomas Maung, Artur Pietruch
Technicians	Chris Andrade, Elias Arias, Isabella Bucci, Larry Greene, Maria Grimaldi, Rich Hammond, Miguel Rivera, Caroline Somera, William South, Rachelle Stern, David Toner

CONSUMER REPORTS/CONSUMERS UNION

President	James Guest
Senior Vice President for Information Products	John J. Sateja
Vice President and Editorial Director	Kevin McKean
Vice President and Technical Director	Jeffrey A. Asher
Vice President for External Affairs and Information Services	Chris Meyer

First printing, September 2005
Copyright © 2006 by Consumers Union of United States, Inc., Yonkers, New York 10703.
Published by Consumers Union of United States, Inc., Yonkers, New York 10703.
All rights reserved, including the right of reproduction in whole or in part in any form.
ISBN-13: 978-1-933524-00-9
ISBN-10: 1-933524-00-6

Manufactured in the United States of America.

CONTENTS

Our tips can help you get the best deal, p. 13

Digital cameras, p. 48

Televisions, p. 62

Cell phones, p. 31

CONTENTS

CHAPTER 05 |
VIDEO & AUDIO GEAR

MP3 players, p. 110

CHAPTER 06 | COMPUTERS & PERIPHERALS

RATINGS & REFERENCE

Speakers, p. 107

PDAs, p. 144

Printers, p. 131

CHOOSING THE BEST ELECTRONICS PRODUCTS WITH THIS GUIDE

Shopping for electronics gear can seem daunting, but it doesn't have to be. There's plenty of help right here, as CONSUMER REPORTS shows you how to make the best buying decisions—even if you don't have the time or inclination to keep up with fast-evolving technologies and rapidly-adopted new products.

If you're still watching that squarish TV and listening to music on a portable CD player, you may be surprised to learn that HDTV sales are on track to surpass those of conventional analog sets in 2006 and that more than 27 million MP3 music players are expected to be produced this year for the U.S. market. Such sales trends demonstrate the appeal of new communications and entertainment products. Consumer electronics have become truly ubiquitous in most American homes, representing a significant amount of discretionary spending. According to the Consumer Electronics Association, a trade organization of makers of such gear, the average U.S. household now owns

26 consumer electronics products and spent an average of $1200 on them in the last 12 months.

As digital technology advances, improvements in performance and convenience, along with dropping prices, are fueling consumer interest across a wide range of products. Results of a recent CONSUMER REPORTS survey of its print and online readers indicate that, of those who made electronics purchases in the previous 12 months, well over half bought cell phones, close to half purchased a digital camera, and just under one in three picked up a new TV.

With the proliferation of consumer electronics gear has come an expansion of features, options, and technical jargon. Reflecting readers' desire for more guidance and testing, for the first time CONSUMER REPORTS magazine will feature consumer electronics on half of its monthly covers in 2006.

Results of the testing and reporting that go into our ongoing consumer electronics coverage are also available in this book.

The proliferation of models in today's superstores and big-box electronics showrooms can make shopping for new electronics gear seem daunting.

USING THIS GUIDE

This CONSUMER REPORTS Electronics Buying Guide 2007 edition will help you take advantage of product trends in the months between back to school and "Auld Lang Syne," the time of year when most electronics are sold. Here you'll find the essential information you'll need to buy a new cell phone, digital camera, television, video or audio gear, or computer.

When considering a purchase in a product category, you can begin with First Things First, a handy summary of product types. Featured articles and brief sidebars fill you in on important buying considerations. Then turn to the back of the book and consult the ratings, charts and summaries of CONSUMER REPORTS' product testing. Ratings are current as this book goes to press.

For the most up-to-date ratings, you can access CONSUMER REPORTS online. The inside front cover of this book provides information on how to activate a free, 30-day trial subscription to *www.ConsumerReports.org.* (You will be asked for a credit card to secure your 30-day trial.)

And before your next electronics purchase, be sure to read the shopping tips, repair-or-replace basics, and recycling update in Chapter 1.

This guide should help you sort through all the choices and ensure that the next electronics purchase you make will turn out to be exactly what you needed and wanted when you get it home.

HOW CR TESTS

Equipment rated in this book is tested at CONSUMER REPORTS' labs in Yonkers, N.Y. The products are bought at retail, just as a consumer would acquire them. Our shoppers buy specific models based on which are top sellers or innovative designs.

CONSUMER REPORTS' tests are rigorous and objective, using constantly refined procedures. In the case of home computers, for example, benchmarks are used to assess how quickly machines can simultaneously run a number of applications, including a word processor, a spreadsheet, and a Web browser.

Much of the work done in the computer labs mimics the way a piece of equipment would be used in your home. Engineers read the owner's manual, try out all the switches, and experiment with the features. They try to answer likely consumer questions: How easy is the system to set up? Can components be replaced with industry standard parts? Are the manuals comprehensive and easy to read? If the computer is marketed for game devotees, how smooth is its 3D graphics capability?

To find the best printers, testers compare text, photos, and graphics, and they gauge the printers' speeds. To assess the image clarity of monitors, engineers do side-by-side comparisons. The quality of digital cameras, scanners, and other imaging equipment is assessed by comparing images created using the product. For instance, engineers inspect glossy 8x10-inch prints created by each digital camera tested, using its best-photo mode. They use the model's supplied software and output all prints to the same photo printer.

For every piece of equipment, testers carefully assess features—do they add to usability or just make an item more complicated? They check ergonomic functions—how does the camera feel in the hand?—and assess battery life.

After all these tests, our engineers analyze the data and results to arrive at the comprehensive Ratings that are published in CONSUMER REPORTS magazine, on *www.ConsumerReports.org.,* and in this book.

Some of the products tested and reviewed here were already being replaced by new models as this book was going to press in the summer of 2006. CONSUMER REPORTS tests many of these products throughout the year, however. Look for the latest test results in monthly issues of CONSUMER REPORTS. And don't forget to see the inside front cover of this book for a free, 30-day trial subscription to *www.ConsumerReports.org.*

At left, our experts look for subtle differences among TVs. At right, an engineer assesses camcorder quality.

GET THE MOST FOR YOUR MONEY

CHAPTER

01

▶▶ There's more to a great deal than the lowest price. You want to make sure your purchase will give you years of trouble-free service.

Ratings: Electronics stores: Internet, p. 10; brick-and-mortar, p. 11

FOLLOW SHOPPING TIPS FOR BEST DIGITAL DEALS

Online retailers do the best job of satisfying their customers

Before you buy, know the store's return policy. It can be a deciding factor.

Electronics are sold practically everywhere these days, from big stationery stores such as Office Depot, OfficeMax, and Staples to mass merchandisers such as BJ's Wholesale, Costco, Sam's Club, and Target. That omnipresence might lull you into thinking it doesn't matter where you buy that digital camera, DVD player, or TV. But don't be fooled: All electronics stores are not created equal.

In fact, retailing powerhouses Best Buy, Circuit City, and Wal-Mart, where much of America shops for electronics, rated only average to below average on price, selection, and service in a June 2005 survey of more than 18,700 CONSUMER REPORTS readers who had purchased an electronics product in the previous 16 months.

So where should you buy that digital camera or personal digital assistant? According to our survey, many online retailers, local independent merchants, specialty superstores, and warehouse chains offer higher levels of customer satisfaction overall. Our survey also found that:

▶ The five Internet retailers at the top of our online store ratings did a better job satisfying customers than most of the brick-and-mortar electronics sellers we rated. Crutchfield, a catalog and Web site that had the best online information and navigability and a great selection, received an exceptionally high score. Two online retailers, Amazon.com and JR.com, offered the holy grail of shopping: low prices and a wide selection.

▶ Local independent stores beat most big electronics chains, warehouse clubs, and mass merchandisers on overall satisfaction. Their prices and selection were only average, but they received top marks for service.

▶ You should expect some trade-offs if you plan to purchase from a traditional brick-and-mortar retailer. None of the stores in our survey offered low prices, a big selection, and great service. For example, warehouse clubs like BJ's Wholesale offered low prices but had subpar selection and

Brick-and-mortar retailers offer hands-on access to electronics, so you can test out what you're buying.

service. Ritz Camera scored tops in selection and service but worst in price.

▸ Among retailers operating both a Web site and a walk-in store, respondents tended to give higher scores to the Web sites.

The Internet has emerged as a powerful tool for consumers in today's electronics marketplace. Not only do online stores provide instant access to lower prices, but they're also good sources for technical specifications, descriptions of model-specific features, and other useful information.

What's more, you can use other Web sites to make the task of culling through all that data a lot easier. "Shopping bots," such as BizRate.com, are sophisticated, specialized search engines that let you compare product features and prices from a wide swath of online retailers. Some bots also furnish you with consumer reviews of products and/or retailers. Other popular shopping bots are mySimon, PriceGrabber.com, PriceScan.com, Shopping.com, and Yahoo Shopping (*shopping.yahoo.com*).

Although most consumers still use the Web primarily as a research tool before heading out to make their purchases at walk-in stores, an ever-increasing number of them are buying products online. The market-research firm Forrester Research in Cambridge, Mass., predicts U.S. online retail sales will total nearly $211 billion in 2006, a $35 billion increase from $176 billion in 2005.

Back in the brick-and-mortar world, specialty superstores, which became "the place" to purchase electronics in the 1980s and 1990s with their sweeping product selections and knowledgeable salespeople, are facing increased competition from mass merchandisers like BJ's Wholesale, Costco, and Target, where low price trumps service. Brand loyalty, too, is playing a less critical role in purchase decisions, as advances in production allow small manufacturers to churn out low-priced copies of commodity products (which helps explain why the best-selling brand of DVD players is CyberHome, a name unfamiliar to most people).

All of this can present potential opportunities or problems for consumers who must navigate a shifting retail landscape that typically offers a choice between service and selection on one side and low prices and inexperienced salespeople on the other. Complicating things further, brick-and-mortar retailers compete with each other as well as with virtual storefronts on the Internet. The following advice will help you find the best deals with

A CONSUMER REPORTS reporter shopped for a digital camera on the Internet and in stores—11 retailers in all. He found the best deal online, saving $30.

the greatest efficiency. Our Ratings of Internet electronics and brick-and-mortar retailers appear on pages 10 and 11.

RESEARCH PRODUCTS, THEN SHOP FOR PRICE

Thanks to today's rapid technological advances, many electronics items are on the shelf for only a short time before being replaced by updated models. This makes it tougher for consumers to shop for electronics than for other types of products, according to Retail Forward, an Ohio-based market-research firm. But if you hope to find a salesperson to bring you up to speed, you'll probably be out of luck at Target, Wal-Mart, and other mass merchandisers with poorly trained, bare-bones sales staff. Seventeen percent of our survey respondents said they had trouble finding sales help, and nearly 80 percent barely relied on salespeople or did not rely on them at all.

That's why it's essential to familiarize yourself with that camcorder or PDA before you think about reaching for your credit card. You can readily find the information you need on the Internet, in magazines and newspapers, and by phoning local retailers and manufacturer help lines. In fact, manufacturer Web sites are among the best sources of product details (such as specifications, accessories, and user manuals).

In the course of your research, you might discover

that the model you've been seeking has reached the end of its product life and has been replaced by the next model in the series, say, the X7 instead of the X6. Compare the features, and price-shop for the new model online. The odds are good it will have more power, more features, or other improvements for a slightly higher—or maybe even lower—price.

When you're satisfied that you have enough information, narrow your prospects to three or four finalists. Write down the brand, the model name or number, and must-have features for each choice. Once you know which models meet your criteria, shop around for the best price. (Low price was our survey respondents' top consideration in choosing a retailer.)

More than half of all purchases by our survey respondents involved browsing first at three to six walk-in and online retailers. But before you plan that trip to the mall to start comparison shopping, it's a good idea to call ahead to find out which stores in your area carry the models you're considering. Most stores don't stock every brand or even every model in a supplier's line. While you're on the phone, be sure to ask for the price, too. But don't be surprised if all the retailers quote you the same minimum advertised price (MAP), and offer the same manufacturer rebates.

NAIL THE BEST DEAL

In addition to calling several local retailers and visiting a few online stores, you may want to look at advertisements from independent electronics dealers in specialty audio, video, and photogra-

---

CR Quick Recommendations

Electronics stores

As a group, Internet retailers had higher overall satisfaction ratings than walk-in stores. But expect trade-offs. Only a few Internet outlets received top scores for price and product selection. No walk-in store scored highly on price, selection, and service. The **Ratings** list stores by overall satisfaction among survey respondents. **Quick Picks** includes venues that scored well for specific attributes.

QUICK PICKS
For the best combination of price and selection:

- 2 **Amazon.com**
- 4 **JR.com**

Amazon.com had better information about its electronics offerings, though respondents were happier with the quality of products they bought at JR.com.

When low price matters most:

- 2 **Amazon.com**
- 3 **Costco.com**
- 4 **JR.com**
- 12 **Costco**
- 14 **BJ's Wholesale**

At Costco and BJ's, remember to factor in membership fees. Costco.com and Costco had the best return policies of all the retailers in our survey.

For top service with the fewest compromises:

- 9 **Local independent store**
- 10 **Tweeter Home Entertainment**
- 11 **Ritz Camera** (cameras only)

These stores also rated high for speedy checkout service.

For top satisfaction and product information online:

- 1 **Crutchfield**

Ratings Internet electronics stores

Better ◄——— Worse

In order of reader score.

Key no.	Web site	Reader score	Price	Product selection	Product quality	Info quality	Ease of use	Return policy (in days)
		0 100						
1	Crutchfield.com	94	○	◒	◒	●	◒	30
2	Amazon.com	92	◒	◒	○	◒	○	30; large TVs can't be returned
3	Costco.com	91	◒	●	○	○	○	Unlimited ⊡
4	J&R.com	91	◒	◒	◒	○	○	30
5	Buy.com	89	◒	◒	○	○	○	30; TVs can't be returned
6	Dell.com	85	○	◔	○	○	○	21
7	CircuitCity.com	85	○	○	○	○	○	14-30
8	BestBuy.com	82	○	○	○	○	◔	14-30

⊡ Computers, 6 months.

phy magazines. If you do, you'll probably see the phrase "call for price" in some ads where you'd normally expect to see a price listed.

Such notations indicate that the retailer has accepted advertising dollars from the manufacturer in exchange for agreeing not to advertise below the MAP. They can sell for less than the MAP, and will quote the lower price over the phone, but they can't advertise it in print. Call for the models you're interested in to check for the lowest price you can get, but be sure to factor in shipping costs. Note, too, that any low prices you're given might include a mail-in rebate you will need to submit.

You're also bound to see "super sale" offers in your local newspaper and in direct-mail catalogs. These are designed to generate traffic for local stores and chains. They are worth looking over in case the model you want is on sale, but keep in mind that these fleeting deals do not constitute serious price shopping.

As you head into the homestretch, you'll need to decide whether to purchase the product from an online seller or a traditional retailer. Remember

Ratings electronics stores

Better ◀————▶ Worse

In order of reader score.

Key no.	Retailer	Reader score (0–100)	Price	Product selection	Product quality	Service	Checkout speed	Return policy (in days)
9	Local independent store	89	○	○	○	●	●	Varies
10	Tweeter Home Entertainment	88	○	◐	○	●	●	None for cameras, camcorders, PDAs
11	Ritz Camera	87	●	◐	◐	●	●	10 for digital & video
12	Costco	85	◐	●	○	●	●	Unlimited ⊡
13	Ultimate Electronics	85	◑	◐	○	●	○	30
14	BJ's Wholesale	84	◐	●	○	●	●	30
15	Staples	84	○	◑	○	○	◑	14
16	Good Guys	83	◑	○	○	◐	○	30
17	Sears	83	○	◑	○	○	○	30
18	RadioShack	83	○	●	●	●	◑	30
19	Office Depot	82	○	●	○	○	○	14
20	Target	82	○	●	◑	●	○	90
21	OfficeMax	81	○	●	○	○	○	14
22	Sam's Club	81	◑	●	◑	●	●	90
23	H.H. Gregg	81	○	○	○	●	○	10
24	Circuit City	80	◑	○	○	○	○	14-21
25	Best Buy	78	◑	○	○	○	◑	14-30
26	Wal-Mart	77	○	●	●	●	●	15-90
27	Fry's Electronics	77	○	○	○	●	●	15-30
28	CompUSA	76	◑	○	○	○	○	21

⊡ Computers, 6 months.

Guide to the Ratings

Based on a survey by the Consumer Reports National Research Center on 23,000 purchases made by 18,700 readers from 2004-2005. The **Reader score** is based on the respondent's satisfaction with their shopping experience. A score of 100 would mean that all respondents were completely satisfied; 80 would mean very satisfied, on average; 60, fairly well satisfied. Differences of fewer than 5 points are not meaningful. Scores for other listed attributes reflect the percentage who rated the chain as excellent or very good on each item. Higher scores mean the chain was rated more favorably compared with the mean score; lower scores mean it was rated less favorably. Note that our readers may not be representative of the U.S. population.

Online prices are often the cheapest, but don't forget to factor in shipping and handling costs. Also make sure you know if you are buying a refurbished item.

that brick-and-mortar stores won't compete with the lower prices available online, although Circuit City stores will match the prices offered by CircuitCity.com, which you can search right on the sales floor. In fact, many specialty stores, mass retailers, and warehouse clubs won't negotiate on price at all, or even consider time-honored haggler's requests, like discounts on accessories purchased with a main item. But some smaller regional retailers, such as H.H. Gregg, will, says Geoff Wissman, a vice president specializing in consumer products at Retail Forward.

If you're considering an online purchase, don't forget to factor in the shipping and handling costs of buying or returning an item, and be wary of super-low prices that could indicate that an item is refurbished or in otherwise less-than-perfect condition.

A store's return policy is another important consideration. Some large retailers, such as Costco, have very liberal, pro-consumer return policies, whereas online retailers may not be subject to the additional rights afforded shoppers under local consumer-protection laws. Walk-in retailers also have the edge when it comes to delivery and installation of large, big-ticket items, especially bulky rear-projection and DLP big-screen TVs, and wall-mounted plasma and LCD wide-screen TVs, for which we recommend professional delivery and installation.

Finally, when you shop can be almost as important as where you shop. In the spring, for example, you'll find the best deals on digital cameras and camcorders; camcorders also go on sale in many places during the winter. Shop for DVD players in April and July, and TV sets in July, November, and in January—pre- and post-Super Bowl.

You Need to Know

Extended warranties may not be a good bet

It has become something of a ritual: Just as you're about to head over to the checkout line, the nice salesperson who just sold you that high-ticket gizmo tries to persuade you to take out some extra insurance in the form of an extended repair warranty. What should you do?

As electronics have become more of a commodity, profit margins have been squeezed. One way specialty electronics retailers boost their bottom line is by selling you an extended warranty, which can yield a sweet 40 to 80 percent profit, industry experts say. With an extended warranty, the insurer must pay to repair or replace the item for a specified period, usually two to five years from the purchase date. Some plans even start on the date of purchase, even though the manufacturer's warranty is also in effect.

CONSUMER REPORTS' long-standing advice is to pass up this costly add-on. Survey data from thousands of our readers have

Your credit card may provide coverage similar to an extended warranty.

shown that on average, the cost of an extended warranty is roughly equivalent to the cost of a repair, which you may never need.

Electronics products are reliable and only a small percentage need repair in the first three years. Possible exceptions include three types of TVs: plasma, LCD, and especially microdisplay rear-projection TVs. Preliminary findings from our user

surveys show a moderately high rate of repair in the first year for microdisplay rear-projection TVs. LCD and flat-panel TVs show no spike in repairs the first year, although it's too soon to say what will happen in later years.

Given the high cost of repairs for these TVs, buying an extended warranty may actually be advisable, particularly for a microdisplay rear-projection model. Nevertheless, the additional coverage should cost no more than 20 percent of the purchase price. For more detailed advice on buying extended warranties for TVs, see "You Need to Know: An extended warranty can be smart for some types of TVs," page 69.

Before you consider paying for an extended warranty, check to see if your credit card provides extra coverage. Such plans, most often found on gold and platinum cards, typically lengthen the original manufacturer's coverage by up to one year.

CONSIDER PAY METHODS AND RETURN POLICIES

Savvy credit-card use can save money and protect your identity

There's more to being a smart shopper these days than finding the best products at the best prices. More often than not, retailers in your area will present you with a maze of incentives and come-ons designed to pull you into the stores and, in some cases, make you spend more than you intended.

For instance, if you've looked at any sales circulars recently, you've probably noticed that many electronics stores are pushing zero-interest financing, typically by having you sign up for a store credit card that carries a high annual interest rate—up to 29 percent. A word of warning: We've found these offers often have a number of gotchas that can end up costing you big bucks if you don't pay installments on time, or if you don't pay the loan in full before the term expires. Even if you've paid $3,000 toward the price of a $4,000 plasma TV, you could be charged interest on the original $4,000 over the full loan period. On a two-year loan with a 24 percent rate, that would tack thousands more onto what was a $1,000 balance. So be sure to check the fine print carefully before you sign up for a deal that might be too good to be true.

Using the credit card that's already in your wallet to make electronics purchases is a good idea, however, because you'll have more leverage to return a product than you would if you were to pay with a debit card or cash. Federal law gives you the right to defend against payment of a credit card charge if you show that the merchant failed to resolve a problem with goods or services satisfactorily. (This applies if the item cost more than $50 and was purchased in your state, within 100 miles of your home, or from the credit-card issuer.)

What's more, you might automatically double the factory warranty on that laptop computer or projection TV if you buy it with a credit card. Check with the card's issuer for details or limitations. You should also use a credit card to purchase items that have to be delivered as well as those that can't be tested until you open the box.

Be aware that a credit card's many conveniences can come at a heavy price: It's easy to become overextended. It's best to always restrict purchases to those you can pay in full when the bill arrives. Also, try to avoid using a credit card if you're already carrying a balance, and steer clear of credit-card advances, which can be a costly way to borrow money.

SAFER ONLINE SHOPPING

You may prefer to use cash or debit cards for some store purchases (especially when buying a gift for someone; if you pay for it by credit card, some stores will not refund cash to the recipient upon the gift's return). But when buying electronics or any other products online, you should always use a credit card. In accordance with the Fair Credit Billing Act, you can dispute charges and withhold payment of the disputed amount while your complaint is being investigated by the creditor. Moreover, most credit-card companies will pay any amount over $50 if your card is used for an unauthorized transaction.

That last benefit can be a true lifesaver. Identity theft is a serious problem, both in the real world and on the Web. (In fact, according to a 2006 survey by the Better Business Bureau and Javelin Strategy & Research, more cases of identity theft

To help protect your identity, use a different password for each Web site where you shop.

occur offline than online.) Still, it pays to err on the side of caution when you offer up personal information online. Anyone can pose as an online company under almost any name. Be suspicious when sellers offer new merchandise at prices dramatically lower than those of legitimate retailers. High-definition TVs and expensive camera equipment are favorite targets of con artists. Don't be afraid to request a paper catalog or brochure if you are not familiar with the merchant.

Before you submit your credit-card information to an online vendor, make sure the site complies with industry security standards by using protection such as Secure Socket Layer (SSL), a technology that encrypts your personal information as it travels across the Internet, safeguarding your transaction. Check the site's security policy, and when it's time to pay, look for an unbroken key or a small padlock image in the bottom-left corner, which indicates your information is secure.

Protect your identity. Make sure you know that a site is secure before you start typing your credit-card number.

Many e-commerce sites require customers to enter with a password. If you have accounts at more than one site, make sure each password is different, and don't use an obvious password, such as your Social Security number or birthday. If you must write down your password(s), don't leave the information in a place where others can find it. Finally, never share your passwords with others.

READ THE FINE PRINT

Before you make your way to the checkout page or empty your shopping cart online, take a few minutes to go over the store's policies. Some retailers have price-matching and sales-adjustment policies; the latter entitle you to a refund or credit if an item goes on sale soon after you buy it. If you're buying a large item, such as a plasma TV or home-theater system, be sure to ask whether the store can deliver and install the product on the same day.

Take some time to go over the retailer's return policy before you walk out the door. Some stores, including Best Buy, charge restocking fees of up to 25 percent for returns of nondefective merchandise. Some online merchants also charge a restocking fee on returned products. CONSUMER REPORTS WebWatch project (*www.ConsumerWebWatch.org/praise-worthy.cfm*) can help you look for online retailers that have pledged to abide by guidelines for improving Web credibility.

Keeping track of any rebates for the products you purchase should be a high priority as well. In-store rebates are no-brainers, but the mail-in variety is more common. Although mail-in rebate offers are fairly straightforward, they can be easy to overlook. Make sure you carefully fill out mail-in rebate forms soon after you get home. Don't forget to include all of the required items, especially UPC codes, and make copies of all rebate materials before you mail them in. Also keep an eye out for your rebate checks in the mail; many arrive in nondescript envelopes that can be mistaken for junk mail.

KNOW YOUR RIGHTS

Even after you've unpacked and used your electronic device, hold on to all your receipts and proofs of purchase. If it doesn't work as advertised, promptly return it and ask for a full refund or replacement. If you are still dissatisfied, contact the merchant and manufacturer in writing.

Effective complaining requires knowing your rights. If you need to call the retailer or manufacturer, get a name, department, and phone number. If the store manager won't help, try the regional sales manager. If e-mail and calls to customer service don't work, contact the sales or product manager. You can find a sample complaint letter in the Federal Citizen Information Center's Consumer Action Handbook, found at *www .consumeraction.gov*. If the matter is not resolved, complain in writing to your local district attorney's office or consumer affairs office.

For online purchases, you should always make printouts of the following:
▸ Web pages indicating the company's name, phone number, and address.
▸ An order-confirmation page, or similar page, with a description of items ordered and your confirmation number.
▸ The site's policies for returns, security, etc.
▸ Any correspondence you exchange with the merchant, including e-mail in which you give notification of product defects and the merchant's responses.

Also make sure that all of these browser-page printout items are dated.

If you suspect fraudulent activity online or worse, if you have fallen victim to a con artist, alert the shopping site and any other organization involved in the transaction, such as Western Union. You should also notify the Internet Fraud Complaint Center, a partnership between the FBI and the National White Collar Crime Center, at *www.ifccfbi.gov*.

SOMETIMES IT'S SMART TO HIRE AN INSTALLER

Consider your own time and skills, then shop for the best deal

A new home-theater system or computer network can provide years of enjoyment, but installing one can cause nearly as much anxiety as getting married or buying a house. That's why many of the larger electronics outlets provide custom-installation services.

All services are not alike, however. While you may groan at the prospect of researching yet another buying topic, the reality is that differences among installation packages are as good a reason to switch stores as product selection, price, or quality of in-store service. Don't take it on faith that most are created equal. There are good installation packages but quality and the terms of the contract will vary.

Even within the same store, the levels of service may differ in a good-better-best scenario. For example, both Circuit City and Best Buy offer levels of service termed Basic, Deluxe, and Premium for various audio- and video-installation packages, while CompUSA offers Bronze, Silver, Gold, and Platinum service and installation plans. The differences among levels involve such things as the number of speakers installed, whether speaker wires are concealed, and the degree of component integration provided. Clearly, it's worthwhile to do some homework when considering installation packages. Be sure you understand the differences among vendors—as well as the differences in service levels available from each vendor.

TYPES OF STORES

If you're planning to purchase installation service for the equipment you buy, a decision you'll face early on is what kind of store to shop in. Larger retailers often employ their own experts to do the work, although many look to third-party contractors. Some retailers, such as Radio Shack, do not offer installations at all, leaving it to customers to work out their own arrangements.

Other retailers only provide Web links to installers. In these cases, it pays to do a detailed Web search and talk to sales reps—preferably more than one, or a manager—at the retailer. You should also try to check the store's Web site a couple of times, since it's easy to overlook a key link.

Local chains are another alternative. Fry's is well known along the West Coast, and MyerEmco is popular in the Washington, D.C., area. One advantage of doing business with a small local chain is that, in the event of a problem, you'll probably have an easier time contacting one of the store's owners or someone who can make a decision on the spot, even one that may lose money for the store. You can't count on such access, of course, but a few visits to a local electronics chain will quickly let you know whether managers are accessible or not.

Single-storefront operations can make it even easier to put you in direct contact with the owner or manager. Getting references should also be easy if the store has a good track record.

Then there's online purchasing. If you're buying from a site like Amazon.com, you'll find links to suppliers of plasma-TV mounting brackets and even independent installation services (*www.installplasma.com*). However, most such sites

Complex setups with many components might mean you need to consult an installer.

shy away from offering to do the installation.

Overall, if you lack the wiring or carpentry skills required to install your home-entertainment or computer system, your best bet is to hire a professional to do the job. Before you sign on the dotted line, however, be sure to ask for and check the installer's references.

For details on hiring an installer for particular types of electronics gear, you'll find more information in related chapters in this book. For installation of a television, see page 85. Installer issues for video and audio systems are discussed on pages 102 and 111. Chapter 6 includes advice on seeking help for setting up PCs and in-home networks, on page 136.

THE OWNER'S DILEMMA: TO REPAIR OR REPLACE?

If it's more than three years old, replacement usually makes sense

Whether it's the vertical lines you see running across the middle of your TV screen whenever you turn on the set; your digital camera not flashing properly; or your DVD player's sudden inability to play most of your movie collection, you'll soon be faced with a decision: Should you bring your damaged electronic device in for repair, or start shopping around for its replacement?

Drawing on the experiences of the 2,300 CONSUMER REPORTS subscribers who answered our latest "repair it or replace it" reader survey, for many products you may be better off replacing your broken item if it's off-warranty and more than three years old. Among the 45 percent of

Aging computer gear might not be worth repairing amid falling prices and increased performance for new models.

respondents who opted to pass on repairing their damaged equipment, the main reason was cost, followed by the availability of low-cost replacements and a desire for models with newer features.

The cost of repairing consumer electronics has been trending upward over the last few years. Consumers are now reporting repairs in the range of $100 to $150 from major repair service companies, according to Ron Sawyer, executive director of the Professional Service Association, a trade group. This is up by as much as 50 percent over the last few years due to increased labor, insurance, and energy costs.

Even if you decide to have your broken product repaired, your satisfaction is far from guaranteed. For example, nearly half of all digital cameras took more than two weeks to fix, and 43 percent of readers said those repairs cost too much, a higher percentage than with any other product. At the same time, 31 percent of our readers who brought their desktop computers in for servicing reported their PCs weren't fixed right the first time or didn't work well afterward.

These days, our basic rule for products in need of repair is to toss any item for which you paid less than $150, and skip any repair that costs more than half the price of a new product—especially off-warranty CD players, cordless phones, inkjet printers, VCRs, and conventional TV sets under 30 inches. In fact, many of these devices aren't even serviceable.

In addition to the high cost of repairs, our readers found other good reasons to replace their broken electronics products, including:

More bang for fewer bucks. Inexpensive imports give consumers more for their money. That's why we no longer recommend out-of-warranty repairs for conventional 27-inch TV sets, which cost about $560 a decade ago and can sell for less than $300 today. Simple DVD players sell for $50 or so, while prices for desktop computers have dropped by about $400 over the past four years and for laptops, by about $200.

The allure of the new. Among readers who didn't seek repairs, 27 percent wanted models offering new features. In TVs, for instance, high-definition and flat-panel sets make upgrades more attractive.

Hard-to-diagnose problems. Readers paid as much as $500 to fix projection TVs, $400 to fix laptops, and $180 to fix digital cameras. That's because most of these products rely on microprocessor-based controls in which failures can be tricky and time-consuming to diagnose. Technicians often have to replace an entire circuit

Many consumers look for sleeker models, like flat-screen monitors, when they replace equipment.

Repair-or-replace timelines

■ Repair   ■ Consider repair   ■ Replace

Product		Age of broken product (<1 yr, 1 yr, 2 yr, 3 yr, 4 yr, 5 yr, 6 yr, 7 yr, 8 yr)	Cost — Replacement	Cost — Repair	Percent with any problems	Hard-to-get parts	Took too long	Bad job	High cost
ELECTRONICS									
Camcorders	Digital		$350-$650	$135-$270	61%		•	•	•
Digital cameras	4-5 megapixels		250-500	50-180	69		•		•
	6-8 megapixels		400-800	50-180	69		•		•
TVs, picture-tube	32-inch		250-550	100-300	45		•		
	36-inch		500-850	100-300	45		•		
TVs, rear-projection	CRT-based		800-1,400	200-500	55	•	•	•	•
Computers	Desktop		500-1,500	90-300	56			•	
	Laptop/notebook		900-2,000	100-400	58		•	•	•

Guide to the timelines

Information is based largely on our 2004 Annual Questionnaire and includes readers' experiences with products that broke while out of warranty and were professionally repaired. Timelines refer to middle-of-the-road products that most people buy. They indicate when repair or replacement makes sense, based on the judgment of our marketing and engineering experts. They take into account the product's age, typical repair and replacement costs, and improvements in new models. **Black** shows when a repair is worthwhile; **gray** signals a judgment call; **red** means we advise against repair. **Replacement** cost is the typical range for new, midpriced products. **Repair cost** is the range readers told us they typically paid. **Problems** indicates how often readers encountered any problems during repair, along with those that cropped up more than average for each product. On average, 10 percent of readers complained about parts availability, 16 percent about lengthy repairs, 16 percent about bad repairs, and 13 percent about excessive cost. Where numbers for repair cost and percent with problems are repeated (say, for 32-inch and 36-inch TVs), data cover both types of product.

board, even though the problem may involve a single blown capacitor.

Fewer repair shops. According to the Professional Service Association, the number of electronics repair shops has dropped from 20,014 in 1992 to 7,153 today. In addition, Sawyer says many repair technicians will now only fix high-end devices because the profit margins are too narrow for repairs on less-expensive products.

Of course, there are situations where it may make sense to have a broken electronic device repaired—especially expensive products that have recently come off warranty, or items that are high in sentimental value (a gift from a friend or family member, for example). If you're considering repairing a damaged product, take the following steps to ease the process:

Make sure it's actually broken. The problem may be a loose plug, improper wiring, a tripped circuit breaker, or a bad surge-protector outlet. Products that rely on microprocessors tend to be especially quirky.

Help yourself. Most instruction manuals have helpful troubleshooting sections. You can also find good advice online, including user forums and downloadable owners' guides on some manufacturers' Web sites. There are third-party sites that offer solutions to common problems and help you find parts, contact companies, and understand how products work. Some useful sites we've seen include RepairClinic.com.

Contact the company. Although 23 percent of the readers in our survey had a hard time getting in touch with the manufacturer of their broken product, and 24 percent complained about the service, some who kept at it were rewarded.

You Need to Know

Prevent wear and tear with some basic care

The longer you can hold on to your CD player, TV, or camcorder, the longer you can put off having to make decisions about repairs or buying a new one. Of course, the longevity of an electronic device largely depends on how well you care for it. Here are some tips that can help you keep those old products up and running well after their warranties have expired:

Camcorders. Store them in protective bags or cases that keep out dust and moisture. Don't aim the lens or eyepiece at the sun. Never use your fingers to clean the lens; use a clean, soft cloth or special lens tissue instead. When loading, press the door gently to avoid bending the cassette carriage. Don't interfere with automatic tape-loading and unloading processes. Remove the cassette (or other media) from the camcorder before storing it.

CD and DVD players. Keep them out of direct sunlight, away from heat, and on a solid, stable surface to prevent jolts and skipping. Always use the tray button to open and close the motorized disc drawer. Pushing the drawer with your hand can strip the gears that move it. Keep CDs and DVDs clean and scratch-free.

Desktop and notebook PCs. Never turn off the power while the computer is running; always let the operating system shut it down. Turn off the monitor before cleaning the screen. Periodically vacuum the keyboard and case openings with a soft brush attachment. Remove the ball in the mouse or the trackball and wash it off with some alcohol (be sure to clean out the ball compartment as well). Make sure the parts are thoroughly dry before using.

Inkjet printers. Keep them covered between uses to keep out dust and dirt. Use at least once a week to prevent ink from clogging the print heads. Don't overload automatic paper feeders.

Picture-tube TVs. Place the set out of direct sunlight and away from heat. Regularly remove dust from the screen and vents. Keep screen brightness and contrast settings low to prolong tube life and to reduce the possibility of "burn-in," a permanent disfiguring of areas of the screen. Place large-screen, 30- to 36-inch sets on a sturdy stand or cart with plenty of room to accommodate the case. Make sure the cart or stand is level and has a raised front lip to prevent the set from tipping over.

Projection TVs. Screens can scratch easily, so be careful when cleaning them. With CRT designs, you must align the three small CRTs as needed for best picture performance. Bumping the set can cause misalignment. Newer microdisplay types (LCD, DLP, or LCoS) and rear-projection television sets don't have these issues, although you should be extra careful when cleaning the screens.

VCRs. Keep the VCR and tapes away from heat, direct sunlight, and dust when not in use. Be sure tapes are free of loose or peeling labels and sticky residue, which can clog a VCR's gears and loading mechanism. Periodically clean the tape heads with a head-cleaning tape.

About 10 percent who complained about a problem got an offer to fix or replace an out-of-warranty product free of charge.

Consider independent repair shops. Readers were equally satisfied with the quality of work done by both authorized and independent repair services. True, manufacturers train authorized technicians on the latest equipment, keep them updated on repair issues, and hold them to performance standards, and this service may be your only choice for a product that's still under warranty. But independents can be good for off-warranty work, especially if you only need a simple repair job or one that doesn't involve proprietary parts from the manufacturer.

Check their credentials. Inquire if the repair service you're considering has been certified by a trade group like the Professional Service Association or the International Society of Certified Electronics Technicians. Membership doesn't ensure integrity, but it does suggest that the shop's technicians are qualified.

The popularity of today's consumer electronics products comes with a serious downside for the environment: e-waste. As consumers replace older products with new models, discarded home electronics are overwhelming landfills and dumps. The only solution is recycling.

What breaks, what doesn't

The chart below indicates the percentage of five-year-old products with and without a warranty that have ever been repaired or had a serious problem. We've also listed a sampling of brands that have been especially reliable over the past few years, along with brands that are among the more likely to have needed repair.

Product	Repair rate	More-reliable brands	Less-reliable brands
Desktop PC		Apple, Dell, Sony	Gateway
Laptop or notebook PC		Apple, Toshiba	Compaq, Gateway
TV: rear-projection		Hitachi, Mitsubishi	RCA
Digital camcorder		Sony D8 and Mini DV	JVC Mini DV
Digital camera		Canon, Panasonic, Sony	Toshiba
DVD player		JVC, Panasonic, Pioneer, Sony, Toshiba	Apex Digital
Picture-tube TV: 30-32"		JVC, Sanyo, Sharp, Toshiba	RCA, Zenith
Picture-tube TV: 34-36"		JVC, Sony, Toshiba	RCA
TV: 25-27"		Sanyo, Sharp, Toshiba	RCA, Samsung

0% 10 20 30 40 50%

THINK GREEN: RECYCLE YOUR OLD ELECTRONICS

States and companies offer more options for consumers

Each old TV or computer system contains between four and eight pounds of potentially brain-damaging lead. Even small electronic products, such as cell phones, personal stereos, and camcorders, pose big hazards. From the mercury in their batteries and the cadmium in their displays, to the arsenic in their circuit boards and the brominated flame retardants (BFR) in their housings, trashed electronics are a toxic time bomb when buried in landfills, leaching carcinogens and other harmful substances into the groundwater.

The Federal Environmental Protection Agency says it is safe to discard TVs in a properly managed landfill, but it strongly recommends recycling to promote resource conservation. Many states and

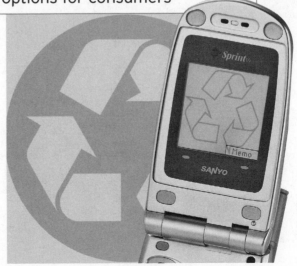

Even small electronics such as cell phones can be donated rather than discarded.

municipalities have banned CRTs from landfills in an effort to reduce the high costs associated with handling such materials.

With an estimated 20 to 24 million unused TVs and computers already gathering dust in homes and offices across the country, more municipal initiatives, state and local laws, and private programs run by manufacturers and retailers are trying to keep this waste out of landfills by enabling or in some cases requiring equipment recycling.

NEW RECYCLING LAWS

Among the recent legislative approaches are four laws passed in California, Maine, Maryland, and Washington.

Under a first-of-its-kind statute implemented in 2004 in Maine, manufacturers are directly billed for the cost of recycling based on the proportion of waste generated by their products. It's a move that recycling proponents believe may provide an incentive for manufacturers to design equipment that lasts longer or is more easily recycled.

Consumers in Maine may pay up to $5 when dropping TV sets or computer monitors off at centralized points. The state estimates that its 1.28 million residents recycle 60,000 to 100,000 TVs and computer monitors annually, according to Carole Cifrino, coordinator for product management programs in Maine's Department of Environmental Protection division of solid-waste management.

In March 2006, Washington followed Maine's example by passing recycling legislation that goes even further. Its law will require manufacturers to assume the costs for collecting, transporting, and processing recycled TVs, computer systems and laptops by January 2009. Residents will not be charged for recycling old equipment, although manufacturers may pass along some of the program's expense in the form of higher prices for electronics items, says Suellen Mele, program director of Washington Citizens for Resource Conservation. "But we're not anticipating any significant increase in prices," she adds.

Consumers Union, the parent company of CONSUMER REPORTS, supports the concept of Extended Producer Responsibility (EPR), which holds manufacturers responsible for costs, requiring them to compete for what portion they pass on to consumers.

Maryland is taking a different approach with its five-year pilot program, which currently applies to computer monitors only but could conceivably be expanded to include TVs. Manufacturers doing business there must pay an initial annual $5,000 registration fee that counties and municipalities will use to promote recycling. If the manufacturer starts a take-back program, the fee for subsequent years is reduced to $500.

In California, buyers of TVs and computer monitors pay a fee of $6 to $10 at the point of sale. The money is then funneled by the state into a collection and recycling system. While that promotes recycling, it creates no incentive for industry to design longer-lasting products, reuse old components, or make equipment easier to recycle, recycling proponents say.

Discarded TVs and computers threaten our landfills unless properly recycled.

National Cristina Foundation

ConsumerReports

Greener Choices
Products for a Better Planet

A variety of organizations online offer information and help in recycling electronics.

California also instituted new waste-disposal rules in February that make it illegal for residents to toss most electronic items in the trash—everything from printers, fax machines, and monitors to cell phones and batteries. Moreover, as of July, cell-phone retailers in the state are required to take back phones from customers for recycling at no fee.

Nevertheless, much work remains to be done. According to Earthworks, a Washington, D.C.-based environmental advocacy group, 98 percent of the 130 million cell phones discarded in the U.S. each year are not being recycled.

Electronics-recycling legislation is currently under consideration in 38 states. The issue is also being addressed by several bills pending in Congress, including the Electronic Waste Recycling Promotion and Consumer Protection Act, which was still in committee when this book went to press. This Senate bill provides tax credits for consumers and companies that invest in recycling infrastructures for electronics products.

MANUFACTURERS' RECYCLING PROGRAMS

Several computer manufacturers, including Apple, Dell, and HP, also provide consumers with computer recycling and donation services.

In April, Apple expanded its recycling program to offer customers purchasing new Macintosh systems free shipping and domestic recycling of their old computer systems. The company also operates a recycling collection facility out of its headquarters in Cupertino, Calif., which is run as a free service for the city's residents. In addition, Apple has partnered with Metech International to let consumers and businesses recycle systems

weighing up to 60 pounds for a flat fee of $30 (including shipping). Apple also provides no-fee iPod recycling services to its U.S. customers through its Apple stores. Customers returning any iPod, iPod mini, or iPod photo will receive a 10 percent discount toward the same-day purchase of a new iPod.

Dell has been offering free computer-recycling services to buyers of new Dimension and Inspiron computer systems since 2004. In September 2006, the company extended free recycling to any Dell-branded product for consumers, regardless of whether a replacement is bought from Dell. The company also arranges for donations of old working computer systems and components to local grass-roots organizations through its partnership with the National Cristina Foundation (*www.cristina.org*).

HP encourages consumers to donate functional computer systems through its partnerships with the National Cristina Foundation and eBay's Rethink Initiative (*http://rethink.ebay.com*). It also provides consumers with an online calculator to quote prices for its recycling service. The company's recycling fees are a bit higher than other manufacturers, (we were quoted $46 for a PC and monitor), but customers are rewarded with e-coupons that can be used toward the purchase of HP products.

CONSIDER DONATING

If you have an obsolete but working computer, digital camera, cell phone—practically any electronic item—why not donate it to a local or national charity or other nonprofit organization? In many cases, you'll even be able to deduct your contribution from your taxes (but be sure to check with your accountant or tax adviser first).

A good place to start is with your local schools, youth and community centers, and charities such as Goodwill Industries and the Salvation Army. You might also decide to donate to a national nonprofit organization, like Recycle for Breast Cancer (*recycleforbreastcancer.org*), which accepts a wide range of working and nonworking electronic items, and even mails out prepaid postage labels for most product categories. Sites such as TechSoup (*www.techsoup.org*), Earth 911 (*www.earth911.org*), and CONSUMER REPORTS' Greener Choices (*www.greenerchoices.org*) can provide you with lists of other nonprofit choices.

A word of advice before you recycle or donate an old computer: Don't forget to reformat all hard drives or use a dedicated program designed to erase all personal data. You should also delete all stored numbers and personal information from any cell phones you donate or recycle, and make sure your service has been deactivated.

WHAT YOU CAN DO

Whether the law mandates that manufacturers pay for recycling, or whether consumers pay a recycling fee when making a purchase, consumers ultimately foot the bill. Voluntary recycling programs might help prevent costly legislative mandates. Here are the steps we recommend you take if you decide to recycle an old TV or computer:

Check with retailers. If the equipment still works, or if you think it can be repaired, check with local thrift stores. You might not want that old console dinosaur, but someone else out there will. If you can't find a thrift store willing to take it, find out if any local charities might be interested. Some of the sites listed in this report include links to groups that accept donated electronics.

Electronics retailers are also getting into the act. Best Buy sponsors recycling events where you can drop off electronics of all kinds, from TVs to fax

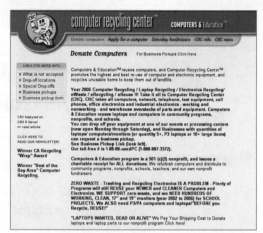

The Computer Recycling Center is a local nonprofit recycler in Northern California. You can search the Net for a recycler in your area.

machines. Check their Web site to see if there is an upcoming event in your neighborhood.

Check for public programs. To see if your town sponsors specific collection days for TVs and other electronics, or if it has a drop-off point for electronics waste, click on the map supplied by the Electronic Industries Alliance (*www.eiae.org*). Kate Krebs, executive director of the National Recycling Coalition, recommends that when you buy a new product, contact the manufacturer to see if it will accept your old item for recycling.

Consider a private recycling firm. You can also take your electronics directly to a private recycling company. You can find lists of such companies on the Electronic Industries Alliance Web page (click on your state, then on Find Reuse and Recycle options). If you go to a private recycler, check the company's credentials first. Some disreputable recyclers simply ship waste overseas instead of recycling it, according to Richard Goss, director of environmental affairs for the EIA. Ask the recycler about its practices, and check with local or state environmental agencies to make sure the recycler is legitimate.

ConsumerReports.org | Product recalls

Despite all your care and research in making electronics buying decisions, a product you've purchased can turn out to be faulty. To find out if a product you own has been recalled by the manufacturer,

you can check among selected recalls listed on *www.ConsumerReports.org*. When you get to the site, just click on the Recalls link.

CONSUMER REPORTS provides these recall notices online as a

service to consumers so that potentially hazardous products can be removed from homes and from the marketplace. News of recent recalls and listings of recalls are also available by product category.

PHONE SERVICES & PHONES

CHAPTER 02

Charge Coverage Area

No Service Area

Looking for Service...

▶▶ **Cell phones are smaller and fancier—some double as cameras or music players. Finding the right provider and plan can be a challenge.**

Ratings: Cell phones, p. 152.

WIRED, WIRELESS & WEB: CHOOSING THE RIGHT MIX

Today's phone choices take work, but you'll be rewarded with lower phone bills and service that fits your family's needs

Before you buy another telephone, it's a good time to review the phone services you use and how often you use them. Chances are you have both a wired line and cell phone, and you may have already made the leap to the Internet-based phone service known as Voice over Internet Protocol, or VoIP. Choosing the right mix of services can help cut your phone bills, protect you in an emergency, and perhaps simplify your phone life.

Here are the two basic steps to fine-tuning your telephone service, with some specific actions we recommend for each.

PICK LANDLINE SERVICE WITH BEST PACKAGE

Keep a landline, regardless. It's possible to forsake local landline service and simply use your wireless phone or VoIP service as your local carrier.

For most people, keeping a landline is still a good idea.

(With VoIP you will need a broadband Internet connection via DSL or cable to access the Internet and make calls, even local ones.)

But we don't recommend dropping your landline, at least not yet. Cell phones don't work everywhere, especially in rural areas. Cell-phone networks also have capacity issues, making it difficult or impossible to place calls when the system is overloaded. What's more, having a cell phone is no guarantee that you'll be able to make calls if your local landline system happens to go down. That's because cell-phone calls may travel over those same wires for part of their journey.

Finally, if you need to dial 911 in an emergency, calling from a landline guarantees that the 911 operator will know your location. Other technologies, like cell phones and VoIP, are more difficult for 911 call centers to locate. VoIP, too, might leave you phoneless in an emergency if, for example, the power goes out or you lose your Internet connection. If you choose to make either wireless or VoIP your primary telephone service, we still recommend maintaining at least basic landline service at your home. For more about emergency service and 911 concerns, see page 28.

Pick the right package. Even though you might have just one local landline telephone company, you probably have numerous packages from which to select. Verizon, for example, was recently offering five levels of local service in suburban Westchester County, New York.

The best way to choose is to check several months' worth of phone bills to see how many minutes of local calling you used. Unless you think your household's calling habits will change markedly in the future, you'll probably do well to choose the plan that most closely matches your current pattern. Because phone companies won't necessarily volunteer that a different plan might suit you better, it's worth a quick call, recent phone bill in hand, to find out.

If you don't make a lot of local calls on your landline or use dial-up Internet service, a basic "measured service" plan may save you money. With these plans, you're either allotted a certain number of calls or you pay for every call you make. Expect to pay about $20 a month, including taxes. Packages with unlimited local calling, sometimes referred to as "flat rate" service, can easily run twice that amount, especially if you add other optional features, such as caller ID and call waiting.

Low-income consumers may be eligible for the Federal Communications Commission's Lifeline Assistance program, which provides discounts on phone service, and the Link-Up America program, which will pay a portion of initial connection fees.

You may also save by switching local carriers. You can find out which local and long-distance carriers offer service in your ZIP code, and what they charge, at *www.telebright.com*, which provides data to our Web site, ConsumerReports.org.

Consider your wireless needs. Generally speaking, you'll get more local calls for your money with a landline than with wireless. But wireless has obvious advantages if you often make calls on the go, especially in this age of disappearing pay phones. Just check your current plan to make sure you aren't paying for more minutes than you actually use each month.

If you've found that you don't use a wireless phone much but would like to keep one around for roadside emergencies and other rare occasions, a prepaid wireless plan may save you money. Companies like Cingular, T-Mobile, TracFone, and Virgin sell them for as little as $30, including the phone itself and a token number of minutes to get you started. After that, you can buy more wireless airtime at prices from about 10 to 50 cents a minute.

Prepaid wireless minutes tend to cost less if you buy more of them. For example, a TracFone card good for 40 minutes recently cost $19.99, or nearly 50 cents a minute, while a 400-minute card was $79.99, or slightly less than 20 cents a minute. Bear in mind that your prepaid wireless minutes may expire. TracFone's, for example, generally expire after 60 days unless you buy more TracFone minutes in the meantime, in which case they roll over into the next time period.

TAKE A LOOK AT THE WAY YOU USE LONG DISTANCE

Look at a few months of phone bills from all of your services, both wireless and landline, to see which of the following best describes your typical usage patterns:

Have you looked for a phone booth lately? For most people, a cell phone has become a virtual necessity.

If you don't make a lot of calls

▸ Typical monthly long-distance usage: well under 100 minutes.
▸ Consider: Wired plus wireless (if you want to make calls on the go), prepaid phone cards, and dial-around services.

Use your wireless minutes. Before running up more minutes on your long-distance landline plan, make sure you've used the ones on your cell plan, unless they roll over to the next month. In fact, if you're happy with wireless voice quality and coverage, you can use it for all of your long-distance calling and jettison your landline long-distance service.

Avoid local/long-distance bundles. MCI, Verizon, and other carriers offer unlimited local and long-distance landline packages for a monthly rate of $30 to $70. But if you tend not to make many long-distance calls, the bundled price may raise your monthly cost. MCI's Neighborhood Unlimited package, with unlimited local and long-distance calling, for example, recently cost $49.99 to $69.99 a month, depending on your state. An MCI package with 200 monthly long-distance minutes and unlimited local calling was $29.99 to $49.99 a month, again depending on your state. If you don't make a lot of long-distance calls and already have a local plan that meets your needs, you could be better off with a long-distance plan that simply bills based on the minutes you use. MCI

Unless you can roll over minutes, be sure to use up your cell phone's long-distance minutes before running up charges on your landline.

had one called Net Value that charged $6.99 a month plus 4 cents a minute for state-to-state calls.

Weigh both monthly fees and per-minute rates. This is good advice no matter how much long-distance service you use, but it's especially important if you don't make a lot of calls. For example, a long-distance plan that charges 5 cents a minute may seem like a bargain, even if it also carries a $3.95 monthly fee. But factoring in that monthly fee, if you use 75 long-distance minutes a month, your actual per-minute charge is more than 10 cents. For just 30 long-distance minutes a month, it's 18 cents.

Use prepaid phone cards. If you make few long-distance calls from your landline phone, say, less than $10 worth a month, consider dropping your long-distance carrier and using a prepaid phone card. (Note that your local phone company may charge you a one-time fee to drop your carrier.) Typically, the more minutes you buy, the less you'll pay for them. Walgreen's, for example, sells its own brand of phone card, recently offering 125 domestic minutes for $10, or 8 cents a minute, while

its 800-minute card cost $40, or 5 cents a minute.

Prepaid cards are a little inconvenient, however, which is why we recommend them only for light long-distance users. You have to enter a toll-free number first, then an authorization code, and finally the number you want to call. Plus, some cards have hefty per-call connection charges and other sneaky fees. Check the terms first, and avoid cards with those charges. Also be sure you know whether, or when, your phone card expires. If you buy a "rechargeable" card, you can add more minutes to it, sometimes at an additional discount.

For the best deals, look to packages containing multiple cards. For example, you could recently buy a pack of 20 100-minute AT&T cards for $69.42 at the Sam's Club Web site; that works out to 3½ cents per minute. Costco's Web site sold a pack of 28 120-minute MCI cards for $99.99, or just under 3 cents a minute. The Costco and Sam's Club cards were top-rated in terms of rates and fees in an analysis of 15 prepaid domestic phone cards published in 2005 by the Consumer Reports Money Adviser newslet-

> **When comparing** long-distance plans, include both per-minute charges and monthly fees.

First Things First

Consider your phone network choices

1 Wired

Also known as a landline. The familiar phone-line system uses cables running under or above the ground. **Pros** Best voice quality. Fewer problems making and keeping a connection than with wireless. Most reliable of the three types and most likely to work in a power outage. Well-established 911 service provides a voice connection and reports your location to emergency responders. A single unified system connects wired phones in the U.S. **Cons** Wires can be damaged by weather and other forces, disrupting service. Add-on features, taxes, and fees can boost your bill substantially. Even cordless phones are portable only within a limited range.

2 Wireless

Also known as cellular or mobile. Uses a network of radio towers to connect your call to the wired network. **Pros** Mobility. Offers many additional services, including text and picture messaging, music streaming, games, e-mail access, and TV snippets, depending on your service carrier and your phone's capabilities. **Cons** Incomplete coverage and incompatible network technologies among service providers create "dead zones" where service is unavailable. Your phone may work in a local electrical power outage but not in a widespread outage. 911 location capability not fully implemented as of yet. Voice quality not as good as on a wired network.

3 Internet

Also known as Voice over Internet Protocol, or VoIP. Your digital telephone hooks up to the Internet using a broadband connection. **Pros** Relatively inexpensive, especially for long-distance calls. Some services, such as caller ID and call waiting, may be free of charge. You can use your phone anywhere a broadband Internet connection is available. **Cons** May not work in an electrical power outage. Reliability depends on your Internet service provider. Voice quality may not be as good as a wired service's. Providers are required to forward 911 calls to the proper operators, along with your location, but how well that works depends on several factors.

ter. Phone cards are also available for international long-distance calls.

Check out "dial around" services. With these long-distance providers, you bypass a regular long-distance carrier by calling a toll-free number beginning with 10-10 and then making your long-distance call. The dial-around provider's charges will generally appear on your local phone bill. Well-known names in this business include Telecom USA (part of MCI) and Lucky Dog (AT&T). Lucky Dog, for example, recently charged 5 cents a minute for state-to-state calls, plus a 59-cent fee per call. So a 15-minute call, for example, would cost $1.34. As with phone cards, dial-around services add some extra number-punching to the process of making a call. You have to decide whether the potential cost savings outweigh the added hassle. Before you drop your regular long-distance carrier in favor of dial-around service, be sure to test the service to make sure that it works from your phone.

If you're an average caller

▸ **Typical monthly long-distance usage: roughly 100 minutes**.
▸ **Consider: Wired bundles, wireless, and possibly VoIP (Internet phone service), especially if you want to try out this relatively new technology.**

Weigh local/long-distance bundles. The more calls you make on your landline, the more beneficial a combined local/long-distance bundle will be. If you're spending more than $30 to $70 a month for local and long-distance plans and no other cost-cutting strategy works for you, then consider a bundle.

Find a better wireless plan. If you regularly exceed the minutes in your calling plan or pay high roaming charges, switch to a plan with more minutes. Choose a national (not regional) plan, which typically has no roaming or long-distance charges. Also consider when you tend to call; a cell plan with unlimited night and weekend minutes is more of a bargain if that's when you typically make your calls. You may not want to choose a carrier solely by price, of course; knowing you found a bargain rate will be of little comfort if you can't get cell service or if your calls are frequently cut off.

Consider VoIP. If you have a broadband connection, you may want to sign up for VoIP service. It generally costs $25 to $40 a month for unlimited U.S. calling, and prices continue to drop. In our most recent survey of VoIP users, 52 percent said they had saved money on their phone bills by using

the service. Of that group, 94 percent said they were saving at least $10 a month, and 34 percent estimated savings of at least $40 a month. For more about choosing and using VoIP service, see page 39.

If you're a heavy caller

▸ **Typical monthly long-distance usage: substantially more than 100 minutes.**
▸ **Consider: VoIP plus basic wired service and wireless.**

Sign up for Internet phone service. Heavy long-distance users, especially those who make a lot of international calls, should realize the greatest savings from using VoIP service.

Check local/long-distance bundles. If you're not ready to make the move to VoIP, consider a bundled plan from your landline company. These plans are most beneficial to big-time callers and often include free calling features.

Determine how you'll use wireless. If you make most of your long-distance calls from home (or plan to bring your VoIP adapter along on your travels), you may want wireless service almost entirely for local calls. If, however, you expect to make a lot of domestic long-distance calls on your wireless phone, look for a national calling plan with no roaming or additional long-distance charges, along with an appropriate number of minutes.

Make sure you aren't paying for more minutes than you actually use each month.

If you don't make a lot of long-distance calls from your landline, you can save money by dropping your long-distance carrier and using prepaid phone cards instead.

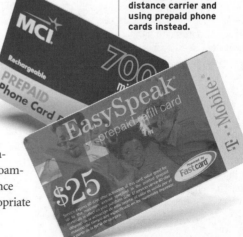

Multiple services can ensure 911 is there when you need it

In the long aftermath of the devastating hurricanes of 2005, few questions became more urgent than whether we can count on our phone systems in times of trouble. More than three million customers' phone lines were knocked out in Louisiana, Mississippi, and Alabama by wind and water during Hurricane Katrina in August of that year. Many of the phone lines that still worked couldn't summon help because 911 call centers or the switching centers that route calls to them went down. Wireless phones also proved useless in many places, as more than a thousand cell sites and their switching centers became inoperative in the wake of the storm.

Some residents of the affected areas managed to reach help using other phone services, including text messaging over their wireless phones, Voice over Internet Protocol (VoIP), and satellite telephony. "Katrina proved that in emergencies you now have multiple ways of communicating," says Rick Jones of the National Emergency Number Association.

The lesson for consumers is that while a single telephone account could suffice for individual emergencies, no one service can currently be counted on to work in a widespread calamity. For that reason, you may want to hedge your bets by subscribing to more than one type of phone service. Here's what to consider:

Landlines are vulnerable. The traditional wired phone system still sets the standard for reliability in emergencies, automatically providing local 911 centers with the caller's address. That can be a lifesaver in the event of a heart attack or stroke, for example. Yet, as was dramatically demonstrated by Katrina, landline service can be disrupted, too. Nearly a month after the hurricane, hundreds of thousands of wired phones were still cut off from service.

Most cell phones can't be located in an emergency. With more than 50 percent of all 911 calls made from wireless phones, and about one-third of cell phones purchased just for emergencies, many consumers depend on mobile telephone

service in times of distress. But mobility has its price, requiring advanced technology to provide a 911 caller's position to local emergency dispatchers.

The Federal Communications Commission, which regulates interstate calls, mandated that by Dec. 31, 2005, wireless 911 callers' position information, accurate to within several hundred feet, had to be available to local emergency responders. At press time, however, the wireless E911 system had not been fully deployed, so be prepared to provide location information when calling 911, which may be tricky at night or in an unfamiliar place. You can check on local compliance at nena.ddti.net.

With landlines down after Katrina, many people reached help through text messaging, wireless phones, VoIP, or satellite.

Internet 911 is improving but still spotty. During Katrina, VoIP worked well in locations where broadband Internet connections were available. For instance, New Orleans city officials were first able to communicate with the outside world via VoIP. The FCC directed VoIP providers to make their services E911-compatible by Nov. 28, 2005. While 911 service for VoIP customers has improved, it's still not as easy for 911 operators to locate. And VoIP service depends on having AC power and an Internet connection; landlines don't. VoIP still may not be a reliable replacement for landline 911 service for many consumers.

911 can call you. One result of the devastation has been greater interest in emergency community notification programs, which use automated outgoing telephone calls, e-mail, and text messages to tell residents about evacuations,

environmental threats, or missing persons. This is usually referred to as Reverse 911, a trademark of Sigma Communications, the firm that originated the underlying technology. The service is already in place in communities from Brookline, Mass., to San Diego, Calif. Note that these systems often rely on landline numbers from phone directories; people with unlisted numbers or wireless or VoIP service must provide their phone numbers to be included.

WHAT YOU CAN DO

First, keep a corded phone and landline service, even if you subscribe to the most basic level. VoIP still isn't ready to replace landline, in our view. Keep your wireless phone's battery charged, have a spare, and/or a car charger, and also consider the following steps:

▶ **Learn to use text messaging.** In Katrina-battered New Orleans, wireless voice calls jammed the few remaining cell sites. But the same damaged telephone system continued to deliver text messages. If you're not familiar with text messaging, consult your phone's instruction book or the nearest teenager.

▶ **Get a locatable cell phone.** If you're using a handset that's more than two years old on the Alltel, Nextel, Sprint, or Verizon wireless systems, it may not have the Global Positioning System (GPS) technology that would help a 911 operator determine your location. Look for the GPS logo in the instruction manual or on the box, or ask your carrier.

▶ **ICE your cell phone.** This idea, which apparently originated with a British paramedic, could assist rescue personnel if you are incapacitated. You create a contact in your cell phone's memory with the name ICE (for "In Case of Emergency"), listing the numbers of people you want to be notified.

Use ICE—In Case of Emergency—in your cell's phone book for emergency workers to summon help.

PICK SERVICE AND PLAN TO FIT YOUR CELL NEEDS

Costs are similar, so base your decision on coverage and network

More than half of cell phone subscribers were less than fully satisfied with their service, according to our latest survey. Only 47 percent of our respondents told us that they were either completely or very satisfied with it, a low showing for any type of service in the U.S.

Perhaps not surprisingly then, 31 percent of the respondents said they were seriously considering changing their providers. Of those who had changed in the past three years, the top reasons for their discontent were poor phone service (54 percent) and price (36 percent). Even the best of today's providers have considerable room for improvement.

Our survey, conducted by the Consumer Reports National Research Center (CRNRC) in September 2005, collected responses from more than 50,000 ConsumerReports.org subscribers who were cell users in 18 metropolitan areas. We asked them about everything from the quality of their calls to how well their inquiries or complaints were handled.

HOW TO CHOOSE

If you're considering a change of carrier, as many of our survey respondents were, what should you

Make sure your prospective provider's coverage area fits your mobile habits before you sign up.

Fed up with all those fees? Here are some you can cut

Phone companies can be as innovative at coming up with new fees as they are with new technology. For example, you could be paying a monthly "subscriber line charge," which rewards your local landline carrier if you make long-distance calls, or the "regulatory programs fee," by which carriers pass along some of their costs under the guise of what seems like a real tax. And there is, of course, no shortage of real taxes.

But all those fees can basically be divided into two groups: those you're stuck with unless you choose to drop your phone service and those you can actually do something about. Here are some examples of where you can cut costs:

Overage charges. Exceeding the number of minutes provided by your wireless plan can subject you to punishing charges of 7 to 45 cents a minute. Avoid them by making sure your plan provides an adequate number of minutes at the time of day that you're most likely to use them.

Roaming fees. Calls made outside what a wireless carrier considers your "home" area could cost you 49 to 69 cents a minute. You may also be subject to long-distance fees. Find out what your plan considers local and regional. Also consider temporarily upgrading to one of your carrier's national plans, with no roaming charges, for lengthy out-of-town trips.

Unused calling features. Optional features such as call forwarding or three-way calling may have seemed like must-haves when you signed up for your landline or wireless service, but if you pay extra and aren't using them, drop them.

Redundant calling features. You may be paying twice for the calling features you do use. Verizon, for example, was recently charging New Jersey customers $7.50 a month for home voice mail, $4.59 for call waiting, and $7.50 for caller ID. Verizon Wireless charged nothing for the same features. So if you have a wireless phone, you could save up to $235 a year simply by eliminating those features from the landline.

look for? Because carriers have become very competitive with one another—which isn't to say that any of them are cheap—we suggest focusing first on service and satisfaction.

Consider our survey findings. Verizon was either the clear leader or among the best in all 18 metro areas we surveyed. But it isn't your only worthy choice. T-Mobile rated about as well in many cities. One important difference between the two: T-Mobile subscribers reported more problems with no coverage and with static.

U.S. Cellular in Chicago and Alltel in Phoenix were statistically tied with Verizon. Those were the only areas for which we had a sufficient sample size to rate the two smaller carriers. But if one of these is available where you live, it may be worth considering.

Check coverage. Ask people who travel the same streets that you do or make calls from the same buildings whether the carrier they use provides consistent service. You can find maps of the carriers' approximate coverage areas and dead zones on their Web sites. We were especially impressed with the accuracy of T-Mobile's. At DeadCellZones.com, an independent site, there are links to many carriers and their coverage maps.

Match networks to your needs. First Things First, below, shows which carriers use which networks. Knowing that can help you figure out whether your phone will work in rural areas or outside the U.S. Generally speaking, a carrier that still offers access to the older, analog network along with the digital networks it uses will provide the best coverage in rural parts of the U.S., although you may have to pay roaming charges.

The digital networks are CDMA (code division multiple access), GSM (global system for mobile), TDMA (time division multiple access), and iDEN (integrated digital enhanced network). The advan-

First Things First

Major wireless carriers compared

We've listed the major carriers in order of overall performance. A carrier's performance should be your first consideration. But if your travels often take you to other countries or rural parts of the U.S., the type of network that your carrier and phone use may also be worth examining.

1 Verizon Wireless

How good Consistently a top performer in our latest survey and in earlier ones. Also did better than other national carriers in responsiveness to customer questions and complaints.

Networks CDMA and analog. But Verizon offers analog access on few of its new phones, which could mean less coverage in some rural areas of the U.S.

2 T-Mobile

How good A solid performer in many of the 18 metro areas we surveyed, but marred by lack of service in some places. Also scored better than all the carriers but Verizon in responsiveness to customer questions and complaints.

Network GSM only. Most phones can be used outside of the U.S.

3 Sprint

How good Sprint and Nextel made their merger final shortly before our survey went out. Sprint was middling and Nextel was low in terms of customer satisfaction.

Networks Sprint uses CDMA but can roam using analog. It may provide the best coverage in rural areas because most of its phones remain analog-capable. Nextel uses iDEN only.

4 Cingular

How good Middling to low levels of consumer satisfaction. Static is a widespread problem. Relatively low marks for helpfulness in handling customer questions and complaints.

Networks Primarily GSM, some TDMA and analog. Most GSM network phones can also be used overseas.

tage of CDMA is that some CDMA phones incorporate analog backup for roaming in areas where a digital signal is unavailable. Most GSM phones provide coverage in other countries, which could be a consideration if you often travel abroad. TDMA is an older system that's no longer widely used, while iDEN is used almost exclusively by Nextel.

Weigh nonvoice differences. Few of the additional nonvoice services offered by carriers are free. Even if they don't add to the cost of your handset, using them will probably increase your cell-service bill. You may also be required to sign a new contract if you wish to switch to a handset with some of the newer features. For more about nonvoice services and which carriers offer them, see page 32.

Price-shop the plans. Once you've decided on a carrier, consult its Web site for the plans it currently offers in your area and any special promotions. If you're looking for a basic, low-cost plan, call the carrier and ask whether any plans other than those featured on the site are available.

While pricing can change frequently, our researchers found some general differences worth noting. Verizon Wireless tended to be somewhat more expensive than, for example, T-Mobile. Sprint offered the best prices for consumers who went over their monthly allotment of minutes, while Cingular allowed its subscribers to roll unused minutes over, which can be a plus if you hate paying for something you don't use.

TODAY'S CELL PHONES DO MORE THAN TALK

Feature-laden models can make it hard to make a simple call

Many cell-phone owners, of course, are no longer using their phones just for talking. They routinely snap pictures or download music or ring tones. Text messaging by phone is also on the rise. More than one-third of the 50,000-plus ConsumerReports.org subscribers surveyed by the CRNRC recently said they have used their phone's text-messaging capability.

New phones offer multimedia messaging, which lets you enliven your messages with photos, video clips, and sound. Some phones can play TV programs downloaded from the carriers' networks and receive real-time news feeds, full-color maps, and other information services.

These and other services are made possible by high-speed cell-phone data networks. Known by the acronyms EV-DO, UMTS, and EDGE, these networks are devoted exclusively to data transmission. Think of them as cell-service counterparts to commuter lanes on the highway.

You may not want the additional capabilities conferred by high-speed networks and the generally

This Motorola is our top-performing, full-featured, advanced phone.

You Need to Know

How to avoid some common cell-service gotchas

A resounding 80 percent of the subscribers we surveyed in September 2005 had at least some trouble shopping for wireless phone services. For example, 49 percent complained that they had to sign up for a long contract to get a better price on a phone, 43 percent said it was hard to compare plans from competing carriers, and 41 percent said it was

hard to figure out the true cost of service. Here's how to get the best deal:

Take advantage of the trial period. Before signing a contract, find out how long a trial period you have. The national carriers offer trials of two weeks to a month. Use that time to assess the service.

Sign up for the shortest contract. We usually

recommend a one-year contract, even if that means paying more for the phone, because that gives you a faster way out if service deteriorates. Early-termination fees typically range from $150 to $200. Consider a two-year contract only if you're renewing with a carrier that has given you good service.

Read the fine print. Check all the terms and conditions

before you sign up. If you don't understand something, you should ask; if you don't like one of the terms and the carrier won't budge, consider another carrier.

If you sign up in a store or at a Web site run by a company other than the carrier, be careful. We found two agents on the Web that have $350 early-cancellation fees on top of the carrier's $200 fee.

fancy phones that work with them. Only 15 percent of ConsumerReports.org subscribers said they used their phone to visit the Web and only 2 percent to send video clips.

The number of basic phones is dwindling as cell-phone manufacturers seek to offer more advanced, and more expensive, models to support the new services. Ironically, many of these fancier phones may actually hamper your ability to make old-fashioned phone calls. For example, their buttons—which often perform double or triple duty—can be-

have unexpectedly if you're in the wrong mode. And the new models cost more than basic phones, even if you take advantage of heavily discounted offers.

Here are some other developments that may affect your choices when you shop:

Higher-resolution cameras. The cameras initially built into cell phones offered only VGA resolution (one-third of a megapixel), OK for viewing on a phone's tiny display but not high enough for good snapshots. Now, many camera phones provide 1-megapixel or greater resolution. Cameras with

Phone carriers keep adding new fee-based services

As cell-phone makers pack new features into their handsets, carriers are launching more fee-based services to cash in on them. Here are some that you're apt to encounter the next time you shop for a phone. Pricing is approximate because many services are part of a bundle. Also bear in mind that features that keep you on the network, such as Web browsing, can eat up plan minutes.

Text messaging (also called SMS, for short message service). You tap out a message on the phone's keypad and send it to another cell phone. **Cost:** From 5 to 10 cents a message or about $20 a month for several thousand text messages, depending on the plan and provider. **Tip:** The meter on the text-messaging toll often runs both ways, charging you for the messages you receive as well as the ones you send. **Best deals:** Sprint and T-Mobile were recently offering unlimited text messaging for $15 per month. For $5 a month, Verizon's IN plan provided unlimited messaging to anyone within the Verizon network.

Multimedia messaging (also called photo and video messaging). You create and send to another cell phone messages that can include photos, sounds, and even video clips. **Cost:** 25 cents per message. **Tip:** Most carriers now carry one another's multimedia messages. **Best deal:** T-Mobile, which wasn't charging extra fees if you had a message package.

E-mail/Web/IM access. Most cell phones have Web browsers, which are needed for e-mail or to buy other services, such as video and games. Major providers offer mobile versions of instant messaging from AOL, MSN, and Yahoo. **Cost:** $5 to $20 per month for Web access; 10 cents to send an e-mail message and 5 to 10 cents

to send an instant message. **Tip:** Dealing with limited graphics and slow networks can wear patience thin, and some plans eat up airtime. **Best deal:** Sprint was offering unlimited access, e-mail, and instant messages for $10 a month. Note that in some areas, Verizon, Sprint, and Cingular have higher-speed networks for Web browsing, e-mail, and TV service, but to use them you'll need a compatible phone and data plan.

You can send multimedia messages that include photos, sound, and even video.

Streaming music and video. A handful of phones have the ability to play music and TV programs streamed over the carriers' networks. TV quality is choppy and programming choices remain limited. **Cost:** $15 and up. **Tip:** Higher-quality video networks, as well as the phones that can handle them, will be available this year. **Best deal:** Sprint currently offers the widest array of streamed entertainment, including music channels and TV programming.

Information services. Cell-phone information services have expanded beyond static weather reports or sports scores. **Cost:** For a monthly fee of $1 to $5, you can now fill your phone screen with full-color maps, real-time news feeds, restaurant reviews, and even product Ratings from CONSUMER REPORTS. **Tip:** You pay third-party sources for the content, plus a monthly Web-access fee to your carrier. Verizon deducts from your airtime for using its data plans. **Best deal:** Sprint PCS Vision or Sprint Power Vision, with unlimited access to its information services for $15 a month.

Games. You can download hundreds of games directly into your phone. The selection depends on your carrier and phone. **Cost:** 99 cents and up per month for each game. **Tip:** Most games can only be rented on a monthly basis. **Best deals:** The most popular games are arcade puzzle classics like Tetris and Frogger. Sprint's prices were the best for those.

Custom ring tones. While most phones already come with a wide selection of free ring tones, you can buy more distinctive sounds, using your phone's browser. **Cost:** $1.49 and up per tone. **Tip:** Read the fine print: In some instances, the fee entitles you to use the ring tone for only a limited amount of time. **Best deals:** T-Mobile, at $1.49 a pop. For $4.99 a month, Sprint lets you create your own ring tones and share them with others.

Ring-back tones. Found on Cingular, T-Mobile, and Verizon, these replace the ringer people hear when they call you with a tune or sound bite. **Cost:** Verizon charged a $1.99 annual fee, plus 99 cents per month. T-Mobile charged $1.49 per month for up to 15 tunes. **Tip:** Choose carefully. Do you want your boss to hear your favorite heavy-metal song when she calls?

higher resolution will typically yield better images, but the lens and other factors can greatly affect quality. Even the best camera phones are no match for a basic digital camera, though.

A boom in Bluetooth. Many cell phones are now Bluetooth-enabled, allowing them to use wireless headsets. Some can also use Bluetooth to exchange information with compatible computers, PDAs, printers, and other devices. Wireless headsets are becoming smaller—as small as a postage stamp, in some cases—and prices are falling. Some new cars and aftermarket add-on kits provide external microphones and speakers that allow hands-free use of Bluetooth-enabled cell phones in cars.

Thin is in. Manufacturers continue to shave as many millimeters as they can from phone thickness. The newest designs, led by the Motorola RAZR and the Samsung "Blade" MM-A900, are less than half as thick as their flip-phone cousins. Thinnest of all

so far is the Samsung T509, a candybar-style phone that's only 0.44 inches thick. A downside to these ultra-thin designs is that they may lack useful features, such as a slot for external memory cards or a standard headset connector.

HOW TO CHOOSE

First decide which service provider you want to go with, which will limit the universe of compatible phones. Next decide how much you want to spend. You can pay as little as $20 for a cell phone or as much as $600. Then select the right phone based on the following steps:

Hold the phone. In the store, pick up the phone and make sure you can comfortably access most keys with one hand. Try to make a test call and access the menu items. We've found that phones with unconventional shapes are difficult to use. So

First Things First

Narrow your choice of phones

1 Basic phone

Choose for voice and text messages only.
Pros Inexpensive or free with a contract. Simple keypad, easy to operate. Usually compact. Adequate capabilities; for example, all allow you to store frequently used numbers and send and receive text messages. Some models have basic cameras, bright screens, and multimedia capabilities.

Cons May not have Bluetooth, which allows you to use wireless headsets. Usually won't support advanced services (video and music).
Expect to spend no more than about $100. Some basic phones are available for as little as $20, or even free, after rebates.

2 Advanced phone

Choose for advanced voice features such as Bluetooth and capabilities such as music, photos, and video.
Pros Capabilities that may include Bluetooth for a wireless headset, an MP3 player, the ability to access music and video services, and memory-card storage for music and pictures. More options for custom ring tones, games,

and other services. Some can connect directly to a printer to print photographs.
Cons Can be larger and more expensive than a basic model. Extra features can make the phone more difficult to use for the basics.
Expect to spend up to $500, depending on features and rebates.

3 Smart phone

Choose if you want a top-of-the-line, advanced cell phone with a built-in personal digital assistant (PDA).
Pros Simple solution if you rely on a PDA and cell phone. Most versatile access to e-mail. Easily tracks appointments and addresses. Synchronizes with a PC. A touch screen and keypad help in entering

text and navigating applications.
Cons Usually bulky and expensive. Hardware can't be upgraded. If a carrier upgrades its network, you'll need a new phone to use it. Some carrier plans are confusing or expensive.
Expect to spend $200 and up.

Cell-phone music services don't deliver great sound

Until recently, music capability on cell phones was mostly confined to ring tones—the pricey song snippets that you order via the phone's Web browser. A few phones allowed you to import music from a computer, but it wasn't possible to download songs directly to a cell phone. Now Sprint, Verizon, and Amp'd, a new cell-service provider, have introduced the first music-downloading services for cell phones.

MAKING THE MUSIC CONNECTION

In our tests, the services worked as promised, but they have drawbacks. Compared with music you buy online or "rip" from CDs, songs you buy from cell-service providers are generally lower in sound quality, usually more expensive to buy, and not as easy to move from device to device.

Don't expect songs downloaded from the phone services to sound as good as those you order from online stores or rip from a CD and listen to on an MP3 player. But in our tests the difference was least pronounced with the Verizon service. Headsets are another issue. The connector the phones use doesn't accept the standard jacks found on better headphones that you can use with MP3 players and the like.

Verizon and Sprint music services are the best, though even they have far fewer songs than online music stores (several hundred thousand, compared with more than one million on iTunes, for example).

CR's TAKE

None of those music services alone justifies upgrading your cell-phone service or your phone. Instead, they offer an extra capability to those considering upgrades for other reasons. Sprint was the best of the bunch overall, given the relative ease with which you could shop for and manage your music. But its compromised sound quality, even compared with other services, and other limitations made it better suited to occasionally supplementing your digital music library than becoming its content hub.

Downloading songs onto your phone can be a handy way to take your tunes on the road, but it's not worth upgrading your phone just to get this service.

Guide to the Chart

Music services are listed in alphabetical order. **Data network** is the extra-cost high-speed data service required for music downloads. **Compatible phones** list those currently available, generally from the provider; prices are for the phone when bought with a two-year contract. **Sound quality** compares the quality of music downloaded with compatible phones playing the same music on an MP3 player. **Music formats** lists the most common types of music files the services support. **Drag and drop** refers to the ability to drag music files from your computer desktop directly to your phone.

Cell-phone music services: How they compare

MUSIC SERVICE	AMP'D LIVE	SPRINT MUSIC STORE	VERIZON V CAST MUSIC
Data network	Unlimited Data Plan ($20 per month)	Sprint Power Vision ($15 to $25 per month, unlimited)	V Cast ($15 per month, unlimited)
Compatible phones (price)	**Jet**/Angel ($99) (black/white Kyocera KX18s)	**Sanyo MM-9000 ($340), Samsung MM-A900 ($350),** Sanyo MM-7500 ($300), Samsung a920 ($300)	**LG VX8100 ($230)*, Samsung SCH a950 ($180)*,** Verizon CDM 8945 ($210)*
Price/song	$0.99	$2.50	$1.99 to $3.99 ($0.99 to a PC)
Sound quality	Slightly worse than MP3 music files	Slightly worse than MP3 music files	As good as MP3 music files
Music formats include:	MP3, WMA, AAC	MP3, AAC	WMA
Drag and drop	Yes	Yes	No
Pros	Least expensive per song; can "push" songs to phone from computer	Very good music search, menus, music management	Very good sound quality; plays copy-protected music (except iTunes)
Cons	Poor song selection, music search; so-so navigation and music management; no Mac support	Downloaded songs sound relatively poor; no Mac support	Poor music search, navigation, music management; no Mac support
Bottom line	Inexpensive, but browsing its limited library is a challenge	Best choice overall, but your own MP3s will sound better	OK; not recommended for iPod owners

* Price includes cost of optional $30 music kit.
Models in bold were those used to test the services.

are keys that are small, oddly shaped, or arranged in unusual patterns, especially if you're trying to dial a number in dim light.

Check the display. Most color screens perform well in dim light, but some are hard to see in daylight. Try the phone outside or under bright light. In our tests, phones that displayed incoming and outgoing numbers in large black type against a white background were the easiest to read under most conditions. Also make sure indicators like battery life and signal strength are clearly visible.

Look for useful features. Phones vary widely in conveniences and design attributes that add to versatility or ease of use. One important factor to look for is an easy-to-mute ringer, which switches the phone from ring to vibrate when you press and hold one key. A built-in speakerphone allows hands-free use in a car or elsewhere. But be wary of using any phone, even hands-free, while driving.

Check for special prices and promotions. Rebates and special offers can be substantial, but they change frequently. To get the best deal, check the carrier's offerings both online and in its retail stores, and then see what independent dealers offer at their Web sites and in their outlets. If possible, buy a new phone when you're switching carriers or signing a new service commitment with your existing carrier. You almost always get a better deal—either a deeply discounted price or even a free phone—when you're signing a contract.

Check the return policy. Make sure you can return the phone if you're not happy with it. Some stores attach stiff service-cancellation fees on top of what a carrier might charge.

Don't buy phone insurance. All major cell carriers offer insurance policies that cover lost, stolen, or damaged phones. These policies typically cost about $4 to $6 a month and carry a $35 to $100 deductible. We don't think insurance is worthwhile for most consumers. The cost of the premium over a year, for example, would be $50 or $60. Tack on the deductible, and you've paid as much as you would have to buy a new phone. In addition, some insurance plans require you to take time to fill out a police report, and damaged phones are often replaced with a refurbished one that may not even be the same model as the original.

FEATURES THAT COUNT

In addition to the useful phone and multimedia features of today's cell phone models, consider whether you need the following:

Voice command. Follows your commands right out of the box, without the usual training, and lets you dial numbers by saying the digits.

Programmable jog dial. Lets you program all the pressure points on a circular jog as shortcuts to the most-used features and functions, such as the address book and text messaging.

Standard headset connector. Also known as

Cell phones that take digital snapshots (above right) have become commonplace. Need a weather forecast for your destination? For a fee you can get it on your cell phone (above left).

a 2.5-mm connector, this is compatible with most wired headsets and speakerphones. As a rule, models with this connector don't come with a headset. CDMA phones designed to play stereo music (such as those compatible with Verizon, Amp'd, or SprintPCS music services) have a 2.5 mm connector with an extra connection for a stereo headset. You can still use a standard headset to make and receive calls with these phones. Wired headsets start at $20. Options include in-ear buds, models that hook over the ear, and those that clip onto your lobe. Look for one that has an answer/end call switch in the cord, so you don't

have to fumble with the phone.

External memory-card slot. Accepts cards that can store pictures and sometimes music, enabling you to transfer contents to computers, printers, and photo kiosks. Types include Multimedia Memory, Secure Digital, and Memory Stick Duo, as used in digital cameras and PDAs. Smaller versions known as Transflash or Micro SD, Mini SD, and Reduced-size MM cards come with adapters so other devices can read them. In some cases, a memory card comes with the phone.

Hearing-aid compatibility. Some phones interfere with hearing aids. Even those with hearing-

---

You Need to Know

Kids' cell phones give parents control, but are controversial

Now that more than one-third of 11-to14-year-olds have their own cell phones, marketers are targeting younger children with phones that lack a keypad but have speed-dial buttons for parents and 911. Parents preset who their child can call and who can call in (kids scroll through names on a screen), and they control costs through prepaid, or pay-as-you-go, plans.

Companies say that the phones help parents keep tabs on children, but some child advocates object. In July 2005, Commercial Alert, a nonprofit consumer group, led 30 health, education, and privacy advocates in asking Congress to regulate how cell phones are marketed to kids. Gary Ruskin, the group's executive director, cited concerns about safety and privacy as the phones become more advanced, including, perhaps, access to external content.

To help you decide if a child's phone is right for your family, we tested the Firefly (sold at *www.fireflymobile.com*, Target, Wal-Mart, Limited Too, and Toys R Us, and through Cingular and smaller carriers); TicTalk (sold at *www.mytictalk.com*); and the LG Migo (available through Verizon Wireless). The results:
▶ Voice quality for all three phones was about as good as an average cell phone.
▶ All three phones lack voice mail and text messaging, though TicTalk can receive a text message sent through its Web site.
▶ Firefly's battery permitted more than seven hours of talk between charges,

Cell phones for kids have programmable speed-dial buttons instead of a keypad but are more costly than basic cell phones.

TicTalk's, about eight hours. But Migo permitted only about three hours.
▶ To activate the Firefly or TicTalk phones, parents just call an 800 number. Firefly includes 30 minutes initial talk time; TicTalk does not. Parents must add minutes to either phone using a credit card (Firefly or TicTalk) or buying prepaid minutes card (Firefly only). Migo requires buying a Verizon phone plan.
▶ Entering phone numbers into memory is

tedious. Parents can use a PIN to control the calls a child gets and makes; new phone numbers can't be entered without first entering the PIN.
▶ Features may include flashing lights, sounds, and animation. TicTalk has educational games. All three phones lack key locks to prevent unintended outgoing calls.

If you're thinking about buying any child's cell phone, consider:

Age. Kids need to be mature enough to use the phone responsibly.

Cost. The Firefly and TicTalk sell for about $100, the Migo for $50; all include a travel charger. For Firefly, Cingular and regional carriers have various contract-billing plans, which may offer a discount on the phone cost. But we recommend that you go with a prepaid plan. They are available directly from Firefly Mobile, TicTalk, or participating retailers. Firefly's prepaid plans come with 30 minutes of airtime; TicTalk does not include any free minutes. You can buy additional time for either Firefly or TicTalk in blocks of 25 cents a minute, which expire after 90 days. Don't buy more minutes than your child is likely to use. For the Migo, Verizon's cost per minute will vary depending on the plan you purchase.

Health concerns. Studies looking for a link between cell phones held close to the head and tumors are inconclusive, but if a link is found, children could be especially vulnerable. Have them use a headset.

Other options. Instead of buying a child's phone, consider a regular cell phone with prepaid minutes and without expensive features.

aid-compatible designations are not guaranteed to work with all hearing aids. Your doctor can help you choose a phone compatible with the one you use. Or go to *www.accesswireless.org/reference/Wireless PhonesandHearingAidAccessibility.htm.* Ask the salesperson for a home trial to test the phone.

MINIMIZE THREE CELL-PHONE RISKS

Here is the latest advice on how best to protect against potential road, electromagnetic, or fire hazards when using a cell phone:

Don't drive and talk. Using a handheld phone is now illegal in at least three states—Connecticut, New Jersey, and New York—plus the District of Columbia and in several cities, including Chicago. Some 30 other states are considering similar laws. Banning handheld cell-phone use while driving has been backed by studies showing the practice to be hazardous.

But there's growing evidence that it may be no safer to talk on a cell phone using a hands-free device than using a handheld phone. For example, an Australian epidemiological study published in the August 2005 issue of the British Medical

Journal concluded that using a hands-free device with a cell phone didn't reduce the risk of a serious road crash.

For safety's sake, pull your car over to the shoulder or other safe place off the road before making a call.

Reduce radiation exposure. Scores of studies have reported a range of effects of cell-phone radiation on living things, but their health significance remains unclear. Two studies should shed more light on the subject: a 13-nation analysis by the World Health Organization (WHO), which is expected to be completed in 2006, and an animal study by the National Institute for Environmental Health Sciences, which is scheduled for release in several years. The preliminary findings from the WHO study suggest little or no risk of brain cancer in the first 10 years of cell-phone use, but risks from exposure longer than 10 years haven't been ruled out.

If you're concerned about radiation, you can follow these precautions:
▶ Use a hands-free device, such as a headset or speaker phone, to keep the phone's antenna away from your head and body.
▶ Limit use by children and teens. Encourage them to wear a headset or send text

Which shape: The swivel and slider join the familiar flip and candy bar

Most cell phones fall into two tried-and-true designs: compact-folding or "flip" phones, and candy-bar models.

Flip phones, the most common type, tend to offer the best voice quality in noisy surroundings. A cover keeps keys from being pressed accidentally. Number keys are usually laid out in a standard pattern, making them easy to use. However, many flip phones have an external antenna that's susceptible to damage. In addition, with the case closed, you can't always see who's calling.

With candy-bar phones, voice quality is often low in noisy surroundings. You answer calls by pressing any key. But unless you lock the phone, number keys can easily be pressed by accident. Also, some candy-bar phones have unorthodox keyboard layouts, which can be confusing. The antenna is usually tucked inside the phone, making it less susceptible to damage.

Here are two of the newest designs, generally found on phones with multimedia

features, megapixel cameras, and music players.

SWIVEL
Pros Compact. Opens like a pen knife. Display is always visible. Most have internal antennas.
Cons Thicker than folding or candy-bar phones. Can be clumsy to operate. In noisy places, voice quality isn't as good as on folding phones.

SLIDER
Pros Tend to have innovative designs with multimedia capabilities. Display is always visible. Most have an automatic lock to prevent you from pressing keys accidentally.
Cons Thicker than folding or candy-bar phones. In noisy environments, voice quality is not as good as on folding phones. Some have external antennas that are susceptible to damage.

At last count, 18 states had partial or total bans on talking on a cell phone while driving. Even in places without such laws, we recommend not phoning while driving, even with a headset.

messages, both of which keep the phone away from the head.

Avoid cell-phone fires. Our engineers offer these safety tips for cell-phone batteries:

▶ Keep the battery away from contact with metal, such as coins, keys, or similar objects in your pocket, which could cause it to short-circuit.

▶ Buy only the battery and charger designed for your phone, from your wireless provider or a reputable retailer. An unusually inexpensive battery or charger carrying what appears to be a brand name may well be a counterfeit and may not be properly manufactured.

▶ Keep the phone and battery away from sources of extreme heat, such as a stove, radiator, or glove compartment.

▶ If you drop a phone with a fully charged battery, there's a small chance it could overheat and explode. Leave it on the ground for a few moments to make sure there's no problem.

▶ Don't let your phone or battery get wet. The circuitry could corrode and pose a safety hazard.

Bluetooth headsets eliminate the tangled wire problems

Bluetooth, the technology that allows cell phones to be used with wireless headsets, eliminates fumbling for the phone when it rings, and it's much more convenient than being tethered to (and often tangled up in) a wired headset. When paired with a cell phone that has voice activation (like virtually all Bluetooth models), the earpiece has all the functionality needed to make or take calls. The phone itself can be as far as 30 feet away.

Here are some tips on buying a Bluetooth headset, including some caveats and recommendations based on our latest tests:

Compactness will cost you. Small is indeed beautiful in an earpiece, and it helps you avoid the disconcerting tendency of long, bulky headsets to "flap" in the wind or when you turn your head. But modest size often comes at an immodest price. A small, sleek earpiece can cost about

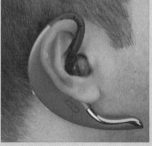

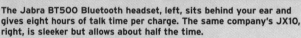
The Jabra BT500 Bluetooth headset, left, sits behind your ear and gives eight hours of talk time per charge. The same company's JX10, right, is sleeker but allows about half the time.

$150—as much or more than a Bluetooth phone. Also, smaller models tend to have smaller batteries–and thus a shorter talk time on a charge than their bulkier cousins.

Expect some setup time and effort. Headsets and Bluetooth phones need to be electronically introduced in a sometimes tricky procedure known as pairing. Some models have a dedicated pairing button that simplifies the process. As this procedure's name implies, most Bluetooth

devices are monogamous. If you buy a new Bluetooth headset or wish to connect your phone to another Bluetooth device, like a printer or PDA, the phone must sever ties with the original headset and pair with the new device.

Consider charging convenience. As with other portable devices, Bluetooth headsets require periodic recharging–an added chore when you're already managing the energy needs of the cell phone and perhaps other mobile gear. All mod-

els come with wall chargers; a dedicated car charger is typically $10 to $30 extra. Of course, you'll minimize recharging if you choose a model with maximum talk time on a charge. While most headsets let you gab for four to five hours between charges, the best in our tests—two from Jabra and one from Motorola—operated for eight or more hours before fizzling out.

Look for useful features. Call mute and/or call hold is common. Equally important, and not always present, is an audible low-battery warning, which can help you avoid dropped calls. Most Bluetooth phones will voice-dial once you teach them that "Mom," let's say, equals a certain number. Phones with voice command follow your commands right out of the box without the usual training. With voice command you can also dial a number by saying the digits and instantly summon voice mail and other common applications.

INTERNET PHONING CAN CUT YOUR PHONE BILLS

Survey shows happy customers, but there are some drawbacks

Consumers tired of paying big bills for traditional landline telephone service are increasingly turning to the Internet for some financial relief. Many are saving $20 to $50 or more a month by using Voice over Internet Protocol, often called VoIP. It transmits your voice calls over the same Internet lines that carry your e-mail.

Phone companies, cable operators, and newcomers such as Vonage offer VoIP service. Unlimited local and domestic long-distance plans cost $25 to $40 a month. Most include typical phone features—such as voice mail, caller ID, and call waiting—plus others you can't get with a landline, such as the ability to make local calls using your home phone number even if you're thousands of miles away.

The combination of price and features sounds unbeatable. Does VoIP deliver? To find out, we surveyed 201 consumers who use VoIP service. This small but nationally representative sample consisted mostly of users who'd had this emerging technology for a year or less. Their reaction was generally positive. More than half of those surveyed said they had cut their phone bills, and an equal number were highly satisfied with VoIP.

But there are a number of drawbacks, including issues regarding emergency 911 service. We strongly recommend that you keep a basic landline even if you get VoIP for day-to-day use.

WHAT VoIP USERS THINK

About half the users we surveyed said reducing local and domestic long-distance phone bills was a factor in their decision to try VoIP. They weren't disappointed. Almost 80 percent of those with lower bills saved at least $20 a month, and 34 percent saved $40 or more. Most of those surveyed didn't have to put up with poor sound quality or unreliable connections to realize those savings.

VoIP vs. landline. About 57 percent of consumers with both VoIP and landline service said Internet phone calls sounded at least as good as calls made on their traditional phone line. But 43 percent said the landline sounded better.

Half the users with VoIP and a landline found no difference in their ability to make and receive calls reliably. But the rest were almost evenly split in rating VoIP or landline as more reliable.

VoIP vs. cell phone. Generally, survey respondents who used both VoIP and a cell phone said Internet phoning offered more-reliable connections than their cell phone and comparable voice quality.

While many of the users we surveyed had no trouble with VoIP, almost one-third had at least one dropped call or difficulty in making or receiving calls within a week of the survey. Some also had occasional problems hearing callers or being heard.

BEFORE YOU PLUNGE IN

If the generally positive experience of users piques your interest in VoIP, here's what

Phoning over the Internet requires a broadband connection.

you should know before signing up:

You might have a new "phone company." Some traditional landline and wireless phone companies, such as AT&T and Verizon, offer VoIP service, but you'll encounter other names not normally associated with telephones. Those include cable companies like Cablevision and Time Warner Cable, as well as businesses that specialize in VoIP. One of the biggest mainstream providers is Vonage, a VoIP-only company.

You can use regular phones. You can use any standard touch-tone phone with VoIP, and the person you're calling does not need special equipment or Internet access. You typically plug your phone into an analog telephone adapter, called an ATA, which you can buy at a retail store for $100 or less; some companies provide one at little or no cost. The adapter connects to a router or modem, which in turn hooks up to the cable or DSL line that serves as your broadband connection.

Only one phone must be connected to the VoIP adapter. To have more than one phone on the line, you can use a cordless phone with several handsets or a multiple-jack device with the adapter. You may be able to use the existing phone wiring and jacks to plug your phones into the VoIP line, but only if you give up your landline, which we don't recommend.

You may be able to keep your phone number for the VoIP line. You can have your phone number reassigned to the VoIP line, but only if you terminate your landline service. It may take a few weeks for the transfer, so you'll have to use a temporary number during the transition. One exception: If your broadband access is through DSL, you may have to keep your current number for that line and get a new number for the VoIP line.

If you'd rather get a new phone number for the VoIP line, you can usually choose the area code. Say you live in Detroit but most of your callers live in Chicago. Get a number with their 312 area code, and you'll be a local call for them but a long-distance call for everyone in your town. Your number may or may not be listed in a 411 directory and a phone book, depending on the provider. Check with the company to see.

You'll probably get reliable service and decent sound quality. Judging by our survey group, frequent dropped calls and poor voice quality didn't seem to be the typical experience. Still, don't be surprised if you have problems occasionally.

VoIP plans compared

	AT&T CallVantage	Optimum Voice	Time Warner Cable	Verizon VoiceWing	Vonage
Unlimited calling plan	$30/mo.	$35/mo.	$40/mo.	$35/mo.	$25/mo.
Limited calling plan	$20/mo. for unlimited local calls; 4¢/min. for long-distance.	none	none	$20 for 500 min.; 4¢/min. for extra time.	$15 for 500 minutes; 3.9¢/min. for extra time.
Voice mail	free	free	$3.95/mo.	free	free
Additional numbers	$5/mo.	not available	not available	$8/mo.	$5/mo.
Coverage area	U.S., Puerto Rico, Canada	U.S., Puerto Rico, Canada	U.S., Puerto Rico, Canada	U.S., Puerto Rico, Canada	U.S., Puerto Rico, Canada
Broadband type	cable or DSL	cable	cable	cable or DSL	cable or DSL
Availability	nationwide	parts of NY, NJ, CT	various markets in 27 states	nationwide	nationwide
Activation fee	$30 by phone or online; no fee at store.	no	no	$40 by phone; no fee for online orders.	$30 by phone or online; no fee at store.
Termination fee	No fee if canceled within 30 days or after 1 yr.	no	no	No fee if canceled within 30 days or after 1 yr.; otherwise $20.	No fee if canceled within 30 days or after 1 yr.; otherwise $40.
Installation	do it yourself	by company	by company	do it yourself	do it yourself

SAMPLE OF INTERNATIONAL RATES *(per minute, to landline)*

	AT&T CallVantage	Optimum Voice	Time Warner Cable	Verizon VoiceWing	Vonage
Hong Kong	5¢	8¢	10¢	3¢	4¢
Kingston, Jamaica	12	32	45	12	12
Mexico City	7	8	9	7	6
New Delhi, India	16	23	36	15.7	17
Philippines	16	17	22	20	18
United Kingdom	5	7	7	3	4

REASONS TO GET VoIP

Like any technology, VoIP has pros and cons. Here are some of its good points:

It costs you less. Unlimited calling plans start at $25 a month—sometimes less as part of a promotion—and plans with a limited number of minutes may be even cheaper. A plan with 500 minutes of talk time, for example, might cost $15 or $20.

While international calls are not covered by flat-rate plans, per-minute rates are often far lower than you'd otherwise pay. Verizon VoiceWing, for example, bills calls to Kingston, Jamaica, at 12 cents a minute; Verizon's lowest rate for a traditional landline plan is 38 cents a minute. Some providers offer unlimited in-network calling among subscribers, even if they're in different countries.

One reason VoIP costs so much less than standard phone service is that it's not subject to all the taxes, surcharges, and other regulatory fees that jack up your landline and cell-phone bills. But the Federal Communications Commission and Congress are examining various tax and regulatory issues, so that is changing.

You'll get services not found on landline. Because VoIP is an Internet-based service, it offers more capabilities than traditional phone lines. Depending on the provider, you may be able to have voice messages e-mailed to you as sound files, which you can click on to hear; view details of calls on an online log; forward calls to other numbers—say, your cell phone and office—if you expect an urgent call; and set up do-not-disturb times during which calls go directly into voice mail.

You can use your home phone service from anywhere. Travelers or people with more than one home can use any broadband Internet connection to place calls from their VoIP number, no matter where they are. To do so, you bring your VoIP adapter on your trip, connect it to a cable or DSL modem providing broadband access, and plug in a phone.

INTERNET PHONING HAS ITS DRAWBACKS

While it has many positive attributes, VoIP still isn't for everyone. Among the reasons:

It requires a broadband Internet connection. If you don't have cable or DSL broadband and get it specifically or primarily for VoIP, the typical $30 to $45 monthly fee will cancel out the savings.

You need some computer savvy to get VoIP up and running. Two-thirds of the group we surveyed installed VoIP themselves, and about 40 percent of those do-it-yourselfers had problems. Things may not go smoothly even if a pro installs it. About 40 percent of that group said setup took more than two hours, or it required two visits or replacement hardware.

Your VoIP phone won't work if you lose power or Internet access. Like a cordless phone, VoIP won't work during power outages. For about $45, you can buy a battery that provides four to six hours of talk time. But there's no way you can restore phone service if your cable or DSL broadband Internet access is disrupted.

There are possible security risks. Because

> **Many people are saving money** with VoIP, usually at least $10 a month, according to our most recent survey.

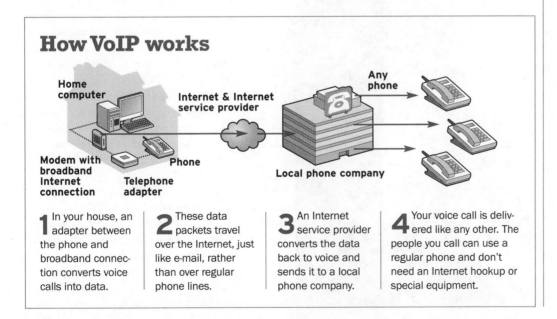

How VoIP works

Home computer

Internet & Internet service provider

Any phone

Modem with broadband Internet connection

Phone

Telephone adapter

Local phone company

1 In your house, an adapter between the phone and broadband connection converts voice calls into data.

2 These data packets travel over the Internet, just like e-mail, rather than over regular phone lines.

3 An Internet service provider converts the data back to voice and sends it to a local phone company.

4 Your voice call is delivered like any other. The people you call can use a regular phone and don't need an Internet hookup or special equipment.

VoIP is Internet-based, it's potentially vulnerable to viruses, hackers, and denial of service. No incidents have been reported, but the risk is there.

THE BOTTOM LINE

If you can deal with the potential problems, VoIP can cut your phone bills, increase your talk time, and add useful new services. However, we urge you to keep a corded phone (requiring no power) and a basic landline plan for emergencies.

VoIP may save you money if you spend more than $60 for local and long-distance service. Assuming you're already paying for broadband, you can get an unlimited VoIP plan for $25 and a basic landline for about $20 and still save.

CORDLESS CAN WORK WITHOUT A PHONE JACK

Higher frequencies and more handsets make them indispensable

It's easier than ever to have a phone where you want one. The newest breed of cordless phone lets you put a handset in any room in the house, even if no phone jack is nearby.

Manufacturers, though, still offer a bewildering array of phones: inexpensive models with just the basics; multihandset, full-featured phones with a built-in answering machine; single-line and two-line phones; digital and analog phones, and different frequency bands. In many instances, a phone will have a phone-answerer sibling.

Many phone-answerers come in a phone-only version. If you have a cordless phone that's several years old, it's probably a 900-MHz phone. Newer phones use higher frequencies, namely 2.4 or 5.8 GHz. They aren't necessarily better than the older ones, but they may provide more calling security and a wider array of useful capabilities and features.

WHAT'S AVAILABLE

AT&T, GE, Panasonic, Uniden, and VTech account for most of the market. VTech owns the AT&T Consumer Products Division and now makes phones under the AT&T brand as well as its own name.

The current trends include phones that support two or more handsets with one base, less expensive 2.4- and 5.8-GHz analog phones, and full-featured 2.4- and 5.8-GHz digital phones. Some of the multiple-handset-capable phones now include an additional handset with a charging cradle. About a third of the cordless phones sold include a digital answering machine.

A major distinction among cordless phones is the way they transmit their signals. Here are some terms that you may see while shopping and what they mean for you:

Analog. These phones are the least expensive type available now. They tend to have better voice quality and enough range to let you chat anywhere in your house and yard, or even a little beyond. They are also unlikely to cause interference with other wireless products. But analog transmission isn't very secure; anyone with an RF scan-

Young consumers have never known a time without cordless phones.

ner or comparable wireless device might be able to listen in. Analog phones are also more likely than digital phones to suffer occasional static and RF interference from other wireless products. Price: $15 to $100.

Digital. These offer about the same range as analog phones, but with better security and less susceptibility to RF interference. And like analogs they are unlikely to cause interference to other wireless products. Price: $50 to $130.

Digital spread spectrum (DSS). A DSS phone distributes a call across a number of frequencies, providing an added measure of security and more immunity from RF interference. The range may be slightly better than that of analog or digital phones. Note that some DSS phones—usually the 2.4-GHz or the multiple-handset-capable phones with handset-to-handset talk capabilities—use such a wide swath of the spectrum even in standby mode that they may interfere with baby monitors and other wireless products operating in the same frequency band. Price: $75 to $225 (for multiple-handset systems).

Frequency. Cordless phones use one or two of the three available frequency bands:

900 MHz. Some manufacturers still make inexpensive 900-MHz phones, usually analog. They are fine for many households, and still account for about one-quarter of the market.

2.4 GHz. The band most phones now use. Unfortunately, many other wireless products—

baby monitors, wireless computer networks, home-security monitors, wireless speakers, and microwaves ovens—use the same band. A 2.4-GHz analog phone is inherently susceptible to RF interference from other wireless devices, and a 2.4-GHz DSS phone may cause interference in other products. However, DSS phones billed as "802.11-friendly" are unlikely to interfere with wireless computer networks.

5.8 GHz. The band that newer phones use. Its main advantage: less chance of RF interference because few other products currently use this band.

Some phones are dual-band, but that only means they transmit between base and handset in

In addition to a cordless handset and an answerer, this model from Uniden includes a corded handset that works during power outages.

You Need to Know

How to minimize wireless interference

Many wireless products, such as cordless phones, home networks, and baby monitors, share the 2.4-gigahertz (GHz) radio frequency bands. As a result, they're likely to interfere with each other. Interference can cause static on a cordless phone, a baby monitor, or wireless speakers; it can also disrupt a wireless computer network.

Here's how to minimize interference in your household:
Make sure you can return it. Ask if the store will let you exchange the phone, in case

you can't get rid of interference. **Choose a cordless phone that uses the 5.8-GHz or 900-megahertz (MHz) band.** These frequency bands are not as widely used as 2.4-GHz and, therefore, are less likely to cause or receive interference. DSS phones billed as "802.11-friendly" are unlikely to interfere with wireless computer networks, but they may interfere with other wireless devices. Keep a 2.4-GHz analog phone out of the kitchen, if possible. It can pick up interference from a

microwave oven that's running. **Change the channel.** Most wireless products allow you to change channels to solve interference problems. On some, it's as easy as pushing a button or sliding a switch. Changing channels on a wireless router requires using your computer. **Keep your distance.** If channel changes don't work, try keeping the conflicting wireless devices as far from each other as possible, such as in different rooms.

A 5.8-GHz phone is not as likely to interfere with other wireless devices.

one band and receive in another; you can't switch to or choose one band or another.

FEATURES THAT COUNT

Standard features on most cordless phones include handset earpiece volume control, handset ringer, last-number redial, a pager to find the handset, a flash button to answer call waiting, and a low-battery indicator.

Some phones let you support two or more handsets with just one base without the need for extra phone jacks. Additional handsets including the charging cradle are usually sold separately, although more phones are being bundled with an additional handset and charging cradle.

An **LCD screen**, found on many handsets and on some bases, can display a personal phone directory and other useful information such as the name and/or number dialed, caller ID, battery strength, or how long you've been connected.

Caller ID displays the name and number of a caller and the date and time of the call if you use your phone company's caller ID service. If you have caller ID with call waiting, the phone will display data on a second caller if you're already on the phone.

A phone that supports **two lines** can receive calls for two phone numbers—useful if you have, say, a business line and a personal line that you'd like to use from a single phone. Some of the phones have **two ringers**, each with a distinctive pitch to let you know which line is ringing. The two-line feature also allows conferencing two callers in three-way connections. Some two-line phones have an **auxiliary jack data port** to plug in a fax, modem, or other phone device that can also be useful.

A **speakerphone** offers a hands-free way to converse or wait on hold, and lets others chime in as well. A **base speakerphone** lets you answer a call without the handset; a **handset speakerphone** lets you chat hands-free as long as you stay within a few feet of the handset.

A **base keypad** supplements the keypad on the handset. It's handy for navigating menu-driven systems, since you don't have to take the phone away from your ear to punch the keys. Some phones have a **lighted keypad** that either glows in the dark or lights up when you press a key or when the phone rings. This makes the phone easier to use in low-light conditions. All phones have a **handset ringer**, and many phones have a **base ringer**. Some let you turn them on or off, adjust the volume, or change the auditory tone.

> **Some answerers have advanced playback controls for fast or slow playback or rewind, making it easier to retrieve messages.**

Taking a message has never been so easy

Digital answering machines come as stand-alone devices or as part of a phone/answerer combo unit. The main advantage of a combo unit—less clutter—has to be weighed against the loss of one part if the other goes bad. Answerers usually have standard features and capabilities such as a selectable number of rings and a toll-saver, on/off control, call screening, remote access from a touch-tone phone, and a variety of ways to navigate through your messages. Most have a message day/time stamp, can delete all messages or just individual ones, allow you to adjust the speaker volume, and can retain messages and greeting, after a momentary power outage.

Other features you may want to consider are the number of mailboxes, advanced playback controls, remote handset access, conversation recording, a counter display that indicates the number of messages received, and a visual indicator or audible message alert that lets you know when you have new messages.

In CONSUMER REPORTS tests, most answerers delivered very good voice quality for recorded messages and good quality for the greeting. Phones that let you record your greeting through the handset usually sound better. Some let you listen to your greeting through the handset, too, as opposed to the base speaker. That gives you a better indication of how the greeting will sound to callers.

Price: $20 to $80 (stand-alone units); $30 to $240 (combos).

Many cordless phones have a **headset jack** on the handset and include a **belt clip** for carrying the phone. This allows hands-free conversation anywhere in the house. Some phones have a headset jack on the base, which allows hands-free conversation without any drain on the handset battery. Headsets are usually sold separately for about $20.

Other convenient features include **auto talk**, which lets you lift the handset off the base for an incoming call and start talking without having to press a button, and **any-key answer**.

Some phones provide a **battery holder for battery backup**—a compartment in the base to charge a spare handset battery pack or to hold alkaline batteries for base-power backup, either of which can enable the phone to work if you lose household AC power. Still, it's wise to keep a corded phone somewhere in your home.

Some multiple-handset-capable phones allow conversation between handsets in an **intercom mode** and allow conferencing handsets with an outside party. In intercom mode, the handsets have to be within range of the base for handset-to-handset use. Others lack this capability; they allow you to transfer calls from handset to handset but not to use the handsets to conference with an outside caller. Still other phones allow direct communication between handsets, so you can take them with you to use like walkie-talkies.

HOW TO CHOOSE

Decide how much hardware you need. The basic options are a stand-alone phone, a phone with a built-in answerer, or a phone that supports multiple handsets from one base. A stand-alone phone is best suited for small families or people in small apartments with little need for more than one phone. The built-in answerer, a common choice, adds a big measure of convenience. A multiple-handset phone is good for active families who need phones throughout the house. This type of phone lets you put handsets in a room that doesn't have a phone jack.

Select the technology and frequency band. A 900-MHz phone should suit most users, but that type may be hard to find because 2.4- and 5.8-GHz models dominate. You're likely to find the widest range of models and prices with 2.4-GHz phones. But if you want to minimize problems of interference with other wireless products, look for a 5.8-GHz or 900-MHz phone. Analog phones, more likely to be less expensive than digital, are fine for many people. But if privacy is important, choose a DSS or digital phone.

To be sure you're actually getting a DSS or digital phone for its voice-transmission security, check the packaging carefully. Look for wording such as "digital phone," "digital spread spectrum" (DSS) or "frequency-hopping spread spectrum" (FHSS). Phrases such as "phone with digital security code," "phone with all-digital answerer," or "spread spectrum technology" (not digital spread spectrum) all describe phones that are less secure.

Phones that use dual-band transmission may indicate only the higher frequency in large print on the packaging. If you want a true 2.4- or 5.8-GHz phone, check the fine print. If only the frequency is prominently shown on the package, it's probably analog.

Settle on the features you want. You can expect caller ID, a headset jack, and a base that can be wall-mounted. But the features don't end there for both stand-alone phones and phone-answerers. Check the box or ask to see an instruction manual to be sure you're getting the

If your home is large, having an extra handset in a room far from the base is convenient.

capabilities and features that matter to you. As a rule, the more feature-laden the phone, the higher its price.

Performance variations. CONSUMER REPORTS' tests show that most new cordless phones have very good overall voice quality. Some are excellent, approaching the voice quality of the best corded phones. In our latest tests, most fully charged nickel-cadmium (NiCd) or nickel-metal hydride (NiMH) batteries handled eight hours of continuous conversation before they needed recharging. Most manufacturers claim that a fully charged battery will last at least a week in standby mode. When they can no longer hold a charge, a replacement battery, usually proprietary, costs about $10 to $25, and may be difficult to find. Some phones use less-expensive AA or AAA rechargeable batteries.

(To find a store that will recycle a used battery, call 800-822-8837. Or go to the Rechargeable Battery Recycling Corporation's Web site, at *www.rbrc.org.*)

Give the handset a test drive. In the store, hold the handset to see if it feels comfortable. It should fit the contours of your face. The earpiece should have rounded edges and a recessed center that fits nicely over the middle of your ear. Check the buttons and controls to make sure they're reasonably sized and legible.

Don't discard your corded phone. It's a good idea to keep at least one in your home, if only for emergencies. A cordless phone may not work if you lose electrical power, and a cell phone won't work if you can't get a signal or the circuits are full. A corded phone draws its power from the phone system and can function without household AC power.

ConsumerReports.org | Compare plans online

Because phone service providers and plans vary from area to area, it's difficult for CONSUMER REPORTS print publications to include all of your options. But national long-distance plans and cellular plans in the top 70 U.S. markets can be compared for your area at *www.Consumer Reports.org.*

Both the long-distance plan selector and the cellular-plan selector are powered by Telebright, an independent provider of such information. The long-distance selector offers listings and comparisons of plans for your area code and prefix; the cellular selector provides plan listings by ZIP code. For long-distance, click on Personal finance on our home page, then on Long-distance service (under Shopping & spending), and finally on the link to the long-distance calling-plan

selector. For cellular, click on Electronics & computers on our home page, on Cell phones decision guide, and then on Cellular-plan selector (under Choosing a cell-phone plan).

As a buyer of this guide, you are entitled to a free one-month subscription to *www.Consumer Reports.org,* allowing you to use the paid as well as free areas of our site.

DIGITAL CAMERAS & CAMCORDERS

▶▶ **Forget film. Digital cameras let you take control of every aspect of picture-taking, from shooting the images to editing and printing them.**

Ratings: Camcorders, p. 148; digital cameras, p. 154.

DIGITAL CAMERAS OFFER VERSATILITY & CONTROL

From shooting to sharing, these photos leave film behind

Digital cameras give you extraordinary control over images. You can transfer them to your computer, then crop, adjust color and contrast, and add textures and other special effects. You can make prints at home on a color inkjet or snapshot printer, drop off the memory card at one of a growing number of photofinishers, use a self-service kiosk at your local drugstore to select, edit, and print pictures instantly, or upload images to an online photofinisher. Final results can be e-mailed, made into cards or T-shirts, or uploaded to a photo-sharing Web site for storage, viewing, and sharing with others.

LCD viewers are very accurate in framing the shot you want, but they use more battery power than an optical viewfinder alone.

Like camcorders, digital cameras have LCD monitors for composing shots or viewing those already taken. Many digital cameras can also shoot video with sound. While some camcorders can shoot still photos, a typical camcorder's resolution is no match for a good still camera's.

WHAT'S AVAILABLE

The leading brands are Canon, Fujifilm, HP, Kodak, Nikon, Olympus, and Sony. Other brands come from consumer-electronics, computer, and traditional camera and film companies.

It's easier than ever to go to extremes with a digital camera. Small is bountiful, and big is also booming. The smallest cameras we tested recently, **subcompacts,** weigh 5 to 8 ounces and can fit in a pocket. Price: $185 to $450.

Too big to pocket, but small enough for most handbags and glove boxes, are mainstream **compacts.** The ones we tested recently weigh 7 to 14 ounces. Price: $140 to $480.

More serious cameras have the versatility and power to capture fast action or create photographic art under the most demanding light conditions. **Advanced compact** cameras are typically larger and heavier than compacts, with versatile controls and long zoom lenses. Price: $280 to $850.

Super-zoom cameras are characterized by a very long zoom range—10x or greater. While traditionally larger and heavier than compacts, a few new models are designed to be smaller and lighter than older models. Price: $250 to $700.

SLRs (single-lens reflex), the largest and heaviest type, offer the most versatility and power, including interchangeable lenses. Price: $600 to $1,700 for consumer models; professional models can cost thousands.

FEATURES THAT COUNT

Digital cameras are distinguished by their **resolution**—how many pixels, or picture elements, the image sensor contains. One megapixel equals 1 million picture elements. A 4-megapixel camera can make excellent 8x10s and pleasing 11x14s. There are also 5- to 10-megapixel models, including point-and-shoot ones. These are well-suited for making larger prints or for maintaining sharpness if you want to use only a portion of the original image. Professional digital cameras use as many as 16 megapixels. Price: $100

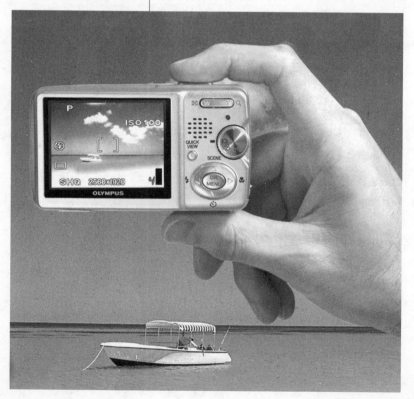

Expert • Independent • Nonprofit

to $400 for 4 megapixels; $150 to $500 for 5 and 6 megapixels; $300 to $1,000 for 7- to 10-megapixel point-and-shoot models, and up to $1,700 for 10-megapixel SLRs.

Most digital cameras are highly automated, with features such as **automatic exposure control** (which manages the shutter speed, aperture, or both according to available light) and **autofocus.**

Instead of film, digital cameras record their shots on **flash-memory cards.** Compact Flash (CF) and SecureDigital (SD) are the most widely used. Once quite expensive, these cards have tumbled in price—a 256-megabyte card can now cost less than $20. Other types of memory cards used by cameras include MemoryStick Duo and xD.

To save images, you transfer them to a computer, typically by connecting the camera to the computer's USB or FireWire port, or inserting the memory card into a special reader. Some printers can take memory cards and make prints without putting the images on a computer first. Image-handling software, such as Adobe Photoshop Elements, Jasc Paint Shop, Microsoft Picture It, and ACDSee, lets you resize, touch up, and crop digital images using your computer. Most digital cameras work with both Windows and Macintosh machines.

The file format commonly used for photos is **JPEG,** which is a compressed format. Some cameras can save photos in the uncompressed TIFF format, but this setting yields enormous files. Other high-end cameras have a RAW file format, which yields the image data with no processing from the camera and might also be uncompressed.

The optical viewfinder is becoming increasingly rare, replaced by larger color LCD **monitors.** (Some are now as large as 3 inches.) Monitors are very accurate in framing the actual image you get—better than most optical viewfinders—but they use more battery power and might be hard to view in bright sunlight. You can also view shots you've already taken on the LCD monitor. Many digital cameras provide a video output, so you can view your pictures on a TV set.

Many new models let you capture **video** and **sound.** Some let you record video in high-quality MPEG4 format, up to 30 frames per second, up to the memory card's limit.

A **zoom lens** provides flexibility in framing shots and closes the distance between you and your subject—ideal if you want to quickly switch to a close shot. The typical 3x zoom on mainstream cameras goes from a moderately wide-angle view

All compact digitals have zoom lenses, which adds flexibility in framing shots.

First Things First

Match the camera type to your needs

Excellent cameras come in several types. To narrow your search, decide which factors are most important to you. Then find the best model by checking the cameras in the Ratings on page 154.

1 Advanced compact cameras

Best for challenging lighting, such as sunsets and dimly lighted subjects.
Pros Versatile controls and long zoom.

Can store RAW images.
Cons Relatively large and heavy.
Expect to spend $280 to $850.

2 Super-zoom cameras

Best for travel, nature, and sports.
Pros Very long zoom range, with powerful telephoto setting.

Cons Usually larger, bulkier, and heavier than a compact model.
Expect to spend $250 to $700.

3 SLR cameras

Best for all of the above and artistic photography.
Pros Instant startup, minimal shutter lag, interchangeable lenses, large image sensor, fast, contin-

uous shooting, RAW images, excellent battery life.
Cons Large, heavy, and expensive.
Expect to spend $600 to $1,700.

This SLR-style camera features a zoom range from wide-angle to medium telephoto.

(35 mm) to moderate telephoto (105 mm). You can find cameras with extended zoom ranges between 8x and 15x, giving added versatility for outdoor photography. Other new cameras go down to 24 or 28 mm at the wide-angle end, making it easier to take in an entire scene in close quarters, such as a crowded party.

Optical zooms are superior to digital zooms, which merely magnify the center of the frame without actually increasing picture detail, resulting in a somewhat coarser view.

Sensors in digital cameras are typically about as light sensitive as ISO 100 film, though many let you increase that setting. (At ISO 100, you'll probably need to use a flash indoors and in low outdoor light.) A camera's **flash range** tells you how far from the camera the flash will provide proper exposure. If the subject is out of range, you'll know to close the distance. But digital cameras can tolerate some underexposure before the image suffers noticeably.

Red-eye reduction shines a light toward your subject just before the main flash. (A camera whose flash unit is farther from the lens reduces the risk of red eye. Computer editing of the image may also correct red eye.) With **automatic flash mode,** the camera fires the flash whenever the light entering the camera registers as insufficient. A few new cameras have **built-in red-eye correction** capability.

Some cameras with large LCDs, and some with powerful telephoto lenses, now come with some form of **image stabilizer.** (Optical-image stabilizers are the best type; some cameras use simulated stabilization to try to achieve the same effect.) Stabilizers compensate for handheld camera shake, letting you use a slower shutter speed than you

otherwise could for following movement. But an image stabilizer won't compensate for the motion of subjects.

Most new 6- to 10-megapixel cameras come with full **manual controls,** including independent controls for shutter and aperture. That gives serious shutterbugs control over depth of field, shooting action, or shooting scenes with tricky lighting.

HOW TO CHOOSE

The first step is to determine how you will use the camera most of the time. Consider these two questions:

How much flexibility to enlarge images do you need? If you mainly want to make 4x6 snapshots, a camera with 4- or 5-megapixel resolution should be fine. It will also make an 8x10 print of an entire image without alteration that won't look much different than one from a 6- or 8-megapixel model. But to enlarge the image more or enlarge only part of it, you'll want a camera with resolution of 6 megapixels or greater.

Checklist

Digital cameras

Size

☐ Medium   ☐ Pocket   ☐ SLR

Number of megapixels? _____

Optical zoom? _____

Manual aperture? _____

Shutter speed? _____

Manual focus? _____

Macro focus? _____

This checklist can help you focus on the features of digital cameras that best meet your shooting style.

An interactive version of this checklist, including prices and brands, is available online at *www.ConsumerReports.org*. The digital camera product selector produces a list of models that fit the criteria you have entered. This decision tool can be found by going to ConsumerReports.org's index page for digital cameras and clicking on the link for Product Selector. One of many online resources available to members only, you can access it by activating the 30-day free trial subscription offered on the inside cover of this guide.

How much control do you want over exposure and composition? Cameras meant for automatic point-and-shoot photos, with a 3x zoom lens, will serve casual shooters as well as dedicated hobbyists much of the time. The full-featured cameras in the advanced compact and superzoom categories offer capabilities that more-dedicated photographers will want to have. Two of the more important capabilities are a zoom range of 5x to 10x or more, which lets you bring distant outdoor subjects close and also lets you shoot candid portraits without getting right in your subject's face, and a full complement of manual controls that let you determine the shutter speed and lens opening.

Once you've established the performance priorities that you need from a camera, you can narrow your choices further by considering these convenience factors:

Size and weight. The smallest, lightest models aren't necessarily inexpensive 4-megapixel cameras. And the biggest and heaviest aren't necessarily found at the high end. If possible, try cameras at the store before you buy. That way, you'll know which one fits your hand best and which can be securely gripped. In our tests, we found that some of the smallest don't leave much room even for small fingers.

Battery type and life. All digital cameras run on rechargeable batteries, either an expensive battery pack or a set of AAs. In our tests, neither type had a clear performance advantage. The best-performing cameras offer at least 250 shots on a charge, while the worst manage under 100. We think it's more convenient to own a camera that

How much memory does your camera need?

The paltry memory cards supplied with new digital cameras—typically enough to hold fewer than 20 still shots—are more inadequate than ever now that 5-plus megapixel resolution is common and more cameras can take storage-hogging video clips. Here's a guide to buying (and wisely using) supplemental storage for your new camera:

Buy at least 256 megabytes of storage. For most cameras, don't consider a card smaller than 256 MB, which can hold around 100 JPEG images, depending on image content and camera settings.

Allow more storage for more demanding uses. For a 6-megapixel camera shooting at maximum resolution and the highest quality level, consider a 1-GB card, which costs about $55 and can hold several hundred JPEG images.

Also factor in the demands of any video you might shoot. Allow roughly 1 GB of storage for each hour of MPEG-4, 30-frames-per-second, 640x480 video, if the scene

isn't very dynamic, or 1 GB for each half-hour for a rapidly changing scene, such as a basketball game.

Don't pay more for high speed. High-speed cards touted by some manufacturers are overkill for most point-and-shoot cameras, which can't take advantage of them. They aren't worth buying for video, either. But they are worth considering for some new SLRs.

There might be one reason to consider these higher-end cards, however: Some of them come bundled with software for recovering corrupted image files. So if, for example, you corrupted files by opening your camera's battery compartment while the camera was turned on and saving an image to the memory card, the software should be able to get those photos back for you. (It's especially risky to open the compartment if you're using AA batteries, since they disconnect once the compartment is open.)

Vary resolution and compression to suit your needs. It's all too easy to leave a camera on the default storage

settings, which may sometimes be more than you really need. Lowering a camera's resolution setting or increasing its compression, even temporarily, increases the number of images that fit on a card.

Most cameras let you set resolution and compression. For example, if you set a camera to its highest resolution, you might also be able to select from among two or even three levels of compression.

For pictures to e-mail or post online, quality is less of an issue. Choose the lowest resolution your camera allows, combined with maximum compression (usually indicated by a quality measure such as Fine, HQ, etc.). Some new cameras let you choose a preset option tailor-made for e-mailing or for posting on the Internet.

For 4x6 snapshots, where detail matters more, use 4 megapixels and midlevel compression. For 8x10 prints or larger, or smaller prints made from heavily cropped images, use the highest resolution possible and the least compression.

Be sure you know your camera's memory and type; media come in several incompatible shapes and sizes.

accepts AA batteries. You can buy economical, rechargeable cells (plus a charger) and drop in a set of disposable lithium or alkaline batteries if the rechargeables run down in the middle of shooting.

Camera speed. With point-and-shoot cameras like the ones we tested, you must wait after each shot as the camera processes the image. Most models let you shoot an image every few seconds, but a few make you wait 5 seconds or more. They may frustrate you when you're taking photos of a subject that is very active, such as a child.

Your other cameras. If you own a film camera with interchangeable lenses, you can probably use those lenses on digital SLRs of the same brand. Some new Olympus digital SLRs require a special $100 adapter to use film lenses, but you'll only be able to focus those lenses manually.

The road-ready digital camera: Buying and accessorizing

Getting ready to take that new digital camera on the road? Here's advice to help you make the most of your camera when you're away:

Bring extra batteries. A camera that runs out of juice when you're miles from a store or power outlet ranks high on the list of photographic frustrations. If your camera accepts standard AA batteries, pack two sets and, if necessary, a charger. If your camera uses only a proprietary battery, consider buying a second one to take along. Keep it charged so it's ready should the primary battery give out. The $20 to $50 cost will be well spent if it allows you to snap an unforgettable sunset that you'd otherwise miss.

▸ **Parting tip:** Don't forget to pack the charger, and to plug it in every night. If you're traveling abroad, make sure it's compatible with local outlets. If not, you'll need an adapter and possibly a converter.

Plan photo storage. A full memory card is the digital-camera counterpart to running out of film. Make sure your card (or cards) have sufficient capacity, especially if you haven't brought along a laptop. For most consumers, a 1-GB card—good for hundreds of shots from a 5-megapixel camera at full resolution and maximum quality—should be plenty. Card prices have dropped of late; you can now buy a 1-GB card for $50 or so; 512-MB cards run $30 or less. If you're buying a new camera, the memory provided with it is probably too small to meet your needs. Buy at least one additional card.

▸ **Parting tip:** Before heading out, make sure you transfer the shots from your last ski trip to your computer and purge them from the card so you start out fresh.

Pack the video cable. You can share your photos with friends and family by using your camera's video-output jack to display them on the nearest TV set. Most cameras even let you set up a slide show, so you can kick back while everyone savors the day's sights.

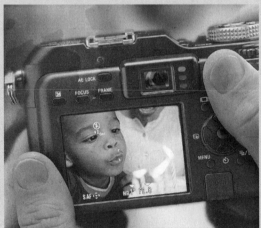

Digital cameras are handy for framing that once-in-a-lifetime shot. Whether you're on the road or at home, make sure you have extra batteries.

Consider using photofinishers as you go. If getting home from vacation typically triggers a printing marathon on the home inkjet, consider using in-store photofinishers along the way, thus giving you the option to enjoy and share your shots as you go, typically with an hour or less waiting time. Be aware though, that even the best are less consistent in high photo quality than the best online photofinishers, so you might want to wait and try online photofinishers when you get home. (See "You have many options for printing your pics," page 55.)

Consider buying a snapshot printer. These pint-sized printers—often smaller than a few DVD-movie cases stacked atop each other—are small enough to take along on vacation and provide a great way to share shots with friends and family away from home. Some can even run on rechargeable batteries. Prices run from $80 to $200. They generally print only 4x6-inch photos, though a few models can also produce 5x7-inch prints or 4x12-inch panoramas.

They've become more numerous in recent years, and printing costs have dropped. Most snapshot printers now have per-photo costs of about 25 to 40 cents, comparable to full-sized inkjets.

▸ **Parting tip:** Stock up on supplies for your snapshot printer—they're typically sold bundled in a package—before you go, since stores that stock them may be scarce where you go.

Another option if you'll have access to a computer when you travel is to upload your photos to a photosharing or photofinishing Web site. You can even order shots that will be ready for you when you get home, or have prints sent ahead to a store at the next stop on your itinerary, where you can pick them up.

▸ **Parting tip:** Research and set up your account with the online site before you leave home to minimize any hassles you might encounter on the road.

EDIT & STORE PHOTOS AT NO ADDITIONAL COST

Everything you need to edit and store your images is probably on your computer already or available to download for free

There are two major advantages to digital photography: You can shoot and store many images at little cost, and you can edit your favorite photos on the computer, a process that once required a darkroom. Of course, these advantages raise new questions: How will you organize the hundreds of shots so that you can easily print or share them? And what software will you use to edit your photos? The good news is that your computer probably has everything you need to organize your photo collection already, and you can download free software that has all the editing tools most people need.

ORGANIZING IMAGES

Newer Mac and Windows-based computers provide ways to organize your photos without spending extra. If you're more serious about organizing, there are software packages costing $50 to $100 that offer options you might not know about, such as sending eye-catching slide shows to almost any computer or creating virtual photo albums to suit any mood or purpose.

Photofinishers like Kodak offer free photo-sharing Web sites, which is their way of driving sales of their printing services. They hope that visitors will buy prints of shots they view.

Handheld electronic albums, like the Apple iPod Photo and the Epson P-1000, can store and organize thousands of pictures and display them on an LCD screen. Prices run from $300 to $500.

If you take few photos, use simple folders. The simplest way to organize photos will work on any computer, even those running old versions of Windows or Mac OS. You copy photos from your camera to folders that you create using the computer's operating system. A basic plan is to store the shots for an event in a folder you create and name for that event. Or store folders for a time period, such as a month or a year, in a folder named for that time period.

Windows XP includes software, with a friendly user interface, that automatically copies image files from your camera to a folder called My Pictures. It also performs other chores, such as displaying thumbnail images of shots, displaying images individually, rotating and zooming, displaying photos in sequence as a slide show, or printing them in a variety of common formats, such as 4x6 or 5x7.

If you use a Mac, try iPhoto. Mac OS X 10.1 or later includes iPhoto, a program with very easy controls that can turn static photo collections into self-launching slide shows, complete with captions, background music, and video clips from a camcorder. It can rename groups of files, saving considerable time over the simple folder approach. iPhoto also has a very efficient system for creating albums—onscreen collections of photos that you can flip through just like physical photo albums—because it can link one photo to several albums simultaneously.

You can download free software for editing photos.

These two cameras—the Nikon Coolpix L3 and S6—will do some editing for you by automatically fixing red-eye. They will also improve photos that are underexposed or have too much backlight.

If you use Windows, download free software. A number of free software packages for Windows-based computers have features similar to iPhoto's. We recommend Picasa 2 from Google (available at *picasa.google.com*). It's especially handy if you already have lots of photos on your hard drive. Immediately after installation, it scans your entire hard drive and automatically organizes all your photo folders according to year and month. You can do that with other programs, but the process is less straightforward.

If you find free software to try from an unfamiliar site, make sure your computer is well-protected against viruses and spyware before downloading it.

If you need integration, buy retail software. iPhoto and Picasa provide most of the organizing features you'll probably need. But there are advantages to buying products like Adobe Photoshop Elements ($80 to $100) and ACDSee 7.0 PowerPack ($80). They integrate organizing features with the ability to share and edit photos. And their photo-editing features are more extensive than those in free software.

Most retail products have convenient controls for burning albums onto a CD, attaching them to e-mail, and compressing files to speed uploads over dial-up Internet connections. But the most efficient way to share photos with a wide group of people is to post them online.

EDITING PHOTOS

Most digital cameras no longer come with full photo-editing software. At best, you get an application for transferring images to your computer.

But if you know where to look, you can find several free tools to help you crop, correct color, brighten, and sharpen images—the kind of editing that many people want to do to improve the photos they take. You might already have the tools you need on your computer's hard drive.

If all you want are 4x6 snapshots, you might be able make all the adjustments you need right in the camera, without editing software. A few cameras can remove red eye, crop material at the edges, or rotate an image from portrait to landscape.

The camera alone usually can't correct exposure or color balance after you've taken the picture. But if you have photo-editing software that came with an older camera, you have all you need for routine fix-ups. If not, try these options:

For serious editing, start with free software. The first choice for Windows users should be a free download called IrfanView (*www.irfanview.com*). It has an easy-to-use interface and many useful features, including one that corrects the color balance of photos shot in artificial or dim light, and another that adjusts brightness and contrast. IrfanView can also resize files for e-mailing or posting to the Internet.

But IrfanView lacks some advanced features and the range of touch-up tools that commercial software offers. And don't expect much technical support.

For advanced uses, buy an editing program. Consider Adobe Photoshop Elements or Corel Paint Shop Pro X, two widely used, moderately priced packages that have done well in our previous tests. Photoshop Elements sells for $80 to $100 and works with Windows and Macintosh. Paint Shop Pro works with Windows only and sells for about $100.

Both have features unavailable in a download like IrfanView. The "fill flash" tool, for example, brightens areas of an image. Other features include sharpening or editing for selected portions of an image, 16-bit color depth to render a wider range of colors, and the ability to process RAW files, images stored as the camera's sensors captured them.

YOU HAVE MANY OPTIONS FOR PRINTING YOUR PICS

In-store and online photofinishers supplement home printing

This year photographers will take more digital images to photofinishers than they print themselves. Using a photofinisher can be cheaper than printing at home, and it spares you paper jams, depleted ink cartridges, and other annoyances.

With in-store processing, you use a terminal or kiosk to order (and even edit) prints stored on a memory card. If the terminals intimidate you, you can usually hand the memory card to a clerk, just as you do with film canisters. With online services, you upload your photos to a Web site where you, or anyone you choose, can view them and order prints. (In some cases, visitors can even download your images.)

Photofinishers can be a major time-saver for large photo batches. They can also print on items that would be challenging on a home printer (calendars, photo albums) or downright impossible (puzzles, mugs, custom postage stamps).

Based on our tests of 12 online services and in-store services at eight retail chains, you're more assured of getting high-quality prints online. But features for sharing and managing your images vary by site. Also, in our experience, if your images look "too professional," online services might make you sign an affidavit verifying that you're not violating a copyright.

At the retail chains, service was speedy, as promised. But testers said other customers could too easily view images on terminal screens, and noticed out-of-order terminals in about 20 percent of the stores.

Whatever service you choose, ask about prepaying for 100 or more prints, which might save you a few cents per print. Also, while you can fix imperfections like red-eye at photofinishing sites or terminals, it's best to make the edits beforehand, using photo-editing software.

HOW TO CHOOSE

If quality matters most, go online. In our tests, the best online photofinishers produced excellent prints more consistently than the best in-store services. Just make sure you have access to a broadband connection; it's painfully slow to upload photos using dial-up access.

If sharing is a priority for you, look for sites that make it easy to store images and organize them into virtual albums or even slideshows, complete with captions and colorful borders. But there are other services, like Flickr.com, that offer more sophisticated sharing than the photofinishers.

Not all sites allow your visitors to download your images to their computers for home printing, especially for free.

For speed and price, go to a store. In our tests using standard delivery, prints ordered online arrived in four to seven days—well within the promised time. In-store prints arrived in 15 to

Kiosks like this one in pharmacies and big retailers walk you through the process of printing your photos. We found that quality varies.

CR Quick Recommendations

Photofinishers

While all types of photofinishers can yield fine results, print quality is more consistent from those online. Quality for in-store labs varied widely among outlets that used the same equipment.

Fujifilm's Printpix kiosks are not in the Ratings because of limited availability; those we tested had poor to good prints. Eckerd service was not included; stores have a variety of equipment, including Kodak and Fujifilm minilabs. Note that Yahoo fulfills Target's online prints and Snapfish does Walgreens'.

Retailers listed in the online Ratings allow you to upload through their online service for in-store processing, as does CVS at CVS.com.

QUICK PICKS

Best online choices overall:

1 Kodak
3 Target
4 Yahoo

All offer excellent inexpensive 4x6 prints and versatile album-management and editing tools. Kodak is best for Mac users. Target orders are handled by Yahoo; both offer $1.99 8x10s. For best results, turn off the color-enhance feature on online photo sites.

If online image sharing is a high priority:

2 Shutterfly
5 Webshots

Though relatively pricey, these offer excellent prints and allow you to move, copy, or add images to albums. Shutterfly offers a handy album-search feature, and Webshots allows free downloads for your album visitors.

Best in-store choice for most people:

17 Wal-Mart minilabs

This chain uses Fuji minilab equipment, which yielded very good or excellent prints. Only the members-only Costco (13) and Sam's Club (15) beat it on price.

When speed is paramount:

24 Wal-Mart kiosks

You get prints in 15 minutes or so, but quality is inconsistent. Members-only Sam's Club (15) aside, this was the lowest-priced chain with kiosks, which produced fair to very good prints.

Ratings Online processing

Excellent ● Very good ◕ Good ○ Fair ◔ Poor ●

Services listed in performance order. Magenta key numbers indicate Quick Picks. Services with equal scores are listed alphabetically.

Key number	Photofinisher	4x6 glossy print	8x10 glossy print	Shipping (25 prints)	Overall score	Print quality	Managing albums	Editing	Free downloads	Mac batch uploads	Date stamp
1	Kodak EasyShare Gallery (kodakgallery.com)	15¢	$3.99	$2.49	86	●	◕	●		◕	●
2	Shutterfly (shutterfly.com)	19	3.99	2.49	84	●	●	◕		◕	
3	Target Photo Center (target.com)	15	1.99	2.29	84	●	◕	●			●
4	Yahoo Photos (yahoo.com)	15	1.99	2.29	84	●	◕	●			●
5	Webshots (webshots.com)	19	3.49	2.75	83	●	◕	○	●	◕	●
6	Ritzpix.com (ritzpix.com)	19	3.89	2.50	81	●	◕	◕	●	◕	●
7	EZ Prints (ezprints.com)	19	1.99	1.95	79	●	○	○			●
8	Costco Photo Center (costco.com)	17	1.49	0.00	71	◕	◕	●		◕	
9	Snapfish (snapfish.com)	12	2.99	1.97	71	●	◕	●			●
10	Walgreens Photo Center (walgreens.com)	19	3.99	1.97	71	◕	◕	●	●	◕	
11	Sam's Club (samsclub.com)	11	1.58	1.80	68	●	◕	◕			
12	Wal-Mart Digital Photo Center (walmart.com)	12	1.96	2.00	65	◕	○	◕	●		

Guide to the Ratings

Overall score is based mainly on 8x10 print quality, with album management and editing also considered. **Print quality** assesses color balance, sharpness, and other factors for nine glossy photos purchased and home-delivered in a five-week period. **Managing albums** reflects capability of arranging images online. **Editing** includes the number of basic tools, like red-eye removal and cropping. **Free downloads** allow visitors to online albums to copy images at no charge. All allow batch uploads from PCs and single-image uploads from Macs; we show those that allow **batch uploads from Macs**. The **date stamp** provides information about the print. **Price** is approximate retail. **Shipping** is the cost of standard delivery (4-7 days) for 25 4x6 prints.

In-store processing

Chains listed alphabetically within groups.

Key number	Retail chain	Price	Paper finish	Date stamp	Name on print	Print index
	These use Fujifilm self-service minilabs. Print quality: ◔ to ●. Timing: typically an hour or less.					
13	Costco	17¢	glossy		●	●
14	Ritz	29	glossy	●		
15	Sam's Club	15	matte	●	●	
16	Walgreens	29	glossy	●		
17	Wal-Mart	19	matte	●	●	
	These use Kodak self-service minilabs. Print quality: ◔ to ●. Timing: typically an hour or less.					
18	CVS/pharmacy	29	glossy		●	
19	Target	20[1]	glossy		●	
	These use Kodak self-service kiosks. Print quality: ◔ to ◔. Timing: typically 15 minutes or less.					
20	CVS/pharmacy	29	glossy			
21	Ritz	35	glossy			
22	Sam's Club	24	glossy			
23	Target	36	glossy			
24	Wal-Mart	28	glossy			

[1] Price is for basic prints. Premium prints cost 29 cents.

Guide to the Ratings

Print quality reflects the range, by equipment manufacturer, from tests in which staffers printed the same set of 4x6 photos at retailers in different cities. The typical time listed reflects staffers' experiences. **Date stamp, name on print,** and a thumbnail **print index** are useful extras. **Price** is the approximate cost we paid; it may vary by location.

---

60 minutes. Still too slow? In-store processing chains that also offer online photofinishing usually allow you to upload images to their site ahead of time. The images are then ferried to your local store, where they're ready when you arrive. The least expensive in-store services are actually cheaper than most online photofinishers once you factor in online shipping costs of about 10 cents a print.

For best quality, use a minilab with Fujifilm equipment. With minilab service, the terminal you use is connected to the lab behind the counter. Orders typically take 15 minutes to an hour to complete. In our tests, the quality from minilabs was better than from kiosks, the other in-store photofinishing technology available. Also, minilab prints are water-resistant, as are online prints. The prints we got from the kiosks we tested weren't.

Major retailers are supplied with minilab equipment by Fujifilm or Kodak. You can expect prints that are at least very good if you use a minilab with Fujifilm equipment. In our tests, minilabs with Kodak equipment were more uneven, with the worst prints having flaws such as washed-out colors, out-of-focus images, and orange-tinted flesh tones.

For speed (and speed alone), use a kiosk. Kiosks are essentially stand-alone terminals that deliver prints like ATMs dispense money. In our tests, they typically delivered prints in 15 minutes or less. But quality is generally lower (and costs higher) than with other options, and you may have to wait for your photos—or fish awkwardly for them—while the next customer uses the machine.

DIGITAL CAMCORDERS TAKE OVER THE MARKET

Quality and ease of use help digital moviemakers win out

You can do a lot more with videos shot on digital or analog camcorders than play them back, unedited, on your TV. You can edit and embellish them with music using your computer, then play your productions on your DVD or PC. Or even send them to friends or family via e-mail.

Digital camcorders, now the dominant type, generally offer very good to excellent picture quality, along with very good sound capability, compactness, and ease of handling. Making copies of a digital recording need not result in a loss of picture or sound quality. You can even take rudimentary still photos with most digital camcorders.

Analog camcorders, now a small part of the market, generally have good picture and sound quality and are less expensive. Some analog units are about as compact and easy to handle as digital models, while others are a bit bigger and bulkier.

WHAT'S AVAILABLE

Sony dominates the camcorder market, with multiple models in a number of formats. Other top brands include Canon, JVC, Panasonic, and Samsung. Most digital models come in the MiniDV format, but there are also the disc-based DVD-RAM, DVD-R, and DVD+RW formats. Newer models record to flash memory or a hard drive. Some digital models weigh as little as 1 pound.

MiniDV. Don't let their small size deceive you. Although some models can be slipped into a large pocket, MiniDV camcorders can record very high-quality images. They use a unique tape cassette, and the typical recording time is 60 minutes at standard play (SP) speed. Expect to pay about $6.50 for a 60-minute tape. You must use the camcorder for playback—it converts its recording to an analog

Look for an LCD viewer that's free from glare and big enough for you to see clearly.

signal that can be played directly into a TV or VCR. If the TV or VCR has an S-video input jack, use it to get a high-quality picture. Price: $350 to more than $1,000.

Disc-based. Capitalizing on the popularity and capabilities of DVD movie discs, these formats offer benefits that tape can't provide: long-term durability, compactness, and random access to scenes as with a DVD. The 3¼-inch discs record standard MPEG-2 video, the same format used in commercial DVD videos. The amount of recording time varies according to the quality level you select, from 20 minutes per side at the highest-quality setting for DVD-RAM to about 60 minutes per side at the lowest setting. DVD-RAM discs are not compatible with most DVD players, but the discs can be reused. DVD-R is supposed to be compatible with most DVD players and computer DVD drives, but the discs are not rewriteable. DVD-RW and DVD+RW are reusable, rewriteable disc formats. Disc prices range from about $4 to $20. Price: $600 to $1,000.

Most analog camcorders now use the Hi8 format; VHS-C and Super VHS-C are fading from the market. Blank tapes range from $3.50 to $6.50. Analog camcorders usually weigh around 2 pounds. Picture quality is generally good, though a notch below digital. Price: $200 to $300.

> **Digital camcorders** deliver consistent quality regardless of recording speed.

FEATURES THAT COUNT

A **flip-out liquid-crystal-display (LCD) monitor** is common on all but the lowest-priced camcorders. And a **wide-screen LCD monitor** is becoming more common. You'll find it useful for reviewing footage you've shot and easier to use than the eyepiece viewfinder for certain shooting poses. Some LCD monitors are hard to use in sunlight, a drawback on models that have only a monitor and no eyepiece.

Screens vary from 2½ to 4 inches measured diagonally, with a larger screen offered as a step-up feature on higher-priced models. Since an LCD monitor uses batteries faster than an eyepiece viewfinder does, you don't have as much recording time when the LCD is in use.

An **image stabilizer** automatically reduces most of the shaking that occurs from holding the camcorder as you record a scene. Most stabilizers are electronic; a few are optical. Either type can be effective, though mounting the camcorder on a tripod is the surest way to get steady images. If you're not using a tripod, try holding the camcorder with both hands and bracing both elbows against your chest.

Full auto switch essentially lets you point and shoot. The camcorder automatically adjusts the color balance, shutter speed, focus, and aperture (also called the "iris" or "f-stop" with camcorders).

Autofocus adjusts for maximum sharpness; manual focus override may be needed for problem situations, such as low light. (With some camcorders, you might have to tap buttons repeatedly to get the focus just right.) With many models, you can also control exposure, shutter speed, and white balance.

The zoom is typically a finger control—press one way to zoom in, the other to widen the view. The rate at which the zoom changes depends on how hard you press the switch. Typical optical zoom ratios range from 10:1 to 26:1. The zoom relies on optical lenses, just like a film camera (hence the term "optical zoom"). Many camcorders offer a digital zoom to extend the range to 400:1 or more, but at a lower picture quality.

For tape-based formats, analog or digital, every camcorder displays **tape speeds** the same way a VCR does. Every model, for example, includes an SP (standard play) speed. Digitals have a slower LP (long play) speed that adds 50 percent to the recording time. A few 8mm and Hi8 models have an LP speed that doubles the recording time. All VHS-C and S-VHS-C camcorders have an even slower EP (extended play) speed that triples the recording time. With analog camcorders, slower speeds worsen picture quality. Slow speed

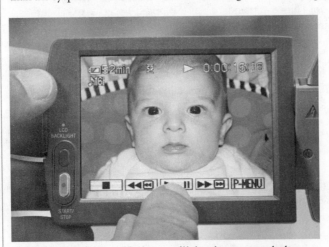

Some camcorders have LCD viewers with touch-screen controls.

usually doesn't reduce picture quality on digital camcorders. But using slow speed means sacrificing some seldom-used editing options and might restrict playback on other camcorders.

Disc-based formats have a variety of modes that trade off recording time for image quality.

Quick review lets you view the last few seconds of a scene without having to press a lot of buttons.

For special lighting situations, preset **auto-exposure** settings can be helpful. A "snow and sand" setting, for example, adjusts shutter speed or aperture to accommodate high reflectivity.

A **light** provides some illumination for close shots when the image would otherwise be too dark. **Backlight compensation** increases the exposure slightly when your subject is lighted from behind and silhouetted. An **infrared-sensitive recording mode** (also known as night vision, zero lux, or MagicVu) allows shooting in very dim or dark situations, using infrared emitters. You can use it for nighttime shots, although colors won't register accurately in this mode.

Audio/video inputs let you record material from another camcorder or from a VCR, useful for copying part of another video onto your own. (A digital camcorder must have such an input jack if you want to record analog material digitally.) Unlike a built-in microphone, an external microphone that is plugged into a microphone jack won't pick up noises from the camcorder itself, and it typically improves audio performance.

A camcorder with **digital still capability** lets you take snapshots, which can be downloaded to your computer. The photo quality is generally inferior to that of a good still camera, although higher-cost camcorders typically offer better photo quality than lower-cost ones.

Features that might help editing include a **built-in title generator**, a **time-and-date stamp**, and a **time code**, which is a frame reference of exactly where you are on the recording media—the hour, minute, second, and frame. A **remote control** helps when you're using the camcorder as a playback device or when you're using a tripod. **Programmed recording** (a self-timer) starts the camcorder recording at a preset time.

The newer digital DVD format in this camera is more durable than tape.

HOW TO CHOOSE

Pick your price range and format. The least-expensive camcorders on the market are analog. All the rest are digital.

Once you've decided which part of the price spectrum to explore, you need to pick a specific recording format. That determines not only how much you'll be spending for tapes, discs, or mem-

---

CR Quick Tip

Three ways to keep your home videos playable for years

Maybe you bought your original camcorder so you could record your children's first steps and first words. The kids now have their learner's permits, and the old camcorder has played its last tape. What can you do to preserve those old videos?

Tape won't last forever, even with proper archival care. DVDs are considered inherently more stable. And as tape wanes and the machines to play it disappear, DVD will be the only playback option. If you want to transfer tapes to discs, these are your choices:

Make your own DVD copies. With the right hardware and cables to connect everything, you can transfer old videos to DVD. You'll need a DVD recorder or a computer with a DVD-R/RW or DVD+R/RW drive. (For more on transferring video to DVD, see "DVD recorders give new life to old videos," page 97.)

Archive as you go. If you have a digital camcorder and a reasonably new computer equipped with video-editing software and a DVD burner, you can back up each new tape to a DVD.

Pay for the service. There are hundreds of services nationwide that will transfer tape to DVD. Local camera stores or photofinishing outlets may handle the work (check the phone book); you can also find mail-order services via the Internet. Prices we've seen range from $18.95 to $39.50 and more (depending on what extras you want) for a 60-minute tape. The biggest risk of using a service: The original tape could be lost, damaged, or erased before the copy is made.

To guard against mishaps,

make a backup tape first and think twice before entrusting original tapes to a company you know nothing about.

Whether they're originals or duplicates, store all home videos properly to make sure they last. Avoid dust and extreme temperature and humidity. Keep the tapes or discs in their cases so they don't get damaged. If you really want to be thorough, our experts recommend keeping duplicate discs. As future technologies emerge, consider upgrading to the newest format.

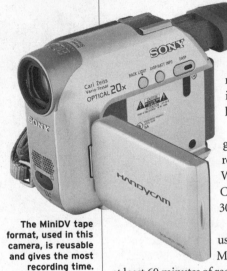

The MiniDV tape format, used in this camera, is reusable and gives the most recording time.

ory, but also how much recording time you'll get. The tape-based digital formats are typically superior in picture quality to analog tape-based formats.

With analog, you can get 120 to 300 minutes of recording on a Hi8 cassette. With the SVHS-C or VHS-C formats, you can get only 30 to 120 minutes.

With digital formats that use MiniDV, Digital 8, or MicroMV tapes, you can get at least 60 minutes of recording on a standard cassette. MiniDV and D8 cassettes are the least expensive and easiest to find.

Digital DVD camcorders from Panasonic and Hitachi can accommodate DVD-RAM discs, which can be reused but aren't compatible with all DVD players. All brands also use DVD-R, one-use discs that work in most DVD players. The standard setting yields 60 minutes of recording; the "fine" setting, 20 to 30 minutes.

With digital formats using memory cards, the amount of video you can record at the highest quality level can vary from 15 minutes to 1 hour on 256-MB to 2-GB cards. (To get a more precise estimate, check a camera's specifications.) Hard-drive based camcorders are limited only by the capacity of the hard drive and the quality settings. On typical models, you can store several hours of video at the highest-quality setting or more than 10 hours at lower-quality settings.

If you're replacing an older camcorder, think about what you'll do with the tapes you've accumulated. If you don't stay with the same format you've been using, you will probably want to transfer the old tapes to an easily viewed medium, such as a DVD.

If you're buying your first camcorder, concentrate on finding the best one for your budget, regardless of format.

Check the size, weight, and controls. In the store, try different camcorders to make sure they fit your hand and are comfortable to use. Some models can feel disconcertingly tiny. You'll need to use a tripod if you want rock-steady video, no matter which camcorder you choose. Most camcorders are designed so that the most frequently used controls—the switch to zoom in and out, the record button, and the button for still photos—are readily at hand. Make sure that the controls are convenient and that you can change the tape, DVD, or memory card and remove the battery easily.

Check the flip-out LCD viewer. Most measure 2.5 inches on the diagonal, but some are larger, adding about $100 to the price. If the viewer seems small and difficult to use or suffers from too much glare, consider trading up to a similar model or a different brand to get a better screen.

Think about the lighting. A camcorder isn't always used outdoors or in a brightly lighted room. You can shoot video in dim light, but don't expect miracles. In our tests, using the default mode, most camcorders produced only fair or poor images in very low light. Many camcorders have settings that can improve performance but can be a challenge to use.

TELEVISIONS

CHAPTER

04

▶▶ **From huge wall-mounted plasma TVs to tried-and-true conventional picture tubes, you have lots of choices to fit your space and lifestyle.**

HDTV IS MAINSTREAM THANKS TO PRICE DROPS

The challenge is to choose the best type, screen size, and brand

If you're in the market for a main TV, there's little reason to hold off buying a high-definition set. Prices have fallen sharply over the past few years, and there are more sets from which to choose, including sleek flat panels and eye-catching big screens. These trends have made digital TVs the mainstream choice for home viewing. In fact, CONSUMER REPORTS no longer tests standard analog televisions, which have become low-priced commodities.

Buying an HDTV involves a number of decisions. Here's our expert advice on finding the best set at the best price.

As brands proliferate, be open to some new names but wary of others. The number of TV brands has skyrocketed. In the LCD category alone, there are more than 50 on the market, many of them names you might not recognize.

Brands such as Kreisen and Vizio are sold mainly online and at warehouse stores. Other TVs have labels better known for audio (Akai, Audiovox) or computers (Dell, Hewlett-Packard). Store brands have joined the fray, among them Best Buy's Insignia, Wal-Mart's ILO, and Target's TruTech.

Some off-brands cost much less than major brands. You might expect them to be mediocre, and you'd be right in many cases. But several of the low-priced LCD sets we tested did surprisingly well.

Check our Ratings online, then decide whether you're comfortable buying an unfamiliar brand or would prefer an established line that has more of a track record.

Time your purchase to take advantage of expected price drops. The lesser-known brands aren't the only ones playing the price card. Major brands are becoming less expensive, too, and price erosion is likely to continue, especially for the biggest, priciest sets: plasma TVs with 50-inch screens, LCD flat panels larger than 40 inches, and rear-projection microdisplays using LCD, DLP, and LCoS technology. Prices for the best-selling flat-panel sizes—42-inch plasmas and LCD sets 34 inches or smaller—should fall as well, as these products become more common. Little change is likely for picture-tube TVs and CRT-based rear-projection sets. Those mature products are close to bottoming out in price as they're replaced by newer technologies. But don't be paralyzed by fear of buyer's remorse. There are always going to be bigger, better, and possibly cheaper, TVs on the horizon, but at some point you have to jump in and start enjoying an HDTV.

Not all programming is in high definition yet, but within the next few years all will be in digital format, meaning clearer pictures.

Price isn't everything when picking a store

To see how merchants stack up when it comes to TVs, we dug deeper into the survey data from the report "Follow shopping tips for best digital deals," on page 8.

Decide where to shop. Among the brick-and-mortar retailers, local independent stores got top scores from buyers of high-end TVs, as did the Tweeter Home Entertainment chain for overall satisfaction, service, and checkout speed. Sears, Circuit City, and Best Buy were rated high for overall satisfaction and product quality, but average for service, price, and selection. Costco, also highly rated overall, was judged best for low TV prices but with limited product selection and service.

Few of the TV buyers we surveyed bought their sets online, but it may be worth considering. Amazon.com, Costco.com, Crutchfield, and JR.com scored high with electronics buyers, and they offer low prices. But if the site charges for shipping (some don't), the cost can wipe out any price advantage. Installation and set-up services and extended warranties may be available at extra cost.

Many sites have product information and buying advice, and you can call for information or sometimes "chat" with a service representative online. One caveat: Some Web retailers, such as Amazon.com, don't accept returns on large TVs.

Whether you shop online or at a store, the expert evaluations of a TV's picture and sound quality in our online Ratings are invaluable. Even if you see a TV in a showroom, it can be hard to judge its performance. The type of content displayed, the connections used, the TV settings, the viewing angle and distance, and the store lighting all affect the picture quality. Ask if there's a viewing room, or see if a salesperson will work with you to adjust the set.

Keep your eye on the price. Many retailers have a low-price guarantee, so scour ads before and after shopping. If you see the same TV at a lower price, take the ad to the store. Chains such as Best Buy, Circuit City, and Sears will match a local rival's price and give you 10 percent of the difference within a few weeks of purchase. Some will also refund the difference if they sell the TV at a lower price within a given time. So keep your receipt handy.

Before buying a TV, see whether your credit card extends warranty coverage. Such plans, most often found on gold and platinum cards, typically lengthen a standard war-

Price depends on weight.

For a more complicated setup—say, hooking up multiple video devices and a sound system—costs can run into several hundred dollars.

The ultimate service is wall-mounting a plasma or LCD set and hiding wires, which takes considerable expertise that doesn't come cheap. For more on setup options, see "How to set up your TV once you get it home," page 85.

Think about the stand. When buying a new stand that requires assembly, see if the store personnel will put it together when

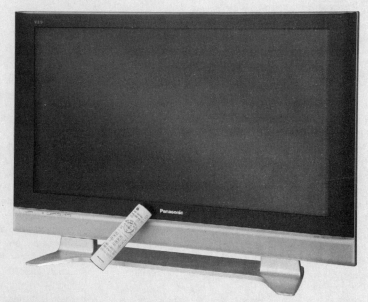

Plasma TVs are thin, but a 42-inch set can weigh 100 pounds. See if the retailer will deliver the set, and look into professional installation if you wall-mount it.

ranty by up to a year at no cost. American Express adds up to a year of protection to standard warranties. MasterCard and Visa may do so, depending on the issuing bank and type of card.

Weigh delivery and setup options. With big-screen TVs, delivery is worth considering. Most sets are heavy, and the cartons are too large to fit in many vehicles. The most basic service is curbside delivery, available from some big-box stores such as Wal-Mart.

they deliver the TV. That usually costs about $50 or so. Otherwise, buy the stand ahead of time so you can assemble it before the TV arrives. If you plan to put the new TV into an existing cabinet or stand, measure carefully to make sure it fits. Also check that the furniture can support the TV's weight. With any stand, old or new, make sure it's sturdy and stable to reduce the chance it could tip over, especially if there are young children in the house.

Buy a big screen to see the best HD. One of the newest developments is the supersizing of flat-panel TVs—as large as 82 inches for LCDs and 103 inches for plasmas. It will be a while before those sets are available and affordably priced. But you can already find LCD TVs with screens 40 inches or larger, and 50- to 60-inch plasma screens. If you don't want to wall-mount your TV, you have more options. Rear-projection TVs offer the most choice in big-screen sets, including some DLP, LCD, and LCoS models with 55- to 71-inch screens.

Even if you don't opt for a jumbo TV, don't buy too small a screen. Our survey of 500 HDTV owners showed that viewing enjoyment increased with screen size, and many wished they'd purchased a bigger set. Generally, we'd recommend at least a 34- or 37-inch screen for a primary TV you'll watch

often. And opt for a 16:9 wide screen, rather than a squarish screen with a 4:3 aspect ratio. The 16:9 shape is better suited to viewing HD programs and DVDs, and was strongly preferred by the consumers we surveyed.

But don't go overboard. A big-screen TV will look larger in your home than in the store. For optimal viewing, sit at least 4 feet from a 37-inch or smaller HD set and 5 to 9 feet from a 40- to 65-inch screen. If you're any closer, the images might appear coarse.

Consider which digital-tuner setup best suits your needs and budget. As of July 2006, all TVs with screens 25 inches and larger must have a built-in ATSC digital tuner, to comply with a government ruling. At this point, only LCD and picture-tube sets with smaller screens still don't

First Things First

HDTV types

1 LCD flat-panel HDTV

Good choice if you want a thin, light set with a small or midsized screen.

Typical prices $1,000 to $1,500 for a 26-inch wide-screen set; $1,200 to $2,000 for a similar 32-inch model; $2,000 to $2,500 for a 37-inch model. A growing number of LCD TVs have even larger screens—up to 50 inches or more—and prices go up along with size.

Points to consider LCD flat panels are the thinnest, lightest TVs available. Even the biggest weigh less than 50 pounds, half as much as a plasma TV, so they're good for wall-mounting.

The best LCD TVs display excellent, bright HD images, and the antireflective surface minimizes the reflections and glare that often plague plasma screens.

But LCD TVs haven't caught up with plasma TVs for viewing angle, color accuracy, and the ability to display the deepest black. Also, fast motion may blur. As a result, their picture-quality scores aren't as high as those for plasma sets.

At this point, a plasma TV still offers more for the money in 42-inch sizes and larger. If a 32- or 37-inch screen would do, an LCD is a good choice for a main TV. Smaller LCD TVs would be best as second sets or in small rooms.

If low price matters most, consider some of the bargain-priced LCD TVs being sold at chains such as Costco, Wal-Mart, Best Buy, and Circuit City. We tested half a dozen low-priced brands and recommend several of them.

However, the newer brands don't have any track record at this point. We have preliminary data for some established brands of LCD TVs that raised no repair concerns during the first year of use, though we have no long-term data yet.

2 Plasma flat-panel HDTV

Good choice if you want a big, thin set.

Common screen sizes 42 to 60 inches.

Typical prices $2,000 and up for a 42-inch HDTV, $3,000 and up for a 50-inch model.

Points to consider These flat panels are thin and can be wall-mounted, but they're not light—a 42-inch set weighs 100 pounds.

The best have excellent picture quality, with good brightness and contrast from any angle. However, a plasma TV's shiny surface can produce reflections, and static images displayed for a long time—such as stock tickers or video games—can burn in.

You'll find a growing selection of 50-inch screens and larger on the market. But these cost considerably more than comparably sized microdisplay projection sets.

If you're willing to compromise on picture quality to get a lower-priced plasma TV, consider an enhanced-definition (ED) set. These don't have high-enough native resolution for true HD but can display HD signals at lower quality. The best do well, but for top quality, you're better off with an HD set. The price advantage of ED sets is shrinking as plasma TV prices continue to dip.

Less-familiar brands of plasma TVs being sold at chains such as Costco, Wal-Mart, Best Buy, and Circuit City cost much less than major brands, which is tempting. But those we've tested have been mediocre, so you'll trade quality for price.

As with LCD TVs, we have limited repair data on plasma TVs at this point. A few major brands have been reliable in their first year of use, according to initial survey results, but we don't yet have long-term reliability information.

have such tuners. By March 2007, all new TVs sold in the U.S., regardless of size and type, must include a digital tuner. Here's a rundown on the types of HD-capable TVs on the market:

HD monitors. Some manufacturers are getting around the government ruling by introducing sets called "monitors," which have no tuner of any type. These require a cable box or satellite receiver, or an external set-top box and antenna, to get any programming, not just HD content.

HD-ready sets. The few HD-ready sets still being sold have a tuner that enables them to display standard-definition programs (which still account for most non-prime-time TV broadcasts) on their own. To display digital programs, they require an external digital tuner that can decode those broadcasts. If you're getting your HD programming from cable or satellite, your digital cable box or satellite receiver will provide the necessary digital decoder.

All you have to do is connect your HD-ready TV to the box and you're all set. Cable companies charge a small rental fee for digital or HD-capable boxes. To receive HD by satellite, you need an HD receiver and special dish antenna(e). Together, these cost about $300, but you might be able to get them from a satellite company at little or no charge as part of a promotion.

You can also get digital broadcasts, including HD, over the air, via an antenna. To do so, you'll have to buy a set-top box containing an ATSC tuner; these cost a few hundred dollars. You won't get the channels available only on cable or satellite, but there's no charge for service. To receive digital programming by antenna, you must be fairly close to a transmitter, with nothing blocking the signal. With digital signals, you'll either have a clear picture or none at all. Marginal reception will result in intermittent picture dropout.

3 Rear-projection HDTV

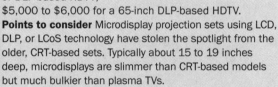

Good choice if you want a big-screen TV that costs less than a plasma set.
Common screen sizes 50 to 65 inches.
Typical prices About $1,000 for a 51-inch CRT-based set; $2,200 to $3,000 for a 50-inch LCD- or DLP-based HDTV; $5,000 to $6,000 for a 65-inch DLP-based HDTV.
Points to consider Microdisplay projection sets using LCD, DLP, or LCoS technology have stolen the spotlight from the older, CRT-based sets. Typically about 15 to 19 inches deep, microdisplays are slimmer than CRT-based models but much bulkier than plasma TVs.

The best offer excellent picture quality, but you don't get the deep black and unlimited viewing angle of a plasma TV. With DLP sets, there's the risk that you may be bothered by the "rainbow effect"—a perceived flash of color some viewers see when moving their eyes along the edges of bright objects on a dark background.

The big news is the arrival of 1080p sets with native resolution of 1920x1080. Some we tested displayed very fine detail, but others didn't make the most of the resolution.

Reliability is a concern. CRT-based models have been much more repair-prone than picture-tube TVs, and initial survey data show that microdisplays have been even less reliable during their first year of use.

4 Front-projector HDTV

Good choice if you want a giant screen and can deal with a potentially complex setup.
Common screen sizes Screen, bought separately, typically 70 to 200 inches. Can use a wall instead. Projector has a 9x12-inch footprint or smaller.
Typical prices $2,000 and up for HD projector; $1,200 and up for enhanced standard definition. Several hundred dollars for screen.
Points to consider A front projector comes closest to giving you a theaterlike experience, with images up to 200 inches diagonally. We've found 110 inches to be optimal for size and brightness; in larger sizes, the picture dims. The best can produce excellent images, but they're best used in a dark room, and so aren't ideal for every day. You must hook up a cable or satellite box, or a DVD player, to get a picture, and speakers, so you'll need a sound system. Mounting a projector and screen takes skill, but you can set it on a table. Most DLP units are subject to the "rainbow effect"—a perceived flash of color some viewers see when moving their eyes along the edges of bright objects on a dark background. We have no data on reliability.

5 Picture-tube (CRT) HDTV

Good choice if you want a low-priced, midsized set, even though it's bulky.
Common screen sizes 26 to 36 inches.
Typical prices About $800 for a 32-inch 4:3 HDTV; $1,200 for a similar 34-inch 16:9 set.
Points to consider Although there are fewer new tube TVs, they're still worth keeping in mind. The best display top picture quality, with excellent detail, color, and contrast, and they have an unlimited viewing angle. Proven long-term reliability of this technology is another plus, although in 30- to 32-inch sets, RCA and Zenith were among the most repair-prone brands. Maximum screen size is limited to 36 inches, and larger sets are big and heavy.

Viewing TV models in a retailer's showroom lets you make side-by-side comparisons of picture quality.

integrated sets require an external HD-capable cable box or satellite receiver; their built-in digital tuner works only for off-air digital broadcasts.

Digital-cable-ready (DCR). Some integrated models, called digital-cable-ready (DCR) sets, can receive unscrambled digital-cable programming without using a set-top box. For HD and premium cable programming—and possibly for any digital programming—you must insert a CableCard into a slot on the set. You usually have to pay a few dollars a month to rent the card from the cable company. However, there's a downside to this setup: It doesn't provide the features offered by a cable box, such as an interactive program guide, video on demand, or pay-per-view ordering via remote. Second-generation DCR-TVs and CableCards are expected at some point, and they're likely to have two-way capability, allowing for interactive features. Integrated sets typically cost more than HD monitors, with digital-cable-ready models costing the most.

You might be able to watch HDTV on some enhanced-definition (ED) sets, which usually cost less than an HDTV. EDTVs, mostly plasma sets, have a lower native resolution than true HDTVs, but many can display HD signals (provided they're used with a digital tuner). The picture

Integrated HDTV sets. These have an ATSC digital tuner built in, which enables them to decode digital signals, including HD, with no equipment other than a roof antenna. As noted earlier, you may be able to receive the major networks' HD offerings transmitted over the air in your area, but you won't get the premium channels available on satellite and cable. To get HD via cable or satellite,

How much screen for how much green

Here's what you can expect to pay for a major-brand HDTV set that offers solid performance and mainstream features—the sets we're likely to recommend. There are more-expensive and cheaper sets out there, but you can find good choices in these ranges. (Prices are for HD sets with 16:9 wide screens, unless noted as enhanced-definition or 4:3 screens. Pricing was current as of June 2006, but is likely to drop.)

TV types	up to $500	$500-$1,000	$1,000-$1,500
LCD TVs Thin and light. Common sizes: 20 to 40 in.	20-in. LCD TV	23-in. LCD TV	26-in. LCD TV
PICTURE-TUBE TVs Lowest-priced midsized screens but bulky. Common sizes: 26 to 36 in.	27-in. tube TV (4:3)	26- to 30-in. tube TV (16:9), 32-in. (4:3)	34-in. tube TV (16:9), 36-in. (4:
PLASMA TVs Thin, fairly large screens. Common sizes: 42 to 50 in.			
REAR-PROJECTION MICRODISPLAYS Fairly slim big screens that cost less than plasmas. Common sizes: 42 to 62 in.			
REAR-PROJECTION CRT-BASED TVs Lowest-priced large screens; big and bulky. Common sizes: 47 to 65 in.		up to 50-in. projection TV	51- to 57-in. projection TV

quality won't match that of true HD, but it can be quite good on the best sets.

Decide whether to pay top dollar for a state-of-the-art 1080p TV. A number of LCD and microdisplay rear-projection TVs with native resolution of 1920x1080 recently hit stores, and plasma models are coming, too. With the highest native resolution so far, these 1080p TVs are the first with the potential to display all the detail in 1080i signals, the most common HD format. That's because they have more pixels per square inch than other TVs of the same size. Until now, the top resolution was 1366x768, and many sets are 1280x720. Because 1080p TVs have more pixels, they can display sharper images, and the pixel grid is very faint. The improvement is most evident on big screens—50 inches and larger—and in close-up viewing.

In our initial tests of 1080p sets, some showed very fine detail, but others didn't make the most of the high resolution. The best were very impressive. But the improved detail related to 1080p resolution alone doesn't guarantee excellent images. A TV must do well with contrast, black level, color, and other factors to achieve overall excellence in picture quality.

The new TVs look their best when displaying 1080p HD signals, which transmit all lines in an image consecutively, rather than in two sweeps as with 1080i signals. But some of the first 1080p TVs can't accept 1080p signals from external sources like Blu-ray and HD-DVD players and Sony's Playstation 3, all due out this year. Instead, the sets

Checklist

Televisions

TV Type

☐ LCD ☐ Plasma ☐ Rear-projection

☐ Front-projection ☐ Picture tube

Screen size (in.) _____

Screen:

☐ EDTV ☐ HD monitor ☐ HDTV

To help you find the right TV for your needs from among the scores of available sets, we've put some useful information on our Web site.

Click on Electronics and Computers at the top of the ConsumerReports.org home page. Under "TV Decision Guide," click on the type of TV you want to learn about.

Once you've decided on one of the TV types, you'll find an interactive product selector for it online. Choose among brands, prices, and other options, and CONSUMER REPORTS' Web-enabled database can suggest models matching your criteria.

To access these interactive buying aids, you need to be a subscriber to ConsumerReports.org, or you can activate a 30-day free trial subscription offered on the inside front cover of this guide.

1,500-$2,000	$2,000-$2,500	$2,500-$3,000	More than $3,000
2-in. LCD TV	37-in. LCD TV		40-in. and up LCD TV
42-in. enhanced-definition plasma TV	42-in. plasma TV		50-in. and up plasma TV
42-in. microdisplay	46- to 52-in. microdisplay	55- to 62-in. microdisplay	
57- to 62-in. projection TV	65-in. projection TV		

A thin-profile large-screen TV is easier to carry than older projection or picture-tube models.

will accept 1080i signals from those sources, then convert them to 1080p. Future 1080p TVs are expected to accept these signals. It's not a major worry. So whether or not the TV can accept 1080p signals, you can still enjoy top picture quality.

If you want the best quality and cost is no issue, buy a 1080p set. Also consider one if you want the best resolution for use with a computer. But if excellent picture quality is your top priority, you can save by buying one of the best non-1080p TV sets instead.

Consider differences in reliability. Some of the repair data we're gathering on newer types of TVs are encouraging, but there is some cause for concern. Our limited survey data show that LCD and plasma TVs have been as reliable as picture-tube TVs during their first year of use. We found no unusual repair issues for flat-panel LCD TVs from Panasonic, Samsung, Sharp, Sony, and Toshiba, or for Panasonic and Sony plasma sets.

Microdisplays using LCD, DLP, or LCoS technology have been the most repair-prone type of TV during the first year of use. Toshiba DLP sets have been less repair-prone than most.

Conventional picture-tube TVs from most major brands have been very reliable over time. RCA and Zenith were among the more repair-prone brands in the 30- to 32-inch category. Rear-projection TVs using CRTs have had twice the rate of repairs for five-year-old sets. The brands for which we have data (Hitachi, Mitsubishi, Sony, and

Talk the Talk

Definition defined: A brief guide to the jargon

High definition. HDTVs display digital signals in 720p, 1080i, or 1080p definition—three technical specs for true HD. Images are sharper and more detailed than standard-definition images.

Enhanced definition. ED refers to 480p, a spec between standard and high definition. Some ED plasma sets (and, less common, LCD TVs) do a very good job down-converting HD signals to a resolution they can display.

Standard definition. Refers to the analog signals in the 480i format, which regular TV content has used for decades.

Native resolution. The number of pixels on an LCD or plasma screen, or in LCD, LCoS (liquid crystal on silicon), and DLP (digital-light processing) microdisplay rear-projection TVs and front projectors. Expressed as horizontal by vertical pixels, such as 1280x720 or 852x480. HDTVs have a vertical resolution (the second number) of 720 and above; ED sets have a vertical resolution of 480.

1080p. A number of LCD and microdisplay TVs with native resolution of 1920x1080 recently hit stores, and plasma models are due soon. With the highest native resolution so far, these

1080p TVs are the first with the potential to display all the detail in 1080i signals, the most common HD format. These TVs have more pixels per square inch than other TVs of the same size. Until now, the top resolution has been 1366x768, and many sets are 1280x720. Because 1080p TVs have more pixels they can display sharper images, and the pixel grid is very faint. The improvement is most evident on big screens—say, 50 inches and larger—and in close-up viewing. No TV broadcasts currently use 1080p resolution; some high-def DVDs with 1080p are starting to come on the market.

Toshiba) were comparable. For CONSUMER REPORTS' advice on added coverage for possible repairs, see "An extended warranty can be smart for some types of TVs," below.

Make sure you have what you need to get HDTV. Simply buying an HDTV doesn't get you HD. The four things you need are:

▶ Programming that's recorded in HD
▶ Transmission in the original HD format by the broadcaster, cable company, or satellite provider
▶ A TV capable of displaying HD
▶ A digital tuner (which may or may not be built into the TV) that can receive and decode the signals

You Need to Know

An extended warranty can be smart for some types of TVs

An extended warranty doesn't make sense for conventional picture-tube TVs and digital cameras. These products are unlikely to break during the warranty period, and if they do, the typical repair often costs no more than the warranty.

The decision isn't so easy with a flat-panel LCD or plasma TV, or a rear-projection TV using LCD, DLP, or LCoS technology. These pricey sets are too new to have a long track record, yet most have a one-year manufacturer's warranty, just like proven products.

Deciding whether an extended warranty makes sense depends on a few factors: how likely it is you'll have a problem, the cost of repairing the TV or replacing it in a few years at a price that might be lower than it is now, the cost of a warranty, and what it covers. Peace of mind is also a consideration if you're worried about the cost of a major repair.

There's no solid information yet on these new TVs, but here's our advice, based on initial repair data from our 2005 survey of subscribers, data from experts, and anecdotes from the ConsumerReports.org TV forum:

Conventional and tube-based rear-projection TVs. Don't buy an extended warranty. Decades of data show that conventional TVs have been very reliable, and newer HD sets appear to be as reliable. Rear-projection sets using CRTs have been considerably less reliable. Still, we don't recommend a service plan for either type considering the repair data and relatively low price.

LCD and plasma flat-panel TVs. Don't rule out an extended warranty. Our data suggest that LCD and plasma sets have been no less reliable in their first year of operation than tube-based TVs. But it's too early to know what might happen in later years. The cost of repairs is also an issue. Even replacing the fan that cools a hot-running plasma set can run $400. At worst, repairs can cost as much as a new TV. Replacing the driver board that regulates entire rows or columns of pixels costs $500 to $1,000—far more if the board is integrated into the flat panel. Image burn-in, a concern with plasma sets, is typically excluded from warranties. An extended warranty isn't essential, but it's worth considering if the price is reasonable, especially for no-name brands and expensive sets.

Rear-projection microdisplay bulbs must be replaced periodically, at $200 or more each.

Microdisplay-projection TVs (LCD, DLP, or LCoS). Seriously consider an extended warranty. Our data show that microdisplay-projection sets have been the most repair-prone types of TVs in their first year of use. As with LCD and plasma flat-panels, integration of components can lead to high repair costs. Manufacturers are increasingly housing color wheels (among the components likely to fail on DLP sets) with other components in a unit known as a light engine.

If any component in the light engine fails, the entire unit must be replaced, at a cost rivaling that of the set itself.

Most warranties cover the TV's light-bulb, a compelling reason to spring for a plan. Bulbs are rated to last 2,000 to 6,000 hours. You'll hit the 2,000-hour mark in just over a year if the set is on nightly from 6 p.m. to 11 p.m. A bulb costs $200 to $400. You can replace it if you're handy with a screwdriver, but you must avoid touching the bulb. If you're skittish, add $200 or more for a service call.

HOW TO BUY A WARRANTY
If you want an extended warranty, you almost always have to buy it when you purchase the TV. Follow these steps:

Check the terms. See when the warranty starts and what it covers. Most begin when you buy the set, overlapping with the standard warranty for the first year. So a three-year plan might give you only two extra years of coverage. But an extended warranty might cover things the standard warranty doesn't, such as damage from electrical surges. Check to see whether the warranty provides in-home service, typical for larger screen sizes, and a replacement set if your TV needs to go to the shop or can't be repaired.

Negotiate the cost. The markup on extended warranties is high, and you may be able to bargain for a lower price. Refuse at least the first sales pitch for a warranty, then signal you might buy at a lower price.

Pay no more than 15 to 20 percent of the TV's cost. That's the highest cost that makes financial sense. A three- or four-year plan priced at $400 is reasonable for a $2,000 TV. For TVs that cost less than $1,500, only a very low-priced plan would be worth it.

LCD PRICES GO DOWN, SIZE AND QUALITY GO UP

Slim models with big screens challenge the plasma TV market

Once available only with small screens, LCD (liquid-crystal display) TVs now come with bigger screens suitable for a household's primary set. The introduction of 37- to 50-inch sets has positioned LCD TVs as strong competition to flat-panel plasma sets. In fact, Sony has stopped offering plasma TVs for the consumer market, instead focusing its flat-panel effort on LCD sets. That illustrates the growing importance of this category.

LCD TVs cost more than comparably sized plasma sets, but the gap is gradually narrowing. Differences in picture quality are narrowing as well. Recent improvements in LCDs address earlier weaknesses at displaying deep black levels, accurate colors, and fast motion. The introduction of some LCD sets with 1080p resolution—the highest currently available—has also raised the bar for picture quality.

Regardless of screen size, LCD TVs are only a few inches thick, giving them a small footprint. They're also relatively lightweight—30 pounds or less for midsized models, 60 pounds or so for big-screen sets—so they're easily moved or wall-mounted. But LCD technology, like plasma technology, is fairly new, so long-term reliability of these TVs is still a question. However, preliminary data are encouraging.

LCD TVs don't have the glare issues that plasma TVs have.

WHAT'S AVAILABLE

Top-selling brands include Sony, Sharp, Samsung, Panasonic, Magnavox, and Westinghouse. Prices have been dropping steadily, thanks in part to the arrival of low-priced brands from computer makers such as Dell and store brands from major retailers such as Best Buy, Circuit City, Wal-Mart, and Target.

Most LCD TVs with screens larger than 20 inches or so are high-definition (HD) models. HDTVs can display the sharpest, most detailed images. On most high-def sets, the resolution is 1024x768 or1366x768. Recently, some 1080p HDTVs have been introduced. With a native resolution of 1920x1080 pixels, the highest so far, 1080p TVs are the first with the potential to display all 1,080 lines in the most common high-definition format, called 1080i. The improvement is most noticeable on large screens, say, 50 inches and up.

In smaller sizes—screens of 20 inches or less—enhanced-definition LCD TVs are also available. ED sets, which are digital, have picture quality that's slightly better than standard definition but not as good as HD; these can accept 480p signals like those from a progressive-scan DVD player. Standard-definition TVs are analog models that can display only 480i signals like those used for most TV broadcasts. Analog TV broadcasts will cease on Feb. 17, 2009, when all broadcasters must switch to digital. An analog set you buy now will be able to receive digital programming when used with an external digital tuner, such as that in a cable or satellite box, or a set-top box and antenna.

Major-brand LCD HDTVs with 26-inch screens typically start at $1,000; $1,200 to $2,000 for a 32-inch set; and $2,000 to $2,500 for 37-inch set. In all size categories, you'll see less-familiar brands selling for hundreds less. A growing number of LCD TVs have even larger screens—up to 50 inches or more—and prices go up along with size.

FEATURES THAT COUNT

LCD TVs typically have all the usual features you expect on a TV. Other features are more specific to

this type of set. The location of the **speakers** is one example. On some LCD models, the speakers are located on both sides of the screen; on others they're below it. That affects the overall width of the set and could determine whether it will fit into a niche in an entertainment center, for example. On some LCD TVs, speakers are detachable. That can be a plus if you want to fit the TV into a particular space or simply position the speakers away from the screen. The ability of a panel to tilt and swivel also varies, so see whether a given model can be adjusted as much as you'd like.

Some LCD sets have a **memory-card slot.** This enables you to view still photos or videos from a digital camera. You can connect a camera or camcorder directly to the TV if it has a **USB** or **IEEE 1394/Firewire input**.

With more sources for video available all the time, it's handy to have a feature that allows you to customize settings for each source, such as the cable box or the DVD player. If you watch many DVD movies with your DVD player in nonprogressive-scan mode, look for a **film-mode feature** on HD sets. This feature is also called **3:2 pull-down compensation,** or brand-specific names like **CineMotion** and **Film Mode.** This can make moving images that were converted from film to video look less jerky and jagged. On 16:9 sets, stretch and zoom modes will expand or compress an image to fill the screen shape better. This helps to reduce the dark bands that can appear on the sides or top and bottom of images if you watch content that isn't formatted for a wide screen. (The picture may be distorted or cut off a bit in the process of stretching or zooming.)

HOW TO CHOOSE

Consider what level of picture quality you're willing to pay for. The best LCD TVs are capable of excellent picture quality, although blacks may not be quite as deep as on a good plasma set. For a main TV or one you'll watch often, we'd strongly recommend an HD set with resolution of at least 1024x768. On screens larger than 30 inches or so, 1366x768 has the potential to offer better quality, though native screen resolution in and of itself

Viewing angles on many new LCD TVs have improved, so they display a better image from off-center than older models did.

doesn't guarantee a certain level of picture quality. Check our Ratings online to see which models make the most of their resolution. It's probably not worth paying the premium for a 1080p set with 1920x1080 resolution for screens much smaller than 50 inches. The quality difference isn't as noticeable below that size. We'd recommend an ED or standard-definition LCD TV only for small sets used for casual viewing in the kitchen, for example, where you wouldn't want the cable or satellite box you generally need to receive HD signals. The picture quality almost certainly won't be as good as what you'll get with an HD set.

Check the viewing angle. Viewing angles have improved, so many new LCD TVs display a better image from off-center than older sets did—a must if the TV will be watched by several people at once. Some sets have wider viewing angles than others. Before buying one, see how the picture looks if you step off to the side or move up and down. With some, you'll see a dimmer, somewhat washed-out image as your viewing position angles away, particularly in a vertical direction.

Look for easy-to-use inputs. On many LCD televisions, the connections are on the side or rear of the panel and might be hard to reach. Some larger models have a separate control unit to which you connect all your external audio/video devices, such as a DVD player or cable box. You then have only one cable going from the control box to the panel itself. That's a plus for wall-mounting and can make the inputs easier to access. But it does give you another box to contend with.

Native resolution alone doesn't guarantee a certain level of picture quality. Check our Ratings online to see which models make the most of their resolution.

Consider a set that doubles as a computer display. If you need a computer display as well as a TV, check connectivity options. An HD set with high native resolution is best for computer use. A standard VGA connection works with all computers; a Digital Visual Interface (DVI) input would be compatible with newer midrange computers.

Our preliminary survey data found no repair problems during the first year of use for LCD sets from Panasonic, Samsung, Sharp, Sony, and Toshiba, but it's too early to comment on other brands or on long-term reliability for any brand.

SLEEK PLASMA PANELS OFFER TOP-NOTCH VIDEO

More, and bigger, screens are adding variety to the category

Plasma TVs make a blockbuster first impression. A scant 6 inches thick or less, these sleek flat panels display bright images on screens measuring about 3 to 5 feet diagonally. With more models 50 inches and larger now available, plasma TVs have become a viable alternative to rear-projection sets for anyone seeking a jumbo screen.

A plasma screen is made up of thousands of pixels containing gas that's converted into "plasma" by an electrical charge. The plasma causes phosphors to glow red, green, or blue, as dictated by a video signal. Thanks to improvements in plasma technology, the best sets have excellent picture quality. They offer a wider viewing angle than most rear-projection sets and LCD TVs, along with deeper blacks and smoother motion than you get with LCD sets.

The picture isn't all rosy, however. Like projection TVs using CRT (cathode-ray tube) technology, plasma sets may be vulnerable to screen burn-in, although new screen-saving technologies minimize the risk. And because plasma sets are relatively new, their long-term reliability is still a question, although preliminary data are encouraging.

WHAT'S AVAILABLE

When buying a plasma TV, you'll face a choice between HD (high-definition) and ED (enhanced-

Major manufacturers say recent models of plasma TVs can be used for 60,000 hours before they start to lose their brightness. That's about 29 years of heavy use.

definition) sets, which cost less. The two types differ in native resolution, meaning the fixed number of pixels on the screen. In a spec like 852x480, note the second number. If it's 480, the set is ED; 720 or higher, it's HD. Most 42-inch plasma HDTVs have resolution of 1024x768; 50-inch sets typically have 1366x768. Some new plasma TVs coming on the market have a still-higher resolution of 1920x1080. These so-called 1080p TVs have the potential to display all 1,080 lines in the most common high-definition format, called 1080i. The improvement is most noticeable on large screens, say 50 inches and up.

Both HD and ED sets should be capable of up- or down-converting signals to match their native resolution. ED sets can display the full detail of 480p signals, such as those output by a DVD player. When connected to an HD tuner, many can down-convert HD TV signals, which are 720p or 1080i, to suit their lower-resolution screens. The picture quality can be very good, even though it's not true HD. If you sit too close to an ED set, though, images may appear coarser than on an HD set, as if you were looking through a screen door. ED sets are likely to become less common as HD prices continue to fall.

As of July 2006, all TVs with screens 25 inches and larger—a range encompassing all plasma TVs—must have a built-in ATSC digital tuner to comply with a government ruling. By March 2007, all new TVs sold in the U.S., regardless of size and type, must include a digital tuner. Some manufacturers are getting around that ruling, however, by introducing sets called "monitors," which have no tuner of any type. These require a cable box or satellite receiver to get any programming, not just HD content.

Among the leading brands in the plasma TV category are Panasonic, Hitachi, Philips, Pioneer, and Samsung. Sony recently stopped making plasma TVs to concentrate instead on LCD sets. Prices have dropped sharply over the past year or two. HD models with 40- to 44-inch screens, the best-selling size, cost $2,000 or more. TVs with screens 50 inches or larger cost $3,000 and up. Look for prices to fall further now that more brands of plasma TVs are available, many priced aggressively.

FEATURES THAT COUNT

Plasma TVs have all the usual features you expect on a higher-priced television, as well as others more specific to this type of TV. For example, some

Some plasma sets have speakers on the sides; others, like this Panasonic, have speakers below. This could be important to consider if you are fitting the set into a cabinet.

sets have screensaver-type features to prevent burn-in from static images. On some models, the speakers are on both sides of the screen; on others they're below it. That affects the overall width of the set and could determine whether it will fit into a niche in an entertainment center, for example. Some plasma sets have a memory-card slot. This enables you to view still photos or videos from a digital camera. You can connect a camera or camcorder directly to the TV if it has a **USB** or **IEEE 1394/Firewire input**.

With more sources for video available all the time, it's handy to have a feature that allows you to customize settings for each source, such as the cable box or the DVD player. If you watch many DVD movies with your DVD player in nonprogressive-scan mode, look for a **film-mode feature** on HD sets. This feature is also called **3:2 pull-down compensation,** or brand-specific names like **CineMotion** and **Film Mode.** This can make moving images that were converted from film to video look less jerky, with less jaggedness around the edges. **Stretch and zoom** modes will expand or compress an image to better fill the screen shape. This helps to reduce the dark bands that can appear on the sides or top and bottom of images if you watch content that isn't formatted for a wide screen. (The picture may be distorted or cut off a bit in the process of stretching or zooming.)

Picture-in-picture (PIP) lets you watch two channels at once, one in a small box, the other a full-screen image. It's useful if you want to browse the onscreen guide while keeping an eye on the program you're watching. A single-tuner TV requires another device with a tuner, such as a VCR or cable box, to display two programs at once; dual-tuner models can display two programs simultaneously on their own.

HOW TO CHOOSE

Decide whether you want true HD or the next best thing. HD sets generally perform better than ED sets with all types of signals. They're worth the higher cost if you're a purist who wants the best image quality. Most ED plasma sets can down-convert an HD signal to fit their lower resolution, so you can still enjoy HD programming. While it won't be true HD quality, it can be very good. For a main TV or one you'll watch often, we'd strongly recommend an HD set, which would have resolution of at least 1024x768. On screens 50 inches or so, 1366x768 has the potential to offer better quality, though native screen resolution in and of itself doesn't guarantee a certain level of picture quality. Note that the shiny surface of a plasma TV can produce annoying reflections, especially in brightly lighted rooms. Many of these sets look best in low light.

Weigh screen size against price. If you're buying a plasma TV, an important question is how much screen you can afford. All other things being equal, the bigger the screen, the bigger the price tag, and the greater the viewing distance you need to

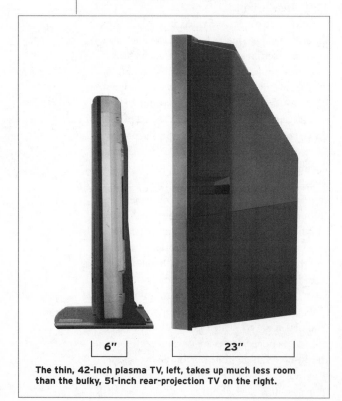

6"   23"

The thin, 42-inch plasma TV, left, takes up much less room than the bulky, 51-inch rear-projection TV on the right.

see optimal picture quality. You'll enjoy the best viewing experience if you sit at least 6 feet away from a 42-inch HD set, and a little farther from an ED set or larger screen.

Beware of burn-in and burnout. Plasma TVs may be prone to burn-in, much like CRT-based rear-projection TVs. Over time, static images displayed for long periods (such as a video game or a stock ticker) may leave permanent ghosted impressions onscreen, so minimize the risk as much as you can.

You may have seen reports, in print or online, suggesting that plasma TVs may not last as long as other types of TVs. Overall longevity and reliability are not yet proven because the technology is so new. Major manufacturers now tout 60,000 hours of use or more before a recent-model plasma screen loses half its brightness. Even in heavy use (40 hours a week), that's about 29 years.

Don't get hung up on specs. Ads touting high-contrast ratios and brightness (cd/m^2, or candelas per square meter) may sway you to one set or another. But don't let this be the deciding factor. Manufacturers arrive at specs differently, so they may not be comparable. Try adjusting sets in the store yourself to compare contrast and brightness.

Determine what's included when comparing prices. Some plasmas are monitors only; they don't include speakers or a tuner for any type of TV signal. You won't have to pay for a tuner if you'll be using a cable box or satellite receiver, which will serve as the tuner for all programming. Otherwise, you'll need a set-top box to work with an antenna. If the plasma TV has no speakers, you'll have to buy them separately unless you plan to connect the set to your existing sound system.

Consider the logistics. Ads for plasma TVs might not show any wires, but you'll probably be connecting a cable box or satellite receiver and a DVD player, and possibly a DVR, DVD recorder, VCR and audio receiver. You can tuck wires behind the TV if you place it on a stand. With wall-mounting, you can run the wires behind the wall or through conduits, a task that might be best handled by a professional. Often weighing 100 pounds or more, plasma TVs need adequate support and ample ventilation because of the heat they can generate. Ask the retailer to recommend an installer or contact the Custom Electronic Design & Installation Association (800-669-5329 or *www.cedia.net*). Figure on paying $300 to $1,000 for labor, plus a few hundred dollars for mounting brackets.

REAR-PROJECTION TVs GET SLIMMER, BETTER

These big-screen TVs are not as bulky as they used to be

Most new rear-projection TVs are microdisplay sets that use liquid-crystal display (LCD), digital-light processing (DLP), or liquid crystal on silicon (LCoS) technology to create images on screens that can be 71 inches or larger.

These TVs are slimmer, lighter, and more expensive than projection sets using cathode-ray tube (CRT) technology, which used to be the norm. CRT-based projection sets are declining in popularity, but some are still available. They tend to be the cheapest type of big screen, but they're notoriously big and heavy.

WHAT'S AVAILABLE

Major brands include Hitachi, JVC, Mitsubishi, Panasonic, Philips, RCA, Samsung, Sony, and Toshiba.

The smallest sets measure about 42 inches diagonally. Rear-projection sets with 50- to 59-inch screens are the best sellers. The largest of these TVs have screens measuring 71 inches or more. Keep in mind that a set with a 57-inch screen could be overwhelming in a modest-sized room. Most rear-projection sets now on the market are digital (HD-capable) sets. Most have a wide-screen 16:9 aspect ratio that resembles a movie-theater screen.

Virtually all projection sets now sold are HD models, typically with resolution of at least 1280x720. One of the newest developments in this category has been the introduction of 1080p models. These sets have resolution of 1920x1080 pixels, giving them the potential to display all 1,080 lines in the most common high-definition format, called 1080i. The improvement is most noticeable on large screens, say, 50 inches and up.

FEATURES THAT COUNT

Most projection TVs have the features that are now standard on higher-priced TVs. **Picture-in-picture** (PIP) lets you watch two channels at once, one in a small box, the other a full-screen image. It's useful if you want to browse the onscreen guide while keeping an eye on the program you're watching. A single-tuner TV requires another device with a tuner, such as a VCR or cable box, to display two programs at once; dual-tuner models can display two programs simultaneously on their own. Some projection sets have a **memory-card slot**. This enables you to view still photos or videos from a digital camera. You can connect a camera or camcorder directly to the TV if it has a **USB** or **IEEE 1394/Firewire input**.

On CRT-based models, **auto convergence** provides a one-touch adjustment to automatically align the three CRTs' images to form an accurate picture. It's much more convenient than manual convergence, which can require time-consuming adjustments. **Manual convergence** does allow finer control, though. The best bet is a set that has both manual and automatic convergence. (Convergence is not necessary on LCD, DLP, or LCoS models.)

If you watch many DVD movies with your DVD

Rear-projection TVs are bulky, but when they're built into a wall unit, their size isn't an issue.

player in nonprogressive-scan mode, look for a **film-mode** feature on HD sets. This feature is also called **3:2 pull-down compensation** or brand-specific names like **CineMotion** and **Film Mode**. This can make moving images that were converted from film to video look less jerky, with less jaggedness around the edges. **Stretch and zoom modes** will expand or compress an image to better fill the screen shape. This helps to reduce the dark bands that can appear on the sides or top and bottom of images if you watch content that isn't formatted for a wide screen. (The picture might be distorted or cut off a bit in the process of stretching or zooming.) On CRT-based sets (but not LCD, LCoS, or DLP models), the dark bands can be more than just a minor distraction. Like any image left on the screen for a long time, the bands can leave "burn in"—ghosted images on the screen.

The trend is toward rear-projection TVs using high-tech microdisplay technology instead of CRTs.

HOW TO CHOOSE

Here are some points to consider when choosing a rear-projection TV:

Consider space before settling on screen size. You might be tempted by the biggest screen, which can span as much as 71 inches or more, but take a breath—and some measurements—first. Figure out how much floor space you can spare, and plan to view the TV from about 7 to 9 feet away for optimal picture quality.

Weigh depth and price in choosing a display type. Once you know how much room you have, decide whether size or price is more important. CRT-based sets are floor-standing models with deep cabinets mounted on casters. Some take up as much space as an armchair or loveseat. Most microdisplays require a stand, which you must buy separately for a few hundred dollars or more. Would you prefer to save money with a bulkier CRT set or spend more for a slimmer microdisplay?

Consider reliability. Rear-projection TVs using CRT technology have been much more repair-prone than conventional picture-tube TVs. As noted, any pattern left on a CRT screen for long pe-

---

Talk the Talk

Projection TV terms & technologies

You might wonder why rear-projection sets are called that, given that there's no projector anywhere in sight. It's because the projector is inside the cabinet. An image is created within the set and projected onto the rear surface of the screen (hence the name "rear projection"). By contrast, direct-view sets (picture-tube TVs and flat-panel LCD and plasma displays) create images right on the screen, not internally.

Different technologies are used to create the images on projection TVs.

MICRODISPLAYS

This is an industry term sometimes used to describe rear-projection sets using LCD (liquid-crystal display), DLP (digital light-processing), or LCoS (liquid-crystal on silicon) chips and a bright lamp to create images. This space-saving "light-engine" technology makes microdisplays slimmer and lighter than CRT-based sets. Most microdisplays are 15 to 20 inches deep, weighing about 100 pounds. Here's a look at the three types of microdisplays:

LCD. These TVs have three tiny LCD panels inside. Don't confuse LCD-based rear-projection TVs with LCD flat panels, though. These big TVs are more than a foot deep. The best of the LCD-based projection sets we've tested displayed excellent picture quality. None of the sets, however, were able to display the deep black levels of TVs using other technologies, and the contrast wasn't as good as we've seen on other types of TVs. Price: $2,200 to $4,500.

DLP. These sets create images using a digital light-processing chip with thousands of tiny mirrors. Rear-projection DLP sets have one chip and a rotating color wheel, which might cause some viewers to perceive annoying flashes of color—what's called the rainbow effect. The best of the DLP projection sets we've tested displayed excellent picture quality. Price: $2,200 to $6,000.

LCoS. These sets share some attributes with LCD and DLP, using both tiny mirrors and liquid-crystal technology. The technology's rollout has been hampered by production and cost problems, prompting companies like Intel and

Philips to abandon their LCoS plans. Because LCoS sets have been slow to reach the market, we've tested only a few so far. The best had very good picture quality. JVC has an LCoS variant that it calls HD-ILA; Sony calls its version SXRD. Price: $3,000 to $6,000.

CRT MODELS

This type of projection TV contains three CRTs, or cathode ray tubes—one each for red, green, and blue—making the cabinet big and heavy. Most CRT-based models are floor-standing sets 24 inches or more deep, and many weigh about 200 pounds. Three beams converge on the inside of the screen to form an image. You must periodically align the CRTs, using the TV's controls, to ensure a sharp image. This is known as convergence. All but the cheapest sets now have an automatic convergence feature that makes this a quick and easy process. Manual convergence usually allows for finer tweaks. The best of the sets we've tested had very good picture quality. Price: $1,000 to $2,500.

riods—such as a stock ticker or video game—can burn into the tubes of a CRT-based model, producing a permanent ghosted image on the screen. Most warranties don't cover burn-in.

This problem doesn't affect other types of rear-projection TVs. Microdisplay technologies are newer and haven't established a track record for long-term reliability. But preliminary data show they're even more repair-prone than CRT-based projection sets during their first year of use. They're not vulnerable to screen burn-in, but they might require lamp replacement, which can cost a few hundred dollars.

Focus on picture quality. The best rear-projection sets can deliver excellent picture quality with HD content and very good picture quality for DVDs and regular TV programming. Within the microdisplay category, we haven't found that any one projection technology was consistently better than another.

Check the viewing angle. Some new models display a better image from off-center than older

sets did—a must if the TV will be watched by several people at once. Some sets have wider viewing angles than others. Before buying one, see how the picture looks if you step off to the side or move up and down. With some, you'll see a dimmer, somewhat washed-out image as your viewing position angles away, particularly in a vertical direction.

Expect fine sound quality. Many people connect big-screen TVs to an audio system to provide surround sound, so the quality of the TV's speakers may not be an issue. It may reassure you to know that virtually all the sets we've tested recently produced excellent sound. That's largely because projection sets have bigger speakers than direct-view TVs and bigger cabinets with superior acoustical properties.

Consider installation. Because rear-projection sets are floor-standing , installation is easier than with front-projection systems or wall-mounted plasma TVs. Still, rear-projection sets are large and might be harder to set up than smaller TVs, so consider delivery and professional installation.

FRONT-PROJECTOR TVs OFFER BIGGEST PICTURE

But they are probably not the best choice for everyday use

For a truly theaterlike experience, you can't beat a front projector paired with a screen that stretches 100 inches or more diagonally. That's about twice the size of a plasma TV, with image quality that's just as good and prices that are comparable, starting at about $2,500 for a high-definition (HD) projector designed for home-theater use.

But front projectors aren't the best choice for typical, everyday viewing. They look best in a dark room, and the need to add a screen, speakers, and a TV tuner increases the cost and complexity of setup.

WHAT'S AVAILABLE

In years past, the only real choice for a big-screen home theater was a bulky CRT-based projector that cost tens of thousands of dollars. Most new projectors are compact units using LCD, DLP, or LCoS technology—the same display technologies used in rear-projection microdisplay TVs. Among the best-

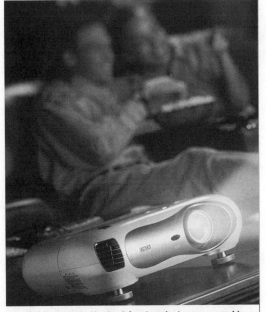

In a big, dark room, the best front projectors can provide an excellent picture on a jumbo screen.

Most front projectors lack built-in audio capability, so you must connect them to external speakers.

Image sizes up to 300 inches are possible with some front-projection models, but our tests show that as the image gets larger, it also gets dimmer.

selling brands of home-theater projectors are BenQ, Epson, InFocus, Optoma, Panasonic, Sanyo, Sharp, and Sony. Technically display devices rather than TVs, front projectors require a separate screen (or a smooth wall) as a display surface. You can vary the picture size—from about 50 inches to about 300 inches—by moving the projector closer to the screen or farther back, and using the zoom control. Consequently, you're not locked into a specific screen size as you are with every other type of TV. The images are best viewed in dark rooms, so you need to turn off lights or use blackout shades for daytime viewing.

To get TV programming, you need to connect an external tuner, such as a cable or satellite box. For movies, you could hook up just a DVD player. In either case, you generally have to provide speakers, because most projectors don't have built-in audio capability. Even when speakers are included, they're generally not of the highest quality, so you'd probably want to use a sound system in any case.

Front projectors can be placed on a table or other flat surface and stored when not in use. Most can also be mounted to the ceiling. If you mount the projector, be sure to place it at the distance recommended by the manufacturer, angled to prevent the rectangular shape of the image from being distorted. Hiding cables and wiring behind walls or above the ceiling may require construction work. Price ranges from $1,200 and up for enhanced-definition (ED) models to $2,000 and up for HD models.

Don't confuse home projectors with the cheaper models designed for conference-room use. Those units, which sell for less than $1,000, might have lower resolution, which won't give you the detailed, big-screen TV images most home viewers want. Data projectors also tend to lack typical TV features, such as aspect-ratio controls (including zoom or stretch) or the more common color controls.

FEATURES THAT COUNT

Maximum image size. Manufacturer specs indicate the largest image you can get from a given model, which may be as large as 200 to 300 inches. To achieve the maximum size, you have to move the projector farther back from the screen. But as the image gets larger, it also gets dimmer. In our tests,

we found an image size of about 110 inches (measured diagonally, for a 16:9 widescreen display) to be the sweet spot for impact and brightness.

Distance to screen. To fill a 110-inch screen size, you'd typically place a projector 10 to 15 feet away. If you want to project a 50-inch image on a wall, about half that distance would do. Recommended placement varies by model, so see what the manufacturer specs indicate.

Keystoning. If you tilt the projector up or down to raise or lower the projected image, the sides of the image will start to angle away from 90 degrees. That turns what should be a rectangular shape into a trapezoid. A keystoning control feature compensates for this, but resolution can suffer depending on the amount of correction applied to the image.

Lens-shift mechanism. Some projectors have this feature, which lets you move the image horizontally or vertically without tilting the projector. This allows you to avoid the shortcomings of the keystone adjustments. The electronic shift adjustment on some projectors tends to have a very limited range. When exceeded, images could be cropped.

Stretch and zoom modes. These aspect-ratio controls will adjust the image size to fill the screen shape better. This helps reduce or eliminate the dark bands that can appear above, below, or on the sides of the image. (The picture may be distorted or cut off a bit in the process of stretching and zooming.)

Inputs. Most front projectors have composite-video, S-video, and component-video inputs. In addition to those connections, most HD-capable sets have a Digital Visual Interface (DVI) or High-Definition Multimedia Interface (HDMI).

HOW TO CHOOSE

First make sure that a front projector is the right choice for your viewing needs, given the logistics involved. These devices have special requirements, but if you can deal with them, you can enjoy a high-quality, theaterlike experience at a reasonable cost. Here's what to consider in choosing among models:

Go for HD. Enhanced-definition models have lower native resolution (the number of pixels that make up an image) than HD units. That limits image quality, especially on larger screens. If you're going to the effort of setting up a front-projection system, we recommend an HD model. An ED projector could do if cost is paramount, but plan to sit farther away to compensate for the coarser images.

Weigh the pros and cons of LCD and DLP

projectors. In general, projectors using LCD technology aren't as good as DLP models at reproducing true black, but some LCD models do quite well. As with rear-projection TVs using DLP technology, you may experience a "rainbow effect" when watching a DLP front projector. This is a flash of color that may be visible mainly when you move your eyes across bright objects on a dark background. The rainbow effect isn't obvious, but once seen, it can be annoying. Take a video with high-contrast scenes to the store so that your family can see whether it's a problem. All DLP projectors using a single chip (including all models in the Ratings online) are affected. Only the priciest DLP units avoid the problem by using three chips to produce red, green, and blue.

See which model suits your room arrangement. Before buying a front projector and screen, figure out how you'll set up the room. The room dimensions and anticipated seating positions will influence what screen sizes are practical. Some projectors give you more flexibility in where you can place the projector to get a certain image size; see what the manufacturer recommends. The larger the image you want, the more distance needed between the projector and screen, though the projector's zoom feature will provide some flexibility here. Also consider where you'll sit to watch the TV. With a 110-inch screen and an HD image, the optimal viewing distance is about 14 feet.

Check the inputs. Consider where you'll place and connect the cable or satellite box that will serve as the TV tuner, a sound system, and probably a DVD player or recorder. All the tested models have the usual analog inputs, such as component-video, and some add HDMI or DVI digital inputs. If you want to use the projector for playing games, make sure it has a computer input.

Think about the screen. In our tests, we used a 110-inch screen that cost $400. It has a matte-white viewing surface 4½ feet high by 8 feet wide. There are screens with more reflective finishes designed to enhance brightness, but you might compromise the wider viewing angle of a matte screen. Other so-called dark screens are designed to enhance contrast by improving black-level performance, but they do take a small hit on overall brightness.

RELIABLE PICTURE TUBES STILL WORTH A LOOK

As new technologies take over, conventional television models dwindle in number but deliver a lot of bang for your buck

Proven reliability is a hallmark of picture-tube televisions.

Familiar picture-tube TVs continue to be big sellers, mostly at prices below $500. In the HDTV arena, they're being overshadowed by flat-panel LCD and plasma sets and big-screen projection models.

With manufacturers shifting their focus to these newer TV technologies, there are fewer new tube TVs coming on the market. Still, the best tube-based HDTVs offer outstanding performance and proven reliability at low prices. But the maximum screen size is limited to 36 inches, and these are getting harder to find.

WHAT'S AVAILABLE

Among the better-selling brands are JVC, Magnavox, Philips, RCA, Samsung, Sanyo, Sharp, Sony, and Toshiba. Picture-tube TVs can be either analog (the kind of set you've been watching for years) or digital models (including HD sets). Analog TVs can display only standard-definition signals, like those used for most TV broadcasts. Standard definition is called 480i because images contain up to 480 lines that are drawn on screen in an interlaced pattern (hence the letter "i"), first the odd lines and then the even, 30 times a second.

Most digital tube TVs can display HD signals with a resolution of 1080i (1,080 lines with an interlaced scan) or 720p (720 lines scanned progressively, in one sweep). These HD images are much sharper and more detailed than standard definition. A few manufacturers have introduced standard-definition (SD) digital models, not to be confused with HDTVs. These accept not only SD signals but also HD signals, which they convert to 480i. Picture quality may be slightly better than with an analog set because digital signals tend to be cleaner than analog.

Size and shape. Most picture-tube TVs have a screen that measures 13 to 34 inches diagonally. There are fewer of the largest sets, with 36-inch screens, possibly because other technologies such as plasma and LCD are coming on strong. HD sets generally have screens 26 inches or larger. On analog sets, the screens are usually squarish, with an aspect ratio of 4:3, meaning they're four units wide for every three units high. Some HD sets have a 4:3 screen, but more have a 16:9 wide screen with proportions similar to that of a movie-theater screen. One of the downsides to picture-tube sets is that they're relatively bulky and heavy, about 2 feet deep and up to 200 pounds in larger sizes. A few slim-

mer sets that measure about 16 inches deep were recently introduced. Samsung's 30-inch widescreen SlimFit HDTV sells for about $800. Though slimmer, these sets are no lighter.

Features. Generally, the larger the screen, the higher the price and the more features and inputs for other video devices. Most sets with screens measuring 26 inches and larger have flat screens, high-quality video inputs, universal remotes, and simulated surround sound.

Price. Analog-tube TVs that display only standard definition are the least-expensive type of set, but they're becoming less common as HD models attract more interest. Analog 13-inch sets start at $75 or so; 27-inch sets start at $200; 32-inch sets start at about $350; and 36-inch sets start at $600. A 27-inch HDTV monitor capable of displaying HD typically sells for $400 to $600. Most 30-inch wide-screen HDTVs start at $800.

FEATURES THAT COUNT

Many new TVs have a **flat-front-screen** CRT, which reduces reflection and glare but doesn't necessarily improve picture quality. **Adjustable color temperature** lets you shade the picture toward the blue range ("cooler" is better for images with outdoor light) or the red ("warmer" is preferred for movie-theater realism). Some sets can memorize custom picture settings for each video input, a useful features because signal qualities often differ when you switch video sources, say, from a DVD player to a cable box or antenna.

Picture-in-picture (PIP) lets you watch two channels at once, one in a small picture alongside the full-screen image. A single-tuner TV requires another device with a tuner, such as a VCR or cable box, to display two programs at once; dual-tuner models can display two programs simultaneously on their own. Some sets have a **memory-card slot.** This enables you to view still photos or videos from a digital camera. You can connect a camera or camcorder directly to the TV if it has a **USB** or **IEEE 1394/Firewire input.**

Stereo sound is standard on sets 27 inches or larger, but you'll generally hear little stereo separation from a TV's built-in speakers. **Ambient sound** is often termed "surround sound," but it isn't like that from a multispeaker home-theater system. It's an effect created by special audio processing. You can turn it off if you don't like it. For a better stereo effect or true surround sound, route the signals to a sound system. An **automatic**

The biggest picture-tube TVs are starting to disappear from store shelves as slimmer and lighter models take over.

Expert • Independent • Nonprofit

You'll need a deep cabinet to house most large-screen models, but slimmer picture-tube sets are also available.

volume leveler compensates for the volume jumps that often accompany commercials or changes in channel.

HD sets may have a **film-mode feature,** sometimes referred to as **3:2 pull-down compensation** or by brand names like **CineMotion.** This can make moving images that were converted from film to video have less jaggedness around the edges of objects. Look for this feature if you watch many movies with your DVD player in nonprogressive-scan mode. On 16:9 sets, **stretch and zoom modes** will expand or compress an image to fill the screen shape better. This helps to reduce the dark bands that can appear on the sides or top and bottom of images if you watch content formatted for a screen shape other than 16:9. (The picture might be distorted or cut off a bit in the process of stretching or zooming.)

HOW TO CHOOSE

Televisions using the familiar picture-tube technology are the least-expensive option, and some offer fine picture quality.

Decide on a screen size. TVs with small screens (less than 27 inches) are likely to have fewer bells and whistles than larger sets. You also need to consider the size of your room to allow for enough distance so that you don't see the lines that make up the images.

Decide whether you want HD image quality. HDTVs can display sharper, finer images than conventional analog TVs, whether you're watching HDTV programming, standard TV programming, or DVD movies. Even with standard (non-HD) signals from a good cable connection, a satellite signal, or a DVD player, the picture quality can be better than a conventional set's. But with a poor analog signal, like the worst channels from regular cable, an HDTV can make the images look worse because the digital circuitry can't always differentiate the noise from the real signal.

While standard-definition TVs can't match HD for picture quality, some offer very good or excellent non-HD images that may suit you fine. Only firsthand experience will enable you to decide whether the extra quality of HD is worth the extra cost. Though HD sets cost less than they used to, they still command a premium over a comparable analog set.

Decide between an HD monitor and an integrated HDTV. If you're among the majority of consumers who get their HD via cable or satellite, you can save money by buying an HD monitor, which requires an external tuner to receive any TV signals. Integrated sets cost more, and they generally require a cable box or satellite receiver anyway. Digital-cable-ready sets that use CableCards are the most expensive type, and as noted above, this first generation doesn't offer interactive program guides or video-on-demand via remote control.

Consider the shape. A screen with the familiar 4:3 aspect ratio is a good choice for regular TV programming, which is formatted for this squarish shape. Most DVD movies and a growing number of HDTV programs are formatted for wide screen. We believe a wide-screen TV will give you a better HD experience now and be preferable for all viewing in a few years. But 4:3 sets cost less. Content formatted for one screen shape must be modified to fit the other, so you might see bars on two sides or above and below the image. Most 16:9 HD sets can stretch or zoom images to eliminate the bars, but this can distort the picture or cut off the edges.

> **While standard-definition TVs** just can't match HD for picture quality, some offer very good or excellent non-HD images.

CUSTOMERS WEIGH IN ON CABLE VS. SATELLITE

Satellite earns higher scores, but digital cable has come on strong

In our most recent national survey of more than 1,750 cable and satellite-television subscribers, satellite continued to lead the pack in overall satisfaction, followed by digital cable and then analog. Our 2005 survey also confirmed what we found two years earlier, that digital cable is making significant strides. It has narrowed the gap in overall satisfaction between it and satellite to just 8 points.

We expect digital cable will gain further ground in the future, in part because of two features in which it holds a clear advantage: reliable, high-speed Internet access and the ability to receive and record high-definition (HD) programs with a minimal investment in hardware.

One area where cable companies need to do some work, however, is customer service. Only 75 percent of digital-cable and 68 percent of analog-cable subscribers told us they received good or excellent service when they phoned their provider with a question or problem.

Your choice of cable or satellite will be dictated to some extent by where you live. Satellite TV from

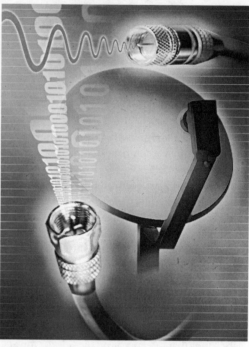

Cable and satellite differ not only in delivery but also in cost, customer satisfaction, and programming.

First Things First

Cable vs. satellite

Find out which types of service are available in your area, then make your choice.

1 Analog cable

Pros Least expensive. Fewest disruptions in service, according to our survey.
Cons Fewest channels. Provides lowest picture and sound quality of the three types.
Price $46 a month was the average amount paid in our survey.

2 Digital cable

Pros Selection of channels now rivals satellite's. Only way to get HD programs via cable; requires less investment than satellite.
Cons Most expensive per month.
Price $70 a month was the average amount paid in our survey.

3 Satellite

Pros Most channels. Provides best picture and sound quality, according to our survey.
Cons Must buy pricey hardware; might get free gear with a long-term commitment.
Price $54 a month was the average amount paid in our survey.

the two major carriers, DirecTV and Dish Network, is available nationwide to households with an unobstructed view of the southern horizon. But you won't be able to get service if tall buildings, trees, or mountains block signals beamed by the satellites. Cable is available in most parts of the country, but about 30 percent of the satellite subscribers we surveyed, mostly living in rural areas, said cable wasn't available to them. Where cable is offered, you can generally get it in either the digital or analog variety.

There is, of course, the venerable option of over-the-air (antenna) reception. These days there's a new twist: With the right antenna and a digital tuner, many households can receive digital signals from local stations broadcasting digitally and can view their HD programming on an HDTV set. There's no ongoing cost, but programs are limited to broadcast TV.

HOW TO CHOOSE

For additional programming, consider satellite or cable and weigh the following:

Decide which channels you want. Not surprisingly, our survey showed a strong correlation between interesting programming and overall satisfaction. Although satellite once had many more channels than cable, digital cable is now competitive.

Bear in mind that if you're like most people,

you'll probably watch only a small fraction of the channels you get. In our survey, satellite customers watched about 15 channels in a typical week, although they received well over 100. For digital-cable subscribers, the numbers were similar. Analog subscribers got more than 50 channels on average but watched only 11.

Statistics like those have fueled the debate over whether cable consumers should have to pay for large packages of programming they don't want or be allowed to select a smaller, à la carte list. (For more on channel choice and other cable-TV issues, go to *www.HearUsNow.org*, a project of Consumers Union, publisher of CONSUMER REPORTS.)

Consider hardware costs. For basic analog cable, you generally don't need any hardware at all. You can plug the cable directly into a TV and use the TV remote. For analog cable with premium channels and for digital service, you'll usually need a set-top box and a remote, which rent for about $5 to $8 a month. With a digital-cable-ready TV and a CableCard, you won't need a box. A card rents for a few dollars a month.

To get satellite TV, you need a dish antenna and a receiver designed to work with the chosen service. You can buy the hardware from a satellite company, an electronics store, or a satellite-system dealer/installer for about $100 and up. Promotional deals often provide free gear if you commit to programming for one or two years.

You Need to Know

What's on TV: Cable and dish programming compared

These are the principal areas in which the programming lineups of satellite and cable providers differ:

Local channels. In its early years, satellite didn't offer any local channels, but that has changed. Both DirecTV and Dish Network now carry local channels in many markets. But that includes only the local affiliates of the major networks. To get community-access and other local channels, you'll still need to have cable.

Movies. Satellite and digital cable offer more movies than analog cable or off-air reception. They have numerous HBO and Showtime channels (comedy, action, Spanish-language, and more) and pay-per-view movies. Some offer both regular and HD versions of TNT, Cinemax, and Starz.

Sports. In addition to ESPN, Fox Sports, and other specialized sports channels, the two satellite providers and many digital-cable services offer regional sports channels and subscription sports packages

that the analog-cable services don't provide.

High-definition programming. Cable companies typically pass along the major-network broadcasts that originate in HD as part of their digital-cable service. That includes prime-time dramas and sitcoms. Satellite companies have trailed in their HD offerings, especially for the major broadcast networks, but they're working to change that. Both digital-cable and satellite packages generally include extra HD channels, like Discovery HD Theater, ESPN

HD, HBO HD, HDNet, and Showtime HD. Satellite typically offers more pay-per-view movies in HD.

Video on demand. Digital cable has much more extensive offerings than satellite, which has limited you to select content that has been downloaded to your DVR. VOD is more versatile than traditional pay-per-view: You have access to the program for a 24-hour period of your choosing, during which you can replay it, pause, rewind, and fast-forward, as with a DVD recording.

With both cable and satellite there are added costs for an HD setup, digital-video recording, or broadband Internet access.

Weigh the extra costs for HD. To get HD via cable, you must subscribe to digital cable and rent an HD-capable cable box or CableCard for each HDTV. With some providers, you get both standard-definition and HD versions of the channels in your digital-cable package at no extra charge. Other cable companies charge $10 or so a month for HD.

With satellite, you need an HD receiver, and you might need to modify your dish or add a second one to receive HD channels. That setup can run hundreds of dollars unless you get a reduced-cost promotional offer. An HD programming package costs $10 a month from Dish Network, $11 from DirecTV.

Note that both Dish Network and DirecTV are switching to a new signal-compression format, MPEG-4, so they can transmit more high-definition channels. Current HD set-top boxes and dishes might have to be replaced. Non-HD subscribers of either shouldn't be affected immediately, but eventually more channels might use MPEG-4, requiring new equipment. So check with your provider before buying any HD hardware.

Decide whether you want recording capability. Many cable companies now rent cable boxes with integrated digital video recorders (DVRs) that store TV programs on a computer-type hard drive. For satellite, you might have to buy the unit—a costly investment we don't recommend at this time, given that it's a fast-changing technology. Prices start at $300, although you might be able to get a DVR free or at a low cost as part of a promotion. With satellite, there's generally a monthly fee of about $5 for recording capa-

bility; with cable, it's about $10. Some of the DVRs available through cable and satellite can record HD programs.

Decide whether you want Internet access with your TV service. Most cable companies offer high-speed Internet access for $40 to $50 a month. You may be able to trim that by as much as $15 if you also subscribe to the provider's TV service. The other primary broadband service choice is DSL, high-speed access over telephone lines. The satellite services have partnered with phone companies to provide DSL. It usually costs about $30 to $45 a month, but you may be able to save $10 a month by ordering it with satellite TV.

Both cable and DSL Internet services have pluses. Cable broadband scored higher for speed and reliability than DSL in a recent survey of our subscribers. DSL was reasonably fast and reliable, and it costs less.

DirecWay, a company partly owned by DirecTV, offers Internet access via satellite. It costs about $600 for equipment plus $60 a month. This service did relatively poorly for speed and reliability in our Internet provider survey, so we suggest that you consider it only if you can't get cable or DSL.

Consider reliability. In addition to its problem with physical obstructions, satellite service is more subject to weather-related woes. About 31 percent of the satellite-television subscribers in our survey reported a loss of alignment or line of sight with the satellite for one reason or another, and 12 percent cited problems with snow or ice buildup. But more digital-cable than satellite users reported losing service for a day or longer: 17 percent vs. 11 percent. To find out how reliable your local television service is, ask your neighbors about their experiences.

> **High definition** will cost you extra with both cable and satellite. Be sure to factor in these costs when selecting a service.

ConsumerReports.org | Chat with other TV buyers

You can learn more online about selecting and buying a new TV from other CONSUMER REPORTS readers. That's the purpose of the "Choosing a new TV set" forum in the Discussions/Forums area on *www.ConsumerReports.org*. You can access it from the main Electronics & Computers

page by clicking on the TV-shopping link under Discussions/Forums.

TV types—including LCD, HDTV, direct view (CRT), plasma, and rear projection—are covered in separate sections of this Discussions section. This is one of the electronics topics currently open in Discussions, the

place for members to share and exchange ideas on topics related to being a wise consumer.

These kinds of resources are among the reasons to activate the 30-day free subscription to *www.Consumer Reports.org* included with this guide (see inside front cover).

HOW TO SET UP YOUR TV ONCE YOU GET IT HOME

There's more involved than plugging it in and turning it on

Your new large-screen TV or HDTV is a big investment. Hooking it up to your satellite or cable box, your antenna, DVD player, or your audio or home-theater system takes time and effort. Plus, many sets are just plain heavy. For all these reasons you might prefer to leave installation of your new screen to a professional. Our experts explain what you can expect from a professional installation, and how to hook up your new TV yourself, should you choose to. You'll also find out how to fine-tune your HDTV, an adjustment anyone can tackle. (If you will be connecting your new TV to a home-theater system, see "Installing a home-theater system" on page 102.) And don't fall for pitches for expensive cables; for sensible wiring advice go to "Premium cables are not necessary" on page 104.

PRO INSTALLATION

Many stores "bundle," or combine, various installation services, sometimes as limited-time offers. If you're considering buying a new large-screen TV or HDTV, check with each store in your area—by phone, in person, or on the Web. This is the only way to find out precisely which charges will apply.

Here's a checklist of the different services you might require for an installation:
▸ Delivery, unboxing, and installation (if needed) of TV; removal of your old TV
▸ Assembly of mounting stand or wall-mounting
▸ Hookup of TV to electrical and audio components
▸ Set up of video recorder
▸ Installation of satellite dish and service activation, if required
▸ Hook up to existing video source (satellite, cable, or antenna)
▸ Programming remote to operate all devices
▸ Checking that all components are working properly; making picture adjustments as required
▸ Demonstration of the system and all controls.

Many of these services overlap, although the installation price may include limits on hookups. For example, a simple delivery might include hooking up the TV to a single video source and to the audio system. A basic installation might add hookup to multiple components, a system check, programming the remote, and a demonstration.

You can expect to pay the following:
▸ Delivery: less than $50
▸ Assembly of mounting stand (if required): about $75
▸ Basic installation: $100 to $200
▸ Wall-mounting (rather than using a stand): $150 to $200, under 30 inches; $250 to $300, over 30 inches.

For many home-theater enthusiasts, placing an LCD or plasma TV on top of a stereo cabinet doesn't cut it. For them, a wall-mount TV is the only way to go. Circuit City will charge $299 to $399 to wall-mount a TV under 30 inches, or $399 to $499 for a set that's over 30 inches.

Typical installation packages include a 90-day warranty, meaning you can get anything that

Some electronics gear is easy enough to hook up yourself. But when faced with complex wiring, hiring an installer might be a better idea.

wasn't properly installed repaired or done over. This is another advantage of going the professional route, but again, it's important to go over the warranty details before you sign up to ensure there's no misunderstanding.

DO-IT-YOURSELF HOOKUP

New TV sets have different types of inputs that handle varying levels of picture quality. That's because manufacturers have added new connections as higher-quality signals have become available and left the other inputs in place to work with older equipment. Using the appropriate input can improve picture quality.

Highest-quality HD signals can be carried by a component-video, DVI, or HDMI input, or by an RF input on an integrated HDTV (with built-in digital tuner) used with an antenna. From most basic to best, here are the inputs you're apt to see:

Antenna/cable, VHF/UHF, or RF (radio frequency) inputs are the most basic, and they can be used with almost any video source. An RF input may be the only way to connect an antenna and some older cable boxes and VCRs. It's one of the few inputs (along with HDMI) that carries both picture and sound. The others require separate audio inputs for the sound.

Composite-video inputs carry only the video signal, providing better picture quality than RF. They're often used to connect a VCR, cable box, camcorder, or game console.

S-video inputs split the video signal into two parts, color and luminance. This lets you take advantage of the improved picture quality from a satellite system, DVD player, or digital camcorder.

Component-video inputs split the video signal into three parts: two for color and one for lumi-nance. This provides slightly better picture quality than S-video. These inputs are often used with DVD players, high-definition satellite receivers, and cable boxes.

DVI and HDMI inputs provide a high-quality digital connection to DVD players, satellite receivers, and other digital devices. DVI signals carry only video; HDMI signals carry audio and video on one cable. The digital-to-digital connection may ensure optimal picture quality. These digital connections may allow the content providers to control your ability to record certain programming. If you plan to buy a high-def DVD player, make sure the TV you buy has an HDMI input. These players may be able to output HD signals only through HDMI; component-video, normally able to carry HD, may output only enhanced definition if the content was flagged by the producer.

VGA inputs let the TV accept signals from virtually any computer. DVI inputs are compatible with newer midrange computers. USB and/or IEEE 1394/Firewire connections let you hook up digital cameras, camcorders, and other devices. A memory card slot lets you insert a card from a digital camera and view your photos or videos onscreen.

Many sets have more than one of type of input. Having two or three S-video or component-video inputs is a plus. For a camcorder or video game, front-panel A/V inputs are helpful. Audio outputs let you direct a TV's audio signal to a receiver or self-powered speakers. HDTVs usually have a Dolby Digital output for surround sound (available from some broadcasts). An automatic volume leveler compensates for the jarring volume jumps that often accompany commercials or changes in channel. A headphone jack, if available, lets you listen to a TV without disturbing others.

Stick with low-priced cables. You'll need various

Single-plug composite and S-video connections are common in older video gear. Three-plug component video offers better quality and can convey HD signals. All three require separate audio inputs. HDMI, an HD-capable digital connection, carries audio and video.

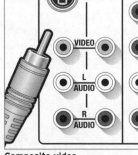

Composite video

S-video

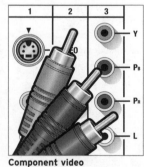

Component video

HDMI

cables to connect your TV to your cable or satellite box, DVD player, VCR, and sound system. If you don't have them already, buy them when you purchase your TV so you can get up and running right away. Prices range from $1 to $35 or more a foot for a 12-inch length. Retailers often tout the advantages of high-priced cables with gold plating or THX certification. Most consumers don't need these features. (See "Premium cables are not necessary" p. 104.) Most mainstream brands sold in electronics stores should fit the bill for typical use.

FINE-TUNE YOUR HDTV

You don't have to be a video expert to finesse the picture settings on your new HDTV. Follow these tips from our expert testers to tune your set for optimal performance.

Picture mode. Most TVs have a menu of picture modes with descriptions like "vivid," "natural," or "cinema." When you select one of these modes, brightness, contrast, and sharpness are automatically adjusted to preset values optimized for different viewing environments. We've found that modes with names like "natural," "cinema," and "pro" generally provide the most-balanced settings. We suggest you stay away from "vivid," "dynamic," and similar modes, which tend to dramatically boost contrast and sharpness and lower brightness to less than optimal levels.

In most cases, you can modify a particular setting within a mode to tweak the picture's appearance. On other sets, if you try to change the settings, your picture mode will automatically change to a "custom" or "preference" mode allowing you to adjust picture settings individually.

To get the best picture quality from your TV, we suggest you adjust the individual picture settings yourself rather than use a preset mode. These picture settings are described below.

Brightness level. This is also called black level, and it's critical to top picture quality. Ideally, a TV should be able to display deep black without losing the detail within the darkest areas. To help you achieve the right balance, freeze-frame a nighttime scene like one from a "Batman" movie. Turn the brightness/black level up until you can see the details in the image's darkest areas. Then turn it down so the black gets as black as possible without obscuring the details in the dark areas. With LCD sets, you won't get as deep a black as with other display technologies.

Contrast. Also called white level, contrast af-

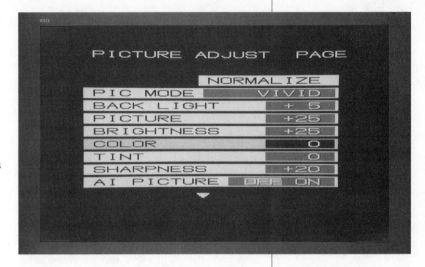

You can adjust your picture quality onscreen.

fects how bright the picture looks. Find an image with lots of white—a wedding gown, a man's dress shirt, or a sky full of puffy white clouds. Lower the contrast until you can see all the detail, such as the shadows in the folds of the gown, the buttons on the shirt, or the subtle gray shadings in the clouds. Then raise it to get the brightest picture possible without washing out the subtle, near-white details described. For the best picture quality, it's generally best to set contrast below the maximum level.

Color and tint. Once the black-and-white quality is optimized, it's time to adjust the color settings. Start with color temperature, sometimes called color tone. We recommend choosing the "warm" or "low" setting, so whites don't appear too blue. Then adjust the tint/hue control so that flesh tones look natural, neither too red nor too greenish-yellow. This generally works best when it's set in the middle of the range. Adjust the color-level control ("saturation") so that colors look vivid and realistic but not excessive (glowing). All these settings may interact with one another, so repeat the process as necessary.

Sharpness and more. Manufacturers often set the sharpness control rather high and turn on noise-reduction and other image-enhancement modes. These are rarely needed when you're watching high-quality HD programming or a DVD movie. In most cases, resist the temptation to crank up sharpness to enhance HD's fine detail. The best HDTVs need little or no help to show all the resolution in HD images.

If you set the sharpness control too high, the background will start to look grainy, and a halo will appear around the edges of objects, making the overall image appear less natural. We suggest you turn the sharpness control down to zero, then add sharpness sparingly only if the image looks soft.

Most TVs out of the box need to be adjusted for the dimmer lighting conditions at home, rather than the bright showrooms for which screens are preset.

Also turn off any noise-reduction and image-enhancement modes that tend to reduce image detail.

But if your TV viewing consists mainly of standard-definition programs with typically noisy picture quality, then you may want to explore the noise-reduction modes to determine if they work for you. These modes are typically found in the menus for picture adjustments, advanced picture settings, or setup.

Consider the source. You may have to tweak picture settings for each video source, depending on the signal and the TV input it comes in on. Each TV input has different circuitry that processes various types of signals, so brightness, color, and other picture attributes may vary. You may find that a DVD player connected to the S-video input yields a different quality picture than the same player connected to the component-video input. When you switch sources, you'll get the best picture quality with settings customized for each input. Some TVs let you store the settings; others, unfortunately, do not.

Do-it-yourselfers who want to calibrate their TV picture in a more precise way can use a calibration DVD such as the AVIA Guide to Home Theater ($50 from Ovation Multimedia, *www.ovationmultimedia.com*), or Digital Video Essentials ($25 from Joe Kane Productions, *www.videoessentials.com*). These will walk you through an easy step-by-step picture alignment process, eliminating guesswork.

For the ultimate fine-tuning, consider a professional calibration—but be prepared to pay hundreds of dollars for the expert touch. In most cases, we don't think it's worth it.

 ConsumerReports.org | **TV Ratings online**

Note to our readers: The latest TV models were introduced too late for us to test in time for the publication of this book. You'll find up-to-date Ratings and recommendations for LCD, plasma, rear-projection, and front-projection TV sets at *www.ConsumerReports.org*. Look on the inside cover of this guide to find out how to get a 30-day free subscription to *www.ConsumerReports.org*, and try out all our features.

VIDEO & AUDIO GEAR

CHAPTER 05

▶▶ **The latest technology is all about choices—more choices in *what* you watch and listen to as well as *where* you enjoy your music and video.**

Ratings: DVD players, p. 158; MP3 players, p. 165.

DVD PLAYERS ARE A HIT; HIGH-DEF IS HERE AT LAST

Conventional players are cheap while two HD formats compete

Great picture and sound quality, plus relatively low prices, have made digital videodisc, or DVD, players, among the most successful consumer-electronics products ever. The vast majority of U.S. households have one or more DVD players. Prices have dropped so low that they're now sold seemingly everywhere—even in supermarkets and drugstores, like everyday commodities.

But conventional DVDs may soon seem quaint as high-definition (HD) content becomes the norm. The first HD players are now on the market, following delays caused by technical issues and competition between the two incompatible formats, HD-DVD and Blu-ray. Toshiba has launched its HD-DVD players, Samsung has introduced a Blu-ray player, and Sony is due to follow with its Blu-ray players. But as with most new technologies, initial prices are high: $500 for Toshiba's low-end model

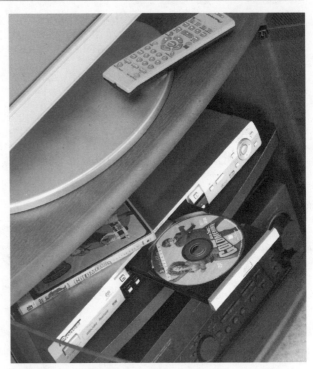

Playing those movies you buy or rent is the main job of DVD players, but they can also play music on CDs.

First Things First

Consider video and audio play functions

Decide whether you just want to play one DVD at a time or multiple CDs as well. Also consider whether you still need videocassette playing capability. To save money and avoid unnecessary features, go with the simplest type of machine that will meet your needs.

1 ### Single-disc DVD player $25 and up

Best for people who simply want an inexpensive machine for watching DVDs.

2 ### DVD changer $100 to $400

Best for people who also want to play multiple CDs. But these units are larger and more expensive.

Expert • Independent • Nonprofit

and an estimated $1,000 for Sony's Blu-ray device. All but the most passionate videophiles might want to wait for prices to drop.

There's another even more compelling reason to wait for the dust to settle: HD-DVD players won't be able to play movies that support the Blu-ray format, and vice versa. One of these formats might not survive, and if you back the losing candidate, you'll have paid a lot of money for obsolete technology.

WHAT'S AVAILABLE

Panasonic, Sony, and Toshiba are among the biggest-selling brands of DVD players. Virtually all new DVD players are progressive-scan models. When used with a conventional TV, these players provide the usual high DVD picture quality. With a TV that can display high-definition or enhanced-definition (ED) images, image quality is slightly better. (That's because HD and ED sets support the player's progressive-scan 480p mode, drawing 480 consecutive lines on the screen. By comparison, with a conventional TV, every other line is drawn and then interlaced or combined, a resolution referred to as 480i.) A player can be connected directly to your TV for viewing movies or routed through your receiver to play movies and audio CDs on your sound system.

Progressive-scan models come in single-disc and multidisc versions. The few nonprogressive-scan players now on the market are mostly single-

disc models; those tend to be the cheapest type.

Single-disc consoles. Even low-end models usually include all the video outputs you might want. Price: about $25 to more than $300.

Multidisc consoles. Like CD changers, these players accommodate more than one disc at a time, typically five. DVD jukeboxes that hold 400 or so discs are also available. Price: $100 to $400.

Portables. These DVD players generally come with a small wide-screen format LCD screen and batteries that claim to provide three hours or more of playback. Some low-priced models don't come with a screen; they're intended for users who plan to connect the device to a television. You pay extra for portability either way. Price: about $100 to $800.

HD players. When used with HDTVs, HD players can potentially convey even better picture quality than you get with regular DVDs. Note that you might need to use an HDMI input on a TV to get HD resolution. High-def players may be able to output HD signals only through an HDMI connection; component-video connections, normally able to carry HD, may output only enhanced definition if the content on a particular disc was encoded that way by the producer. Price: $500 to $1,000.

FEATURES THAT COUNT

DVD-based movies often come in various formats. **Aspect-ratio control** lets you choose between the 4:3 viewing format of conventional TVs (4 inches wide for every 3 inches high) and the 16:9 ratio of newer wide-screen sets.

A DVD player gives you all sorts of control over the picture—control you might never have known you needed. **Picture zoom** lets you zoom in on a specific frame. **Black-level adjustment** brings out the detail in dark parts of the screen image. If you've ever wanted to see certain action scenes from different angles, **multiangle capability** gives you that opportunity. Note that this feature and some others work only with certain discs.

A DVD player enables you to navigate the disc in a number of ways. Unlike a VHS tape, most DVDs are sectioned. **Chapter preview** lets you scan the opening seconds of each section or chapter until you find what you want. A related feature, **chapter gallery**, shows thumbnails of section or chapter opening scenes. **Go-to by time** lets you enter how many hours and minutes into the disc you'd like to skip to. **Marker functions** allow easy indexing of specific sections.

> All but the most passionate videophiles might want to wait to buy a high-definition DVD player.

3 DVD player/VCR
$90 to $140

Best for people who want both machines but have room for only one. But combination models often have fewer functions than separate units.

To get the most from a DVD player, you need to hook it up to the TV with the best available connection. A **composite-video connection** can produce a very good picture, but there will be some loss of detail and some color artifacts such as adjacent colors bleeding into each other. Using the TV's **S-video** input can improve picture quality. It keeps the black-and-white and the color portions of the signal separated, producing more picture detail and fewer color defects.

Component-video, sometimes not provided on the lowest-end models, improves on S-video by splitting the color signal, resulting in a wider range of color. If you connect a DVD player via an S-video or component connection, don't be surprised if you have to adjust the television-picture setup when you switch to a picture coming from an antenna, a VCR, or a cable box that uses a radio-frequency (RF, also called antenna/cable)

connection or a composite connection.

Two newer outputs found on some players, **Digital Video Interface (DVI)** and **High-Definition Multimedia Interface (HDMI),** are intended for use with digital TVs with corresponding inputs. They may be used to pass digital 480p, up-converted higher-resolution video signals, and HD signals. These connections potentially allow content providers to control your ability to record the content.

Another benefit of DVD players is the ability to enjoy movies with multichannel surround sound. To reap the full sound experience of the audio encoded into DVD titles, you'll need a Dolby Digital receiver and six speakers, including a subwoofer. (For 6.1 and 7.1 soundtracks, you'll need seven or eight speakers.) Dolby Digital decoding built-in refers to a DVD player that decodes the multichannel audio before the audio receiver. Without the

DVD portables: Go-anywhere video for less than $150

Portable DVD players give new meaning to the phrase "Taking the show on the road." The ability to play a movie anytime, anywhere can help you survive a long flight or forestall backseat tantrums. Portable DVD players have come down in price considerably, with some selling for less than $150.

Portables resemble small laptop computers minus the keyboard. Everything you need

to watch a movie is housed in a slim, lightweight case.

You can play movies on a fairly new laptop, but portable DVD players are smaller, lighter, and less expensive. Most portables are also competitive in price with dedicated car-video hardware.

If you use a portable DVD player in a car, be sure to buy a mount ($20 to $40) to secure it on the center armrest or suspend it between

the front seats. This will keep it from flying around if you stop short or are involved in even a minor accident.

Weigh screen size against portability and price. Screens on the tested portables measure 7 inches diagonally; that's as small as we'd recommend. You can buy models with 4- to 6-inch screens, but they're a tad too small for comfortable viewing and won't save you much money. Players with 9- or 10-inch displays are a bit heavier and more expensive— $500 or more. They might be worth it, especially if more than one person wants to watch a movie.

Go for good picture quality. The LCD screens on these portable players couldn't display the kind of excellent picture quality that DVD technology produces. None of the portables we

tested had a picture that was as sharp as that of a very good LCD TV set. The better ones should be fine for playing DVDs in the car or on a plane. All the pictures washed out in bright light. All the screens tilt to help you find the best viewing angle.

Try before you buy. Listen to the player in the store through the built-in speakers and with your headphones (bring your own) to check the audio. These portables can produce very good sound through headphones, but sound from the built-in speakers is merely OK.

Insist on long battery life. Because most movies run at least two hours, be sure your player won't run out of juice too soon. Most claim a three-hour battery life from their built-in rechargeables.

Consider construction and warranty. Warranties are usually 12 months on parts and 3 months on labor. We'd avoid those with only three months on parts.

You can take it with you: A light, portable DVD player lets you bring a mini-movie theater on the road or on vacation.

You can transfer camcorder recordings or your old home videos to a DVD player and archive them onto a DVD.

built-in circuitry, you'd need to have the decoder built into the receiver or, in rare instances, use a separate decoder box to take advantage of the audio. (A Dolby Digital receiver will decode an older format, Dolby Pro Logic, as well.) Most players also support Digital Theater System (DTS) decoding for titles using 5.1-, 6.1- or 7.1-channel encoding format. When you're watching DVD-based movies, dynamic audio-range control helps keep explosions and other noisy sound effects from seeming too loud.

In addition to commercial DVD titles, DVD players often support playback or display of many other formats. They include CD-R/RW recordings of standard audio CDs; the recordable DVD formats DVD+R/RW, DVD-R/RW, and DVD-RAM; Video CD (VCD); and DVD-Audio and Super Audio CD (SACD). They can also play CD-R/RW discs containing MP3 and Windows Media Audio (WMA) files and JPEG picture files. Make sure the one you're considering plays the discs and formats you use now or might want to use in the future.

DVD players also provide features such as multilingual support, which lets you choose dialog or subtitles in different languages for a movie. Parental control lets parents "lock out" films by rating code.

HOW TO CHOOSE

Hold off on a high-def player. Given the current high prices of the first models and the incompatibility between the two rival formats, we strongly recommend that you wait awhile for things to shake out.

Buy a progressive-scan model unless the lowest price is your highest priority. Although you won't see progressive-scan picture quality on a conventional analog TV, it's worth spending a little extra for a progressive-scan player if you might get a digital (probably HD) TV at some point. You'll have a wider choice of products as well, since al-most all new players are progressive-scan. It's definitely worth getting a progressive-scan player for use with a digital TV, which is capable of displaying the smoother picture these players can deliver.

Choose a multidisc model if you want continuous music. A single-disc player is fine for movies and CDs one at a time. But if you want this to be your main music player, consider a multidisc player. Note, though, that multidisc models are typically about 1 to 2 inches taller and 6 to 7 inches deeper than single-disc players.

Make sure there are enough types of the connections you want. Virtually all DVD players now have outputs for optimal connection to most TV sets. A few players have DVI or HDMI connectors that are compatible with some new TVs, though these don't necessarily offer improved picture quality. If you want to use digital-audio connections from the DVD player to a receiver, make sure the DVD player's digital-audio outputs match the receiver's inputs. Some receivers use a coaxial input; others, an optical input. If you have an older receiver that lacks 5.1 surround-sound decoding, look for a player with a decoder for Dolby Digital.

Consider which, if any, special playback formats matter. All DVD players can play pre-recorded DVDs and CDs. Most models also play several types of discs you record yourself, such as DVD-R, DVD+R, and CD-R/-RW. Most can read DVD+RW, but the ability to read DVD-RW discs depends on how they were recorded. Some can also play DVD-RAM discs. Most models play CD-audio and MP3 music recorded on discs you burn yourself. You'll need to shop around more if you want to play Windows Media Audio (WMA) files, video CD, and high-resolution SACD and DVD-Audio discs in their original format.

Do you want to present slide shows on your TV? Then choose a model that can read JPEG image files that you've captured with a digital camera and burned onto a disc. Some models have built-in card readers that accept various memory cards.

FORMATS ARE EVOLVING FOR DVD RECORDERS

Prices for machines and media will probably continue to drop

While DVD players are playback-only devices, DVD recorders record onto removable discs as well as playing them. Prices have dropped considerably in the past few years, with entry-level models now selling for less than $150. At the highest-quality setting, the quality of most DVD video recordings is better than that of a VCR and comparable to what you can get with a hard-drive-based digital video recorder. DVD recorders also offer more ways to navigate recordings than a VCR, with no need to rewind or fast-forward. With certain disc types, some DVD recorders can perform functions that no VCR can match, such as letting you start watching a program from the beginning while you're still recording the end. They also offer a way to convert

A visual index of scenes lets you quickly access the content you've burned onto a disc with your DVD recorder.

First Things First

Decide which recording technology you need

1 DVD recorder

Best for those satisfied with VCR-like capability on a digital platform.
Pros The least-expensive way to record on DVDs. Doubles as a DVD player. No extra monthly fees.
Cons Requires the purchase and labeling of blank discs (25 cents and up per disc). No models for recording HD content.
Expect to pay $130 to $300 for most.

2 DVD recorder with built-in VCR

Best for for people who own a lot of home videos on VHS that they want to transfer to DVD.
Pros Versatile. Handy for transferring content from VHS tape to DVD and vice versa.
Cons Relatively expensive. Loss of picture quality if you copy a DVD to tape. You can't transfer most prerecorded tapes and DVDs.
Expect to pay $270 to $400 for most.

Expert • Independent • Nonprofit

camcorder tapes or homemade VCR recordings to a digital format.

DVD recorders are still relatively new, so there will probably be more changes involving disc types, and prices for machines and for blank storage media may drop further. At press time, there were no DVD recorders capable of recording high-definition (HD) content. High-def recorders are in development and could be on the market late in 2006 or in 2007. There are some digital-video recorders capable of recording HDTV programs, available mainly from satellite and cable companies. They use hard discs, not removable DVDs.

WHAT'S AVAILABLE

DVD recorders are available from many of the same manufacturers that make DVD players. Cyberhome, Panasonic, Philips, Sony, and Toshiba are among the biggest brands. Some DVD recorders store content only on DVDs. Others can also use VHS tapes, hard drives, or both. Price: DVD-only recording, about $130 and up.

FEATURES THAT COUNT

A recorder's **storage capacity** varies in actual usage. DVD recorders store content at different compression settings and thus at different quality levels. For the best image quality, you have to record programming at the device's lowest compression, yielding as little as one hour of recording. To get the maximum capacity advertised—typically six or eight hours—you have to use the highest level of compression, which gives the lowest quality.

All rewriteable DVD formats let you edit, to varying extents, what you've recorded. DVD-RW in VR mode and DVD-RAM recorders let you edit more extensively than DVD+RW or DVD-RW in video mode. Besides letting you watch one program while recording another, recorders with DVD-RAM capability and some with DVD-RW in VR mode let you watch an earlier section of a program while you're still recording it.

As with VCRs, DVD recorders might use **VCR Plus** to ease the setup of time-shift recordings. Some also come with **TV Guide On-Screen**, a free interactive program guide that gets several days of listings at a time from your broadcast TV signal and many cable services. It offers point-and-click setup of recording events.

In addition to commercial DVD titles, DVD recorders often support playback or display of many other disc formats. They include CD-R/RW discs containing standard CD-audio information;

3 Digital-video recorder (hard-drive based)

Best for those who are interested only in TV recording and those who record often.
Pros Easiest TV-recording option. No need to buy blank discs. Some models can record HD broadcasts.
Cons For archiving, you need a VCR or DVD recorder. Most models require a monthly rental or programming fee and a phone connection to update the program guide. You can't edit recordings.
Expect to pay Up to $200 plus programming fees for a TiVo box, $800 and up for HD models. About $5 to $10 a month to rent cable-box versions.

4 DVD/hard-drive recorder

Best for people who often want to archive TV recordings to DVD.
Pros Can hold many hours of video. Combines ease of recording to hard drive with ability to archive to DVD.
Cons Expensive. Better, less-expensive models will probably be available soon.
Expect to pay $300 to $800 for most.

DVDs are sectioned so you can move quickly to a particular place.

the recordable DVD formats DVD+R/RW, DVD-R/RW, and DVD-RAM; Video CD (VCD); and DVD-Audio and Super Audio CD (SACD). They can also play CD-R/RW discs containing MP3 and Windows Media Audio (WMA) files and JPEG picture files. Make sure a model you're considering plays the discs and formats you use now or might want to use in the future.

DVD-based movies often come in various formats. **Aspect-ratio control** lets you choose between the 4:3 viewing format of conventional TVs (4 inches wide for every 3 inches high) and the 16:9 ratio of newer, wide-screen sets.

A DVD recorder gives you all sorts of control over the picture—control you may never have known you needed. **Picture zoom** lets you zoom in on a specific frame. **Black-level adjustment** brings out the detail in dark parts of the screen image. If you've ever wanted to see

certain action scenes from different angles, multiangle capability gives you that opportunity. Note that this feature and some others work only with certain discs.

A DVD recorder, like a DVD player, enables you to navigate the disc in a number of ways. Unlike a VHS tape, most DVDs are sectioned. **Chapter preview** lets you scan the opening seconds of each section or chapter until you find what you want. A related feature, **chapter gallery**, shows thumbnails of section or chapter opening scenes. **Go-to by time** lets you enter how many hours and minutes into the disc you'd like to skip to. Marker functions allow easy indexing of specific sections.

HOW TO CHOOSE

Decide whether you want to record on removable media. DVD recording is the best option for those who want to share video recordings with other users or those who want unlimited storage, allowing recordings to be saved indefinitely. They're also space efficient, since they can replace a separate DVD player. But if none of these attributes is important to you, consider a hard-drive-based DVR instead. If you've decided on DVD recording, here's what you should consider in selecting a unit:

Choose between a DVD-only recorder or a combo unit. DVD-only models can cost about half the price of units with a second recording platform such as a hard drive or VCR. The combos

Deciphering all those DVD formats

DVDs come in five varieties: DVD-R, DVD-RW, DVD+R, DVD+RW, and DVD-RAM. If you want to record on discs that are compatible with the most DVD players, only two matter: DVD-R and DVD+R. Their main limitation is that you can record on them only once.

The multirecordable formats, DVD-RW and DVD+RW, are more expensive and may not be compatible with older

players. But they can save money if you reuse them as you would a tape. DVD-RAM discs, which are also rerecordable, are the least compatible.

However, they do play on Panasonic models, a growing number of players from JVC, Toshiba, and others, and on some computer drives.

Forget about high-definition DVD recording—for now. Today's discs and recorders lack the

capacity to provide adequate playing time at HD resolution. You may start seeing HD-DVD formats, such as Blu-ray and HD-DVD. When they do arrive, expect high prices and renewed format wars.

HD-ready recorders that record on a hard drive are already available, either for purchase or by monthly rental from some satellite providers or local cable companies.

are pricier and bulkier but more versatile.

Look for "time slip" capability. It allows you to pause your viewing of a TV program you're recording while the unit continues to record. You can resume viewing where you left off. Time-slip models also let you view a previously recorded program while recording another. A feature of all hard-drive-equipped recorders, time slip is also available on most stand-alone DVD recorders that record to DVD-RAM discs, one of five disc types recorders use. (All models use at least one write-once and one rewriteable disc type; DVD-RAM discs are rewriteable.) However, DVD-RAM discs can be played on fewer recorders or players than discs using formats that are more widely compatible. Some models that record to DVD-RW discs in VR mode also have time-slip capability.

Decide what kind of TV-programming capabilities you want. When it comes to programmed recording, a typical DVD recorder can do everything a VCR can. And as with VCRs, some DVD recorders can control a cable or satellite box, allowing you to program the unit to record from various channels without setting the box to the correct channel before each recording. DVD/hard-drive recorders designed to work with TiVo, the subscription programming service, also offer automatic recording of your favorite shows (or performers) whenever or wherever they're on. But that added functionality has a cost: a monthly fee of about $13 (longer terms may be available). TV Guide On-Screen is a free interactive program guide available on some models that works with broadcast TV and many cable services. While not as versatile as the TiVo programming guide, it does offer point-and-click recording ability.

Weigh the importance of video editing. A DVD-only model that records to DVD-RAM discs or to DVD-RW discs in VR mode allows scenes to be subdivided and rearranged onscreen. But the discs aren't compatible with all players, and even if they do play, edits you make on those discs might not show up. DVD/hard-drive models, except for tested models allied with the TiVo service, give you the ability to edit video on the hard drive. You can then burn images to a range of disc types for maximum compatibility with other players.

If you want to burn DVDs on your computer and play them on your living-room DVD player or recorder, make sure the two devices can read the same DVD-recordable format.

DVD recorders give new life to old videos

Making the transition from an obsolete format to a new one is never completely painless. The emergence of the CD, for instance, forced many of us to go out to buy digital versions of the music we had already purchased as LPs. The switch from VHS tape to DVD is no different. But while you can always find a DVD boxed set to replace those episodes of "Seinfeld" you've taped, what can be done to preserve your one-of-a-kind wedding day video and other home movies?

For most consumers, the simplest solution would be to buy a DVD recorder. Prices have dropped considerably over the past few years, with entry-level models now selling for less than $150. Your choice essentially comes down to a basic single-drive DVD recorder or a combo unit, which adds a second recording platform, either a VCR or an internal hard drive. If your VCR still works well, you might want to opt for a basic DVD recorder. Such units are about half the cost of combo decks, which are bulkier but more versatile with convenient dubbing and editing features.

If your PC is equipped with a DVD burner, you can make digital copies of your home movies on your computer, but it is more complicated than using a DVD recorder. But if you want to edit your tapes extensively or add sophisticated effects and transitions, it may be worth considering.

Capturing and editing video on a PC requires considerable processing power.

To keep old home videos playable, a DVD burner offers the easiest way to transfer VHS recordings to discs.

For the best results, your computer should have a fast CPU (2.8 GHz or faster is recommended), at least 512 MB of RAM, and plenty of available hard-drive space (at least 26 GB per hour of edited video). You'll also need a video-capture card or an external capture device, many of which sell for about $100, to handle all the necessary connections from your VCR or camcorder to your PC. Video-editing software is also needed to control the video capture, edit your videos, and burn them to the disc. These software packages vary in complexity and can be purchased for as little as $30 or as much as $1,500. Again, this approach is clearly not for everyone, and is best undertaken by more technically savvy users.

Whether you use a DVD recorder or PC to transfer your tapes, be sure to use the highest quality setting your equipment allows. While it may be tempting to squeeze eight hours of video onto a single disc, the added compression will result in degraded video and sound performance, which is not recommended for archival purposes.

DVRs USE A HARD DRIVE TO LET YOU SCHEDULE TV

Love TV? Hate commercials? Digital-video recorders are for you.

Digital-video recorders don't have a slot for removable discs or tapes; they record only on a hard drive, much like the one in a computer, and can't play prerecorded media. Some combination units pair a DVR with a DVD player/recorder so you can play (and copy to) removable media. Many models have space for 100 hours or more of programming at high quality, and more than 300 hours at a low-quality setting.

You can get a stand-alone DVR or one that's integrated into a digital-cable box, satellite-TV receiver, or DVD player/recorder. Depending on which type you choose, you might pay for the service as well as the equipment—either a one-time charge or a monthly fee on top of your current cable or satellite-TV bill.

Because they can record and play at the same time, DVRs allow you to pause (and rewind or fast-forward) the current show you're watching, picking up where you left off. If you pause a one-hour show for 10 or 15 minutes at the beginning, you can resume watching it, skip past all the commercials, and catch up to the actual "live" broadcast by the end of the show. Dual-tuner models can record two programs at once, even as you're watching a third recorded program.

Many digital video recorders offer recording capability with the convenience of a TV program guide. Onscreen TV program guides are customized according to which broadcast channels are available in your area and which cable or satellite service you have. A DVR does not replace your usual programming source. You must still get broadcasts via cable, satellite service, or antenna.

Zapping has never been easier with DVR technology.

WHAT'S AVAILABLE

If you get your DVR functionality in a digital-cable box leased from your cable company, you're typically limited to the cable operator's choice of hardware. For hard-drive recording in a satellite receiver, you might be able to buy or lease the hardware directly from the Dish Network or DirecTV, or buy it from a retailer, depending on the model you choose.

For stand-alone DVRs, TiVo is the main service provider. Hardware prices depend mostly on how many hours of programming you can store; service charges vary. You can buy TiVo equipment directly from TiVo or a number of electronics retailers. TiVo functionality is incorporated into DVRs from Sony, Toshiba, Pioneer, and Humax. Basic TiVo service is included with some of those products at no additional charge, but TiVo's regular

This Pioneer combines a DVR with a built-in DVD recorder, best for recording and archiving to a DVD.

subscription rates apply for full functionality. Price: about $50 to more than $500 for a player that also incorporates a DVD player and VCR. Some TiVo units are free when you sign up for service at $13 per month; longer terms may be available.

Most combination DVD recorder/DVR models lack an onscreen program guide. But a few manufacturers, such as Panasonic, Pioneer, and Toshiba, offer some combination DVD recorder/DVR models that use a free program guide service, such as TV Guide On-Screen, that works with broadcast TV and many cable services.

FEATURES THAT COUNT

Stand-alone DVRs resemble VCRs in size and shape but don't have a slot for a tape or disc. (The internal hard drive is not removable.) Combination units that add a DVD player or recorder will have the requisite media slots. Depending on the model, it can be connected to your television using HDMI, composite, S-video, component, or possibly RF antenna outputs to match the input of your set.

A recorder's **hard-drive capacity** varies in actual usage. Like digital cameras, many DVRs record at different compression settings and thus at different quality levels. For the best image quality, you have to record programming at the DVR's lowest level of compression. To get the maximum capacity advertised, you have to use the highest level of compression, which gives the lowest quality. For example, a model that advertises a 30-hour maximum capacity will fit only about nine hours at its best-quality setting.

The program guide is an interactive list of TV programs that can be recorded by the DVR for the next three to 14 days, depending on the program guide type. You can use it to select a show currently being broadcast to watch or record, or you can to search it by title, artist, or show type for programs you want to record automatically in the future.

Custom channels, available with some models, are individualized groupings of programs that interest you. The feature allows you to set up your own "channel" of favorites, such as crime dramas or appearances by David Caruso, whether on "NYPD Blue" reruns or on "CSI: Miami." A DVR can also record a specific show every time it runs.

A **remote control** is standard. Common features include instant replay, fast-forward, rewind, and pause for either recorded or live programs.

HOW TO CHOOSE

Ultimately, a DVR's picture quality, like a VCR's, depends on the quality of the signal coming in, whether that's via your cable or satellite provider, or antenna.

Do you want the most programming features? The services from TiVo may have more features and functionality than some of the offerings of cable and satellite companies. But you will have to buy another box, deal with another remote, and possibly pay another monthly fee.

Would you prefer to have fewer boxes and service providers to contend with? Inquire whether a cable box equipped with DVR functionality is available. If satellite service is an option, consider getting a receiver that includes a DVR. Keep in mind that you may have to pay a separate fee for the DVR service. And some satellite and cable DVRs work only with the service provider's programming and won't record from other sources, such as an antenna.

Do you want to edit recordings or store camcorder video? Then you need a DVD recorder or DVD recorder/hard-drive combo. Both capabilities are available in some boxes that come with TiVo or some cable companies.

Do you want to record HD content? Your best option right now is a DVR that's incorporated into your cable box or satellite receiver. Stand-alone DVRs that can handle HD are few and far between and are still quite expensive.

Systems like TiVo can quickly show you what programs it recorded.

HOME THEATER IN A BOX STREAMLINES SHOPPING

Get an all-in-one system to add to your TV with few setup hassles

Even the priciest digital TV can't convey the rich multichannel sound you'll find on most DVD movies and high-definition television programs. To remedy that, you have two basic choices: You can buy components and assemble your own system, or opt for a home-theater-in-a-box system.

Good speakers and the components for a home-theater system cost less than ever, so assembling your own system can be a good idea, especially if you already own some of the pieces. But selecting separate components can be time-consuming, and connecting them can be a challenge. You can avoid some of the hassle by buying a prepackaged system that combines a receiver with a set of matched speakers, wiring, and often a DVD player. The package will be cheaper than building your own system from scratch. Unless you're a serious music listener, you'll probably find the sound quality to be just fine.

WHAT'S AVAILABLE

Home-theater packages include a receiver that can decode digital-audio soundtracks and six to eight compact speakers—two front, one center, two to four surround speakers for the rear, and a subwoofer—that have been matched for sound. Some systems have wireless surround speakers or speakers with flat styling to complement a flat-panel TV. You get all the cables and wiring you need, usually color-coded or labeled for easy setup.

Most systems include a progressive-scan DVD player, either built into the receiver or as a

Unless you're very demanding, you won't compromise much on quality by getting a home-theater package.

separate component, and a powered subwoofer. Some bundle in a VCR as well. Price: $50 to $1,500 for typical systems, and $2,000 or more for systems aimed at audiophiles. Panasonic and Sony are among the best-selling brands in the market.

FEATURES THAT COUNT

The receivers in home-theater-in-a-box systems tend to be on the simple side. They usually include both **Dolby Digital** and **DTS decoders** for handling the surround-sound track when playing a DVD. **Controls** should be easy to use. Look for a **front panel** with displays and controls grouped by function and labeled clearly. An **onscreen display** lets you control the receiver by the television screen.

Switched AC outlets let you plug in other components and turn on the whole system with one button. The receivers have about 20 or more presets you can use for AM and FM stations. Most receivers also offer a sleep timer, which turns them on or off at a preset time. **Remote controls** are most useful when they have clear labels and different-shaped, color-coded buttons grouped by function. A universal remote can control a number of devices.

An HDMI or **component-video output** on the receiver that can connect to the TV allows for the best picture quality if you choose to switch video signals through your receiver. You can also use an **S-video output**, which is a tad below a component connection but better than a composite-video or RF (antenna) connection.

Both let you pipe signals from an external DVD player, digital camcorder, or certain cable or satellite boxes through the system. Any player that you might want to connect will need the same digital-audio connections, either optical or coaxial, as those of the included receiver. And if you want to make occasional connections—perhaps for a camcorder or an MP3 player—you'll find front-panel inputs handy.

DSP (for digital-signal processor) modes use digital circuitry to duplicate the sound quality of, say, a concert hall. Each mode represents a different listening environment. A bass-boost switch amplifies the deepest sounds.

A **subwoofer** may be powered or unpowered. Either type will do the job, but a powered subwoofer often provides more control over bass.

An **integrated DVD player**, available with some models, typically has fewer features than does a stand-alone DVD player. Features to expect are **track programmability** (more useful for playing CDs than DVDs), **track repeat,** and **disc repeat.** If you want more features, a stand-alone DVD player might be the wiser choice.

HOW TO CHOOSE

Decide whether you want a DVD player. If not, you could save money by buying a system without one. If you want a DVD in the bundle, consider whether you need a multidisc model that will provide uninterrupted CDs and DVD movies, or if a single-disc player will do. All the DVD-equipped systems we tested have a progressive-scan player. These offer regular DVD picture quality when used with a conventional TV but can deliver a smoother image when paired with a TV capable of displaying high-definition (HD) or enhanced-definition (ED) signals. Some bundled DVD players can play multichannel DVD-Audio and SACD music discs, some even in their original, high-resolution format.

Do you want a separate DVD player or one integrated with a receiver? Systems that integrate the DVD player and the receiver in one box tend to offer a bit less functionality and fewer connections than those that have two separate components. Integrated units are somewhat simpler to set up, but they may not allow you to connect video devices other than a TV to the receiver. Other devices, such as a digital-video recorder, would have to be hooked up directly to the TV.

Make sure there are enough inputs. You might want to route video as well as audio signals through your home-theater receiver so you can easily switch among sources such as a VCR, cable or satellite box, and digital-video recorder. Before buying, consider which devices you'll want to channel through the home-theater unit and which ones you can hook up directly to the TV, and make sure you have enough of the appropriate inputs and outputs.

Each type of connection is capable of conveying

Speakers, receiver, and DVD player: Plug in your TV and all you need is popcorn to complement your home-theater system.

a different level of video quality. If you'll be connecting a DVD player to your TV through the receiver, look for a model with S-video, component-video, or HDMI connections, which should give you better picture quality than a composite-video hookup.

With audio inputs, you'll need a digital-audio input for relaying undecoded digital audio from your DVD player, digital-cable box, or satellite receiver. Make sure the input on the home-theater system matches the output on the other device. Some of these units have an optical digital-audio output, while others have a coaxial digital-audio output. (An HDMI connection carries the audio along with video in one cable).

If you want to connect a turntable, see if the one you have requires a special phono input, which is hard to come by. Look for a front-video input on the receiver if you want to make occasional connections—perhaps for a camcorder or a game system—and your TV doesn't have accessible front-panel inputs.

Get features that suit your needs. With any system, you can be assured of such basics as AM/FM tuners, Dolby Digital and DTS surround-sound support, and enough speakers for at least a 5.1 surround setup. Some systems now include an integrated XM satellite-radio tuner or a USB port for connecting an iPod or other portable music player so you can listen to your music through the sound system.

Extras such as switched AC outlets are less

Installing a home-theater system

Setting up a home-theater system is only as complicated as your own audio/video needs.

Does a home-theater-in-a-box merit professional installation? Not really. You could probably get the retailer to sell you a basic installation package, but unless you are very uncomfortable with technology, chances are you won't need it. Setup is a matter of plugging in the speakers and the power cord. Many systems use color-coding and clear labeling to simplify the process. On the other hand, a high-end system consisting of many separate components usually demands professional help.

SHOP FOR SERVICE
Most retailers sell home-theater installation and setup services. Given the range of options, it's no surprise that several offer various levels of service to cover their customers' needs. Best Buy, Circuit City, and CompUSA, for example, have variations on Basic, Deluxe, and Premium packages. The packages are similar in scope, although Best Buy and CompUSA list each service as a flat rate, while Circuit City provides a price range for most of its services.

With Best Buy's $399 Deluxe Home Theater installation package, for instance, the installer hooks up everything, mounts and conceals wires for up to three speakers, and explains how the system works. Circuit City's Deluxe Home Theater

package, which ranges from $299 to $399, includes installation, demonstration, programming the remote, and wall-mounting with wire concealment for up to two speakers.

The Circuit City package also gives you a minimum-maximum installation time. When considering such a package, make sure you ask what happens if the installation runs longer than expected. Do you then pay more? The same question should be asked for flat-rate packages. The key issues are: who pays if the project takes longer than estimated, and what kind of fees apply if the installer comes out and cannot complete the installation—for whatever reason. Wherever possible, check the fine print on your purchase agreement for details like these. At the very least, asking some basic worst-case-scenario questions before you leave the store can help avoid any major surprises later on.

Once the installers begin their work, unanticipated issues may come up, and it's best to understand your options ahead of time. For example, an installer might say: "This speaker can't be hidden because of the brick wall. I'll either have to mount it on the brick surface or place it a couple of feet over, where the drywall and studs permit me to hide it." If you want to say no to those options, you need to understand that the installers might

refuse to do the job your way and bill you for the visit anyway, or that it might cost more to do it your way.

CompUSA's home-theater installation prices range from $99.97 for a Basic Video Component Installation to

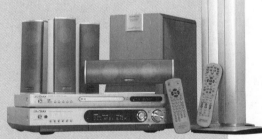

You're not being lazy if you get a professional to install one of today's multicomponent home-theater systems.

$539.97 for the Premium +7 Home Theater Package with in-wall mounting of up to seven speakers and the subwoofer, plus complete installation, demonstration, and remote programming. CompUSA promises a flat rate for its installation service no matter how long the job takes, which eliminates some uncertainty. But the details on home-theater installation are hard to find on CompUSA's Web site. The best bet is to get an in-store or online sales rep to help you find them.

common than on component receivers, so make sure a system has what you want. An onscreen display is handy for setting up and adjusting various functions using the TV screen rather than a small display on the console. Among our tested systems, only those with a DVD player integrated with the receiver had an onscreen display.

A few models offer newer Dolby and DTS surround formats that process 6.1 or 7.1 channels, which support an additional one or two rear-surround speakers, respectively. Those formats still aren't widely used in movies but could become more common in the future.

Also consider the warranty. Manufacturers provide 24 months of coverage, rather than 12 months, on some models.

RECEIVERS ARE THE HUB OF HOME MEDIA SYSTEMS

In addition to accommodating new audio sources, today's receivers connect to your television and DVD player/recorder

The receiver is the heart of a contemporary home-entertainment system. It connects video sources such as a TV, DVD player, VCR, and cable and satellite boxes, as well as audio components such as speakers, a CD player, cassette deck, and turntable.

Receivers started out as audio equipment, providing AM and FM radio tuners, stereo and surround sound, and switching capabilities. But as they have taken on a pivotal role in home entertainment, they've lost some audio-related features that were common in the past, such as tape monitors and phono inputs. Manufacturers say they must eliminate those less-used features to make room for others. Even so, a stand-alone receiver generally provides more functionality than one bundled with speakers as a home-theater-in-a-box system.

The receiver plays a pivotal role in any home-theater system.

WHAT'S AVAILABLE

Sony is by far the biggest-selling brand of receivers. Other top-selling brands include Denon, JVC, Onkyo, Panasonic, Pioneer, RCA, and Yamaha.

Most receivers sold today are capable of handling the multichannel audio in DVDs and some TV programming, but stereo receivers are still available. Here are the different types you'll find:

Stereo. Basic receivers accept analog-stereo signals and provide two channels of amplification for a pair of speakers. For a simple music setup, you can add a DVD or CD player to play CDs. A basic home-theater setup consists of a TV and DVD player, a receiver, and a pair of speakers. This simple, inexpensive setup gives you the most noticeable improvement in TV audio. Stereo receivers typically output 50 to 100 watts per channel. Price: $125 to $250.

Multichannel. Most of the action today is in the multichannel category. This is the type of receiver you'd want for a full-featured home-entertainment system. Most new receivers have 6.1 or 7.1 channels; some have 5.1. Here's what that means: Dolby Digital 5.1, the longtime standard for multichannel audio, has five full channels—front left and right, front center, and two rear—plus a .1 channel for low-frequency bass effects from a separate powered subwoofer.

Dolby Digital is used on DVDs and digital TV programming. A rival format, DTS, also offers 5.1 channels. It's used on some DVD movies. Dolby Digital EX and DTS-EX are newer formats that add one or two rear channels to the 5.1 setup, for a total of 6.1 or 7.1 channels.

Any receiver with 6.1 or 7.1 channels can also support 5.1 as well as audio formats with fewer channels, including the Dolby Pro Logic family of analog-multichannel decoders. This enables them to take a two-channel stereo source from your TV and transform it into a soundtrack with 4 to 7.1 channels.

Of course, all this requires that you have the necessary speakers. To take advantage of true surround-sound capability, you need the appropriate number of speakers in a setup capable of reproducing full-spectrum sound. Some new receivers support Dolby Headphone decoding, which provides a surround-sound experience with standard headphones.

Power output for multichannel receivers is typically 75 to 150 watts per channel. Price: $200 to $500 or more.

THX-certified. Some high-priced multichannel receivers have been certified to meet THX standards. This indicates that they can replicate theater-like sound in a home environment. The higher cost of these receivers generally isn't worth it unless you have a very elaborate home theater. Power for THX models is typically 100 to 170 watts per channel. Price: $500 to $2,500 and up.

FEATURES THAT COUNT

Some models have expanded their repertoire to accommodate newer technologies, such as satellite radio. Others include a tuner for the XM Radio

Premium cables are not necessary

Cables are an essential part of any audio/video system. They're needed to connect the components in your stereo system, and your TV to your cable or satellite box, DVD player, and other A/V gear.

Audio and video cables are made differently, with video being more particular. However, both have the required electrical shielding inside their jacket.

The audio/video cable marketplace is populated with manufacturers that try to capitalize on the mystique of cables. For example, they may use silver or exotic materials for an infinitesimal reduction in signal degradation. Retailers mark up accessory prices substantially, and sales reps often steer customers to purchase these premium-priced, high-end cables, which can cost $100 or more. But are they really worth the money?

In most cases, they're not. While you should avoid flimsy, thin cables with cheap construction and low-quality connectors, most name-brand cables sold in electronics stores should be fine for short runs of up to 10 feet—and they'll save you a bundle.

Choose cables with connectors that have a large enough grip to allow you to hold it comfortably as you plug or unplug it from your device. The connectors should fit snugly when inserted into the mating connector. Always disconnect a cable from your TV or stereo device by holding the connector, never by pulling on the wire.

But there are situations where high-end cables may make sense. Consider a premium brand if:
▶ you have a long cable run (over 100 feet);
▶ you are picking up interfer-ence and need cables with better shielding;
▶ you'll be repeatedly disconnecting/reconnecting and need more-rugged connectors.

Gold plating might also be a good choice in urban environments with polluted air or oceanfront homes with salty air.

For digital signals, the decision is very simple. Use the cheapest video cable of reasonable construction you can get. For DVI or HDMI, any cable that's designed to handle those signals should work fine. One caution: The signal may degrade too much when these cables are extended with adapters to long lengths (greater than 35 feet).

For the best performance, go with a shielded cable to protect against electrical interference, and consider a coaxial-type video cable for long cable runs.

satellite-radio service; fewer support competitor Sirius. (To receive satellite radio, you need to purchase an external antenna and pay an ongoing service fee to XM or Sirius.)

On higher-priced new models, you may also find support for HD Radio, a free digital form of AM/FM. We expect to see this feature in more models, at lower prices, in the future.

A growing number of models also permit **Apple iPod docking**. The receiver will charge the iPod, play its audio and video (using the receiver's remote or console controls), and perhaps show track selections on the console display.

Some receivers have a **USB port**, allowing you to playback music stored on your computer. A few models can route video and still images stored on a computer or on a memory card inserted into a slot on the receiver to a TV.

Another example of versatility is the ability to play music in more than one room. Many receivers have a **B-speaker connection** that lets you power a remote pair of stereo speakers so you can listen to the same source in a few locations.

A step up from that is **multizone capability**. This enables you to listen to different input sources in different rooms—say, play the radio in the bedroom (Zone 2), while another family member watches a DVD movie in the living room, where the receiver is located (the main zone). A few high-priced models have three-zone capability. A remote control for the additional zones is sometimes available. Some receivers provide power for the additional speakers; with others, you might need a separate power amplifier.

Connections matter more on a receiver than on any other component of your home theater. A stereo receiver will give you **analog-audio inputs** and **outputs**; many will have **analog-video inputs** and **outputs** as well. Multichannel receivers will typically have several types of analog-video connections, including **composite-video** and **S-video**, and **component-video**. Newer models might have HDMI inputs and outputs, important if you are planning to get an HD-DVD or Blu-ray HD player. All these video jacks let you route video signals through the receiver to the TV. Some multichannel receivers convert composite-video or S-video input to component-video or HDMI output.

Multichannel receivers may also have **analog 5.1** or **7.1 audio inputs**. These accept input from a DVD player with its own built-in digital-audio decoder, an outboard decoder, or other components

To ensure that your receiver has enough oomph to provide adequate volume, plan on at least 50 watts per channel in a typical 12x20-foot living room.

with multichannel analog signals, such as a DVD-Audio or SACD player. USB inputs, as mentioned earlier, allow connections to a computer.

Controls are another important consideration. **Tone controls** adjust bass and treble, letting you satisfy your personal preferences; you can adjust these using the remote as well as the console. A graphic equalizer breaks the sound spectrum into three or more sections, giving you more control over the audio spectrum. Instead of tone controls, some receivers come with tone presets such as Jazz, Classical, or Rock, each accentuating a different frequency pattern. Often you can also craft your own styles.

DSP (digital-signal processor) modes use a computer chip to duplicate the sound characteristics of a concert hall and other listening environments. A **bass-boost switch** amplifies the deepest sounds, and midnight mode reduces loud sounds and amplifies quiet ones in Dolby Digital encoded music or soundtracks.

Sometimes called "one touch," a **settings memory** lets you store settings for each source to minimize differences in volume, tone, and other settings when switching between sources. A similar feature, loudness memory, is limited to volume settings alone.

Onscreen display lets you view the receiver's menus on a TV screen, a squint-free alternative to using the receiver's LED or LCD display. **Switched AC outlets** (expect one or two) let you plug in other components and turn the whole system on and off with one button.

Automatic setup and speaker balancing features are improving, appearing even on low-priced models. More models also have onscreen setup to simplify the process.

A **tape monitor** lets you listen to the recording as it's being made if your recorder has that capability, or patch in signal-processing equipment such as an outboard graphic equalizer. **Automatic** or **seek-radio tuning** searches for the next in-range

Most receivers are designed for six-channel surround-sound formats that are encoded in most DVDs and some TV programs.

Receivers often have front-panel inputs for headphones and other devices you may want to connect temporarily.

station at the touch of a button. Most models have a **station-preset feature** that lets you store 20 to 40 of your favorite stations for easy recall.

To catch stations too weak for the seek mode, receivers also have a **manual mode**. Direct tuning of frequencies lets you tune a radio station by entering its frequency on a keypad.

HOW TO CHOOSE

First, don't assume that pricey brands outperform less costly ones. We've found fine performers at all prices. Points to consider:

How many channels do you want? A receiver with 5.1 channels is suitable for most of the entertainment available today. Down the road, content with 6.1 or 7.1 channels will be more common. A receiver that can support the additional channels will give you some future-proofing but will probably cost a bit more than a 5.1 model. Remember that you need the appropriate speaker setup to get the full effect of 6.1 or 7.1 channels.

How many devices do you want to connect? Even low-end multichannel receivers generally have enough video and audio inputs for a CD or DVD player, a VCR, and a cable box or satellite receiver. Mid- and high-priced models usually have more inputs, so you can connect additional devices, such as a camcorder, a digital-video recorder such as TiVo, or a game system.

The number of connections isn't the only issue; the type also matters. Composite-video inputs, the most basic type, can be used with everything from an older VCR to a new DVD player. S-video and component-video inputs are used mostly by devices that provide better picture quality such as DVD players, digital-cable boxes, and satellite receivers. To get high-definition TV programming or enhanced-definition output from a progressive-scan DVD player, you must use a component-video input or an HDMI input. If you have or plan to buy an HDTV and an HD-DVD or Blu-ray Disc player (once they're available), look for an HDMI input.

A receiver should have the same impedance rating as the speakers it will power. Mismatched equipment could cause overheating, and protection circuitry will shut down the receiver.

All video inputs require or can use a companion audio input. The basic left/right audio inputs can be used with almost any device to provide stereo sound. To directly connect a turntable without the need for a separate phono amplifier, you need a phono input.

To get multichannel sound from DVD players, digital-cable boxes, and satellite receivers, you generally use a digital-audio input. With this input, digitally encoded multichannel sound is relayed on one cable to the receiver, which decodes it into separate channels. The input on the receiver must be the same type—either optical, the more common type, or coaxial—as the output on the other device, or you will need a converter. You usually have to buy cables, about $10 and up, for digital-audio, S-video, and component-video connections. You often have to buy speaker cables as well.

What kind of music do you like? Any receiver can reproduce stereo sound. Most multichannel models have digital-signal processing (DSP) modes that process two channels to simulate a sound environment such as a concert hall. For multichannel music from SACD or DVD-Audio discs and players, get a receiver with 5.1 analog inputs.

How big is your room? Make sure a receiver has the oomph to provide adequate volume: at least 50 watts per channel in a typical 12x20-foot living room, or 85 watts for a 15x25-foot space. A huge room, plush furnishings, inefficient loudspeakers, or high volume levels all call for more power.

Is the receiver compatible with your speakers? If you like to blast music for hours on end, get a receiver rated to handle your speakers' impedance. Most receivers are rated for 6-ohm and 8-ohm speakers. If used with 4-ohm speakers, such a receiver could overheat and its protection circuitry would shut it down.

Is it easy to use? Most receivers have legible displays and well-labeled function buttons. Some add an onscreen menu, which displays settings on your TV screen. An auto-calibration feature adjusts speaker sound levels and balance to improve the surround effect. Models with a test-tone function for setting speaker levels help you balance the sound yourself.

Two tips: When deciding where to place your receiver, allow 4 inches or so of space behind it for cables and at least 2 inches on top for venting to prevent overheating. And if setting up a home theater is more than you want to tackle, consider calling in a professional installer. Retailers often offer an installation service or can refer you to one.

BE SURE TO BUDGET FOR GOOD SPEAKERS

Select quality brands to get the most out of your system

The best array of audio or video components will let you down if matched with poor-quality speakers. Good speakers don't have to cost a bundle, though it is easy to spend a lot. For a home-theater system, you can start with two or three speakers and add others as need dictates and budget allows. Size is no indication of quality.

WHAT'S AVAILABLE

Among the hundreds of speaker brands available, the major names include Advent, Bose, Infinity, JBL, KLH, Pioneer, Polk Audio, and Sony. Speakers are sold through mass merchandisers, audio/video stores, and "boutique" retailers. You can also buy speakers online, but be prepared for shipping charges of up to $100 because they can be fairly heavy.

Speakers are sold as pairs for traditional stereo setups, and singly or in sets of three to six for equipping a home theater. To keep a balanced system, buy left and right speakers in pairs rather than individually. The center-channel speaker should be matched to the front (or main) speakers. For the best effect, the rear speakers should also have a sound similar to the front speakers.

Each type of speaker serves a different purpose. The front speakers are used for stereo music playback; in a home-theater setup, they provide front left and right sounds. The center (or center-channel) speaker chiefly delivers movie dialog and is usually placed on top of or beneath the TV in a home theater. Rear speakers, sometimes called surround or satellite speakers, deliver rear ambient effects such as crowd noise. A subwoofer carries the lowest tones, such as explosions in an action movie.

Bookshelf speakers. These are among the smallest speakers, but at 12 to 18 inches tall, many are still too large to fit on a shelf, despite their name. A pair of bookshelf speakers can serve as the sole speakers in a stereo system or as the front or rear duo in a home theater. One can serve as the center-channel unit provided it's

Decide just how "surrounded" you want to be when selecting the number of speakers.

magnetically shielded so it won't interfere with the TV. Small speakers like these have made strides in their ability to handle deep bass without buzzing or distortion. Any bass-handling limitations would be less of a concern in a multispeaker system that uses a subwoofer to reproduce deep bass. Price: $50 to more than $800.

Floor-standing speakers. Typically about 3 to 4 feet tall, these large speakers can also serve as the sole speakers in a stereo system or as the front pair in a home-theater system. Their big cabinets have the potential to do more justice to deep bass than smaller speakers, but we think many listeners would be satisfied with smaller speakers that scored well for bass handling. Even if floor-standing models do a bit better, their size and cost may steer buyers toward smaller, cheaper bookshelf models. Price: $200 to more than $1,000.

Center-channel speaker. In a multichannel setup, the center-channel speaker sits on or below the TV. Because it primarily handles dialog, its frequency range doesn't have to be as full as that of the front pair, but its sound should be similar so all three blend well. Dedicated center-channel speakers are short and wide (6 inches high by 20 inches wide, for example) so they perch neatly atop a TV. Price: $100 to more than $500.

Rear-surround speakers. Rear speakers in a multichannel setup carry mostly background sound such as crowd noise. Multichannel formats such as Dolby Digital, DTS, DVD-Audio, and SACD make fuller use of these speakers than earlier formats. You'll get the best blend if the rear pair sounds similar to the front pair. Rear speakers tend to be small and light (often 5 to 10 inches high and 3 to 6 pounds) so they can be wall-mounted or placed on a shelf. Price: $50 to more than $500.

Three-piece sets. Designed to be used as a stand-alone system or integrated with other speakers, these sets combine two bookshelf or satellite speakers for midrange and higher tones with either a center-channel speaker or a subwoofer for bass. Price: $100 to $800.

Six-piece sets. These systems have four satellites (used for both front and rear pairs), one center-channel speaker, and a subwoofer. Six-piece sets save you the trouble of matching the distinctive sounds of six speakers. That's a daunting task at home, and harder in a store without a listening room. Price: $400 to more than $1,000.

Other shapes and sizes. A "power tower" is a tower speaker, usually priced above $1,000, with a side-firing, powered subwoofer in its base.

Speakers come in different sizes for different spaces, so think about where they will sit in your room.

HOW TO CHOOSE

Lovers of loud sound should pay attention to a speaker's measured impedance. It should be matched with the receiver; check your receiver manual. Power range refers to the power-handling capability of the speaker, usually expressed in RMS (average power) and peak power (maximum surge power). Speakers placed near a TV set should have magnetic shielding so they won't distort the picture.

Consider size. Speakers come in all shapes and sizes, so see how they'll fit in your room. Floor-standing speakers might overwhelm smaller spaces. Bookshelf speakers are often a better fit, but some are quite large, so make sure the model you choose will fit the shelf or niche you've earmarked for it. And don't fear that you're giving up quality for compactness. Many small speakers do a fine job. Style may factor into your decision as well. Some speakers are sleekly shaped, with silver finishes. Others are more conventional black boxes.

Focus on accuracy, not advertising. The most critical attribute of any speaker is accuracy—the ability to reproduce sound frequencies without over- or underemphasizing any part of the audio range. As our tests have shown time and again, some of the lowest-priced speakers can be among the most accurate. Ads often tout two-way or three-way drivers and the size of the cone inside a speaker, but you can't judge sound quality by these attributes.

Listen for the differences. Even speakers with comparable accuracy scores can sound quite different. One model may overemphasize treble, while another underemphasizes it. There's no substitute for hearing speakers, so bring a CD with a familiar piece of music to the store. Pay special attention to the front pair because those speakers do the most work.

Speakers will sound different at home because of your room size, shape, and furnishings, so see if the retailer will allow a home trial or ask about the return policy. If you're torn between two choices, buy the cheaper. Stores may be more open to a return if you want to trade up to a pricier set.

Check impedance. If you like to play music loudly, make sure your receiver is rated to handle the impedance (generally from 4 to 8 ohms) of the front speaker pair.

Headphones prevent a war of decibels

With audio and video gear taking center stage in many households, it's bound to happen: You're relaxing to a classical CD when your kids start blasting hip-hop music or an action-packed DVD movie. Rather than resorting to a duel of decibels, you can keep the peace by doling out headphones.

Most home/studio headphones look like earmuffs, with earpieces on a headband. They can be corded or wireless. Corded sets, which account for 9 out of 10 sales, have a wire about 8 feet long that connects to your receiver, DVD player, or TV. Wireless sets have a battery-powered headset and an AC-powered transmitter that connects to your audio or video gear.

Prices for home/studio headphones range from $20 for basic models to more than $1,000. We've tested a range of models in recent years, and our general findings still apply:

▶ Most of the corded sets had good sound quality, and a few were very good.

▶ Among the wireless sets, only a few had good sound quality. All were prone to interference from devices such as cordless phones, resulting in static, hissing, or clicking.

▶ Price isn't always the best gauge of sound quality. Some low-priced corded headphones performed as well as sets costing far more.

WHAT'S AVAILABLE

There are a few hundred different headphone models on the market. Sony is the market leader; other leading brands include Koss, Panasonic, JVC, and Philips.

Home/studio headphones come in a few basic designs and range in price from $20 to $1,000:

Closed over-the-ear sets cup your ears, and creating a seal that reduces the amount of sound that escapes. They also muffle ambient sound. But you may miss some things that you want to hear, like a doorbell.

Open over-the-ear models don't press as firmly on the sides of your head and are usually lighter. They let more sound in and out, so late-night listening could keep your spouse awake.

On-ear headphones have earpieces designed to lay flat on your ears, with no gaps. Models can be open or closed. They let more sound in and out than closed over-the-ear headphones.

Comfort is subjective, depending on such things as the shape of your head and ears. Weight can affect comfort as well. Prolonged listening with any headphones can make your ears warm; closed models might be more likely to do so.

On some wireless sets, including all those we tested, the transmitter uses radio frequency (RF) to communicate with the headphones. Other sets use infrared, much like a TV remote, which requires a line of sight between the headphones and the base. RF can pass

Try on headphones before buying to judge comfort and sound quality.

through walls and floors, allowing you to use the headphones in other rooms or outside. Although the range can exceed 150 feet, the farther you go from the base, the more the sound degrades. The downside to RF is interference between devices on the same frequency. A cordless phone could cause static and clicking on your headphones and vice versa. Because you wouldn't know this until you tried the headphones at home, we recommend that you buy wireless sets only if they can be returned for a refund.

Portable headphones for use with portable audio devices such as CD and MP3 players vary mostly by whether the earpieces sit on or go into your ears. Because many sacrifice

sound quality for size, serious listeners might prefer a home/studio model even with a portable player. They range from about $10 to $300.

Noise-canceling headphones are designed to block out ambient noise. They come with all types of ear covers (closed, open, in-ear, and buds). Price: $50 to $350.

HOW TO CHOOSE

Headphones should feed you clear, accurate sound with sufficient volume. Sound quality on the models we tested ranged from very good to fair. Critical users might want to stick with the best-sounding corded models. Most of the corded models and a few wireless sets are fine for watching TV or, if you're not too fussy, for music. Like speakers, headphones may emphasize various parts of the audio spectrum.

Among the wireless models, all but the best had some background hissing and/or dynamic range compression that flattened sound to some extent. The best differed from the other wireless models we tested in two ways: digital rather than analog, and operating at 2.4 GHz rather than at 900 MHz.

But devices such as 2.4-GHz cordless phones, microwave ovens, and wireless computer networks operating in the vicinity caused a jarring crackle. Other wireless sets also suffered from interference, notably from 900-MHz DSS phones.

Headphones should produce adequate volume with any home-audio device, but those with lower sensitivity might not do so with all portable players.

Headphones don't have many features, but among those that are useful are volume and mute controls. On wireless models, multiple channels are also a plus; you can switch channels to minimize interference.

We recommend trying headphones before buying them to judge the comfort as well as the sound quality. Online shoppers should be sure to check out return policies. Sites such as *headroom.headphone.com* and *www.crutchfield.com* have a wide selection and offer refunds within 30 days.

MP3 PLAYERS DO MORE THAN JUST PLAY MUSIC

Newer models with color displays can show photos and videos

The MP3 player continues its evolution from simple audio player to complex multimedia device. More and more players come with color displays and the ability to show digital photos transferred from your computer, sometimes while the music is playing. Such models usually also play music videos, TV shows, and short films.

As digital players morph, one thing remains constant: The brand name that's on most of them. Apple's iPod players still account for more than three out of four MP3 players sold. Hardware alone doesn't explain Apple's dominance. While iPods score well in our tests, so do players from other manufacturers, some of which offer capabilities and features that iPods lack.

Apple's success rests in part on its creation of a self-contained digital-entertainment system. iTunes, its content-management software, works seamlessly—only with iPods—a fact that's prompted the French government to sue Apple for monopolistic practices. Its online iTunes store offers by far the largest library of online video content, supplementing its dominance over online music sales. Its content includes many exclusives and also offers comprehensive one-stop access to podcasts, the booming (and mostly free) online downloads that offer everything from National Public Radio broadcasts to music-preview shows to weekly self-help recordings. And while you can play content obtained from the store (and use iTunes software) on virtually any computer, including Windows PCs and Macs, you need an iPod to enjoy it portably.

Not that all innovative content comes from Apple. Other legal online content sources include BuyMusic (WMA), MusicMatch (WMA), Napster (WMA), and Yahoo (WMA), and retailers like Wal-Mart (WMA), as well as electronics giant Sony (ATRAC). Unlike iTunes, some of these sites also offer subscription-based services, typically for less than $10 per month, that let you listen to music on your computer in real time (streaming). Napster, a pioneer of free peer-to-peer music-sharing, now allows you to stream music free from its (now legal) site, for up to five listens per song. With the subscription and Napster services, downloading music that you transfer to an MP3 player or CD costs extra, but those fees are generally lower than the ones for nonsubscribers.

We've found that MP3 players perform very well at their key task: producing near-audio-CD quality from a headphone jack. Many models also have small screens to display photo and video files.

Free online music-sharing, still the most popular way for acquiring MP3 music, has been driven underground by a flurry of record-industry lawsuits and a 2005 U.S. Supreme Court ruling. (The justices unanimously ruled that the popular music-sharing site Grokster, as well as similar operations, could be held liable if their networks were used to illegally distribute copyrighted music.)

Before you buy any digital player, be sure your computer can handle it. New computers shouldn't be a problem, but make sure any player you're considering is compatible with your older Windows or Macintosh computer (including its operating system). Keep in mind that some operating-system upgrades can exceed the price of a player. Your computer must have a USB port. Consider high-speed Internet access if you plan to download much of your music. Also keep in mind that getting started can be tricky with some players. Even if compatible with the player, an older computer may not recognize it easily, so you might have to seek help from the manufacturer.

WHAT'S AVAILABLE

Major brands of MP3 players include Apple, Archos, Cowon, Creative Labs, iRiver, Philips, RCA, Samsung, SanDisk, Sony, and Toshiba. Brands from smaller companies are on the market as well. And MP3 playback has been incorporated into other handheld portable products, including CD players, cell phones, and personal digital assistants (PDAs).

Flash-memory players. These are the smallest and lightest players, often no bigger than a pack of gum, and they weigh no more than 2 or 3 ounces. They're solid-state, meaning they have no moving parts and tend to have longer audio playback time than players that use hard-disk storage. Storage capacities range from 128 megabytes to 6 gigabytes (or about 30 to 1,500 songs). Some flash-memory players also have expansion slots to add more memory via card slots on the player. Common expansion-memory formats include Compact Flash, MultiMedia, Secure Digital, and SmartMedia. Sony players may use a MagicGate MemoryStick, a copyright-protected version of Sony's existing MemoryStick media. Memory-card capacities range from about 32 MB to 2 GB. Memory costs have gradually dropped. Price: $40 to $280 for the player; $45 to $50 for a 1-GB memory card.

Hard-disk players. There are two types: microdrive and standard hard-disk. The palm-sized microdrive players have a tiny hard drive with a storage capacity of 3 to 8 GB (about 750 to 2,000 songs). They weigh about a quarter-pound. Standard hard-disk players are about the size of a deck of cards, and they have a storage capacity of 10 to 60 GB (about 2,500 to 15,000 songs). They typically weigh less than half a pound. Some hard-disk players with video capability have relatively larger displays, and as a result tend to be the bulkiest models. Price: $140 and up.

Creative Zen Vision M outdoes the same-priced iPod Video with a built-in FM radio and microphone for recording memos.

Professional MP3-file installation can save hours of ripping

The MP3 player has given rise to a new type of custom-installation service: one that converts, or rips, the audio tracks on your CDs to MP3 or other digital-music file formats that can be read by your player. The service, offered primarily by online firms like MusicRip (www.musicrip.com), RipDigital (www.ripdigital.com), RipIt Digital (www.ripitdigital .com), and Riptopia (www .riptopia.com), might seem extravagant at first, given the relative ease of creating files for a music player. But when faced with the prospect of ripping a CD collection of several hundred discs, it might sound like a great idea.

Most of these services work the same way: for about $1 per disc, they will mail you empty spindles and postage-paid packaging to hold all your CDs. Once you've removed the discs from their jewel cases, loaded them onto the spindles, and packed them up, you mail them to the ripping service. The default format conversion for CDs is MP3, although most services will rip to a different format if requested. The entire process typically takes between two and seven days after your package is received.

Along with your CDs, the services will mail back to you a DVD data disc containing your freshly ripped MP3 files, which makes it easy to transfer them first to your PC and then onto your MP3 player. (Many services will also load the files onto the player itself or a portable hard drive for an additional cost.)

If you're thinking about using a CD-ripping service, be sure to ask what sampling rate is used. An MP3 ripped at high rate like 256Kbps provides better musical reproduction, but a higher bit rate also requires more storage space on your hard drive. Consider a sampling rate of 128Kbps to offer the best balance between quality and storage.

The Apple iPod has become synonymous with MP3 music players. Nearly four out of five digital music players sold are iPods.

CD players with "MP3" compatibility. Flash-memory and hard-disk portable players aren't the only way to enjoy digital music. Many of today's portable CD players can play digital music saved on discs and may support the copyright-protected formats from online music stores. Controls and displays are comparable to portable MP3 players, and you can group songs on each disc according to artist, genre, and other categories. A CD, with its 650- to 800-MB storage capacity, can hold more than 10 hours of MP3-formatted music at the standard CD-quality setting. You can create MP3 CDs using the proper software and your PC's CD burner. Price: $25 and up for the players; 15 cents to 75 cents or so for blank CDs.

Cell phones. An increasing number of phones have built-in MP3 players, some with controls and features that rival stand-alone players. Sprint, Verizon, and other cell-phone providers let subscribers download music over their networks. But music phones are pricey, and most can't store more than 150 songs. Price: 99cents to $2.50 per song; $150 and up for a phone with a two-year contract, or $500 without one.

Satellite radio. Some pocket-sized XM and Sirius receivers have built-in memory for recording up to 50 hours of satellite programming, and might also let you add your own MP3 songs to the mix. Not all models let you listen to live programming on the go; some must be docked at home. Price: $200 to $400 for the receiver; about $13 a month for satellite service.

FEATURES THAT COUNT

Software and hardware. Most MP3 players come with software to convert your CDs into the audio playback format the player can handle. You can also organize your music collection according to artist, album, genre, and a variety of other categories, as well as create playlists to suit any mood or occasion. All come with software to help

you shuttle content between your PC and the player via a Universal Serial Bus (USB) connection. All players work with a Windows PC, and some support the Macintosh platform.

Player upgradability. On most models, the firmware—the built-in operating instructions—can be upgraded so the player does not become obsolete. Upgrades can add or enhance features, fix bugs, and add support for other audio and video formats and operating systems. This is particularly important for models with video playback because of the evolving nature of video formats.

Display. Most MP3 players have a display screen that allows you to view the song title, track number,

Checklist

MP3 players

iPod or not iPod?_____
Onboard memory (MB/GB)_____
or
Audio playback time (hr.)_____
Width (in.) _____
Height (in.) _____
Depth (in.) _____
Weight (oz.) _____
Plays online music? _____
Mac compatible? _____
Color display? _____
Video playback? _____
Plays online video? _____
Slideshow capability? _____
FM radio? _____
Built-in microphone? _____

This list can help you choose features for an MP3 player that best meets your needs. You'll find an interactive version of this checklist, including prices and brands, at *www.ConsumerReports.org*. This MP3 product selector produces a list of models that fit the criteria you have entered. This resource is available by going to ConsumerReports.org's index page for MP3 players and clicking on the link for Product Selector. It's one of many buying-decision aids available to members only, and you can access it by activating the 30-day free trial subscription offered on the inside cover of this guide.

amount of memory remaining, battery-life indicator, and other functions. Models with color displays also let you store and view pictures taken with your digital camera, and in some cases, video clips.

Some displays present a list of tracks from which you can easily make a selection, while others show only one track at a time, requiring you to advance through individual tracks to find the desired one. On some of the models you can access the player's function controls by a wired or infrared remote control. Most players have built-in management of songs that can be accessed via album, artist, or genre. Individual playlists of songs are usually created on a computer and transferred to the player, though many let you manage the music on the player, allowing you to edit playlists and delete files.

Photo playback. Virtually all players with color screens can play JPEGs, the default photo format of most digital cameras. Some can handle TIFFs, BMPs, and lesser-known formats as well. Many let

you view your photos in slideshow fashion, complete with fade-outs, scrolls, and other transitions, as well as with music.

Video playback. A growing number of hard-drive players with color displays can also store and play back video. The video is in a format that compresses about three hours of video into 1 GB of hard-disk space. Popular content sources include CinemaNow and iTunes, which let you download music videos, TV shows, and short films for $2 apiece. But iTunes only works with iPods, and CinemaNow only supports players that can handle copy-protected Windows formats. Virtually all video players come with software that converts nonprotected movies into a format the player can handle.

As for the viewing experience itself, MP3-player screens are relatively tiny—even when compared with portable DVD players—and are hard to see in outdoor light. Players with the largest screens, up to 3 inches wide, are easier to watch for longer periods and some come with built-in speakers. But they

Safetywise

Music players at high volume can cause hearing loss

Portable music players can damage your hearing, recent research suggests. Many players can reach potentially damaging volumes, and many users might be cranking the sound up that high regularly.

In a study published in December 2004, Brian J. Fligor, Sc.D., and L. Clarke Cox, Ph.D., of Boston University measured the volume levels of six portable CD players through both the original headsets, if any, and five others purchased separately. At their highest settings, most of the 35 possible player-headset combinations were loud enough to cause irreversible noise-induced hearing loss if used regularly for as little as a few minutes per day.

The measurements were taken shortly before iPods became popular. Fligor, now director of diagnostic audiology at Children's Hospital Boston, said preliminary results indicated that the volumes produced by iPods and other MP3 players are "in the same ballpark" as that of the CD players.

In a separate study published in April 2005, Warwick Williams of Australia's

Keep music low to preserve your hearing. These headphones block outside ambient noise.

National Acoustic Laboratories measured the noise coming from the personal music players of 55 randomly chosen passers-by at two busy city intersections. The volume

averaged about 86 decibels—a bit too high, say CONSUMER REPORTS' noise experts, for extended daily listening. Some players were turned up much higher than that.

To avoid hearing loss, our experts say you should never set your music player's volume higher than the same level as a vacuum cleaner or a noisy restaurant—about 85 decibels. Be sure to judge the volume conservatively: Music you like tends to sound softer than an annoying sound with the same decibel level.

Our experts also say that people whose living and working environments are otherwise quiet can safely listen to 85-decibel music for several hours a day. But if you're regularly exposed to other loud sounds—whether from machinery, transportation, or live music—you should wear hearing protection at those times if you want to enjoy music from your portable player at other times. That's because damage from noise exposure is cumulative. If you have any concerns about hearing loss, see an audiologist soon.

can weigh as much a pound and are often too bulky to stuff into a shirt pocket.

Sound enhancement. Expect some type of equalizer, which allows you to adjust the tone in various ways. A custom setting through separate bass and treble controls or adjustable equalizers gives you the most control over the tone. Some players have presets, such as "rock" or "jazz," as well as channel balance control.

> **Downloaded songs** typically cost less than $1 each, or $10 for an album.

Playback controls. Volume, track play/pause, and forward/reverse controls are standard. Most portable MP3 players let you set a play mode so you can repeat one or all music tracks, or play tracks in a random order, also referred to as "shuffle" mode. An A-B repeat feature allows you to set bookmarks and repeat a section of the music track.

Useful extras. In addition to playing music, most MP3 players can function as external hard drives, allowing you to shuttle files from one PC to another. Some players can act as a USB host, which lets you transfer images, data, or music directly from a memory-card reader, digital camera, or another MP3 player without using a computer. A few of these, however, won't let you play or view the files you transfer. Some allow you to view text files, photos, and videos on their display screens. Other convenient features include an FM radio tuner, a built-in microphone or line input for recording, and adapters or a line output for patching the player into your car's audio system.

HOW TO CHOOSE

Decide whether to get an iPod. With Apple's family of players so ubiquitous, and so similar in many ways, it's worth considering the advantages and shortcomings of iPods before going further with your buying decision. iPods are easy to use, thanks to superb integration of the players and the company's iTunes software. The iTunes Store offers the largest selection of legal digital content on the Web, including virtually all the available downloads of major TV

iPod accessories: from sublime to ridiculous

Few electronic products have dominated their category the way the iPod models have. Almost five years after its introduction, Apple's compact digital music system still accounts for more than three out of four MP3 players sold.

As a de facto standard, the iPod has spawned a cottage industry for accessory makers. From boom box-like docking stations to FM transmitters, and

A docking station with speakers lets you recharge the player's battery and listen to your music files without headphones.

more frivolous gadgets, here's a sampling of what's available:

To outfit an iPod with room-filling sound, CONSUMER REPORTS recommends the Bose SoundDock ($300) and Altec Lansing inMotion iM7 ($250). Weighing in at 5.6 pounds and 10.7 pounds, respectively, these two portable remote-controlled systems produce loud, clean sound with decent bass handling. Both accommodate all dockable iPod versions and recharge players as they play.

Hate waking up to your least-favorite song? The iHome iH5 ($100) is a stereo AM/FM clock radio that lets you use your iPod as a morning alarm. It also has built-in charging circuitry. (This and models that follow have not been tested by CONSUMER REPORTS.)

Want to listen to your tunes while behind the wheel? There are plenty of products that let iPods play wirelessly over the FM

band of your car radio. Maxell's 191205 ($40), for instance, works with all docking iPods and connects to your car's cigarette adapter to charge the unit while it plays. Belkin's TuneDok ($30) and Macally's FMCup ($45) transmitters are both designed to mount inside most car cup holders; the FMCup additionally provides a back-lighted LCD display and charges units via car cigarette-lighter adapters.

And then there are the less essential iPod add-ons, such as Tavo Products' iPod gloves ($35), lightweight fleece liners with conductive thumb and index fingertips that let you control your iPod's Click Wheel in cold weather.

Among the silliest accessories is Speck Products' iGuy ($25), a rubberized protective case with bendable arms and legs that turns any iPod nano into a Gumby-like ipal.

shows. And with the use of iTunes software so widespread, it's very likely that a friend or family member from whom you might want to borrow content already uses it—meaning you'll need an iPod to enjoy their songs or videos.

iPods also have a plethora of accessories to extend their use, from boomboxes and clock radios with iPod slots to iPod cases that come in every color and fabric imaginable. Few other brands of players have custom aftermarket equipment (al-

though generic gear will, for example, allow you to pipe any player into a component sound system or a car stereo).

As for drawbacks, iPods typically cost a little more than non-Apple players with comparable capacity. They lack bells and whistles; no iPod has a radio, for example, or a built-in voice recorder (you need to buy a $70 accessory). And iTunes has some special limitations, such as the inability to easily transfer music from your iPod to any other device. And

New players expand your video options

Many of the latest color-display MP3 players can now show downloaded music videos, movies, and TV programs. If you like the idea of totally portable entertainment and don't mind a little squinting at a smallish screen, you might want to check out one of the following models.

Three players in our current roundup offered good to very good video performance, intuitive controls, and other conveniences. They are the Apple iPod (30 GB) and Archos Gmini 402 Pocket Multimedia Center (20 GB), both $300, and the Creative Zen Vision (30 GB), $400.

Some details to bear in mind before you buy a player:

You'll need a fast Internet connection. Video downloads take much longer than music, so you'll need a broadband connection that can deliver download speeds of 1 megabit per second or faster. Even then, a one-hour show can take up to an hour to download.

You'll need to recharge frequently. Watching videos can slash playback time dramatically. On the 30-GB iPod we tested, for example, video playback time was only three hours–about what it takes to charge the unit. When playing music, that iPod ran for 15 hours before needing a recharge.

Not all content works on every player. Major content sources for video players currently include CinemaNow.com, MSN Video Downloads, and iTunes.com. Prices range from nothing to $15 per download, depending on the site, the content, and whether you rent or buy. While their offerings are growing, iTunes content works only with iPods (for portable applications), and CinemaNow and MSN Video support only players that can handle copy-protected Windows formats.

The tiny screen takes some getting used to. Screens are typically between 1 and 3 inches–relatively microscopic compared with other video-ready devices such as portable DVD players

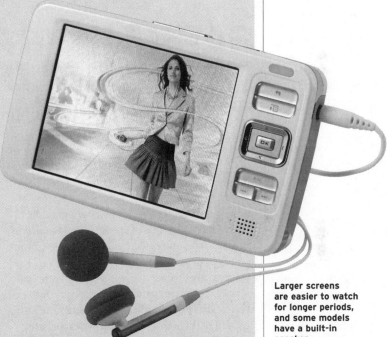

Larger screens are easier to watch for longer periods, and some models have a built-in speaker.

and laptop computers. Watching videos at off-angles or under direct sunlight could also be challenging. And you might be disappointed with the sharpness and resolution.

You'll need a bigger pocket. Small as their screens may be, most video MP3 players are bulkier and heavier than current nonvideo models. Some can weigh about a half pound. The exception is the latest iPod, which is smaller and lighter than previous models.

Finally, whichever player you choose, look for one with firmware that can be upgraded for adding or enhancing player features, as well as accommodating newer encoding schemes or variations of compression. This is particularly important for models with video playback because of the evolving nature of video formats.

The Cowon iAudio U3 is a compact rival to Apple's iPod Nano, with an FM radio and recording capability to boot.

some non-iPod players allow you to drag and drop music files into the player without opening music-management software.

Weigh capacity vs. size. Consider a flash-memory model (holding up to 1,500 songs) if a lower price, smaller size, lighter weight, and long playback time are more important to you than a vast selection of tunes. Look for flash models that can accept external memory cards if you want expanded song capacity. If you have a large music collection that you want to keep with you, a hard-disk player might make

more sense. Those players can hold up to 15,000 songs and could serenade you for weeks without repeating a tune. However, a hard-disk player can be more complicated to manage than a flash-memory player. For some, navigating through the menus or directories (folders) of songs might also take longer.

Hard-disk players vary in size, generally in step with capacity. Microdrive players are about the size of a credit card, and a 4-GB model can hold about 1,000 songs, whereas models with 20-GB hard disks are about the size of a deck of cards and can hold about 5,000 songs.

SATELLITE RADIO OPENS NEW WORLD OF MUSIC

Subscribers say extra programming is worth the monthly fees

The signals have never been stronger for satellite radio, the subscription service that beams hundreds of "stations" to your car or home. Is it time to consider satellite radio? To help you answer the question, we surveyed a nationally representative sample of several hundred current satellite-radio subscribers who listen in their cars, where most satellite radio is heard. Overall, 71 percent said they were highly satisfied with their service. That's comparable to the satisfaction levels satellite-TV subscribers recently reported to us, and ranks high among all services we have rated. They also gave satellite radio high marks for ease of setup and use.

But paying for radio rankles even satellite devotees. The cost of the service—$12.95 per month or $142 a year from the two providers, Sirius and XM—topped the list of their com-

Forty-two percent of satellite radio subscribers in our survey listened to it at home, through satellite receivers, plug-and-play models that you can shuttle between car and home, and handheld portables.

plaints. More than a third considered satellite radio to be only fair or poor for cost. Still, a whopping majority plans to continue getting satellite anyway; 89 percent said they would definitely or probably renew their subscriptions. Other points to weigh if you're considering satellite radio:

Expect to discover new content. Half of the survey respondents said that satellite had made them more likely to listen to types of music they had not listened to before, especially country, rock, and jazz. Satellite's hundreds of channels are remarkably diverse, exploring not only genres but multiple subgenres; for example, XM's flavors of country music include traditional, bluegrass, and progressive. With that many choices, it's hard not to stumble on unfamiliar ones as you surf, and it's easy to find a few that stick with you.

You'll hear fewer commercials. While all music channels are commercial-free, most other satellite-radio channels, such as sports, news, and talk, aren't.

Sports is a main attraction. Sports was a major draw for 10 percent of the respondents. Both Sirius and XM provide play-by-play of all games for the professional sports they cover.

Thirty-three percent of the respondents said they had taken advantage of this capability to follow their favorite teams.

Equipment choices have grown. As satellite programming has diversified, so have equipment options. You can buy aftermarket receivers that integrate into your car's stereo. You'll find numerous models of new cars with satellite-capable radios as optional equipment, often with a starter subscription—from three months to a year—included in the car's purchase price.

It's not just for the car. Of our survey respondents, 42 percent said they listened to satellite radio at home. There are several ways to do this. Sirius and XM let subscribers listen to broadcasts on their Web sites using any Internet-enabled computer. There are also home satellite receivers, plug-and-play models that you can shuttle between car and home, and handheld portables that let you listen virtually anywhere you can receive a strong signal.

New portables for either Sirius or XM have powerful and controversial new recording features. You can record content, save individual songs, schedule show recordings, pause, rewind, fast-forward live programs, and create the type of mixes that have popularized Apple's iPod. Satellite-radio services and manufacturers view those functions as perfectly legal time-shifting. The recording industry defines it as illegal downloading and has filed lawsuits to curb such use.

For now at least, choose satellite radio if you want a lot of diversity radio plus static-free sound. Serious music and sports fans are most likely to appreciate the investment.

HOW TO CHOOSE

Select a provider. While Sirius and XM both fared well in overall satisfaction, respondents reported some differences. They rated XM's sound quality and signal availability more highly and, while complaining about both services' cost, they rated Sirius a slightly better value.

Both Sirius and XM offer scores of music channels, several news outlets, plus traffic and weather

Half of our survey respondents said that, thanks to satellite radio, they were more likely to listen to a type of music they hadn't listened to before.

Satellite radio: Weighing the options

COST VS. PROGRAMMING

What you get:	What you pay:
▶ Diverse, commercial-free music	▶ $12.95 per month or $142 per year
▶ Uncensored talk	
▶ Exhaustive play-by-play sports (i.e., most teams, most games)	▶ Family plans are available for $6.99 per month per additional receiver.
▶ Interviews and live concerts	
▶ Same stations coast to coast	

SIRIUS VS. XM: SOME KEY DIFFERENCES

Category	SIRIUS	XM
Sports	NFL, NBA	MLB, NASCAR (moving to Sirius 1/2007)
Talk radio	NPR	Bob Edwards
Special interest	Gay/lesbian	African-American talk
Trash talk	Howard Stern	Opie & Anthony

Portable units put satellite radio in your pocket or purse.

for 20 metropolitan areas. But each features exclusive content, too (see "Satellite radio: Weighing the options," p. 117). A dual XM and Sirius unit could be available as early as this year from Interoperable Technologies, according to an article on fmqb.com.

Consider car-only options. A car receiver that integrates with your in-dash stereo is easier to use than the other types. Most manufacturers offer only Sirius or only XM as a factory-installed feature. Four—Nissan/ Infiniti, Porsche, Toyota/Lexus/Scion, and Volkswagen—offer a choice of either. These 15 car brands offer only Sirius as a factory- or dealer-installed feature: Aston Martin, BMW, Chrysler, Dodge, Ford, Jaguar, Jeep, Land Rover, Lincoln, Mazda, Mercedes-Benz, Mercury, Mini, Mitsubishi, and Volvo.

These 12 car brands offer only XM as a factory- or dealer-installed feature: Acura, Buick, Cadillac, Chevrolet, GMC, Honda, Hummer, Isuzu, Pontiac, Saab, Saturn, and Suzuki.

Consider where you'll listen. If you plan to listen without using a computer, consider the following types of receivers. (These prices are based on the Sirius and XM Web sites and can vary among retailers.) A handheld portable lets you listen anywhere through a headphone or nearby FM radio. If reception is poor, you can play recorded broadcasts. Sirius offers the S50 for $330, which can play only broadcasts you've recorded—not live ones—when carried by hand. There are several handheld models for XM, priced from $150 to $300.

Console models are for listening only at home. There are several for Sirius, priced from $250 to $300, but just one $250 XM model. Plug-and-play models can shuttle between car and home and install easily in minutes. Some require a home-use kit for $30 to $50 extra.

There are more than a dozen Sirius plug-and-play models, priced $50 to $170; the three XM models are priced $50 to $120.

You can add any of the above receivers to an existing account for $6.99 per month. Sirius allows up to three such additions; XM allows four. The one-time activation charge for each receiver added is $10 online, or $15 by phone.

ConsumerReports.org | Shop from the CR Web site

The Ratings in the back of this book tell you about the best products to buy, but you're on your own when it comes to finding the best deal. That's why CONSUMER REPORTS has provided a way to shop for the best prices from reputable retailers online.

ConsumerReports.org's Shop Online tool offers members easy access to retailers of a variety of products—including video and audio gear. Just click on the icon ⑤ in the Ratings online for the product that interests you; you will leave ConsumerReports.org and be linked directly to Yahoo Shopping. CONSUMER REPORTS has asked Yahoo to sort online retailers by price, lowest to highest, to help you choose. Additionally, to help protect your purchase, only those online retailers who qualify for inclusion in Yahoo's Buyer Protection Plan are listed.

If you are not already a subscriber, you can take advantage of the Shop Online service by activating the 30-day free subscription to *www.ConsumerReports.org* offered on the inside front cover of this guide.

COMPUTERS & PERIPHERALS

CHAPTER

06

▶▶ **Shopping for a computer, monitor, printer, or PDA? You'll be surprised at what your money will buy. Then follow our tips on online security.**

Ratings: Laptops, p. 162; printers, p. 173; scanners, p. 179; software: antispam, p 180; antispyware, p. 181, antivirus, p. 182.

DESKTOP COMPUTERS: POWERFUL AND CHEAP

Tech support may be a deciding factor when you choose

The desktop computer has become just another appliance you use every day. Replacement sales—not first-time purchases—now drive the computer market. Fully loaded desktops selling for less than $700 are common, even among established brands. When choosing a model, it's hard to go too far wrong; the performance of today's computers are uniformly quite high across brands.

With performance so consistently high among all types of computers, differences in reliability and technical support matter more than ever. Repair rates for computers are higher than for most products we track, based on respondents to our Annual Questionnaire. You increase your chances for getting a reliable computer by choosing from brands that have proven reliable in the past.

Technical support may be a deciding factor in which manufacturer gets your business. Tech support remains a hot-button issue judging from our latest subscriber survey of computer users. Apple has maintained its lead in tech support, while other brands continue to show only so-so performance and face some chronic support woes.

Our subscribers still say that tech support is dismal. The most serious complaint from our Annual Questionnaire is that the support people simply can't solve the problem. Major complaints about phone support included being kept on hold too long, being bounced around among support staff, and communication problems. Support via e-mail or the manufacturer's Web site was also lacking. Live-chat online support was problematic, too. To see how readers rated the tech support, see the chart on page 123.

WHAT'S AVAILABLE

There are eight major brands to choose from. Computers from Dell, Compaq, eMachines, Gateway (which owns eMachines), Hewlett-Packard (which owns Compaq), Lenovo (formerly branded as IBM), and Sony all use Microsoft's Windows operating system. Apple is the sole maker of Macintosh models. (A new generation of Macs released in 2006 can run Windows as well as Apple's own OS X operating system). Many small mail-order and store brands also cater to budget-minded buyers. Price: $400 to $3,000.

FEATURES THAT COUNT

The **processor** houses the "brains" of a computer. Its clock speed, measured in gigahertz (GHz), and the chip's design, termed "architecture," determine how fast it can process information. Within a processor family, the higher the clock speed, the faster the computer. But different processor families attain different efficiencies. Pentium 4 processors have the higher speed ratings; other desktop single-processor families, such as Celeron D, Athlon 64, and Sempron, have a slower-rated speed but actually perform on a par with Pentium 4 processors. Dual-core processor families have been introduced recently by Intel (Core Duo) and AMD (Athlon 64 X2). These represent the newest technologies developed to increase processing power

On your next desktop computer, consider front connectors for photo memory, audio, and video inputs.

beyond what a single-chip processor can achieve. Macs have transitioned to Intel core-series processors. In short, the different types of processors make direct speed comparisons difficult, but any type of processor is likely to deliver all the speed you'll need.

All brand-name computers sold today have at least 256 megabytes (MB) of RAM, or **random-access memory,** the memory the computer uses while in operation. Memory upgrades are not expensive. For most users, 512 MB is plenty, but 1024 MB can speed things up for advanced users or those who want to be ready for the Windows Vista operating system due out in early 2007. Video RAM, also measured in megabytes, is secondary RAM that works with the graphics processor to provide smooth video imaging and game play. Gamers may want 128 MB or even 256 MB.

The **hard drive** is your computer's long-term data storage system. Given the disk-space requirements of today's multimedia games, digital photos, and video files, bigger is better. Sizes range from 40 to 500 gigabytes (GB).

Commonly supplied is a **CD-RW (CD-rewriteable) drive,** also known as a "burner," that lets you create backup files or make music compilations on a compact disc. A DVD-ROM drive brings full-length movies or action-packed multimedia games with full-motion video to the desktop. It complements the burner on midline and higher-end systems, allowing you to copy CDs directly between the two drives.

A **DVD drive** will also play CDs and CD-ROMs. Combo drives combine CD-writing and DVD-playing in a single drive, saving money and space. The newest in this family, rapidly becoming a common choice, is the DVD writer, which lets you transfer home-video footage to a DVD disc, or store as much data as six CDs.

There are three competing, incompatible **DVD formats**—DVD-RW, DVD+RW, and DVD-RAM—as well as drives that can create dual-layer DVDs that store twice as much. Some drives can write in more than one format, but all can create a disk that will play on stand-alone DVD players. Just arriving: DVD burners with new technology designed for high-definition video, which will allow storing 25 GB or more on a disk. We recommend waiting until the two competing versions—Blu-ray and HD DVD—sort out their differences.

Many PCs now come with a **memory-card reader** that can also serve for file transfer. You can also get external drives or use a USB memory module to copy files from the hard drive.

The computer's flat-panel **liquid-crystal display** (LCD) or **cathode-ray tube** (CRT) monitor contains the display screen and renders the images sent from the graphics processor—internal circuitry that creates the images. Monitors come in sizes (measured diagonally) ranging from 15 to 21 inches and larger. Seventeen-inch LCD monitors are the most common.

First Things First

Which is right for you—a desktop or laptop?

1 Desktop computers

Pros They start at a lower price. Dollar for dollar, they generally offer more than laptops in terms of hard-drive capacity, memory, and sound quality. They also have more options for expansion and are easier (and less costly) to repair. They allow for a more ergonomically correct work environment.

Modular designs allow them to keep running in the event that a noncritical component, such as a CD drive or external port, fails.
Cons They eat up desk space, even with a thin LCD monitor.
Price $300 to $3,000 plus.

2 Laptop computers

Pros Laptops can do just about anything that desktops can do. They can be carried anywhere and easily tucked away when not needed. According to our surveys of reliability, laptops appear to be less repair-prone than desktops (see Repair history, p. 162).

Cons Laptops cost more than comparably equipped desktop models. Internal components and add-on drives are proprietary and costly to repair. Portability means they're easy to steal and at greater risk of damage.
Price $500 to $3,000 plus.

Apple's iMac comes with a built-in monitor, while its Mac Mini doesn't have one. LCD displays are now the most popular, taking up less space and using less power than CRTs. Better LCD displays can use a Digital Video Interface (DVI) connection, found on many newer PCs. You might obtain a substantial discount on an LCD monitor by buying it bundled with a new computer at a manufacturer's Web site.

All computers have a **graphics adapter,** which might be integrated on the motherboard or on a separate, internal plug-in card. In addition to feeding the computer's display with an analog (VGA) or sometimes a digital (DVI) connection, a graphics adapter may have an additional output to feed video to an external TV (common), or accept video from an external analog source (less common). But it can always display video from whatever source it comes: a file, a DVD, an external analog feed, or a TV tuner.

All desktops and laptops come with a minimum of integrated graphics suitable for watching TV or playing simple games like Solitaire. If you want to run Windows, Vista's new 3D user interface or play more challenging 3D intensive games, like the Sims or World of Warcraft, we recommend the ATI Radeon X1600, the Nvidia GeForce 7600, or higher.

The critical components of a desktop computer are usually housed in a case called a tower. A mini-tower is the typical configuration and can fit either on top of or under a desk. More expensive machines have a midtower, which has extra room for upgrades. A microtower is a space-saving alternative but has less room inside for upgrading. All-in-one computers, such as the Apple iMac, have no tower; everything but the keyboard and mouse is built into the monitor. Apple's Power Mac line of computers has a tower. Apple's desktop model, the Mac Mini, has a space-saving design that puts everything but the monitor, keyboard, and mouse in a case about the size of a hardcover book. Macs are more user-friendly than comparable Windows PCs, and some versions include a DVD writer.

An **"entertainment PC"**—one with a TV tuner built in—comes in a case that is more like an audio or video component, made to fit in with other home-entertainment devices. Some computer makers, including Dell and HP, offer Microsoft's Windows Media Center Edition (MCE) as a standard operating system (or for a small fee) on desktops priced about $500 and above. Media Center's main advantage over other versions of Windows is its simpler interface for playing DVDs, CDs, and MP3s and for viewing photos and video. It can also "serve" this content to an Xbox 360 game system. One of MCE's heralded features, a TiVo-like on-screen guide that can find and record TV programs, is useful only if your PC is equipped to receive TV broadcasts. But a TV tuner and remote are typically a $100 option.

A **mouse,** a small device that fits under your hand and has a "tail" of wire that connects to the computer, moves the cursor (the pointer on the screen) via a rolling ball or a light sensor on its underside. Alternative input devices include a trackball, which is rolled with the fingers in the direction you want the cursor to go; a pad, which lets you move the cursor by sliding a finger; a tablet, which uses a penlike stylus for input; and a game pad, used to play computer games.

Most computers come with a standard keyboard, although you can also buy one separately. Many keyboards have CD (or DVD) controls to pause, playback, change tracks, and so on. Many also have keys to facilitate getting online, starting a search, launching programs, or retrieving e-mail. There are also wireless keyboards and mice that give you flexibility in how you work.

Apple's iMac adds another feature to desktop computers: A built-in camera for video phoning.

Computers for home use feature a high-fidelity **sound system** that plays music from CDs or downloaded music files, synthesized music, game sounds, and DVD-movie soundtracks. Speaker systems with a subwoofer have deeper, more powerful bass. Surround-sound systems can turn a PC into a home theater. Some computers come with a microphone for recording, or one can be added.

PCs come with a **modem** to allow a dial-up Internet connection, as well as an Ethernet port or wireless network card that lets you link several computers in the household to share files, a printer, or a broadband Internet connection. Parallel and serial ports are the traditional connections for printers and scanners but are fading away in newer PCs. Universal serial bus (USB) ports are designed to replace parallel and serial ports and provide a connection to many other devices. FireWire or IEEE 1394 ports are used to capture video from digital camcorders and connect to other peripheral devices. An S-video output jack lets you run a video cable from the computer to a television, so you can use the computer's DVD drive to view a movie on a TV instead of on the computer moni-

tor. Media center PCs that are equipped with TV tuners can capture video from a VCR and allow you to copy tapes to DVDs.

HOW TO CHOOSE

First, decide whether to upgrade your current computer. Upgrading rather than replacing it might make sense if your additional needs are modest—a second hard drive, say, because you're running out of room for digital photos. Adding memory or a CD burner is usually more cost-effective than buying a whole new machine. If your PC has become unreliable, your wish list is more demanding, or if there's software you must run that your system is not up to, a new PC is the logical answer.

Consider a laptop. A desktop computer typically costs less for equivalent performance and is easier to upgrade, expand, and repair. It usually offers better ergonomics, such as a more comfortable keyboard, bigger eye-level display, and enhanced audio. But a laptop merits consideration if portability and compactness are priorities.

Pick the right type of desktop. Most manu-

> **If your PC has become** unreliable, your wish list is more demanding, or if there's software you must run that your system is not up to, a new PC is the logical answer.

Most manufacturers get low marks for tech support

Recently, we conducted a Computer Tech Support Survey among subscribers to CONSUMER REPORTS on their most recent experiences with manufacturers' technical support. The survey covered September 2004 through January 2006.

The survey found that Apple continues to do the best job of solving technical problems on the phone and minimizing the amount of time callers spend waiting on hold.

The charts below give the specifics. If everyone was completely satisfied, the **reader score** would be 100; 80 would mean respondents

were very satisfied, on average; 60, fairly well satisfied. Differences of less than 6 points are not meaningful for desktops, 7 points for laptops.

Solved problem indicates how many people said the manufacturer solved their problem. **Waiting on phone** refers to time waiting and other phone-system problems. **Support staff** is primarily based on how knowledgeable phone representatives seemed and whether they communicated clearly. Because of differences in methodology, the charts are not directly comparable.

Desktops
In order of reader score.

Brand	Reader score	Solved problem	Waiting on phone	Support staff
Apple	82	◉	◉	◉
eMachines	62	○	-	-
Sony	57	○	○	◖
Gateway	54	○	○	○
Dell	54	○	◖	○
HP	53	○	○	○
Compaq	46	●	◖	◖

Based on 7,394 desktop computers bought before January 2006. Note: (-) indicates insufficient sample size.

Laptops
In order of reader score.

Brand	Reader score	Solved problem	Waiting on phone	Support staff
Apple	82	◉	◉	◉
Lenovo (formerly IBM)	69	◉	◉	◉
Toshiba	57	○	○	◖
Dell	56	◖	●	◖
Gateway	54	○	○	○
HP	54	○	○	●
Sony	51	◖	○	◖
Compaq	47	●	●	●

Based on 5,049 laptop computers bought before January 2006.

Better ← → Worse

No matter what the price, you need these basics for a new desktop system: monitor, mouse, tower, keyboard, and speakers.

facturers offer several lines at different prices. Budget computers are the least expensive, and they are suitable for routine work, like e-mail, word processing, and Web surfing. You can also do photo editing. Workhorse computers cost a few hundred dollars more but are faster, more versatile, and upgradable. They can run complex 3D games and edit video. All-in-one models have most of the components in a single case. And entertainment or media PCs can include TV tuners, a remote control, and software that give them the functions of a DVR.

Choose by brand. Our surveys have consistently shown notable differences in reliability and technical support among computer brands. And some brands are generally more expensive than others. Those factors could help you decide which of two similarly equipped computers is the better buy.

Choose between preconfigured and custom-built. You can buy a PC off the shelf in a store or via the Web configured with features and options the manufacturer pitches to average consumers. Or consider purchasing a desktop that you configure to order, either online or in a store. When you configure a computer to order online, onscreen menus typically show you the options and let you see how a change in one affects the overall price. Be sure to double-check your choices before ordering and look for unwanted items that some manufacturers include by default.

Decide between Windows and Mac. More home and entertainment software is available for Windows computers than for Macs. Apple's computers, however, have attractions of their own. The

brand repeatedly scores best in tech support and has been reliable. And according to our last survey, viruses and spyware have been far less likely to target Macs than Windows PCs. The newest Macs let you install Windows as an alternative operating system. In early 2007, Microsoft plans to release a major new version of its flagship Windows operating system called Vista. It promises simpler networking, fewer crashes, better security, and visual features similar to the ones Apple put into Mac OS X a couple of years ago. (To see if a PC you buy now can run Vista when it becomes available, check "New OS needs lots of power and memory," page 127.)

Plan for software. At first glance, virtually any computer you buy will seem laden with useful software for virus scanning, managing finances, and working with audio or image files. But much of it is "teaserware" that works for a limited period or needs an upgrade for full capacity. Especially with Windows computers, check before buying that the selected model includes antivirus and antispyware software that will work (and can be updated) for at least a year. When comparing computer prices, consider any other necessary software as adding to the true cost.

Consider security. Security might not be foremost in your mind when you're shopping for a computer, but it should play a part in your decision. Your choice of hardware and software can affect your ability to deflect intruders and defend your data. Viruses and spyware are far more likely to target Windows PCs than Macs. It's too soon to know, however, whether new Intel-based Macs that Apple has begun shipping are more vulnerable to attack.

Whether you opt for a Windows PC or a Mac, you should use antivirus, firewall, and antispyware programs. Many computers include software such as Norton Internet Security or McAfee Security Center, but those are often limited to 30 to 90 days of use. Upgrade and update these starter packages as necessary or replace them to maintain protection over the long haul. (Also see "Save your computer from online attack," page 140.)

Skip the extended warranty. A recent subscriber survey found that the average cost of a service contract was not substantially less than the average repair cost. That means you might be better off paying for repairs out of your own pocket rather than buying a service contract that you might never use.

LAPTOPS ARE BECOMING THE PRIMARY COMPUTER

Portable models take over as home-office and entertainment devices. Increasing wireless availability adds to their appeal.

Bigger, crisper displays and more usable key layouts have replaced small screens and cramped keyboards. Processors have caught up in speed, and innovative new processors provide some real advantages. Fast CD and DVD recording drives are common, as are ample hard drives. As computers become a repository for digital photos, music, and video, manufacturers are making laptops and the peripherals to which they connect increasingly compatible with home-entertainment systems. And a growing interest in wireless computing plays to the laptop's main strength: its portability. A laptop is the most convenient way to take full advantage of the growing availability of high-speed wireless Internet access at airports, schools, hotels, restaurants, and coffee shops.

Most laptops now have wireless networking capability built in and deliver commendably long battery life. The thinnest laptops on the market are less than an inch thick and weigh just 3 to 5 pounds. To get these light, sleek models, however, you'll have to pay a premium and make a few sacrifices in performance and screen size.

WHAT'S AVAILABLE

Dell, Gateway, Hewlett-Packard (which also makes Compaq), Lenovo (formerly branded as IBM), Sony, and Toshiba are the leading Windows laptop brands. Apple makes Mac OS MacBook and MacBook Pro models. Laptops can be grouped into several basic configurations:

Budget models. These have slower processors, fewer features, and lower screen quality than others but are suitable for routine office work and home software. Price: $1,000 or less.

Workhorse/multimedia models. These have faster processors and more built-in devices, so there's less need for external attachments. They also have larger screens and enhanced sound and video components for home-entertainment uses. They're not lightweight or battery-efficient enough for frequent travelers. Price: $1,000 and up.

Slim-and-light models. These are for travelers.

They are about an inch thick and weigh about 3 to 4 pounds. Some require an external drive to read DVDs or burn CDs. Price: $1,000 and up.

Tablet-style. These sit in your hand like a clipboard and have handwriting-recognition software. Some convert to a "normal" laptop with a keyboard. Price: $1,600 and up.

FEATURES THAT COUNT

Windows laptops generally have a 1.6- to 3.5-GHz processor. Popular processors include Intel Core Solo and Duo and AMD Turion 64. Apple laptops have made the transition to Intel processors and use Intel's Core Duo. The different types of proces-

For intensive applications like gaming, you'll want at least 1 gigabyte of memory and a dedicated graphics chip.

A budget laptop may be all you need for general use.

Some of the accessories you might need for your laptop: a spare power adapter and a carrying case.

sors make direct speed comparisons difficult, but any type of processor will probably deliver all the speed you'll need.

Laptops come with a 40- to 160-gigabyte hard drive and 256 megabytes or more of random-access memory (RAM). We recommend at least 512 MB.

Laptops use a **rechargeable lithium-ion battery.** In Consumer Reports tests, a normal battery provided two to five hours of continuous use when running office applications. (Laptops go into sleep mode when used intermittently, extending the time between charges.) You can extend battery life somewhat by dimming the display as you work, turning off wireless devices when they aren't needed, or only using basic applications.

Playing a DVD movie uses more battery power than usual, but most laptops should be able to play one through to the end. Many laptops can accept an "extended" battery, adding size and weight but giving as much as twice the battery life.

A laptop's **keyboard** can be quite different from that of a desktop computer. The keys themselves may be full-sized (generally only lightweight models pare them down), but they may not feel as solid. Some laptops have extra buttons to expedite your access to e-mail or a Web browser, or to control DVD playback. You can attach a USB keyboard, which you may find easier to use.

A 14- to 15-inch **display,** measured diagonally, should suit most people. Displays that are 17-inches are becoming more common. A resolution of 1280x800 (WXGA) pixels (picture elements) or more is better than 1,024x768 (XGA) for viewing the fine detail in photographs or video but may shrink objects on the screen. You can use settings in Windows to make them larger. Many models are now offered with a display that has a glossy surface instead of a matte one. Those look better in bright ambient light, as long as you avoid direct reflections. A "wide-aspect" display (WXGA or WSXGA) fits wide-screen DVD movies better.

Most laptops use a small **touchpad** in place of a mouse—you slide your finger across the pad to move the cursor. You can also program the pad to respond to a "tap" as a "click," or to scroll as you sweep your index finger along the pad's right edge (or use two fingers). An alternative system uses a pencil-eraser-sized pointing stick in the middle of the keyboard. You can attach a USB mouse or trackball if you prefer.

Laptops usually include at least one **PC-card or Expresscard slot** for expansion. You might add a wireless-network card or a cellular modem, for example, if those are not built in. Many laptops offer a connection for a **docking station,** a $100 to $200 base that makes it easy to connect an external monitor, keyboard, mouse, printer, network and power in one step. Most laptops let you attach these devices anyway, without the docking station. An external display lets you set up your workspace more ergonomically. At least two **USB ports,** for easy hookup of, say, a printer, digital camera, or scanner, is standard. A wired network (Ethernet) port is common, as is a FireWire port for digital-video transfer. Many models have a standard internal wireless-network (Wi-Fi) adapter. An increasingly common option is an internal Bluetooth wireless adapter to link to a cell phone, PDA, or another laptop.

For backing up files or transferring them to other computers, you can use a **USB memory drive** (about $20 and up), which fits on a keychain and holds as much data as a CD-R (60

MB). Or save files on a writeable CD or camera-memory card. The small **speakers** built into laptops often sound tinny, with little bass. Headphones or external speakers deliver much better sound.

HOW TO CHOOSE

Decide if a laptop is right for you. If you're on a tight budget and aren't cramped for space, a comparably equipped desktop computer may be preferable because it costs a few hundred dollars less. It's also a better choice for heavy users who spend hours at the computer each day. Otherwise, consider a laptop. If you'll use it mostly at home, built-in wireless networking lets you use it throughout the house and easily store it.

Windows vs. Macintosh. Many people choose laptops using the Windows operating system because it's what they've always used, but Apple's Mac OS is a fine alternative. In recent subscriber surveys, CONSUMER REPORTS found Apple technical support to be top-notch. According to a recent survey, we also found that Apple computers have been less susceptible to most viruses and spyware than Windows-based computers. Apple's MacBook will suit you if you're interested in basic photo editing, music, video, and office applications, but the 13.3-inch screen is small. The Apple MacBook Pro is suited to more intensive tasks but is relatively expensive as laptops go.

Buy à la carte. Dell and Gateway pioneered the notion that every computer can be tailored to an individual's needs, much like choosing the options for a car. This configure-to-order model is now common practice for laptops as well as desktops.

You can also purchase a computer off the shelf. (You can do the same online if you opt for the default choices of equipment the manufacturer offers.) That's fine if you don't have very strict requirements for how a laptop is outfitted or if you want to take advantage of an attractive sale.

Menus show you all the options and let you see how a change in one affects the overall price. You might decide to use a less-expensive processor, for example, but spend more for wireless capability or better graphics. Configure-to-order will often give you choices you won't get if you buy an off-the-shelf model. And configure-to-order means less chance of overlooking important details. But be sure to double-check your choices before ordering, and look for unwanted items that some manufacturers include by default.

Downplay the processor speed. Speed is no longer the be-all an end-all of personal computers. Current processors deliver all the speed most people need. Spend the money on more memory instead.

Look closely at warranties and insurance. Since the average cost of repair is usually not much more than the average cost of an extended warranty, we don't recommend buying a service you might not use. If you intend to travel a lot, consider buying screen insurance from the manufacturer.

> **Speed is no longer** the most important feature of a personal computer. Current processors deliver all the speed most people need. Spend the money on more memory instead.

New OS needs lots of power and memory

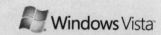

Microsoft's latest operating system, Windows Vista, is due for release in early 2007. But it won't run on just any PC. Loaded with a host of new features, such as desktop search, online security functions, and speech recognition, Vista represents a major step up from Microsoft's previous operating systems, even Windows XP. This new OS requires a considerable amount of processing power and memory to run with its full feature set enabled.

In response to PC makers' concerns that Vista's demanding architecture would lead to a sharp spike in new PC prices, Microsoft will be releasing a stripped-down version of the OS called Vista Home Basic in addition to the full-blown Vista Home Premium.

Manufacturers have already started selling new systems in anticipation of a consumer migration to the new OS by attaching "Vista Capable" stickers on their PCs. It can be a tricky path to navigate, however. Some of those computers—particularly those selling for less than $600—will only be able to run Vista Home Basic. To ensure that a PC can run the full version of Vista, look for PCs that are designated "Vista Premium Ready." The key difference between the two versions will be seen in the graphics performance and the user experience. Vista Home Premium will employ Microsoft's new Windows Aero technology, which adds Mac-like visual elements, such as transparent windows, to the interface.

For Vista Home Basic, the recommended hardware requirements are a CPU of 800 MHz or faster; 512 MB of system memory; a DirectX 9-capable graphics processor; and a 20-GB hard drive with 15 GB of free space. For Vista Premium, Microsoft recommends a minimum system configuration of 1 GHz or faster 32-bit (x86) or 64-bit (x64) CPU; 1 GB of system memory; a dedicated graphics card with at least 128 MB of graphics memory; a 40-GB hard drive with 15 GB of free space; and a DVD-ROM drive.

To see if your current PC will be able to accommodate Windows Vista, Microsoft is offering consumers a small downloadable application, called Windows Vista Upgrade Advisor, which will scan your system and recommend upgrades if needed. You can download this program from: *www.microsoft.com/windowsvista /getready/upgradeadvisor/default.mspx.*

MONITOR PRICES DROP & SCREENS GET BIGGER

LCDs are most popular but CRT monitors offer some advantages

Deciding whether to buy a flat-panel LCD or a standard, fairly fat CRT monitor comes down to this: Do you need more space on the surface of your desk or on the screen? If freeing up space on your desk is a priority, an LCD is the clear choice. But since LCDs are more costly, you might opt for a CRT. And a CRT still has some other advantages (see "There are reasons to consider a CRT," page 129).Desktop computers and monitors are often sold as a package, with some manufacturers offering attractive discounts for monitors bundled with PCs sold online.

WHAT'S AVAILABLE

Apple, Dell, eMachines (which merged with Gateway in 2004), Gateway, Hewlett-Packard (which merged with Compaq in 2002), Lenovo, and Sony all market their own monitors for their computers. Other brands of monitors, such as Acer, Envision, KDS, LG, NEC, Samsung, and ViewSonic, are sold separately. Many brands are manufactured on an outsource basis.

Flat-panel LCD monitors. These have been outselling CRTs for years. Because the monitors have a liquid-crystal display rather than a TV-style picture tube, they take up much less desktop space than CRTs. They operate with analog or digital input, or both. Unlike a CRT, the nominal and the viewable-image size (VIS) of a flat-panel LCD are the same. Desktop models typically measure 17 or 19 inches diagonally and just a few inches deep, and they weigh around 15 pounds, compared with 30 to 50 pounds for a CRT. LCDs with a screen 20 inches

A 20-inch LCD screen is ideal for playing games or watching videos. With a TV tuner card, your computer can turn it into a television screen, too.

or larger are available, but they are still somewhat pricey. Wide-screen LCDs with a 17-inch VIS, specially designed for watching wide-format videos, are also available. These screens have an aspect ratio of 16:9, like those found on most digital TVs, and they're also fairly expensive.

Flat-panel displays deliver a very clear image, but they have some inherent quirks. Their range of color is a bit narrower than a CRT's. And you have to view a flat-panel screen straight on; except for wide-screen models, the picture loses contrast as you move off-center, and fine lines might appear grainy. In analog mode you have to tweak the controls in order to get the best picture, but we have seen some improvements lately regarding the narrow angle. Price: $170 to $300 (15-inch); $150 to $500 (17-inch); $200 to $600 (19-inch); and $250 to $1,500 (20-inch).

CRT monitors. These typically range from 17 to 22 inches. To reduce glare, some CRTs have flattened, squared-off screens (not to be confused with flat-panel LCD screens). The nominal image size—the screen size touted in ads—is generally based on the diagonal measurement of the picture tube. The image you see, the viewable-image size, is usually an inch smaller. Thus a 17-inch CRT has a 16-inch VIS. As a result of a class-action lawsuit, ads must state a CRT's VIS as well as its nominal image, but you might have to squint at the fine print to find it.

Generally, the bigger the screen, the more room a CRT takes up on your desk, with depth roughly matching nominal screen size. "Short-depth" models shave an inch or more off the depth.

A 17-inch monitor, the most frequent choice these days, has almost one-third more viewable area than the 15-inch version now vanishing from the market. The larger size is especially useful when you're using the Internet, playing video games, watching DVD movies, editing photos, or working in several windows.

If you regularly work with graphics or sprawling spreadsheets, consider a 19-inch monitor. Its viewable area is one-fourth larger than a 17-inch model's. A short-depth 19-inch model doesn't take up much more desktop space than a standard 17-inch.

Aimed at graphics professionals, 21- and 22-inch models provide ample viewing area but they gobble up desktop space. Price: $50 to $500 (17-inch); $150 to $650 (19-inch); and $400 to $800 (21- to 22-inch).

FEATURES THAT COUNT

A monitor's **resolution** refers to the number of picture elements, or pixels, that make up an image. More pixels mean finer detail. Most monitors can display at several resolutions, generally ranging from 640x480 to 1600x1200 depending on the monitor and the graphics card. An LCD usually displays a sharper image than a CRT of comparable size when both are viewed at identical resolutions. But that's only if the LCD is set to its "native" resolution—1024x768 pixels for a 15-inch screen; 1280x1024, 1400x1050, or 1440x900 wide-screen for a 17-, 18-, or 19-inch model. On both types of monitor, the higher the resolution the smaller the text and images, so more content fits on the screen. Bigger CRT screens can handle higher resolutions and display more information.

Dot pitch, measured in millimeters, refers to the spacing between a CRT's pixels. All else being equal, a smaller dot pitch produces a more detailed image, though that's no guarantee of an excellent picture. In general, avoid models with a dot pitch larger than 0.28 mm.

A CRT requires a high **refresh rate** (the number of times per second an image is redrawn on the screen) to avoid annoying image flicker. In general, you'll be more comfortable with a 17-inch monitor with a refresh rate of at least 75 hertz (Hz) at the resolution you want. For a 19-inch monitor, you might need an 85-Hz rate to avoid eyestrain, especially at higher resolutions. The refresh rate isn't an issue with flat-panel displays.

Monitors have controls for **brightness** and **contrast.** Most of them also have controls for color balance (usually called color temperature), distortion, and such. Buttons activate onscreen controls and menus.

Bigger CRTs use a considerable amount of juice: about 80 watts for a typical 19-inch model, 65 to 70 watts for a 17-inch model, and about 20 watts for a 15-inch flat-panel LCD, for example. Most monitors have a sleep mode when the computer is on but not in use that uses less than 3 watts.

Some monitors include a microphone, integrated or separate speakers, or composite-video inputs for viewing the output of a VCR or camcorder.

Plug-and-play capability makes it fairly simple to add a new monitor to an existing computer.

HOW TO CHOOSE

Decide between LCD and CRT monitors. If your computer's monitor is hogging the top of your desk, you can reclaim much of that space by replacing it with an LCD. But doing so will cost you about $100 to $300 more than if you bought a new CRT monitor. And LCD screens have an inherent shortcoming: The image appears to fade as you move left, right, up, or down. However, most LCD monitors in

Flat-panel displays deliver a very clear image but they have some quirks. The range of color is a bit narrower than a CRT's, and you have to view the screen straight on, except for wide-screen models.

The bigger the screen, the more desk space a CRT takes up, but gamers will love the image clarity.

There are reasons to consider a CRT

Big and bulky, a CRT monitor can gobble up a huge section of your desktop, be difficult to maneuver or move, and consume twice as much energy—up to 80 watts—as an LCD of comparable size. Nevertheless, for some people, it might still be worth considering for these reasons:

A CRT offers the most screen for the money. A 19-inch model can be on your desk for less than $200, compared with $350 and up for an LCD.

It may perform very well. Two 17-inch models we tested (16-inch viewable-image size) performed better overall than half the LCDs in our Ratings.

It's superior for photographers, designers, and gamers. CRTs generally deliver slightly truer colors, making them the preferred medium for graphic designers and digital photographers. They also render fast-moving objects better than LCDs, making them attractive to serious gamers. And unlike LCDs, they can be readily viewed from extreme angles.

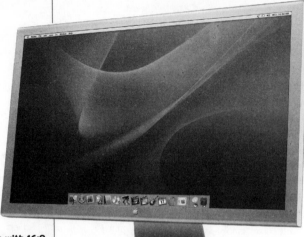

Monitors with 16:9 proportions, like HDTV screens, allow side-by-side views of text pages or a single wide-screen video image.

our recent tests had a wider viewing angle than we've seen in the past. If space isn't an issue but budget is, a CRT monitor is a good choice. Because they deliver truer color and render fast-moving objects better, they are a superior choice for photographers, designers, and gamers.

Settle on size. For most people, a 17-inch CRT is big enough. Larger monitors are best suited for people who need to show photo enlargements or who regularly display multiple windows on the screen.

Consider helpful features. A monitor you can raise or lower can compensate for a desk that's too high or low. It's a feature found on some LCD monitors, but not on CRTs because they're so heavy. Some monitors can be rotated 90 degrees, from a landscape to portrait orientation, with the image automatically adjusting itself. That can be handy for viewing photos and Web pages. Also look for conveniently placed controls that adjust contrast, brightness, and other settings that affect images.

Look for a long warranty. Many monitors, both LCDs and CRTs, come with a three-year warranty on parts and labor. A warranty that long is worth looking for, especially when purchasing a more-expensive model.

Convergence with TV isn't here yet. Manufacturers offer monitors with TV tuners and LCD TVs with computer connections. But big differences remain between monitors and TVs.

Consider budget vs. speed when picking Internet service

If you spend much time online, you're probably using a broadband Internet connection to your home or you are thinking seriously about getting one. Broadband offers near-instantaneous connections and swifter downloads than slower, albeit cheaper, dial-up Internet service.

But if broadband service is becoming almost a utility, it isn't yet as predictable and uniform in performance as that term suggests. In a survey of nearly 26,000 CONSUMER REPORTS subscribers—our largest survey on Internet service providers (ISPs) and the first to rate broadband—we found differences in satisfaction with broadband service.

Here are the highlights of our findings:

There's no best broadband type. The availability of broadband is growing, with virtually all cable-TV companies now offering broadband Internet service and telephone companies wiring more neighborhoods for digital subscriber line (DSL) service. The highest-scoring cable and DSL providers offered comparable, fairly high levels of satisfaction—while the least satisfactory of each received equally ho-hum Ratings overall.

Sharing broadband via a home network makes an Internet connection more economical.

But the two provider types differed in what made their best ISPs score so high. Subscribers to the better-rated cable-broadband providers were more satisfied than most DSL subscribers with the speed of their service, and with its reliability and tech support. But subscribers to the least pricey of the DSL providers were far more satisfied with their monthly bills (around $30) than were subscribers to cable broadband, who paid about $35 to $45 a month.

There's no question about the worst provider in our survey. It was DirecWay (now called HughesNet), the satellite-TV broadband provider, which offers relatively low satisfaction at a very high price—$600 and up for equipment and installation, and $60 a month for service.

At its best, dial-up service is satisfactory. Cost was again a main attraction. It certainly wasn't speed, which was much slower for all the dial-ups than the broadband providers. In fact, the least expensive service, Juno, was among the top-rated dial-ups, while pricey AOL, the biggest ISP, had one of the lowest overall scores.

INKJET PRINTERS RULE, BUT CONSIDER LASERS

All-in-one models can scan, copy, and sometimes fax, too

Inkjet printers have become the standard for home-computer use. They can turn out color photos nearly indistinguishable from lab-processed photos, along with banners, stickers, transparencies, T-shirt transfers, and greeting cards. Many produce excellent black-and-white text. With some very good models selling for less than $200, it's no surprise that inkjets account for the vast majority of printers sold for home use.

Laser printers still have their place in home offices. If you print reams of black-and-white text documents, you probably need the quality, speed, and low per-copy cost of a laser printer. Printers use a computer's microprocessor and memory to process data. The latest inkjets and lasers are so fast partly because computers themselves have become more powerful and contain much more memory than before.

WHAT'S AVAILABLE

The printer market is dominated by a handful of well-established brands. Hewlett-Packard is the market leader. Other major brands include Brother, Canon, Dell, Epson, and Lexmark. Printers designed for printing 4x6-inch snapshots are also sold by Kodak, Olympus, Samsung, and Sony.

The type of computer a printer can serve depends on its ports. The most common by far, a Universal Serial Bus (USB) port, lets a printer connect to Windows or Macintosh computers. A few models also have a parallel port, which allows connections to older Windows computers. All these printers lack a serial port, which means they won't work with older Macs.

Inkjet printers. Inkjets use droplets of ink to form letters, graphics, and photos. Some printers have one cartridge that holds the cyan (greenish-blue), magenta, and yellow inks, and a second cartridge for the black ink. Others have an individual cartridge for each color. For photos, many inkjets also have additional cartridges that contain lighter shades of cyan and magenta inks, or gray ink.

Most inkjet printers output black-and-white text at a speed of 2 to 10 pages per minute (ppm) but are much slower for color photos. Various models we tested took 2 to 11 minutes to print a single 8x10, depending on the complexity of the image. The cost of printing a black-and-white text page with an inkjet varies considerably from model to model, from 2 to 12 cents. The cost of printing a color 8x10 photo can range from 90 cents to $1.60. Printer price: $60 to $700. You can also get them with scanning, copying, and sometimes fax capability. These all-in-one models typically cost more than stand-alone inkjets. Price: $100 and up.

Specialty snapshot printers. For printing photos at home, a speedy snapshot printer can be more convenient than a full-sized model. Most are limited to 4x6-inch snapshots, but a few models can also print on 5x7 paper. These models use either inkjet or dye-sublimation technology. Like most full-sized inkjet printers, most of these models can hook up directly via cable to a digital camera through the PictBridge connection, so you can print without

Inkjet printers are cheaper to buy, but laser printers are cheaper to operate.

using a computer. This is the simplest and quickest way to print at home, provided you don't want to edit the photos. Price: $80 to $300.

Laser printers. These work much like plain-paper copiers, forming images by transferring toner (powdered ink) to paper passing over an electrically charged drum. The process yields sharp black-and-white text and graphics. Laser printers usually outrun inkjets, cranking out black-and-white text at a rate of 12 to 18 ppm. Black-and-white laser printers generally cost about as much as midpriced inkjets, but they're cheaper to operate. Laser cartridges, about $50 to $100, can print thousands of black-and-white pages for a per-page cost of 2 to 4 cents. Price: $100 and up. All-in-one laser

First Things First

1 Text only

Your best choice A laser printer.
Pros Nothing beats a laser for fine, fast text printing. The best inkjet can match the excellent text quality, but lasers print text more quickly and cheaply than most inkjets. As an added plus, lasers are often quieter than inkjets, too.
Cons While tops for text, lasers aren't as versatile as inkjets and they're not suited for printing photos. Even models that can print in color aren't intended for use with glossy photo stock or other specialty papers. They also cost more to buy than inkjets, although you'll probably spend less on supplies over time.
Price $100 and up for black-and-white printers. Multifunction models start at $200, color ones at about $300.
The bottom line A laser printer will be your best choice for fast, low-cost, top-quality black-and-white text. But you'll still need an inkjet or snapshot model if you plan to print photos.

2 Text plus color photos & graphics

Your best choice A regular inkjet printer.
Pros Many offer excellent print quality for both photos and text, and will accept a variety of paper types and sizes. Most can print photos directly from a digital camera.
Cons Supply costs can be high. Inkjet speeds can also be slow, from 2 to 11 minutes for an 8x10-inch photo.
Price $60 and up.
The bottom line Inkjets remain your best all-around choice for printing photos, text, and color graphics, like greeting cards and Web pages.

3 Text, photos & graphics plus copying & scanning

Your best choice An all-in-one inkjet printer.
Pros It combines printing, scanning, and copying in one unit and may be cheaper than buying several separate devices. The best of them can produce excellent color photos and text, and most will print photos without a PC. A few can also fax.
Cons The print quality of some all-in-one machines might not match that of a regular printer, especially for photos. They might also have fewer features than stand-alone printers. As with other electronic devices designed to do more than one job, you'll have to repair or replace the entire unit if one part breaks down.
Price $100 and up.
The bottom line Check out all-in-one machines if you need a printer, scanner, and copier but lack the space for separate units.

4 Snapshots only

Your best choice A snapshot printer.
Pros Snapshot printers are small and fast, with speeds as quick as a minute per print. Some portable types can run on batteries, handy for use on the road. All can print photos from a digital camera or memory card, without requiring a computer. Many models use dye-sublimation (dye-sub) technology to make prints that are more water-resistant than those from inkjets.
Cons Snapshot printers can only print small photos, and they are not intended for printing text or graphics. In our tests, they didn't provide the photo quality of the best regular inkjets, and they tend to cost the same as a full-sized printer.
Price $80 to $300.
The bottom line Snapshot photo printers are speedy and convenient, but you'll sacrifice flexibility and some print quality.

printers add scanning, copying, and sometimes fax capability. Price: $200 and up. Color laser printers are also available, but those now on the market can't print on glossy photo paper, so they're not a good choice for printing photos. Price: $300 and up.

FEATURES THAT COUNT

Printers differ in the fineness of detail they can produce. **Resolution,** expressed in dots per inch (dpi), is often touted as the main measure of print quality. But other factors, such as the way dot patterns are formed by software instructions from the printer driver, count, too. At their default settings—where they're usually expected to run—inkjets currently on the market typically have a resolution of 600x600 dpi. The dpi can be increased for color photos. Some printers go up to 5760x1440 dpi. Laser printers for home use typically offer 600 or 1200 dpi. Printing color inkjet photos on photo paper at a higher dpi setting can produce smoother shading of colors but can slow printing significantly.

Most inkjet printers have an **ink monitor** to warn when you're running low, but they vary in accuracy. Generic ink cartridges usually cost less but most produce fewer prints than the brand-name inks, so per-print costs may not be lower. And print quality and fade-resistance may not be as good. (See "Cheaper ink cartridges don't save money in the long run," page 134.)

For double-sided printing, you can print the odd-numbered pages of a document first, then flip those pages over to print the even-numbered pages on a second pass. A few printers can automatically print on both sides, but it slows down printing.

HOW TO CHOOSE

Be skeptical about advertised speeds. Print speed varies depending on what you're printing and at what quality, but the speeds you see in ads are generally higher than you're likely to achieve in normal use. You can't reliably compare speeds for different brands because each company uses its own methods to measure speed. We run the same tests on all models, printing text pages and photos that are similar to what you might print. As a result, our print times are realistic and can be compared across brands.

Don't get hung up on resolution. A printer's resolution, expressed in dots per inch, is another

potential source of confusion. All things being equal, the more ink dots a printer puts on the paper, the more detailed the image. But dot size, shape, and placement also affect quality, so don't base your choice solely on resolution.

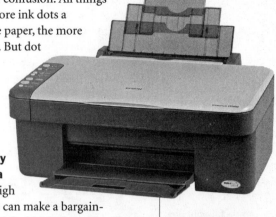

Consider supply costs as well as a printer's price. High ink-cartridge costs can make a bargain-priced printer a bad deal in the long run. Shop around for the best cartridge prices, but be wary of off-brands. We have found brand-name cartridges that overall, have better print quality and fade-resistance, and per-page costs are often comparable.

If you need to copy and scan as well as print, an all-in-one inkjet will save you money and desk space.

Glossy photo paper costs about 25 to 75 cents a sheet, so use plain paper for works in progress and save the good stuff for the final results. We've gotten the best results using the recom-

Software available for your home computer can turn a regular color inkjet printer into a multitalented graphic-arts machine.

mended brand of paper. You might be tempted to buy a cheaper brand, but bear in mind that lower-grade paper can reduce photo quality and might not be as fade resistant.

Decide if you want to print photos without using a computer. Printing without a computer saves you an extra step and a little time. Features such as memory-card support, PictBridge support (a standard that allows a compatible camera to be connected directly to the printer), or a wireless interface are convenient. But when you print directly from camera to printer, you compromise on what may have attracted you to digital photography in the first place—the ability to tweak size, color, brightness, and other image attributes. And with a snapshot printer, you give up the ability to print on larger media.

Cheaper ink cartridges don't save money in the long run

If you print a lot of photos, you might be as fed up with ink costs as you are with gasoline prices. Alternative brands that sell for as little as half the price of brand-name ink seem like a good way to save money. They are—sometimes.

Lower-priced options include store brands, third-party products, and generic inks. You can also have empty cartridges refilled. Inks are sold at office-supply chains, mass-market retailers, franchise stores specializing in printer supplies, and online. Most also sell brand-name inks.

But our tests of hundreds of cartridges from many of these sources found that off-brands often didn't cut photo costs much because they printed fewer photos than brand-name cartridges. Also, they generally didn't match the manufacturers' inks for print quality and fade resistance.

We did find some exceptions. Office Depot cartridges for Hewlett-Packard printers, the top-selling brand, matched HP ink for photo quality and trimmed 20 cents off the cost of an 8x10-inch photo. Staples cartridges for Canon printers and Epson-compatible inks from online suppliers Carrot Ink and PrintPal matched the photo quality of the printer makers' cartridges at slightly lower cost.

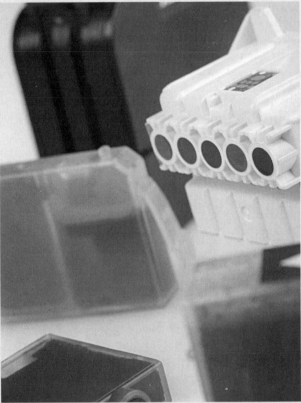

Our tests have found that brand-name inks are worth the cost.

There are trade-offs. Few of the off-brand inks we tested offered manufacturer-level quality for text and graphics as well as photos, and it was almost always a challenge to get them working properly. We often had to run the cleaning utility, which wastes ink, and some samples simply didn't work. In our experience, brand-name cartridges rarely have such issues.

HOW TO CHOOSE

Use brand-name ink for the least risk and hassle. As a rule, brand-name ink produced the best-quality photos, graphics, and text. For top results with all output and for keepsake photos, buy brand-name ink. That might be your only choice for new printers with redesigned cartridges. It often takes three to six months before alternative cartridges for new models arrive.

Consider the best off-brands for economical 8x10s. Alternative inks offer little, if any, savings on snapshots, but they can save you 5 to 10 percent on 8x10s. Stick with one of those we recommend so that you don't sacrifice any print quality.

For cheaper text and less-critical uses, go with an off-brand. When top-quality text and graphics aren't a must–say, for casual home projects–use one of the better off-brands to cut costs.

Refill or recycle. At the franchise stores, you'll get the lowest price by refilling empties or trading them in for new ones. Office Depot and Staples offer a $3 credit for empties; Office Max gives you a ream of paper worth about $4. Some Office Depot, Office Max, and Walgreens stores offer while-you-shop refills, and PrintPal offers refills by mail. (We didn't test store-refilled cartridges for this last group, but prices here reflect the lowest possible, including credit for empties, if available.)

Avoid DIY refill kits. Do-it-yourself kits are low-cost, but most we've tried were messy. The Automatic Ink Refill System from Dataproducts, for $20, was the only one that was fairly easy to use, with no mess.

Weigh convenience features. Most printers can make borderless prints like those from a photo developer. This matters most if you're printing to the full size of the paper, as you might with 4x6-inch sheets. Otherwise, you can trim the edges off.

If you plan to use 4x6-inch paper regularly, look for a printer with a 4x6-inch tray or a second paper tray, which makes it easier to feed paper of this size. With these small sheets, though, the cost per photo might be higher than ganging up a few images on 8½ x11-inch paper.

With some models, if you want to use the photo inks to get the best picture quality, you have to remove the black-ink cartridge and replace it with the photo-ink cartridge. Then, to print text or graphics, you have to swap the black cartridge back in. This process can get tedious. The models that hold all the ink

The Canon Pixma MP800 aced our tests for printing text and photos and copied and scanned well.

Checklist

Printers

Printing method

☐ Inkjet ☐ Laser ☐ Dye sublimation

Copier, scanner? _____

Fax? _____

Print photos? _____

Memory-card slot? _____

Portable? _____

_____

This features checklist can help you narrow your choices when shopping for a printer.

You'll find an interactive version of this product-selector tool online. Specify your preferences among brands, prices, and other options and CONSUMER REPORTS' Web-enabled database can suggest models matching your criteria.

To access this interactive buying aid, you need to be a subscriber to ConsumerReports.org, or you can activate the 30-day free trial subscription offered on the inside front cover of this guide.

At the top of the ConsumerReports.org home page, click on Electronics and Computers. Under Computers Decision Guide, click on Printers. Then, on the introductory page for Printers, click on the link for Product Selector.

tanks simultaneously eliminate that hassle.

Consider connections. Printers with USB 2.0 ports are fairly common now. But they don't enable much faster print speeds than plain USB. All new computers and printers have USB 2.0 ports, which are compatible with plain USB. Computers more than seven years old may have only a parallel port.

Decide whether you need scanning and copying. An all-in-one inkjet unit provides scanning and color copying (and sometimes faxing) while saving space. The downside is that the scanners in all-in-one units might be slower and have fewer features than the latest stand-alone scanners. Stand-alone scanners are best for handling negatives and slides, although some all-in-one units now include a light in the lid and a holder to keep negatives and slides in place. And if one part of the unit breaks, the whole unit must be repaired or replaced.

GET YOUR COMPUTER OFF TO A SMOOTH START

Transfer data from your old computer or set up a home network

Hooking up a new computer to the monitor, keyboard, mouse, printer and other peripherals is quick and easy. But once the hookup is done, you're likely to spend considerable time transferring the data and software from your old computer. Below you'll find a step-by-step guide that can make the move to a new computer easier.

You'll also find advice on setting up a home network in case you now have more than one computer in your home.

TRANSFERRING DATA

Your new PC has an operating system and other software installed that incorporate many items just for your computer. Examples are special "driver" programs installed by the PC manufacturer for your specific hardware components, help files and documentation for hardware and software, utilities to access the manufacturer's online resources, and applications that have been preinstalled, but without supplied reinstallation disks, system and application restore files on a separate hard-drive partition.

For your new PC to operate properly, you must leave such items intact on the hard drive. You can't just clone old drive to new. To prevent overwriting critical operating-system files and the other components, you must transfer data or programs from your old PC carefully and methodically.

Getting connected. A high-speed wired connection is the best way to move large amounts of data from one PC to another. The best compromise among cost, speed, reliability, and complexity is an Ethernet network. For this, both computers need an Ethernet card, also known as an Ethernet port, "10/100-base-T" port, or simply a LAN (local-area networking) port. Both PC ports need to be connected with an Ethernet cable (also known as Cat-5) either to an existing network hub or router, or directly to each other using a special crossover cable.

Another way to connect two PCs that have USB ports is via a USB network cable, such as the Belkin USB Direct Connect F5U104 ($50), or the Micro Innovations USB600A ($18). Make sure it comes with NDIS software drivers that make the link appear to the PCs as a normal TCP/IP network connection.

Once they are physically connected, the PCs need to be set up so the new one can access the old one's hard drive across the network. Chances are that the newer of your PCs has Windows XP, which has a utility called "Network Setup Wizard" (Start, All Programs, Accessories, Communications). This asks a few simple questions, to which you take the default answers. At the end, you're prompted to create a diskette to run on the older PC, which makes it able to talk to the new one.

The long way around. If you can't get wired, you can still transfer your files by writing them to disks on the old PC and reading them into the new one. If the old PC has a CD burner, you can do this with far fewer disks than if you used a diskette drive. If your old computer has a USB port, you can transfer files on a USB memory module.

You may be able to transfer data to your new computer via a wired or wireless home network router.

Backing up is critical. It's good practice to keep a fresh backup copy of personal documents, photos, worksheets, databases, and downloaded files. Back up anything you wouldn't want to lose. That's unlikely to happen from day to day, but it's more likely when you—or anyone else—performs major "surgery" on your PC, including moving large groups of files to another hard drive or system. You're responsible for your own data; don't entrust the backup to others.

▶ First, make a list of the folders containing the files and subfolders you want to back up. This list should include standard locations like Windows' My Documents and any documents you've placed on the desktop. If there is more than one user with a separate log-on to your PC, include everyone's document folders, even though they might be accessible only when they log on.

▶ Don't back up program files for installed programs. They will have to be reinstalled from scratch or moved with savvy program-moving software (see below). Be sure to find the documents or multimedia files (pictures, videos, music) you've created with various applications. They don't always end up in My Documents. Also include your Favorites folder, e-mail from your e-mail program, and address book or scheduler data from any personal information manager you use. Most e-mail and organizer programs, such as Outlook, Netscape mail, and Eudora, have an export or backup feature to save this information to files.

▶ Decide where you want to copy the backup files. If your old PC has a CD burner, use it. If not, but the old PC is networked to another PC with enough space on a shared hard drive to hold the backup files, that's the next best choice. A USB memory module can also store relatively large amounts of data.

If none of those apply, you might need to use diskettes. If you have a lot of files, or many large ones, such as music files or downloaded programs, estimate how many diskettes you will need. To do this, select a group of files or one or more folders, and check "Size on disk" in its property sheet (right-click and select Properties). A CD will hold about 700 MB, a diskette about 1.4 MB.

Be sure to copy, not move, the files, so your originals remain intact. You should be able to drag-and-drop files and folders to the backup drive.

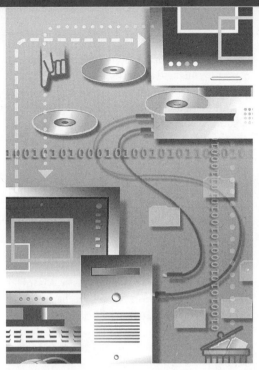

Data transferred to a new personal computer can come from many sources.

Transferring to the new PC. Next, decide on how automated you want the process of setting up the new PC to be.

The first alternative—easiest if only a few removable disks' worth of your old files are needed—is to manually copy your documents and personal files to the corresponding locations on the new PC, creating folders for them if needed. If you've configured the desktop settings to your liking on the old PC, redo those settings. That might not matter if you're also stepping up to a newer version of Windows or Mac OS that doesn't resemble the old one.

▶ Next, in order of complexity, use the Windows XP Files and Settings Transfer Wizard. That can help you through the process of copying personal files, Windows profile and desktop settings, e-mail and contacts from Microsoft Outlook Express, Favorites, and program settings for many common programs. This wizard creates a diskette you run on the old PC that sets it up to automatically copy all these items to the new PC. You can also set up the Transfer Wizard on the old PC directly from a Windows XP installation CD.

The transfer can be over a network, a serial cable, or to a set of transfer diskettes. It can't transfer via a CD burner directly unless the CD-R drive in the old PC has direct-writing software, which uses specially formatted CD-R disks that allow the drive to be

Back up what you don't want to lose. Data loss is unlikely to happen from day to day, but it's more likely when moving large groups of files to another hard drive or system.

treated as a high-capacity diskette drive. (Some names for this kind of software are DirectCD, InCD, and DLA.)

One quirk of the Transfer Wizard is that it assumes you will reinstall all your applications on the new PC, so it transfers the program-launch items on your Start, Programs menu plus shortcuts from the Windows desktop. If you choose not to reinstall some applications, manually delete their launch icons from the new PC.

If your new PC has any of the same applications preinstalled, their transferred launch icons or shortcuts may not work and may have to be deleted, but the preinstalled ones should work. There have been reports of the Transfer Wizard missing some files during a transfer; check each application after you've reinstalled. Make sure it can find all documents or files you expected to transfer. Non-Microsoft applications may require custom settings, such as the default document location, to be corrected after reinstallation.

Moving programs. Moving application programs to a new computer is more complex than reinstalling them. Parts of a Windows application reside in folders other than the program's own folder; configuration data is deeply embedded in a large database called the Registry, which Windows uses to manage the whole PC.

One commercial application, described below, attempts a "one-step" transfer of files, settings, and programs. It is said to work in most cases, but be aware that the underlying technology is so complex and prone to unanticipated problems that the process will probably not go perfectly.

Alohabob PC Relocator *(www.alohabob .com/products/index.asp;* $30 standard, $70 Ultra Control) can transfer recent versions of popular application software over a USB cable (included with the Ultra version); a parallel cable (included with the standard version); a network connection (Ulta version only); or via removable disks. The standard version can't use the network method and doesn't let you select which applications you want to transfer. Alohabob provides extensive technical support. The fee-based premium support is reasonably priced.

HOME NETWORK

If you have broadband Internet service and more than one computer in your home, there's good reason to link them to create a home network. A network allows a single broadband account to be shared throughout the home. (Alas, such network-

ing is impractical with dial-up Internet service—one of several reasons to consider broadband.)

Home networking is also getting a boost from improvements in the range, speed, and cost of wireless networks. If you own a laptop computer that has wireless capability, a wireless network now allows you to surf the Web at broadband speeds from most places in your house, yard, or apartment.

Wired networking is far from obsolete, however, since it still provides the most secure, reliable, and fastest connections. Indeed, for many households the best solution for sharing a broadband connection—or printer, music files, or digital photos—among multiple computers might be a network that includes both wired and wireless.

Such hybrids are easier and cheaper to assemble than they used to be. Routers, the boxes that connect computers and other equipment to the Internet, increasingly support both Ethernet, the primary technology used in wired networks, and Wi-Fi, its wireless counterpart. They typically cost under $100, and are even offered free by some Internet providers when you sign up for broadband service.

Plan your network. You'll probably want to put the router near the source of your broadband service—usually a cable or DSL modem. The router and the modem will be connected by an Ethernet cable. But the connections between the router and the computers in the network might be either wired or wireless.

Choose a wireless router. That is the official term for the models that support both Ethernet and Wi-Fi. Leading brands include D-Link, Netgear, and Linksys. Even if you don't need wireless capability now, acquiring it costs little extra (perhaps $10 or so) compared with a wired model, and you'll avoid having to replace the router if you want to add a wireless device to it in the future.

Stick with the 802.11g wireless standard. Wi-Fi is continually evolving, with new standards designed to increase broadcast range and speed, thus increasing the network's ability to handle new types of information.

The name of the standard is usually listed on the router's package as a letter suffix to the technical term for Wi-Fi, which is 802.11. Currently, the most common standard is known as 802.11g. We think it's the best choice for most people.

Some routers use early variants of the latest Wi-Fi draft standard, 802.11n. Frequently referred to as "MIMO," "Super G," or "pre-n," such models might not be compatible with the actual "n" standard, which is due in late 2006. They also

You may want to choose between the security of a wired home network and the convenience of a wireless one.

require that you buy matching networking adapters, even for computers with built-in 802.11g capability. Consider one of these new routers only if you have range problems that can't be solved in other ways. In our tests, they were better at penetrating walls than 802.11g routers, and some offered data speeds that were twice as fast. But they were just as likely to interfere with (or receive interference from) cordless phones and other devices.

Consider whether you'll share a printer, and how. A network lets you avoid the cost of putting a printer in every room by sharing one. To do this, you can use a printer with built-in network capability. Networked laser printers cost about $275, which is about $100 more than regular models; network-ready color inkjets start at about $130.

It's possible to share a non-networked printer by attaching it to the network via a print server, a device that costs $70 to $100 and is the size of a large paperback. You can even find a print server built into your wireless router. But when we tested two of them, they interfered with some printer-management software. Any PC connected to a printer can also serve as a print server for the other computers on the network, though you must leave that computer on when you're printing.

Check to see if you need to buy adapters. Every computer on your network will require an adapter to allow it to communicate with the network; the question is whether it already has one built in. If you're using Ethernet to connect a computer bought within the past three years or so, the adapter will most likely be built into the unit. The same applies to recent-vintage laptops, which should have built-in 802.11g capability.

If you need to buy a network adapter for your desktop, you can choose either an internal PCI-card version, which requires opening the computer case for installation, or a USB version, which plugs into a USB port. Laptops can use either a PC-card or USB adapter. In all cases, the cost should be no more than $60.

Think twice about professional installation. Computer retailers might try to sell you on professional installation of your new network, starting at a cost of $150 or so. Today's networks are so easy to set up that you shouldn't take them up on the offer if you're comfortable with technology. Network gear usually comes with instructions and access to free 24/7 technical support. And you can always go back to the retailer for help in troubleshooting the network if necessary.

You don't need special expertise to network home computers.

Still, if you have a low tolerance for high-tech frustration, there are a variety of installation services at your disposal. Your options include the phone-based technical support offered by many retailers, in-store specialists (like the Geek Squad "precincts" inside Best Buy stores), remote-control software by PlumChoice (*www.plumchoice.com*), and having a technician come to your home to set everything up.

Most vendors offer multiple installation options. Dell, for instance, has extensive, easy-to-follow network set-up instructions on its Web site. Dell and most other retailers also offer phone set-up support, online FAQ (frequently asked questions), support chat areas, the ability to talk online with a technician, and in-home service.

Although rates will vary depending on where you live, expect to pay about $150 to wirelessly link one PC to a router (and to the rest of your network, if necessary) or $200 for two PCs.

Protect your wireless connection. Wi-Fi's greatest strength is also its weakness. Virtually every network action you take, whether downloading Web pages or printing files, is broadcast a few hundred feet in every direction. In closely spaced homes or apartment buildings, that can be a serious security problem. The most common consequence of using an unsecured wireless network is that a neighbor can encroach upon your broadband connection to surf the Web or send e-mail. That might sound harmless, but it's not if the poacher engages in illegal activities or hogs your bandwidth. A hacker might go further by stealing personal information right off your hard drive or turning your

Computer retailers might try to sell you on professional installation starting at a cost of $150 or so. Don't take them up on their offer if you're comfortable with technology.

computer into a high-speed spamming machine.

Here are some steps for protecting your wireless network:

Activate encryption. Encryption makes all wireless communications look like gibberish to outsiders. No encryption is 100 percent safe. But a technology called Wi-Fi Protected Access (WPA) offers the best protection against hackers. Another, Wired Equivalent Privacy (WEP), will prevent most neighbors from using your connection. But it won't stop a determined hacker. Make sure your network personal ID and password are hacker resistant. They should each be at least 10 characters long and include both letters and numbers.

Change your router's default password. All routers protect their system settings and other controls with factory-set user names and passwords. Since most hackers know them, you should change them at the same time you set up your network.

Disguise your network. Wi-Fi networks continually broadcast a signal called a security-set identifier (SSID) so that any Wi-Fi-equipped computer can find them when it comes within range. You should change the factory-assigned SSID, which gives away more details about your network than it should. Make sure the one you choose is not based on a password or other personal information. You can also prevent hackers from seeing your network by disabling SSID broadcast. But that will also make it harder for you to troubleshoot your network.

SAVE YOUR COMPUTER FROM ONLINE ATTACK

Fight back against computer viruses, spyware, spam, and phishing

Spyware could be on your computer right now and you might not even know it.

Innovative online technologies and the increased availability of fast broadband connections have made the Internet more alluring than ever. But the Web is no longer the urbane information motorway it was five years ago. It's more like a no-holds-barred raceway teeming with unsavory drivers and hardly a police car in sight. Your computer may be at risk of assault through e-mail, Web sites, messaging services, and downloads.

In our 2005 State of the Net survey, we found that American consumers invested more than $2.6 billion in antivirus and Internet-security software over a two-year period ending in 2005, but they spent more than $9 billion over the same period for computer repairs, parts, and replacements to solve problems caused by viruses and spyware. Those problems were so extensive that they prompted almost 8 percent of all consumer computer purchases during that period.

Things haven't improved much since then. The national price tag for cyberinsecurity remains staggeringly high. Because of viruses and spyware, Americans spent at least $7.8 billion for computer repairs, parts, and replacements over the past two years, according to the 2006 Consumer Reports State of the Net, the third annual survey of online activity and threats conducted by the Consumer Reports National Research Center.

A recent rise in prosecutions of online perpetrators might convince you that it's now less likely that you'll suffer computer damage, financial loss, or both due to Internet threats. In fact, according to the survey, your odds of becoming a cybervictim are about 1 in 3, the same as a year ago.

The good news is that there are effective meas-

ures you can take to protect your computer and your data. Through safer online practices and the use of Internet-security software, you can greatly reduce your exposure online.

THREATS ON THE INTERNET

Make no mistake: If you neglect to take the necessary online precautions, your computer runs a substantially higher risk of damage caused by a virus, worm, or spyware. Here's a rundown of the most prevalent online threats and how you can best defend yourself, and your computer, against them. (Note that most commercial antivirus and antispyware programs charge you an annual fee—from $10 to $40—to renew your subscription after the first year.)

Viruses and worms. These are the most destructive of all online hazards. At one time viruses and worms were the product of techno-geek malcontents, but they are increasingly used for criminal purposes. Typically, a virus will infiltrate a PC via an e-mail attachment or a file downloaded from an illicit Web site. Once it has seized control of your computer, the virus could destroy critical files or disable your system, and it can spread to other computers by attaching itself to files and e-mail messages.

A worm is similar to a virus both in design and maliciousness, but unlike a virus, it can spread unaided from one computer to another using your system's file-transport features. A worm's ability to replicate itself on your computer makes these pieces of code potentially more dangerous than viruses. Instead of spreading one copy at a time, as a virus does, an infected computer can send out hundreds or even thousands of copies of a worm in a very short time.

In addition to corrupting your computer's data, some viruses and worms allow hackers to use your computer to send large volumes of spam or attack specific Web sites. Broadband users in our survey were significantly more likely to be infected with a virus or worm than those with dial-up service (likely due to a broadband connection's "always on" state). Of those infected, 46 percent suffered noticeable operating problems or permanently lost files.

Fortunately, there is no shortage of effective

antivirus software on the market. Of the 12 programs we tested, we found Bit DeFender Standard (*www.bitdefender.com*; $30) and Kaspersky Lab's Anti-Virus Personal (*www.kaspersky.com*; $50) to offer the greatest ease of use and comprehensive virus protection. Bit DeFender also scans instant messages.

Spyware. This is a fast-growing and complex threat. As the Federal Trade Commission defines it, spyware gathers data from your PC and may transmit that information or assert control over your PC without your knowledge or consent. By that standard, adware—which interferes with Web browsing by popping up paid advertisements—is spyware if it is installed without proper consent. But often, consent is obtained deceptively or not at all.

Whatever the name, it can infiltrate your computer through e-mail attachments, files downloaded from Web sites, and instant-messaging programs. A common way to unwittingly infect your PC with such software is to download free games, utilities, or ad-supported software; the spyware piggybacks on the freebie. Some sites alert you to the extras, but such notice isn't always prominent or explicit.

Companies that produce and use so-called adware make no apologies. "The bargain is, we'll

Online precautions can lower the risk that your identity will be stolen.

What You Can Do

Good habits help keep your computer healthy and data safe

Protection software isn't perfect, so you should take additional precautions to reduce your vulnerability to online dangers. Here are the measures our experts consider most effective:

Upgrade your operating system. If you use Windows XP, enable the automatic Windows Update feature if you haven't already done so. Go to *www.microsoft.com /protect* to download and install Service Pack 2, which offers enhanced security. Consider upgrading to the next version of Windows—Vista—when it comes out with more security features. For earlier versions of Windows, run Windows Update from the Start menu.

Even though the vast majority of viruses and spyware programs have targeted Windows-based PCs, it doesn't hurt to keep your Mac up to date via the Software Update Control Panel. Also, don't forget to regularly update your Web browser and other major software using the manufacturers' update instructions or features.

Use a firewall. A hardware or software firewall is essential if you're using a high-speed (broadband) Internet connection. (Use the built-in firewall protection found in Windows XP or Mac OS if needed, but you'd probably be better off upgrading to a stand-alone package.) There are a few good software firewalls available free of charge, such as SpyBot Search and Destroy 1.4 (*www.spybot.info*), although most cost $30 to $40. The firewall should provide both incoming and outgoing protection. If you have a home network, your router probably has a built-in hardware firewall. Change its default user name and password and disable "remote administration" to prevent hackers from seizing control of it.

Adjust your browser's security settings. If you use Internet Explorer 6, keep its security level at medium or higher to block Web sites from downloading programs without your authorization or automatically running Windows Activex scripts. Internet Explorer 7 has improved security features, so consider upgrading.

Use a different browser. Since most types of viruses, worms, and spyware applications are specifically written for Internet Explorer, you can cut some of the potential risks by surfing with a non-Microsoft browser, such as Firefox or Opera (both are available free).

Consider an ISP or e-mail provider that offers security. AOL, EarthLink, MSN, and Yahoo offer spam filtering and virus scanning for e-mail at no extra charge for their subscribers. Use them as one layer of a multilayer defense. Check other ISP sites to find out what they provide. Many ISPs now offer full antivirus and firewall software free.

Use antivirus software. You can obtain additional virus protection from ISPs, directly from a manufacturer's site, or at a retail store. Enable the auto-protect and automatic update features and keep your subscription current.

Use more than one antispyware program. None of the products we've tested catches every spyware variant. Using more than one program boosts your coverage,

Software included with a computer is the first step in guarding your files and information.

even if the second product is a free one (try Microsoft's free AntiSpyware beta from *www.microsoft.com/protect*). If you use more than one program, enable the real-time protection for only one product. Keep your subscription to new spyware definitions current and regularly update the definitions or use the automatic update.

Regularly back up personal files. This safeguards your data in case of a security problem. Consider using a plug-in external hard drive as your storage, so that if the computer becomes disabled, you'll already have your files off the machine.

Exercise caution when downloading. Download only from online sources you trust. Be wary of ad-sponsored or "free" screen savers, games, videos, toolbars, music and movie file-sharing programs, and other purported giveaways; they probably include spyware that may damage your PC if it gets through your security. Children who share and download files should do so on a PC that doesn't contain

confidential information or valuable data, such as financial records.

Avoid short passwords. To foil password-cracking software, use passwords that are at least eight characters long, including at least one numeral and a symbol, such as #. Avoid common words, personal information such as your birthday or street address, and using the same password for important e-commerce sites. With a broadband connection, shut off the computer or modem when you aren't using it. Don't post your e-mail address in its normal form on a publicly accessible Web page. Use a form, such as "Jane AT isp DOT com," that spammers' address-harvesting software can't easily read. And never disclose a password online.

Use e-mail cautiously. Never open an attachment that you weren't expecting, even from someone you know. If you use Microsoft Outlook, disable the preview pane to prevent accidental infection from harmful e-mail messages. Never respond to e-mail asking for personal information, and don't reply to spam or click on its "unsubscribe" link; that tells the sender that your e-mail address is valid. Forward fraudulent spam to the Anti-Phishing Working Group at *reportphishing @antiphishing.org*.

Use more than one e-mail address. Use one e-mail address for family and friends, another for everyone else. You can get a free address from Hotmail, Yahoo, or a disposable-forwarding-address service such as SpamMotel. When an address attracts too much spam, drop it. Instead of an e-mail address like janedoe@isp.com, select one with embedded digits, like jane8doe2@isp.com. Report spam to your ISP to improve its filtering.

Don't buy anything promoted in a spam message. Even if the offer isn't a scam, your patronage can help finance and encourage spam.

Look for secure Web sites. To check whether a site is secure with most browsers, look for an icon of an unbroken key or a lock that's closed, golden, or glowing. It will be in your browser's window (usually at the bottom), not within the Web page itself. Double-click on the lock to display the site's certificate, and be sure it matches the company you think you're connected to. Also, make sure the site's address begins with "https:".

give you free software in exchange for your agreement to receive ads," says D. Reed Freeman, chief privacy officer for Claria Corp., an Internet marketing company. Until recently, Claria's adware had been bundled with the popular free version of Kazaa file-sharing software.

But figuring out exactly what you're agreeing to can be difficult. End-user license agreements often contain thousands of words of legalese, and users typically agree to the terms without even reading them. In some cases, the explanations are confusing; in others, there is little or no mention of how the adware can affect your computer. Adware has even been known to come packaged in the software bundles found on some new PCs. Then there is the issue of your 12-year-old agreeing to download software to your computer.

Spyware can track online activities, such as which sites you visit, and report them to marketers. Some of the most widespread pests generate pop-up ads and interfere with your browser, sending you to sites you didn't want to visit. A spyware infestation on your computer will significantly slow down its performance and can even bring things to a standstill. Microsoft estimates that spyware is responsible for up to half of all PC crashes. There are other varieties of spyware as well. Some types can capture screen shots of, say, your electronically filed tax return, online checkbook, and household budget or assets inventory. Other variants can even eavesdrop via your PC's webcam and microphone.

Companies are constantly creating new spyware variants. Computer Associates, maker of eTrust PestPatrol Anti-Spyware, says 350 new samples and 250 variations on existing samples turn up each week. "The mutation rate for spyware is high because companies are behind this, and they are actively working not to be detected by spyware pro-

grams," says Sam Curry, a vice president at Computer Associates.

In addition to avoiding free downloads and not clicking on offers generated by pop-up ads, you should protect your computer with at least one spyware blocker (since the problem is so prevalent and manufacturers tend to focus on different variants, some people use two or more programs). Of the 13 spyware-blocking programs we looked at, F-Secure's Anti-Spyware 2006 (*www.f-secure.com*, $60) and Webroot's Spy Sweeper (*www.webroot.com*; $25) tied for best overall score. Spybot Search & Destroy (*www.spybot.info*) was the highest-rated free anti-spyware program. Pop-up blockers are also incorporated into the popular Internet Explorer toolbars offered by Google and Yahoo; the latter also provides built-in spyware scanning.

Spam and phishing scams. Spam accounts for the majority of Internet e-mail. Our survey results show that the most common complaint about spam is the time it takes. Everyone knows it takes time to sort through it and delete it, and even more time for those with a slower dial-up connection.

The criminal variant of spam, phishing e-mail, appears to come from a financial institution or company requesting personal information such as a password or PIN code. You're asked to click on a link but when you do, you're connected to a fraudulent look-alike Web site. Fifty-three percent of the Internet users we surveyed who received spam said they had received what looked like a fraudulent solicitation.

More than 12,000 active fraudulent Web sites were operating in May 2006, a 31 percent jump from only three months earlier, according to the Anti-Phishing Working Group, an industry association. Symantec says its antifraud filters blocked an average of 40 million phishing e-mail messages per

Spyware can track online activities, such as which sites you visit, and report them to marketers. Some of the most widespread pests generate pop-up ads and interfere with your browser, sending you to sites you didn't want to visit.

Antispam, antivirus, and antispyware programs are must-haves to avoid online threats. See Ratings, p. 180-182.

week in late 2005, compared with 21 million per week at the beginning of the year.

The latest development in phishing is the use of a seemingly blank e-mail, without either a text message or a suspicious link. When you open it on an unprotected PC, however, a silent script is released onto your computer that does nothing until the next time you try to bank online or access a password-protected site. Then it automatically redirects you to the fraudulent site. Even more insidious is a script that operates while you use the

legitimate banking Web site, sending your personal information to identity thieves.

Two effective weapons against spam that we've seen are the spam-blocking capabilities incorporated into Microsoft's Outlook 2003 (*www.microsoft.com*; $90) and Apple's OS 10.4 Mail (*www.apple.com*; $130). Our Quick Picks for add-on packages are a free one, Anti-Spam Pilot from Trend Micro (*www.trendmicro.com*), which works with popular e-mail programs, and Allume Systems' SpamCatcher, which works with any e-mail program.

PDAS ARE MUCH MORE THAN ADDRESS BOOKS

Some handhelds are phones, Net appliances, and video players

Personal digital assistants like the Palm LifeDrive have become personal media centers.

PDAs can store thousands of phone numbers, appointments, tasks, and notes. All models can exchange, or synchronize, information with a full-sized computer. To do this, you connect the PDA to your computer via a cradle or cable. For models that run on rechargeable batteries, the cradle doubles as a charger. Infrared, Bluetooth, and Wi-Fi (wireless) let you synchronize with a computer without wires or a cradle.

Most PDAs can be made to work with both Windows and Macintosh computers, but PDAs with the Pocket PC operating system usually require third-party software for Macs. PDAs with Wi-Fi (wireless) capability can access the Internet. Those without can with the addition of a separately purchased modem. Most PDAs can record your voice, play videos, display digital photos, and hold maps, city guides, and books.

WHAT'S AVAILABLE

Most PDAs on the market are the familiar tablet-with-stylus type that feature a squarish display screen, a design pioneered by Palm Inc. Today the main choices are models that use the Palm operating system (OS)—mostly Palm models—and Pocket PC devices from companies like Dell and Hewlett-Packard. The latter use a stripped-down version of Microsoft Windows. A few PDAs use a proprietary operating system. Hewlett-Packard, Nokia, Palm, Samsung, and Sony Ericsson offer units that combine a cell phone and a PDA, often referred to as smartphones.

Palm OS systems. Equipped with software to link with Windows and (for Palm-brand units) Macintosh computers, Palm units and their clones have a simple user interface. You use a stylus to enter data on the units by tapping an onscreen keyboard or writing in shorthand known as Graffiti. Some models have a tiny tactile keyboard. Or you can download data from your computer.

Most Palm OS-based PDAs can synchronize with a variety of desktop e-mail programs, such as Outlook Express and Eudora. (Palm models with VersaMail software are good at handling e-mail with attachments.) And all include a basic personal information management (PIM) application. Palm OS units are easy to use, although navigation between different programs is cumbersome because of the operating system's "single tasking" nature.

Most models make it difficult or impossible to replace the battery yourself. And beyond the warranty period, you can't be sure the manufacturer will do it for you.

Most Palm OS-based models have expansion slots that let you add memory or attach separately purchased accessories. All Palm OS-based PDAs can be enhanced by adding third-party software applications—the more free memory that a model comes with, the more software it can accommodate. There is a large body of Palm OS-compatible freeware, shareware, and commercial software available for download at such sites as *www.palmgear.com*. Many Palm models come with Documents To Go—word-processing and spreadsheet software similar to that used in Pocket PCs but more versatile. Price: $100 to $400.

Palm's top-of-the-line model, the LifeDrive, combines a 3.7-GB hard drive with many of the best features of the Pocket PC and Palm OS operating systems. When it's connected to a Windows PC, you can drag and drop files to the LifeDrive's hard drive, even on PCs that don't have Palm's desktop software installed. It's also handy for storing photos from a digital camera that uses a MMC/SD (MultiMedia/SecureDigital) memory card and for listening to MP3 music.

Pocket PC systems. These resemble Palm OS-based models but are more like miniature computers. They have a processor with extra horsepower and come with familiar applications such as a word processor and a spreadsheet. Included is a scaled-down version of Internet Explorer, plus voice recording and perhaps some financial functions. The included e-mail program handles Word and Excel attachments easily. Also standard is an application that plays MP3 music files, as well as Microsoft Reader, an eBook application.

As you might expect, all the application software included in a Pocket PC integrates well with the Windows computer environment. You need to purchase third-party software to use a Mac. And you'll need Microsoft Office programs such as Word, Excel, and Outlook on your computer to exchange data with a PDA. Pocket PCs have a color display and rechargeable lithium-ion batteries. Unlike most Palm OS-based PDAs, replacing the battery of most Pocket PCs is usually straightforward. Price: $200 to $600.

Ultra Mobile PCs (UMPCs). These are small, fully functional computers that run a version of Microsoft's Windows XP. An early model, the Samsung Q1, released in early 2006, has a 7-inch display, measuring 5½ inches x 9 inches x 1 inch and weighing 1.7 pounds. It lacks a built-in keyboard and cost about $1,100.

FEATURES THAT COUNT

Whichever operating system your PDA uses, you might need to install programs in your computer to enable the PDA to synchronize with it. This software lets you swap data with leading PIM programs such as Lotus Organizer or Microsoft Outlook.

All PDAs have the tools for basic tasks: a **calendar** to keep track of your appointments, **contact/address software** for addresses and phone numbers, **tasks/to-do lists** for reminders and keeping track of errands, and a **calculator.** A **notes/memo function** lets you make quick notes to yourself. Other capabilities include **word-processing, spreadsheet,** and **e-mail** functions. A **voice recorder,** which uses a built-in microphone and speaker, works like a tape recorder. **MP3 playback** lets you listen to digital-music files stored in that format, and a **picture viewer** lets you look at digital photos. A few models also include a built-in **digital camera** and **keyboard**.

A PDA's **processor** is the system's brain. In general, the higher the processing speed of this chip, the faster the PDA will execute tasks—and the more expensive it will be. But higher-speed processors may require more battery power and thus deplete batteries more

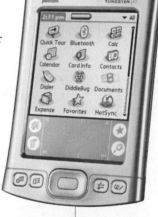

Many PDAs have touch displays, usually with onscreen keyboards.

quickly. Processing speeds are 200 to 624 megahertz (MHz), and models typically have 16 to 256 megabytes (MB) of user memory. Even the smallest amount in that range should be more than enough for most people.

Nearly every PDA offers an **expansion slot** for some form of removable memory card: CompactFlash, MultiMedia card (slots also accept SecureDigital cards), or Memory Stick. Models with two expansion slots can accommodate a peripheral device, such as a Wi-Fi wireless networking card and removable memory. If you plan to transfer photos from a digital camera to your PDA, make sure the two devices use the same type of card.

Some PDAs offer **wireless connectivity.** Models with a capability known as **Bluetooth** can connect wirelessly over short distances to a properly equipped computer or peripheral such as a printer or modem. Models with **Wi-Fi** can connect over medium distances to a Wi-Fi-enabled home network or to the Internet at "hot spots" in certain airports, coffee shops, and hotels. A PDA combined with a **cell phone** can make voice calls or directly connect to the Internet via a wireless Internet service provider. It's possible for a single PDA to have more than one of these types of wireless connectivity.

HOW TO CHOOSE

Consider your ties to a computer. Pocket PCs provide a Windows-like interface that allows simple PC-to-PDA file transfer with drag-and-drop capability. They're also more convenient than Palm OS models for setting up a Wi-Fi (wireless) e-mail connection. Most have replaceable batteries along with accessible flash memory to which you can back up data.

Palm OS models run a wider range of third-party software applications than do Pocket PCs. For the basics, they're still easier to use. While most PDAs can sync with Macs, only Palm models do so out of the box. Programs such as Missing Sync (*www.markspace.com*) and PocketMac (*www.pocketmac.net*) support Palm OS PDAs from Garmin and others, as well as Pocket PCs that run older versions of that operating system, such as the Asus A730W. Currently, neither Missing Sync nor PocketMac support PDAs that run Microsoft Windows Mobile 5.0. Both are priced under $50.

Small size vs. extra features. As a rule, a model with a larger display or physical keyboard won't be the lightest or smallest. A PDA with two slots for memory and peripherals is more expandable but will tend to be larger.

 ConsumerReports.org | Shop directly from CR online

The Ratings in the back of this book tell you about the best products to buy, but you're on your own in finding the best deal. That's why CONSUMER REPORTS has set up a way to shop for the best prices from reputable retailers online.

ConsumerReports.org's Shop Online tool offers members easy access to retailers of a variety of products—including printers and PDAs. Just click on the $ icon in the Ratings online for the product that interests you; you will leave Consumer Reports.org and be linked directly to Yahoo Shopping. CONSUMER REPORTS has asked Yahoo to sort products from online retailers by price, lowest to highest. And to help protect your purchase, only those online retailers who qualify for inclusion in Yahoo's Buyer Protection Plan are listed.

If you don't already subscribe, you can use the Shop Online service by activating the 30-day free subscription to *www.Consumer Reports.org* offered on the inside front cover of this guide.

REFERENCE &RATINGS

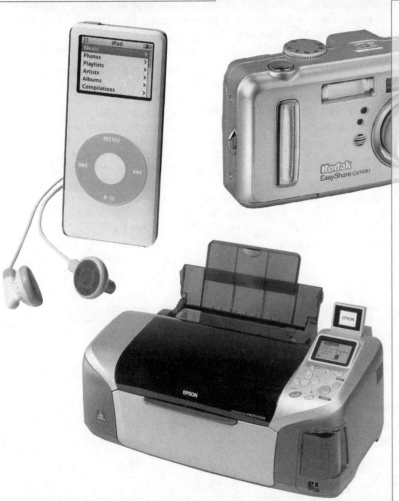

RATINGS

BRAND LOCATOR

GLOSSARY

INDEX

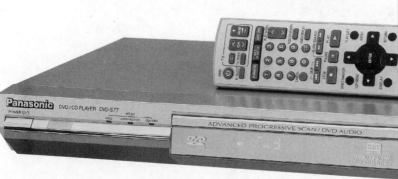

CAMCORDERS

CR Quick Recommendations

Camcorders

You can expect a digital camcorder to deliver very good video, as our Ratings scores demonstrate. Many of the digital camcorders that record directly onto small DVD discs were ranked at or near the top of the Ratings. However, that doesn't automatically make them the best choice. As the Ratings show, most DVD models were not markedly better than many camcorders that use MiniDV tape. The MiniDV camcorders win on price, making them the type that most people should consider first. The DVD models are for people who want ease of playback above all else.

Most camcorders weigh about a pound, give or take a few ounces. As camcorders get smaller and lighter, image-stabilization features become more important. A lightweight camcorder is harder to hold steady than a heavy one. Fortunately, most did an excellent job of minimizing the shakes.

Analog camcorders are a dying breed. Only one model, the Sony CCD-TRV138, at $235, remains in the Ratings, and it's not in the same league as the digitals.

QUICK PICKS
Best values in digital tape:

4 Canon ZR200, $315
13 Sony DCR-TRV280, $275

The Canon ZR200 lacks still-image capture. (A newer sibling, the Canon ZR700, and the similar Canon ZR500 and Canon ZR600 are lighter and smaller but scored lower overall.) The D8 Sony DCR-TRV280, a CR Best Buy, is feature-laden but some thumb-activated buttons are not located well and it has mediocre sound quality. JVC also has some high-scoring, low-priced models; however Sony (D8 and MiniDV) has been the most reliable brand among digital camcorders.

Best value in a DVD camcorder:

5 Sony DCR-DVD92, $500

The Sony DCR-DVD92 has very good picture quality, with an excellent image stabilizer and autofocus. It also has good picture quality in low light if manual settings are used. The location of its strap can make DVD access difficult. We don't have enough data to judge the reliability of DVD camcorders.

If small size is paramount:

16 Sanyo Xacti C6, $495

This model is as small as a subcompact digital camera and provides much better video quality (albeit at a higher price than most subcompact cameras). It captures about 41 minutes of high-quality video onto a 1-GB SD memory card. It also takes 6.1-megapixel still images and has very good image stabilization.

For a model that requires no recording media:

11 Toshiba GSC-60, $750
23 JVS Everio G Series GZ-MG77, $765

These camcorders resemble MiniDV models but capture and store video digitally onto a built-in, nonremovable hard drive. The Toshiba GSC-R60 and the similar GSC-R30 record 13.5 hours and 6.7 hours, respectively, of very good video to the drive (audio quality was only fair, however). Images from the JVC GZ-MG77 were a little worse in quality than the Toshibas—merely good—but the JVC's audio was a little better and the unit has an excellent image stabilizer.

Ratings

Excellent ● Very good ◓ Good ○ Fair ◒ Poor ●

In performance order, within categories.

Key number	Brand & model	Price	Format	Overall score (0-100)	Picture quality	Ease of use	Image stabilizer	Audio quality	Weight (lbs.)	Digital still capable	Optical zoom	LCD size (in.)	Battery life (min.)	Full auto switch	Quick review	Built-in light	AV input	Microphone input
DIGITAL MODELS																		
1	**Canon** DC40	$770	DVD-R/RW	69	●	○	◒	◓	1.2	●	10x	2.7	75	●	●	●		
2	**Hitachi** Ultravision DZGX20A	570	DVD-RAM, DVD-R	68	◓	○	●	◒	1.3	●	10x	2.5	125					●
3	**Panasonic** VDR-M75	630	DVD-RAM, DVD-R	68	◓	○	◓	◓	1.1	●	10x	2.5	125			●	●	●
4	**Canon** ZR200	315	MiniDV	65	◓	◓	◓	◒	1.1	●	20x	2.4	85	●	●		●	
5	**Sony** DCR-DVD92	500	DVD-R, DVD-RW, DVD+RW	65	◓	○	●	◓	1.1	●	20x	2.5	80	●	●		●	
6	**Sony** DCR-HC90	630	MiniDV	65	◓	○	◓	◓	1.1	●	10x	2.7	80	●			●	
7	**Canon** Optura 50	445	MiniDV	63	◓	○	◓	◒	1.3	●	10x	2.5	75	●			●	
8	**Hitachi** UltraVision DZGX3200A	585	DVD-RAM, DVD-R, DVD-RW, DVD+RW	63	◓	○	◓	◒	1.2	●	10x	2.7	125					●
9	**Sony** DCR-HC96	640	MiniDV	63	◓	○	◓	◓	1.2	●	10x	2.7	80	●			●	
10	**Sony** DCR-PC55	500	MiniDV	62	◓	○	◓	◒	0.8	●	10x	3	95	●			●	
11	**Toshiba** GSC-R60	750	Hard Disk	62	◓	○	○	◒	1	●	10x	2.5	110	●	●			
12	**Sony** DCR-PC1000	980	MiniDV	61	◓	◒	●	◓	1.0	●	10x	2.7	80	●			●	
13	**Sony** DCR-TRV280	275	D8	61	◓	○	●	◓	2		20x	2.5	80	●			●	
14	**Hitachi** Ultravision DZMV730A	370	DVD-RAM, DVD-R	60	○	○	◓	○	1.1	●	16x	2.5	70				●	●
15	**Sony** DCR-DVD405	680	DVD-R/RW, DVD+RW	60	◓	○	◓	◓	1.3	●	10x	2.7	85	●			●	
16	**Sanyo** Xacti C6	495	External Memory	59	◓	○	◓	◒	0.4	●	5x	2	60					
17	**Panasonic** PV-GS31	290	MiniDV	58	○	○	◒	◒	1	●	26x	2.5	85	●	●			

Expert • Independent • Nonprofit

Ratings (continued)

Excellent ●   Very good ◕   Good ○   Fair ◔   Poor ●

In performance order, within categories.

Key number	Brand & model	Price	Format	Overall score (0–100)	Picture quality	Ease of use	Image stabilizer	Audio quality	Weight (lbs.)	Digital still capable	Optical zoom	LCD size (in.)	Battery life (min.)	Full auto switch	Quick review	Built-in light	AV input	Microphone input
DIGITAL MODELS																		
18	**Sony** DCR-HC46	$440	MiniDV	58	○	○	●	◕	1	●	12x	2.7	100	●	●			
19	**Panasonic** VDR-D200	490	DVD-RAM, DVD-R, DVD-RW	57	◕	○	○	◕	1.2	●	30x	2.5	120	●		●		
20	**Sony** DCR-DVD7	465	DVD-R, DVD-RW, DVD+RW	56	◕	◕	●	○	0.9	●	10x	2.5	90	●	●	●		
21	**Canon** Elura 100	350	MiniDV	55	◕	○	○	◕	0.9	●	20x	2.7	140	●	●	●	●	●
22	**Canon** ZR700	350	MiniDV	55	○	○	◕	◕	0.9	●	25x	2.7	90	●	●	●	●	●
23	**JVC** Everio G Series GZ-MG77	765	Hard Disk	55	○	○	●	◕	0.9	●	10x	2.7	90					
24	**JVC** Ultra-Compact Series GR-DF550	365	MiniDV	55	○	○	○	◕	1.1	●	15x	2.5	60	●	●	●	●	
25	**JVC** GR-D395	330	MiniDV	53	◕	◕	○	◕	1.2	●	32x	2.5	180	●	●			
26	**Panasonic** PV-GS180	500	MiniDV	53	○	○	◕	◕	1.1	●	10x	2.5	70					●
27	**Samsung** SC-D453	280	MiniDV	53	○	○	○	◕	0.9	●	10x	2.5	80					●
28	**Panasonic** PV-GS39	315	MiniDV	50	○	○	◕	◕	1	●	30x	2.7	80					●
29	**Sony** DCR-DVD305	545	DVD-R/RW, DVD+RW	50	○	○	○	◕	1	●	12x	2.7	75					
30	**Samsung** DuoCam SC-D6550	450	MiniDV	49	○	○	◕	◕	1.2	●	10x	2.5	90					●
31	**Sanyo** Xacti HD1	720	External Memory	34	◕	○	◕	◕	0.5		10x	2.2	60		●			
32	**Samsung** SC-DC164	405	DVD-R/RW, DVD+RW	33	◕	○	◕	◕	1.1	●	33x	2.7	65					●
33	**Samsung** SC-D365	300	MiniDV	30	◕	○	●	◕	0.9	●	33x	2.7	80	●	●	●	●	●
ANALOG MODELS																		
34	**Sony** CCD-TRV138	235	Hi8	51	○	○	NA	◕	2		20x	2.5	115	●		●		

Guide to the Ratings

Overall score mainly reflects picture quality and ease of use. **Picture quality** is based on the judgments of trained panelists who viewed static images shot in good light at standard speed (SP) for tape and "fine" mode for DVDs. **Ease of use** takes into account ergonomics, weight, how accurately the viewers reflected the scene being shot, and LCD contrast. **Image stabilizer** reflects how well the model reduces the shakes in a scene. Most stabilizers are electronic, and some of those are digital (digital stabilization is used on both analog and digital camcorders). Some camcorders have optical stabilization. All three types can be effective, though using a tripod is the surest way to get a steady image. **"NA"** indicates the model lacks this feature.

Audio quality represents accuracy using the built-in microphone, plus freedom from noise and flutter. **Weight** is measured in pounds, and includes the battery and tape (or disc). **Optical zoom** allows the camcorder to fill the frame with far-away objects at the touch of a button. An optical zoom rated at 16x means the camcorder can magnify the image up to 16 times the normal size. **LCD size,** measured diagonally, typically ranges from 2 to 4 inches. **Battery life** is the manufacturer's statement, in minutes, of how long the camcorder can record images continuously with the LCD viewer in use. **Price** is approximate retail. *Based on tests posted on ConsumerReports.org in July 2006, with updated prices and availability.*

REFERENCE & RATINGS

CAMCORDERS

Profiles Model-by-Model

DIGITAL

1 Canon DC40 Very good overall. Excellent picture quality at standard speed and good low-light picture quality. VCR controls are very easy to use. Image stabilizer only slightly effective. Must use provided proprietary cable for S-video connection. Lacks FireWire port.

2 Hitachi Ultravision DZGX20A Very good picture quality and image stabilizer worked very well. Very good picture quality in low-light. A relatively light model that didn't sit in the hand well. Fair audio quality. Uses proprietary A/V cable. Discontinued, but may still be available.

3 Panasonic VDR-M75 Very good picture quality, image stabilizer worked very well. A relatively light model that didn't sit in the hand well. Fair audio quality. Uses proprietary A/V cable. Discontinued, but may still be available.

4 Canon ZR200 Easy to use and hold. Very good picture quality. Image stabilizer and autofocus are excellent. Fair audio quality. Similar model: ZR300.

5 Sony DCR-DVD92 Very good picture quality, with excellent image stabilizer and autofocus. Good picture quality in low light if manual settings are used. Strap location can make loading and unloading DVDs hard. Uses proprietary A/V cable.

6 Sony DCR-HC90 A relatively light, feature-laden model with very good picture quality, audio quality and image stabilizer. Thumb-activated buttons were hard to use. Uses proprietary A/V cable. Among digital camcorders, Sony (D8 and MiniDV) has been the most reliable brand.

7 Canon Optura 50 Feature-laden model with very good picture quality. Image stabilizer is excellent, but autofocus failed to work in many situations. Fair audio quality. Sits awkwardly in hand.

8 Hitachi UltraVision DZGX3200A Very good overall. Easy to use, overall. Determining how to load the disc or battery is obvious. Image stabilizer and autofocus worked very well, but recorded audio had noticeable background noise. Must use provided proprietary cable for S-video connection. Lacks FireWire port.

9 Sony DCR-HC96 Sony (D8 and MiniDV) has been the most reliable brand.

10 Sony DCR-PC55 Very good picture quality. Image stabilizer and autofocus are excellent. Fair audio quality. Uses proprietary A/V cable. Some connectors not on camcorder, only on docking station. Strap design doesn't hold camcorder to hand. Among digital camcorders, Sony (D8 and MiniDV) has been the most reliable brand. Discontinued, but may still be available.

11 Toshiba GSC-R60 Very good overall but poor picture quality in low-light. Determining how to load the tape or battery isn't obvious. Background noise is noticeable in recorded audio. Audio noise was also recorded during zooming. Uses proprietary A/V cable. Lacks manual aperture control, audio fade, video fade, and FireWire port. Similar model: GSC-R30.

12 Sony DCR-PC1000 Very good picture quality and image stabilizer worked very well. A relatively light model that was hard to hold and use. Uses proprietary A/V cable. Among digital camcorders, Sony (D8 and MiniDV) has been the most reliable brand.

13 Sony DCR-TRV280 A CR Best Buy Feature-laden model with very good picture quality. Image stabilizer and autofocus are excellent. Fair audio quality.

Some thumb-activated buttons not located well. Among digital camcorders, Sony (D8 and MiniDV) has been the most reliable brand.

14 Hitachi Ultravision DZMV730A Good picture quality and image stabilizer worked very well. Good low-light picture quality in 'Auto' mode. A relatively light model that didn't sit in the hand well. Uses proprietary A/V cable. Similar model: Ultravision DZMV750A.

15 Sony DCR-DVD405 Good overall. Image stabilizer and autofocus worked very well. But background noise is noticeable in recorded audio. Audio noise was also recorded during zooming. Uses proprietary A/V cable. Lacks: FireWire port.

16 Sanyo Xacti C6 Good overall. Menu is very easy to use. A relatively light model. Included docking station or proprietary cable required for audio-video connections, including S-video output. Audio had noticeable background noise. Lacks backlight compensation switch, manual aperture control, audio fade, video fade, and FireWire port.

17 Panasonic PV-GS31 Autofocus worked very well and menu is very easy to use. Fits hand well, but thumb activators cramped due to larger battery pack. Fair audio quality. Similar model: PV-GS35.

18 Sony DCR-HC46 Sony (D8 and MiniDV) has been the most reliable brand.

19 Panasonic VDR-D200 Good overall. Must use provided cable for S-video output. But background noise is noticeable in recorded audio. Audio noise was also recorded during zooming. Uses proprietary audio-video cable. Lacks quick review and FireWire port. Similar model: VDR-D100.

Profiles Model-by-Model (continued)

20 Sony DCR-DVD7 Very good picture quality and image stabilizer worked very well. A relatively light model that was hard to hold and use. Uses proprietary A/V cable. Lacks still image digital capture.

21 Canon Elura 100 Good overall. Good low-light picture quality (in 'Auto' mode). But menu is hard to use. Audio had very noticeable background noise. Lacks backlight compensation switch.

22 Canon ZR700 Good overall. But menu is hard to use. Audio had very noticeable background noise. Similar models: ZR500, ZR600.

23 JVC Everio G Series GZ-MG77 Good overall. Image stabilizer and autofocus worked very well. Lacks manual aperture control, quick review, FireWire port, and viewfinder.

24 JVC Ultra-Compact Series GR-DF550 Feature-laden model with good picture quality and good low-light picture quality. A relatively light model that didn't sit in the hand well. Fair audio quality. Discontinued, but may still be available.

25 JVC GR-D395 Good overall. But somewhat hard to use, overall. Determining how to load the tape or battery isn't obvious. VCR controls are difficult to use. Menu is hard to navigate. Audio had noticeable background noise. Similar models: GR-D350, GR-D370, GR-D396.

26 Panasonic PV-GS180 Good overall. Menu is very easy to use. Must use provided cable for S-video output. But image stabilizer only slightly effective. Audio had noticeable background noise.

27 Samsung SC-D453 Good picture quality and image stabilizer. Sits in hand well, but record button is crowded by battery. Fair audio quality. Discontinued, but may still be available.

28 Panasonic PV-GS39 Good overall. Autofocus worked very well. Menu is very easy to use. But image stabilizer only slightly effective. Eyepiece was inaccurate at framing scenes. Audio had noticeable background noise. Similar model: PV-GS59.

29 Sony DCR-DVD305 Good overall. But audio had noticeable background noise. Uses proprietary audio-video cable. Lacks: FireWire port. Similar model: DCR-DVD205.

30 Samsung DuoCam SC-D6550 Duocam that adds a separate lensing system for digital stills. Good picture quality and image stabilizer. Padded strap makes it comfortable to hold. Fair audio quality.

31 Sanyo Xacti HD1 Fair overall. Menu is very easy to use. A relatively light model.

Included docking station or proprietary cable required for audio-video connections, including S-video. But fair picture quality at standard speed. Audio had very noticeable background noise. Noise was in recorded audio when zooming. Lacks backlight compensation switch, audio fade, video fade, FireWire port, and viewfinder.

32 Samsung SC-DC164 Fair overall. Must use provided cable for S-video output. But fair picture quality at standard speed. Image stabilizer only slightly effective. Audio had noticeable background noise. Uses proprietary audio-video cable. Lacks quick review and FireWire port.

33 Samsung SC-D365 Fair overall. Must use provided cable for S-video output. But fair picture quality at standard speed. Image stabilizer not very effective. Determining how to load the tape or battery isn't obvious. Audio had noticeable background noise. Uses proprietary audio-video cable. Similar model: SC-D363.

ANALOG

34 Sony CCD-TRV138 Analog Hi8 model. Autofocus is excellent. Good low-light picture quality. Lacks image stabilizer and digital stills. Some thumb-activated buttons not located well.

Brand Repair History

Readers report on some 35,000 camcorders

This graph shows the percentage of digital and analog camcorders that have been repaired or developed a serious problem that wasn't repaired. We don't have enough reader data to judge the reliability of DVD camcorders. Models within a brand may vary, and design and manufacturing changes may affect reliability. Nevertheless, you can improve your chances of getting a trouble-free camcorder if you choose a brand that has been reliable in the past.

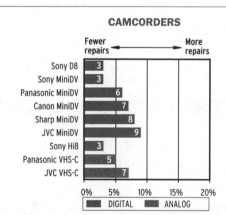

CAMCORDERS

Fewer repairs ← → More repairs

Brand	Value
Sony D8	3
Sony MiniDV	3
Panasonic MiniDV	6
Canon MiniDV	7
Sharp MiniDV	8
JVC MiniDV	9
Sony Hi8	3
Panasonic VHS-C	5
JVC VHS-C	7

0%   5%   10%   15%   20%

■ DIGITAL   ■ ANALOG

Based on 35,181 reader responses to our 2005 Annual Questionnaire about camcorders bought new between 2002 and 2005. Data have been standardized to eliminate differences linked to age and use. Differences of less than 3 points aren't meaningful.

CELL PHONES

CR Quick Recommendations

Cell phones

In the Ratings and in our recommendations we show approximate prices based on a two-year contract. Rebates or "instant savings" can reduce these prices substantially. Sprint Nextel and T-Mobile tend to rely more heavily on these supplemental discounts than other carriers. To find the best price on any phone, check with carriers and retailers, both online and in stores.

All but the Samsungs (21 and 27) and Palm (10) have voice dial for hands-free dialing. The Nokias (15 and 29) lack the convenience of side-mounted volume controls, which are available on all the other models we tested. The Motorolas (24, 28, 30) and the Sony Ericsson (26) are quad-band GSM phones that maximize coverage of the U.S., Europe, and Asia.

QUICK PICKS

Best for Verizon (CDMA):

1 **Motorola E815, $290**
3 **Kyocera KX444, $100**
4 **LG The V, $550**

The Motorola E815 is a top-performing, fully featured advanced phone. Its keypad is easy to read under most lighting conditions, though the display can be hard to see in bright light. It's compatible with Verizon's high-speed EV-DO network, which provides access to video programs and faster Web surfing than with regular cell service. LG's The V is another EV-DO-ready phone that doubles as an e-mail/messaging terminal. Turned on its side, this candy-bar phone flips open to reveal a QWERTY keyboard and larger display that's well-suited for text-based communication. But it's much thicker than most phones. The Kyocera KX444 is a very good basic phone with a simple display that was the easiest to read under any lighting conditions of all the phones we tested. But its bulky rectangular case is cumbersome. It's compatible with Verizon's push-to-talk service.

Best for Sprint (CDMA):

11 **Samsung MM-A800, $500**
13 **Sanyo SCP-200, $175**
16 **Samsung MM-A900, $350**

The Samsung MM-A800 has a high-resolution camera and removable memory card for storing pictures. Its PictBridge interface lets you connect compatible printers via cable to print pictures directly from the camera. But the sliding case is bulky. The Samsung MM-A900 competently stuffs high-speed network access, Bluetooth connectivity and other advanced features into a stylishly thin case. It's the only CDMA phone we've seen that can swap photos, music, and other files with other Bluetooth devices. It's also one of the few phones that can download music from the new cell-phone music services. But battery life is relatively short and internal memory is a puny 48 megabytes. Also, there's no slot for an external memory card, and it lacks the analog backup offered by most CDMA phones. The Sanyo SCP-200 is a good, basic, no-frills phone for use with voice-only plans.

Best for Cingular (GSM):

24 **Motorola Razr V3, $265**
26 **Sony Ericsson W600i, $300**

28 **Motorola V220, $250**

All three phones can make and receive calls on international GSM networks, but unlike CDMA phones, they lack the analog backup that provides better coverage where a digital network is unavailable. The Motorola Razr V3 crams Bluetooth and other advanced phone features into an ultraslim case that slips easily into a tight pocket. Unlike its Verizon cousin, this Razr has a programmable jog dial for instant access to important features. The keypad and display are easy to see in low-light conditions, but just average in bright light. The Motorola V220 is a good basic phone combining very good battery life with solid overall performance. But the display can be hard to read in bright light. The Sony Ericsson W600i has a well-integrated MP3 player that automatically pauses music playback when you answer an incoming call then resumes it when the call ends. As with other Sony Ericsson models, the Bluetooth connection works well with headsets and when transferring pictures and files, but it doesn't work with all hands-free speaker phones. Its 256 megabytes of internal storage can't be expanded with an external memory card, not ideal for a music-enabled phone.

Best for T-Mobile (GSM):

20 **Motorola V360, $200**

Like all GSM phones, this lacks analog backup, but its 850/1900 MHz capability expands domestic coverage. The V360 combines Bluetooth, international roaming, and other advanced features with excellent battery life. Its keypad and display are readable everywhere except in bright light.

Ratings

In performance order, within categories.

	Excellent	Very good	Good	Fair	Poor
	●	◕	○	◔	◑

Key number	Brand & model	Price	Type	Overall score (0-100) P F G VG E	Voice quality: Listening	Voice quality: Talking	Talk time (hr.)	Sensitivity	Ease of use	Easy-to-mute ringer	Speaker phone	Bluetooth	Camera (megapixels)	Analog backup
VERIZON PHONES *Most work on Verizon's or other CDMA networks.*														
1	**Motorola** E815 (Verizon)	$290	Advanced	65	○	◑	4 ¼	◑	◑		●	●	1.0	
2	**LG** VX8100 (Verizon)	275	Advanced	61	○	◑	3 ¼	●	◑	●	●	●	1.0	
3	**Kyocera** KX444 (Verizon)	100	Basic	58	○	○	4 ¼	◑	◑		●		NA	●
4	**LG** The V (Verizon)	550	Advanced	58	○	○	4 ¼	◑	○	●	●	●	1.0	
5	**Motorola** Razr V3c (Verizon, Alltel, U.S. Cellular)	200	Advanced	55	◑	◑	3 ¾	○	○		●	●	1.0	
6	**Kyocera** KX1 (Verizon, Alltel)	115	Basic	54	○	◑	2 ¾	◑	◑	●	●		NA	●

Ratings (continued)

In performance order, within categories.

Excellent ● Very good ◕ Good ○ Fair ◑ Poor ●

Guide to the Ratings

Overall score is based mainly on voice quality and talk time. **Listening** rates the voice quality you hear during a cell-phone conversation. **Talking** rates the quality a person you call hears. Listening and talking tests were conducted in noisy and quiet environments using live phone calls. **Talk time**, in hours, is the average time for calls you should expect, based on our tests with strong and weak signals. **Sensitivity** is a measure of a phone's voice quality when a call is placed using a weak signal. The scores are applicable only within a Ratings group, not between groups. **Ease of use** takes in the design of the display and keypad and the ease with which you can send or receive text messages and the like. **Price** is approximate for a phone purchased from the carrier with a two-year contract in fall 2005. Prices shown are the manufacturer's standard, excluding rebates or special offers, which can be substantial but constantly change. *Based on testing posted on ConsumerReports.org in April 2006.*

Key number	Brand & model	Price	Type	Overall score	Listening	Talking	Talk time (hr.)	Sensitivity	Ease of use	Easy-to-mute ringer	Speaker phone	Bluetooth	Camera (megapixels)	Analog backup
VERIZON PHONES *Most work on Verizon's or other CDMA networks.*														
7	**Samsung** SCH-a950 (Verizon)	$130	Advanced	53	○	◑	3½	○	○		●	●	1.0	
8	**UTS** Starcom CDM 180 (Verizon)	70	Basic	53	○	◑	3¼	○	○		●		0.3	
9	**Kyocera** KX18 Amp'd Jet (Amp'd Mobile)	100	Advanced	52	○	○	3	◑	○	●	●		0.3	
SPRINT NEXTEL PHONES *These work only on Sprint's CDMA network.*														
10	**PalmOne** Treo 650	575	Smartphone	60	○	○	4¼	◑	◑	●	●	●	0.3	
11	**Samsung** MM-A800	500	Advanced	60	○	◑	3½	◑	◑				2.0	●
12	**LG** PM-225	255	Advanced	56	○	◑	3	◑	○		●		0.3	●
13	**Sanyo** SCP-200	175	Basic	55	○	◑	2¾	◑	○		●		NA	●
14	**Sanyo** VI-2300	240	Basic	54	○	◑	3	◑	○		●		NA	●
15	**Nokia** 6016i	150	Basic	53	○	○	3¼	◑	○		●		NA	●
16	**Samsung** MM-A900	350	Advanced	52	○	◑	2½	◑	○		●	●	1.0	
17	**Sanyo** MM-8300	335	Advanced	51	○	◑	2¾	○	○		●		0.3	●
18	**Sanyo** MM-9000	550	Advanced	48	○	◑	3	○	○		●		1.0	
19	**Nokia** 3155i	190	Basic	46	◑	○	3¾	◑	◑		●		NA	●
CINGULAR/T-MOBILE PHONES *These work on Cingular's or T-Mobile's GSM network.*														
20	**Motorola** V360 (T-Mobile)	200	Advanced	67	○	○	7	◑	◑	●	●	●	0.3	
21	**Samsung** e335 (T-Mobile)	535	Basic	66	○	◑	6¾	◑	◑	●	●		0.3	
22	**Nokia** 6101 (T-Mobile)	150	Basic	64	◑	○	6½	◑	◑		●		0.3	
23	**Samsung** SGH-d307 (Cingular)	200	Advanced	64	◑	○	7	◑	◑	●	●	●	NA	
24	**Motorola** Razr V3 (Cingular, T-mobile)	265	Advanced	62	○	○	5¼	◑	◑		●	●	0.3	
25	**Motorola** ROKR E1 (Cingular)	300	Advanced	62	○	○	6¼	◑	◑		●	●	0.3	
26	**Sony** Ericsson W600i (Cingular)	300	Advanced	62	◑	○	6½	◑	◑		●	●	1.0	
27	**Samsung** e635 (T-Mobile)	350	Basic	61	○	○	5½	◑	◑	●	●		0.3	
28	**Motorola** V220 (Cingular)	250	Basic	60	○	○	5¼	○	◑		●		0.3	
29	**Nokia** 6682 (Cingular)	300	Advanced	56	○	○	5¼	◑	○		●	●	1.0	
30	**Motorola** PEBL U6 (T-Mobile)	300	Advanced	54	○	○	3¼	○	◑	●	●	●	0.3	

REFERENCE & RATINGS

DIGITAL CAMERAS

CR Quick Recommendations

Digital cameras

Based on our judgments of uncropped 8x10-inch prints, all the cameras produced images that were excellent. But if we had used only a small portion of the original image and enlarged it to 8x10, the higher-megapixel cameras would have produced better results than the others. The advanced compact and superzoom models have features that demanding photographers will appreciate, such as manual controls, especially long battery life, and a next-shot delay no longer than two seconds.

QUICK PICKS

Best value for most people:

5 Canon PowerShot A520, $160
This CR Best Buy has excellent print quality and battery life, manual controls, and uses AA batteries. It also has 4-megapixel resolution and a 4X optical zoom, but has a small LCD and limited time for each video recording.

For additional flexibility:

1 Canon PowerShot A620, $220
4 Hewlett-Packard PhotoSmart R817, $220

These compacts have excellent print quality and battery life, plus manual controls. The Canon PowerShot A620 has 7-megapixel resolution, a flip-out movable LCD, and uses AA batteries, but doesn't include a charger. The Hewlett-Packard PhotoSmart R817 has 5-megapixel resolution, a 5X optical zoom, short next-shot delay, and includes a charger for its proprietary battery. It also has image advice, in-camera red-eye removal, panoramic shooting with in-camera stitching, and the ability to save as a still image and enhance any frame from a video.

For a camera that fits in a purse:

10 Casio Exilim Zoom EX-Z750, $300
11 Kodak EasyShare V550, $240
14 Canon PowerShot SD450, $260
17 Panasonic Lumix DMC-FX8, $240

All are small and light, with excellent or very good print quality, and include a charger. All except the Casio Exilim Zoom EX-Z750 have 5-megapixel resolution. The Casio has 7-megapixel resolution, excellent battery life, manual controls, an optical viewfinder, and MPEG-4 video at 30 frames per second. But its image stabilizer is simulated (less effective than optical stabilization). The Kodak EasyShare V550 has good battery life, an optical viewfinder, short next-shot delay, and MPEG-4 video at 30 frames per second. But it lacks manual controls and its ISO 800 setting automatically reduces resolution. The Canon PowerShot SD450 has good battery life, an optical viewfinder, and a mode that helps you align shots to stitch together later for panoramic photos. But it lacks manual controls and its image stabilizer is for video only. The Panasonic Lumix DMC-FX8 has excellent battery life, an optical image stabilizer (the most effective type), and a "baby" mode for softer images. But it lacks manual controls.

For an advanced compact camera:

22 Kodak EasyShare P880, $450
23 Fujifilm FinePix E900, $350
25 Panasonic Lumix DMC-LX1, $430

You can't go wrong with any of these advanced compacts. The priciest, the Kodak EasyShare P880, offers a lot to the serious photographer. It has 8-megapixel resolution, a 5.8X optical zoom with wide-angle capability, in-camera red-eye removal, and it can make advanced adjustments to a RAW file and save it as a separate JPEG. But it weighs more than twice as much as the other two models, and its ISO 800 setting automatically reduces resolution. For the best value, the CR Best Buy Fujifilm FinePix E900 has 9-megapixel resolution, excellent battery life, an extremely sharp lens, and less-grainy images than other models at high ISO settings. The 8-megapixel Panasonic Lumix DMC-LX1 is well-suited for displaying photos on widescreen digital TVs if you use its 16:9 aspect mode. Its resolution drops if you use narrower aspect modes. It also has very good battery life, a 4X optical zoom with wide-angle capability and an optical image stabilizer (the most effective type).

For a long zoom range:

28 Canon PowerShot S2 IS, $390
31 Fujifilm FinePix S5200, $260

These 5-megapixel superzoom models are well-suited for shooting situations where distance is a major factor, such as sports and nature photography. Both use AA batteries, which are easily obtained in a pinch. The Canon PowerShot S2 IS has a 12X optical zoom, an optical image stabilizer (the most effective type), high-quality Motion JPEG video recording at 30 frames per second, and can zoom optically during video recording. But it has a small LCD. The Fujifilm FinePix S5200 has a 10X optical zoom, very sharp lens, 1600 ISO setting, and short next-shot delay. But it has a small LCD.

Ratings

			Excellent	Very good	Good	Fair	Poor
			●	◒	○	◓	●

In performance order, within categories.

Key number	Brand & model	Price	Overall score (0–100)	Print quality	Ease of use	Megapixels	Weight (oz.)	Flash range (ft.)	Battery life (shots)	Next-shot delay (sec.)	Shutter lag (sec.)	Optical zoom	Manual controls	Secure grip	Movie mode	Charger	AA batteries	Eyeglasses	Wide angle	Image stabilizer
COMPACT MODELS																				
1	**Canon** PowerShot A620	$220	76	●	◒	7	12	14	500	2	0.7	4X	●	●	●		●			
2	**Kodak** EasyShare Z700	250	76	●	●	4	10	12	200	2	0.7	5X	●	●	●	●	●	●		
3	**Olympus** Stylus 800	330	73	●	◒	8	7	21	400	2	0.8	3X		●	●					●
4	**Hewlett-Packard** PhotoSmart R817	220	72	●	◒	5.1	7	12	260	1	0.3	5X	●	●	●	●				
5	**Canon** PowerShot A520	160	71	●	◒	4	8	11	300	2	1.1	4X	●	●	●		●			
6	**Hewlett-Packard** PhotoSmart R717	260	71	●	◒	6.2	7	16	80	2	1.5	3X	●		●	●				
7	**Nikon** Coolpix S4	330	66	◒	◒	6	9	10	300	3	0.9	10X			●	●				●
8	**Kodak** EasyShare One	210	65	●	◒	4	9	10	120	2	0.6	3X			●	●		●		

Expert • Independent • Nonprofit

Ratings (continued)

In performance order, within categories.

Excellent ● | Very good ◖ | Good ○ | Fair ◗ | Poor ●

Key number	Brand & model	Price	Overall score (0–100)	Print quality	Ease of use	Megapixels	Weight (oz.)	Flash range (ft.)	Battery life (shots)	Next-shot delay (sec.)	Shutter lag (sec.)	Optical zoom	Manual controls	Secure grip	Movie mode	Charger	AA batteries	Eyeglasses	Wide angle	Image stabilizer
SUBCOMPACT MODELS																				
9	**Canon** PowerShot SD500 Digital ELPH	$280	75	●	◖	7.1	7	16	160	2	1	3X			●	●				
10	**Casio** Exilim Zoom EX-Z750	300	72	●	◖	7.2	6	10	320	2	0.5	3X	●		●	●				●
11	**Kodak** EasyShare V550	240	72	●	●	5	6	8	120	1	0.4	3X			●	●				●
12	**Pentax** Optio SV	220	72	●	◖	5	6	14	100	9	1.1	5X	●		●	●				
13	**Canon** PowerShot SD430	450	70	●	◖	5	5	11	150	2	0.8	3X			●	●				
14	**Canon** PowerShot SD450	260	68	◖	◖	5	5	11	150	2	0.9	3X			●	●				
15	**Sony** Cyber-shot DSC-M1	430	66	●	●	5	8	6	160	4	0.3	3X			●	●		●		
16	**Kodak** EasyShare V570	350	65	●	●	5	5	10	140	1	0.4	3X			●	●		●	●	●
17	**Panasonic** Lumix DMC-FX8	240	64	●	●	5	5	6	300	2	0.7	3X			●	●				●
18	**Pentax** Optio S5z	240	64	◖	◖	5	4	11	180	3	0.4	3X			●	●		●		
19	**Fujifilm** FinePix Z1	270	62	◖	◖	5.1	5	10	170	2	0.6	3X			●	●		●		
20	**Sony** Cyber-shot DSC-T7	330	61	◖	◖	5.1	5	9	150	1	0.3	3X			●	●		●		
21	**Canon** PowerShot SD30	270	60	◖	◖	5	4	7	160	2	0.7	2.4X			●	●		●		
ADVANCED COMPACT MODELS																				
22	**Kodak** EasyShare P880	450	73	●	●	8	21	13	260	2	1.5	5.8X	●	●	●	●		●	●	
23	**Fujifilm** FinePix E900 [CR BEST BUY]	350	72	●	◖	9	9	12	280	2	0.8	4X	●	●	●	●	●	●		
24	**Olympus** SP-350	290	70	●	◖	8	8	12	200	7	1.4	3X	●		●					●
25	**Panasonic** Lumix DMC-LX1	430	69	●	●	8.4	7	13	240	2	1.3	4X	●		●	●		●	●	●
26	**Sony** Cyber-shot DSC-R1	760	69	●	◖	10	37	28	500	2	0.5	5X	●	●	●			●	●	
27	**Leica** D-LUX 2	750	64	●	●	8.4	8	6	240	6	1	4X	●		●	●		●	●	●
SUPER ZOOM MODELS																				
28	**Canon** PowerShot S2 IS	350	81	●	◖	5	19	17	550	2	1.1	12X	●	●	●	●		●		●
29	**Kodak** EasyShare P850	380	79	●	●	5.1	16	15	260	4	1.2	12X	●	●	●	●		●		●
30	**Panasonic** Lumix DMC-FZ20S	410	78	●	●	5	22	23	280	1	0.7	12X	●	●	●	●		●		●
31	**Fujifilm** FinePix S5200	260	77	●	◖	5	17	13	500	1	0.6	10X	●	●	●		●	●		
32	**Kodak** EasyShare Z740	220	74	●	●	5	12	16	260	2	0.5	10X	●	●	●		●	●		
33	**Fujifilm** FinePix S9000	550	72	●	●	9	27	18	340	2	1.1	10.7X	●	●	●		●	●	●	
34	**Samsung** Digimax Pro815	700	67	◖	●	8	36	20	460	3	0.9	15X	●	●	●	●		●	●	

REFERENCE & RATINGS

DIGITAL CAMERAS

Guide to the Ratings

Overall score is based largely on picture quality and convenience factors. **Print quality** is based on panelists' judgments of glossy 8x10-inch photos made on a high-quality inkjet printer. **Ease of use** Is our measure of how convenient it is to use the camera's essential features. **Megapixels** shows how many million pixels the image sensor has. As a rule, with more megapixels, you can make larger prints or enlarge parts of an image without losing detail or image quality. **Weight**, in ounces, includes battery and memory card. **Flash range**, in feet, is the maximum claimed range for a well-lighted photo. **Battery life** reflects the number of high-resolution photos we could take with a fresh set of alkaline batteries (or, if included, with rechargeables that were fully charged). The LCD image display was turned off (if possible), the flash was used for half of the shots, and the zoom lens was racked in and out. **Next-shot delay** is the time, in seconds, the camera needs to ready itself for the next shot. **Shutter lag** is the time in seconds from when you press the shutter to the moment the camera takes the picture (after autofocusing and metering for exposure). **Optical zoom** magnifies the image using a real multi-focal-length lens, whereas a digital zoom uses electronics to enlarge the center portion of the image using interpolation. **Manual controls** allow the user to set the aperture (f-stop), shutter speed, or (usually) both. This feature is used to override the automatic exposure settings when more control is needed. **Secure grip** denotes cameras designed with room for your fingers, so you can hold the camera steady and keep your fingers clear of the flash, lens, or autofocus sensor. The **movie mode** feature allows you to record short video clips using your digital camera; some models record with sound while others do not. **Charger** indicates whether the camera comes with a charger. **AA batteries** indicates whether the camera accepts AA batteries. This options allows you to use disposable or rechargeable batteries. **Eyeglasses** denotes cameras with a viewfinder diopter adjustment, which allows some eyeglass wearers to take off their glasses when using the camera. **Wide angle** shows which model has a lens that can zoom as wide as a 28-mm lens. The **image stabilizer** feature minimizes the effect of camera shake. **Price** is approximate retail.

Based on testing posted on ConsumerReports.org in April 2006, with updated prices and availability.

Profiles Model-by-Model

COMPACT MODELS

1 Canon PowerShot A620 Very good overall. 4X optical zoom. Excellent battery life. LCD display flips out and swivels. Has multiple special-scene modes. Has panoramic stitch-assist mode. Can control shooting from PC.

2 Kodak EasyShare Z700 Excellent overall. Has 5X optical zoom and secure grip. Has multiple special-scene modes. Has MPEG-4 video compression. Comes with EasyShare Printer Dock Series 3.

3 Olympus Stylus 800 Excellent overall. Excellent battery life. Has multiple special-scene modes, ISO settings up to 1600, image stabilizer, and all-weather body.

4 Hewlett-Packard PhotoSmart R817 Very good overall. Has excellent battery life, 5x optical zoom, image advice, in-camera red-eye removal, adaptive lighting setting to bring out details lost in shadows, panorama with in-camera stitching, ability to select and save, with enhancement, any frame from a video capture as a still image, and an orientation sensor.

5 Canon PowerShot A520 A CR Best Buy Very good overall. Excellent battery life. Has multiple special-scene modes. Discontinued, but may still be available.

6 Hewlett-Packard PhotoSmart R717 Excellent overall. Has multiple special-scene modes. Can undelete last deleted picture. Has in-camera red-eye correction and in-camera panoramic stiching. Battery life is only fair.

7 Nikon Coolpix S4 Very good overall. 10X optical zoom. Excellent battery life. Has image stabilizer for movies. Has in-camera red-eye removal. Has multiple special-scene modes. Has unique, rotating lens design.

8 Kodak EasyShare One Very good overall. Has large LCD with touch screen, Wi-Fi for uploading images via network, external Wi-Fi antenna, and good battery life. Comes with two batteries.

SUBCOMPACT MODELS

9 Canon PowerShot SD500 Digital ELPH Excellent overall. Has multiple special-scene modes.

10 Casio Exilim Zoom EX-Z750 Excellent overall. Has excellent battery life, multiple special-scene modes, image stabilizer, and MPEG-4 movie compression. Can record past movies that begin five seconds prior to pressing shutter, with continually updated five-second buffer.

11 Kodak EasyShare V550 Excellent overall. Has multiple special-scene modes, image stabilizer for movies, and MPEG-4 movie compression. Can crop photos in camera. Discontinued, but may still be available.

12 Pentax Optio SV Very good overall. Has live histogram that graphically displays image information on LCD. Has special-scene modes (flower, sports, surf & snow, autumn colors, sunset, museum, food, and 3D).

13 Canon PowerShot SD430 Very good overall. One of the few subcompacts with an optical viewfinder. Has panoramic stitch-assist mode, Wi-Fi, and PC remote-control shooting.

14 Canon PowerShot SD450 Very good overall. One of the few subcompacts with an optical viewfinder. Has panoramic stitch-assist mode.

15 Sony Cyber-shot DSC-M1 Very good overall. Swivel LCD monitor and body. Has MPEG4 full-motion video capability with stereo sound. Comes with dock for connections other than battery-charging. Stores images on new MemoryStick Duo Pro and will not accept regular MemoryStick.

16 Kodak EasyShare V570 Very good overall. Has good battery life, twin lens system, ultrawide-angle lens, and large LCD monitor.

17 Panasonic Lumix DMC-FX8 Very good overall. Has excellent battery life, optical image stabilizer, and "baby" mode (for color and softer flash). Can make flip animations.

18 Pentax Optio S5z Very good overall. Has multiple special-scene modes and MPEG-4 movie compression. Discontinued, but may still be available.

Profiles Model-by-Model (continued)

19 Fujifilm FinePix Z1 Very good overall. Has 800 ISO setting. Lacks tripod socket. Discontinued, but may still be available.

20 Sony Cyber-shot DSC-T7 Very good overall. Has multiple special-scene modes. Lacks tripod socket.

21 Canon PowerShot SD30 Good overall. Has 2.4x zoom, small, stylish form, and small LCD monitor.

ADVANCED COMPACT MODELS

22 Kodak EasyShare P880 Very good overall. 5.8X optical zoom. Excellent battery life. SLR-like body. Wide angle. Can convert RAW images to JPEG in camera. Has in-camera red-eye correction. Has multiple special-scene modes. Has album function.

23 Fujifilm FinePix E900 A CR Best Buy. Very good overall. Among the best in picture quality. 4X optical zoom. Excellent battery life. Excellent dynamic range. Lens has excellent sharpness.

24 Olympus SP-350 Very good overall. Can zoom optically when recording movies. Has image stabilizer for movies. Has excellent dynamic range. Has multiple special-scene modes.

25 Panasonic Lumix DMC-LX1 Very good overall. 4X optical zoom. Wide angle. Has image stabilizer. 16:9 sensor aspect ratio. Has multiple special-scene modes.

26 Sony Cyber-shot DSC-R1 Very good overall. 5X optical zoom. Excellent battery life. APS size sensor. SLR-like body. Wide angle. Adobe RGB. Has excellent dynamic range. No movie mode.

27 Leica D-LUX 2 Very good overall. Has 4x optical zoom, wide angle, panoramic 16:9 aspect image sensor, and optical image stabilizer.

SUPER ZOOM MODELS

28 Canon PowerShot S2 IS Excellent overall. Excellent battery life. Has multiple special-scene modes.

29 Kodak EasyShare P850 Excellent overall. 12X optical zoom. Excellent battery life. Can convert RAW images to JPEG in camera. Has image stabilizer. Can zoom optically when recording movies. Has in-camera red-eye removal. Has multiple special-scene modes. Has album function.

30 Panasonic Lumix DMC-FZ20S Excellent overall. Has special-scene modes (sports, scenery, panning, fireworks, party, and snow). Comes with large lens hood,

hot shoe for add-on flash. Image stabilizer. Noise reduction. Discontinued, but may still be available.

31 Fujifilm FinePix S5200 Very good overall. 10X optical zoom. Excellent battery life. Lightweight for its class.

32 Kodak EasyShare Z740 Very good overall. 10X optical zoom. Excellent battery life. Excellent dynamic range. Uses MPEG-4 compression for movie recording. Lacks image stabilization. Has multiple special-scene modes, with descriptions.

33 Fujifilm FinePix S9000 Very good overall. 10.7X optical zoom. Excellent battery life. SLR-like body. Wide angle. Can zoom optically when recording movies. Has image stabilizer for movies. LCD monitor tilts out. Has multiple special-scene modes.

34 Samsung Digimax Pro815 Very good overall. 15X optical zoom. Excellent battery life. SLR-like body. Wide angle. Adobe RGB. Can zoom optically when recording movies. Has large, 3.4-inch LCD monitor. Has multiple special scene modes.

Brand Repair History

Readers report on some 187,000 digital cameras

The graph shows the percentage of digital cameras that have been repaired or developed a serious problem that wasn't repaired. Models within a brand may vary, and design and manufacturing changes may affect the repair history. The graph does not include digital SLR cameras. Digital cameras have been generally very reliable.

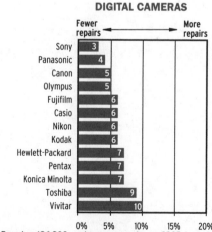

DIGITAL CAMERAS

Fewer repairs ← → More repairs

Brand	Value
Sony	3
Panasonic	4
Canon	5
Olympus	5
Fujifilm	6
Casio	6
Nikon	6
Kodak	6
Hewlett-Packard	7
Pentax	7
Konica Minolta	7
Toshiba	9
Vivitar	10

0% 5% 10% 15% 20%

Based on 186,900 reader responses to our 2005 Annual Questionnaire about digital cameras bought new between 2002 and 2005. Data have been standardized to eliminate differences linked to age and usage. Differences of less than 4 points aren't meaningful.

DVD PLAYERS

CR Quick Recommendations

DVD players

Excellent picture quality is a hallmark of DVD players. For typical use with a conventional (as in standard-definition) TV, most people can safely purchase by disc capacity, features, price, and brand reliability. The Ratings cover a representative sample of players from major brands, selected for value and a wide diversity of features and capabilities. We've listed models in the Ratings chart below not by overall performance but by price within types.

If you're buying a player for use with a high-definition or enhanced-definition TV, you should be choosier. You can use any DVD player with your HDTV. But as our Quick Picks reflect, some players are better than others at smoothing moving images on an HDTV. (On HD sets, DVD images appear in an enhanced-definition mode, known technically as "480p" for 480 lines using progressive-scan formatting that looks better than conventional TV but falls a little short of true high-definition resolution.)

If you want to connect your DVD player to a digital receiver to get surround sound from a multispeaker setup, check that its outputs (as noted in the chart) match those of your audio receiver. Also, if you own an HDTV that has digital video input (HDMI or DVI), note that some models have matching output. Our tests, however, have found that a digital-video connection does not necessarily provide better picture quality than one between the component-video input of any HDTV and the matching output found on almost any DVD player or recorder.

QUICK PICKS

For use with a standard-definition TV:

You could simply start with the lowest-priced models at the top of the category that best meets your needs, and work down to find a player with the features you want.

For use with a high-definition TV:

For widest selection and best value, most HDTV owners should choose among the many models we've identified in the chart column entitled "Well-suited for HDTVs."

In our tests, those players yielded a smoother enhanced-definition (480p) picture with all DVDs. If you often play discs whose content was shot on video cameras, including DVDs of many TV programs and concert videos, consider narrowing your choice to a subset of those models that smoothed video-based content more than others. Those players, listed from least to most expensive: Toshiba SD-3960, $50 (a bargain that's discontinued and may be hard to find); Toshiba SD-5970, $145; Panasonic DVD-S77, $220; and Yamaha DVD-S1500, $310 (also an older and scarce model.)

For a player that can accept a wide range of disc types:

All the players can play audio CDs, including CD-R or CD-RW discs (including those that carry MP3 files). If you expect to use other disc types, check the Ratings chart. Expect to pay a premium for players that can handle high-resolution audio formats such as DVD-Audio and Super Audio CD.

Ratings

Excellent ● Very good ◕ Good ○ Fair ◒ Poor ●

By price, within types.

Key number	Brand & model	Price	Well-suited for HDTVs	Plays DVD-audio discs	Plays SACD discs	HDMI output	DVI output	Coaxial digital audio out	Optical digital audio out	Six-channel decoder	Reads JPEG image files	Plays video CDs	Plays WMA-audio files
	PROGRESSIVE-SCAN, SINGLE-DISC PLAYERS												
1	**Toshiba** SD-3960	$50	●					●			●	●	●
2	**Toshiba** SD-3980	50	●					●			●	●	●
3	**Philips** DVP3500/37	60						●			●	●	
4	**JVC** XV-N310B	65	●					●			●		●
5	**Panasonic** DVD-S27	65	●					●			●		●
6	**Philips** DVP642	65						●	●		●		●
7	**Samsung** P241	65	●					●			●		●
8	**Kenwood** DVF-8100	70	●					●	●		●		●
9	**Panasonic** DVD-S29	70	●					●			●	●	●
10	**RCA** DRC246N	70						●			●	●	●
11	**JVC** XV-N410B	75	●					●			●	●	●
12	**Sony** DVP-NS50P	75	●					●			●		●
13	**JVC** XV-N420B	80						●			●	●	●
14	**RCA** DRC240N	85	●					●	●		●	●	●
15	**Kenwood** Fineline DVF-3250	90	●					●			●	●	●
16	**Pioneer** DV-578A	100	●	●	●			●	●	●	●	●	●
17	**Samsung** P341	100	●					●	●		●		●
18	**Pioneer** DV-588A-S	120	●	●	●			●	●	●	●	●	●

Guide to the Ratings

Features are important attributes that might affect your buying decision, such as whether a model is **well-suited for HDTVs**. Features for players indicate whether it plays **DVD-audio** or **SACD discs**, which have **HDMI output** or **DVI output**, which inputs/outputs have **coaxial digital audio out** or **optical digital audio out**. We note other features, such as **six-channel decoder**, whether the player reads **JPEG image files**, plays **video CDs**, and plays **WMA-audio files**. **Price** is approximate retail. *Based on tests posted to ConsumerReports.org in March 2006, with updated prices and availability.*

Ratings (continued)

By price, within types.

	Excellent	Very good	Good	Fair	Poor
	●	◖	○	◒	●

Key number	Brand & model	Price	Well-suited for HDTVs	Plays DVD-audio discs	Plays SACD discs	HDMI output	DVI output	Coaxial digital audio out	Optical digital audio out	Six-channel decoder	Reads JPEG image files	Plays video CDs	Plays WMA-audio files
PROGRESSIVE-SCAN, SINGLE-DISC PLAYERS													
19	**JVC** XV-N510B	$125	●	●				●	●		●		●
20	**Toshiba** SD-4960	125		●	●			●	●	●	●		●
21	**Denon** DVD-1710	130						●	●		●		●
22	**Denon** DVD-1720	130	●					●	●		●		●
23	**Sony** DVP-NS70H	135	●			●		●	●		●		
24	**Toshiba** SD-5980	140	●			●		●	●		●		●
25	**Samsung** DVD-HD841	145				●	●	●	●		●		●
26	**Samsung** DVD-HD850	145				●		●	●		●		●
27	**Toshiba** SD-5970	145	●			●		●	●		●		●
28	**Toshiba** SD-6980	170	●	●		●		●	●		●		●
29	**LG** LDA-511	175		●				●	●		●		●
30	**Harman** Kardon DVD 22	185						●	●		●	●	
31	**Samsung** DVD-HD950	195		●	●	●		●	●	●	●		●
32	**Panasonic** DVD-S77	220	●	●				●	●	●	●		●
33	**Yamaha** DV-S5860SL	230	●	●	●			●	●	●	●		●
34	**Onkyo** DV-SP502	280	●	●	●			●	●	●	●		●
35	**Denon** DVD-1920	300	●	●	●	●		●	●	●	●		●
36	**Yamaha** DVD-S1500	310	●	●	●			●	●	●	●		●
PROGRESSIVE-SCAN, MULTI-DISC PLAYERS													
37	**Toshiba** SD-5915	90	●					●	●		●		●
38	**Toshiba** SD-6915	100		●	●			●	●	●	●		●
39	**Panasonic** DVD-F86	110		●				●			●		●
40	**Panasonic** DVD-F87	115	●	●				●		●	●		●
41	**Sony** DVP-NC80V	125	●		●			●	●	●	●		
42	**Sony** DVP-CX995V	310			●	●		●	●	●	●		
43	**Onkyo** DV-CP802	410	●	●	●			●	●	●	●		

Profiles Model-by-Model

PROGRESSIVE-SCAN, SINGLE-DISC PLAYERS

1 Toshiba SD-3960 Very basic unit, but among the best choices for use with a high-definition TV; smooths progressive-scan images from DVDs created from many sources, including movies, TV programs, and concert videos. Has center-channel enhancement feature to improve clarity of DVD-movie dialog.

2 Toshiba SD-3980 Provides noticeable smoothing of progressive-scan images from all sources, especially movies.

3 Philips DVP3500/37 There are better choices for use with a high-definition TV;

provides only intermittent smoothing of progressive-scan images from film-based DVDs (such as those of most movie releases). Lacks S-video output.

4 JVC XV-N310B Provides noticeable smoothing of progressive-scan images from all sources, especially movies. Similar model: XV-N312.

5 Panasonic DVD-S27 Provides noticeable smoothing of progressive-scan images from all sources, especially movies. Has center-channel enhancement feature to improve clarity of DVD-movie dialog. Discontinued, but may still be available.

6 Philips DVP642 There are better

choices for use with a high-definition TV; provides little or no smoothing of progressive-scan images from film-based DVDs (such as those of most movie releases).

7 Samsung P241 Provides noticeable smoothing of progressive-scan images from all sources, especially movies. Has LED indicator lights instead of true console display. Discontinued, but may still be available.

8 Kenwood DVF-8100 Provides noticeable smoothing of progressive-scan images from all sources, especially movies. Discontinued, but may still be available.

9 Panasonic DVD-S29 Provides

(continued)

DVD PLAYERS

Profiles Model-by-Model (continued)

noticeable smoothing of progressive-scan images from all sources, especially movies. Has center-channel enhancement feature to improve clarity of DVD-movie dialog.

10 RCA DRC246N There are better choices for use with a high-definition TV; progressive-scan images are a little less clear than those from most other models. Reads CompactFlash, SmartMedia, Memory Stick, Secure Digital (SD), and MultiMedia Card removable media. Lacks DTS digital-audio output and go-to-by-time search function. Discontinued, but may still be available.

11 JVC XV-N410B Provides noticeable smoothing of progressive-scan images from all sources, especially movies.

12 Sony DVP-NS50P Provides noticeable smoothing of progressive-scan images from all sources, especially movies.

13 JVC XV-N420B There are better choices for use with a high-definition TV; provides little or no smoothing of progressive-scan video images from video-based DVDs (such as many TV-show compilations). Similar model: XV-N422S.

14 RCA DRC240N Provides noticeable smoothing of progressive-scan images from all sources, especially movies. Has center-channel enhancement feature to improve clarity of DVD-movie dialog.

15 Kenwood Fineline DVF-3250 Provides noticeable smoothing of progressive-scan images from all sources, especially movies.

16 Pioneer DV-578A Provides noticeable smoothing of progressive-scan images from all sources, especially movies. Has center-channel enhancement feature to improve clarity of DVD-movie dialog.

17 Samsung P341 Provides noticeable smoothing of progressive-scan images from all sources, especially movies. Reads CompactFlash, SmartMedia, Memory Stick, Secure Digital (SD), MultiMedia Card, and Microdrive removable media.

18 Pioneer DV-588A-S Provides noticeable smoothing of progressive-scan images from all sources, especially movies. Has center-channel enhancement feature to improve clarity of DVD-movie dialog.

19 JVC XV-N510B Provides noticeable smoothing of progressive-scan images from all sources, especially movies.

20 Toshiba SD-4960 There are better choices for use with a high-definition TV; progressive-scan images are a little less clear than those from most other models.

21 Denon DVD-1710 There are better choices for use with a high-definition TV; progressive-scan video images are a little less clear than those from most other models.

22 Denon DVD-1720 Provides noticeable smoothing of progressive-scan images from all sources, especially movies.

23 Sony DVP-NS70H Provides noticeable smoothing of progressive-scan images from all sources, especially movies.

24 Toshiba SD-5980 Provides noticeable smoothing of progressive-scan images from all sources, especially movies. Reads CompactFlash, Memory Stick, Secure Digital (SD), MultiMedia Card, and xD-Picture Card removable media.

25 Samsung DVD-HD841 There are better choices for use with a high-definition TV; progressive-scan images are a little less clear than those from most other models.

26 Samsung DVD-HD850 There are better choices for use with a high-definition TV; progressive-scan images are a little less clear than those from most other models.

27 Toshiba SD-5970 Among the best choices for use with a high-definition TV; smooths progressive-scan images from DVDs created from many sources, including movies, TV programs, and concert videos. Discontinued, but may still be available.

28 Toshiba SD-6980 Provides noticeable smoothing of progressive-scan images from all sources, especially movies. Reads CompactFlash, SmartMedia, Memory Stick, Memory Stick Pro, Memory Stick Duo, Secure Digital (SD), Mini SD,

Profiles Model-by-Model (continued)

MultiMedia Card, RS-MMC, xD-Picture Card, and Microdrive removable media.

29 LG LDA-511 There are better choices for use with a high-definition TV; progressive-scan images are a little less clear than those from most other models. Reads CompactFlash, Memory Stick, Memory Stick Pro, Secure Digital (SD), MultiMedia Card, xD-Picture Card, and Microdrive removable media. Loads disc via slot instead of tray.

30 Harman Kardon DVD 22 There are better choices for use with a high-definition TV; provides little or no smoothing of progressive-scan images from video-based DVDs (as are many TV-show compilations).

31 Samsung DVD-HD950 There are better choices for use with a high-definition TV; progressive-scan video images are a little less clear than those of most other models.

32 Panasonic DVD-S77 Among the best choices for use with a high-definition TV; smooths progressive-scan images from DVDs created from many sources, including movies, TV programs, and concert videos. Has center-channel enhancement feature to improve clarity of DVD-movie dialog.

33 Yamaha DV-S5860SL Provides noticeable smoothing of progressive-scan images from all sources, especially movies. Discontinued, but may still be available.

34 Onkyo DV-SP502 Provides noticeable smoothing of progressive-scan images from all sources, especially movies.

35 Denon DVD-1920 Among the best choices for use with a high-definition TV; smooths progressive-scan images from DVDs created from many sources, including movies, TV programs, and concert videos.

36 Yamaha DVD-S1500 Among the best choices for use with a high-definition TV; smooths progressive-scan images from DVDs created from many sources, including movies, TV programs, and concert videos. Has center-channel enhancement feature to improve clarity of DVD-movie dialog. Discontinued, but may still be available.

PROGRESSIVE-SCAN, MULTI-DISC PLAYERS

37 Toshiba SD-5915 Provides noticeable smoothing of progressive-scan images from all sources, especially movies. Provides continuous playback of multiple CDs only when tracks played in random order.

38 Toshiba SD-6915 There are better choices for use with a high-def TV; progressive-scan images are a little less clear than those from most other models. Provides continuous playback of multiple CDs only when tracks played in random order.

39 Panasonic DVD-F86 There are better choices for use with a high-definition TV; provides little or no smoothing of progressive-scan images from video-based DVDs (as are many TV-show compilations). Has center-channel enhancement feature to improve clarity of DVD-movie dialog. DVD-Audio playback is stereo only. Discontinued, but may still be available.

40 Panasonic DVD-F87 Provides noticeable smoothing of progressive-scan images from all sources, especially movies. Has center-channel enhancement feature to improve clarity of DVD-movie dialog.

41 Sony DVP-NC80V Provides noticeable smoothing of progressive-scan images from all sources, especially movies.

42 Sony DVP-CX995V There are better choices for use with a high-definition TV; provides only intermittent smoothing of progressive-scan images from film-based DVDs (such as those of most movie releases). Vertical disc-carousel jukebox automatically sorts discs by type into video, music, and photo folders—and has four user-defined subfolders for further categorization. Accepts IBM-standard keyboard input for disc or folder labeling.

43 Onkyo DV-CP802 Provides noticeable smoothing of progressive-scan images from all sources, especially movies. Poor performance at playing damaged DVD-video discs in our tests. Discontinued, but may still be available.

LAPTOPS

Laptops

The Ratings rank models by performance and features. Quick Picks take into account not only performance but reliability, tech support, and value. All the major brands have had similar repair rates. Apple's tech support has been the best by far, followed by Lenovo (IBM).

QUICK PICKS

If low price is a priority:

1 Gateway NX510S, $740

The Gateway, a CR Best Buy, stands out for good performance, an attractive matte display, and a nice design at a low price. Battery life was fairly long. (You can buy this model only by calling Gateway.)

Good balance of power, speed, and mobility:

7 Dell Inspiron E1505, $1,120

The Dell did well on all counts and has a good 15.4-inch glossy display, decent speakers, and very good multimedia features. As the lowest-priced of the workhorses, it's a CR Best Buy.

Best choices for a desktop replacement or entertainment PC:

11 Apple Macbook Pro 17-inch, $2,800

14 HP Pavilion dv8000t, $1,315

A beautiful 17-inch matte display, very good speakers, and a very good multimedia software bundle make the Macbook Pro the top-scoring model in the Ratings and the best choice for playing music and video. The built-in webcam, microphone, and remote control are handy, and Apple's

superior tech support is a plus. However, this model has no memory-card reader; you'll need an external one. For a Windows model with a 17-inch glossy display and good multimedia features, consider the HP. It's a great deal for a loaded laptop, making it a CR Best Buy. Its big screen and Nvidia video adapter are good for gaming.

Smart pick for on-the-go computing:

19 Sony Vaio VGNSZ140, $1,980

The 4.2-pound Sony balances speed and portability. It has a very good glossy 13.3-inch display with antireflective coating, plus a built-in webcam, microphone, and fingerprint scanner. Its two video cards are a plus: On the Speed setting, an Nvidia adapter delivers fast performance but drains battery life rather quickly. On the Stamina setting, the computer uses a slower but less power-hungry Intel graphics card.

Readers report on some 49,000 laptop computers

This graph shows the percentage of laptop computers bought between 2001 and 2005 that have been repaired or had a serious problem. We have enough data to report on eight major brands. Differences of less than 3 points are not meaningful. Models within a brand may vary, and changes in design or manufacture may affect reliability. Still, choosing a brand with a good repair history can improve your odds of getting a reliable model.

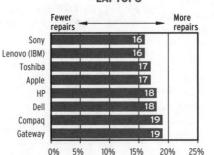

LAPTOPS

Fewer repairs ← → More repairs

Brand	%
Sony	16
Lenovo (IBM)	16
Toshiba	17
Apple	17
HP	18
Dell	18
Compaq	19
Gateway	19

0% 5% 10% 15% 20% 25%

Data are based on more than 49,000 responses to our Annual Product Reliability Survey, conducted by the Consumer Reports National Research Center. Data have been adjusted to eliminate differences between brands solely linked to age and usage.

Ratings

In performance order, within categories.

Excellent Very good Good Fair Poor

REFERENCE & RATINGS

Key number	Brand & model / Similar models, in small type, comparable to tested model.	Processor	Video adapter	Price	Overall score	Ergonomics	Display	Multimedia features	Speed	Speakers	Battery life (hr.)	Weight (lb.)	Memory-card slot	FireWire port	Remote control	Built-in webcam
	15.4-INCH BUDGET MODELS *Relatively low-cost systems for most general uses, including word processing, Web browsing, and e-mail.*															
1 CR BEST BUY	**Gateway** NX510S	Celeron M 420	Intel 950	$740	55	○	○[1]	○	◐	◖	3½	6.4	●	●		
2	**Lenovo** (IBM) 3000 N100	Core Duo T2300	Intel 950	950	53	○	○[1]	○	◐	●	3½	6.1	●			
3	**Dell** Inspiron B130	Pentium M 745	Intel 900	750	51	○	○[1]	○	◐	◖	2	6.6				
4	**Toshiba** Satellite A105	Celeron M 390	ATI 200M	850	51	○	○	○	○	○	1¼	5.8				
	15.4-INCH WORKHORSE MODELS *Have additional memory and storage for more intensive uses, such as 3D games and video editing.*															
5	**Apple** Macbook Pro 15"	2.0-GHz Core Duo	128-MB ATI X1600	2,200	63	◐	◐[1]	◐	◉	◖	3¼	5.5		●	●	●
6 CR BEST BUY	**Gateway** NX560XL	Core Duo T2400	128-MB ATI X1400	1,520	59	○	○	◐	◉	○	4	6.5	●	●		
7	**Dell** Inspiron E1505	Core Duo T2400	128-MB ATI X1300	1,120	58	○	○	◐	◉	○	2½	6.6	●	●		
8	**HP** Pavilion dv5000t / Compaq Presario V5000T	Core Duo T2400	128-MB Nvidia 7400	1,215	58	○	○	◐	◉	○	3	6.8	●	●		
9	**Sony** VAIO VGN-FE590G / VGN-FE690	Core Duo T2400	Intel 950	1,550	57	○	◐	○	◐	◖	3	6.2	●			●
10	**HP** Pavilion dv5000z / Compaq Presario V5000Z	Turion 64 ML-37	ATI 200M	1,145	53	○	○	○	◐	○	2¼	6.7	●	●		
	17-INCH WORKHORSE MODELS *Same as above; larger screen makes these laptops especially suitable as a desktop replacement.*															
11	**Apple** Macbook Pro 17"	2.16-GHz Core Duo	256-MB ATI X1600	2,800	71	◐	◉[1]	◐	◉	◐	4	6.7		●	●	●
12	**Toshiba** Qosmio G35-AV600	Core Duo T2400	256-MB Nvidia 7300	2,400	61	◐	◐	◐	◉	◐	2¾	10	●	●	●	
13	**Dell** Inspiron E1705	Core Duo T2400	256-MB ATI X1400	1,620	60	◐	○[1]	◐	◉	○	3½	7.8	●	●		
14 CR BEST BUY	**HP** Pavilion dv8000t	Core Duo T2400	256-MB Nvidia 7600	1,315	59	○	○[1]	◐	◉	○	4¼	8.2	●	●		
15	**Gateway** NX860X	Core Duo T2400	128-MB Nvidia 7600	1,565	57	○	○[1]	○	◐	◐	2¾	7.9	●	●		
16	**Toshiba** Satellite P100	Core Duo T2400	128-MB Nvidia 7600	1,585	57	○	◐	◐	◐	○	1¼	7.4	●	●		
17	**Averatec** 7160-EC1	Turion 64 ML-32	ATI 200M	1,200	35	●	○	○	○	●	2¼	7.3	●	●		
	12.1 TO 13.3-INCH SLIM AND LIGHT MODELS *Lightweight systems for travelers.*															
18	**Apple** Macbook 13.3"	1.83-GHz Core Duo	Intel 950	1,200	62	○	○	◐	◐	●	4	5.1		●	●	●
19	**Sony** VAIO VGN-SZ140 13.3" / VGN-SZ240	Core Duo T2400	Intel/Nvidia 7400	1,980	60	○	◐	◐	◉	◖	3¼	4.2	●	●		●
20	**Toshiba** Portege R205 12.1"	Pentium M 753	Intel 900	2,150	50	◖	○[1]	○	○	◐	4	2.8	●			
21	**Averatec** 2260-EY1 12.1"	Turion 64 MT-32	Via DeltaChrome	1,000	43	◖	○	○	○	○	2½	4.2	●	●		

[1] Matte display.

Guide to the Ratings

Overall score is based mostly on ergonomics and display quality but considers multimedia features and other factors. **Ergonomics** represents the ease of using the keyboard, touchpad, and switches, as well as case design. **Display** covers screen quality, including clarity, contrast, and viewing angle. **Multimedia features** include hardware (memory-card slots, A/V connections), and software (multimedia playback and editing programs). **Speed** measures performance while running office productivity and content creation applications. **Speakers** covers speaker fidelity, bass response, and loudness. **Battery life** is while running productivity applications. Weight includes optical drives and one battery (no AC adapter). **Price** is approximate retail. Tested models have 1 GB of memory, except budget models, which have 512 MB; 60-GB hard drive for budget and slim and light models, 80-GB drive for workhorse models; a DVD burner for the workhorse models, the Sony (19), and the Veratec (21). All others have a combo drive. All tested models have Wi-Fi and a one-year warranty on parts and labor. *Based on testing in September 2006 issue of CONSUMER REPORTS.*

MONITORS

CR Quick Recommendations

Monitors

Prices for LCD monitors continue to fall, making them (especially in their 17-inch size) the best choice for most people. Choose a model 19 inches or larger if you have poor vision and prefer a larger screen, routinely edit photos, play games often, or frequently run several programs at once. Models differ in display quality, features, warranty, and how well designed their controls are. Full-featured models typically include both adjustable height and tilt to reduce neck strain. They also include the ability to rotate from landscape mode, which is best for photography and video, to portrait mode, which is best for Web pages and text documents. If more than one person will often view the monitor at the same time, consider a model that has a wide viewing angle. Most models have a DVI input, a computer interface that makes it easier to configure the monitor for the best picture quality.

QUICK PICKS

For a full-featured 17-inch LCD:

1 Samsung SyncMaster 740T, $380

An excellent performer that is easy to use and has excellent display quality. It can be rotated from landscape to portrait mode and adjusted for height, and has a DVI input along with a three-year warranty.

Best values in a 17-inch LCD; both are CR Best Buys:

5 eMachines E174T4, $270
6 HP L1706, $250

Both are very good performers and are attractively priced for 17-inch models, with a wider viewing angle than most displays. The eMachines is a bit easier to use, but it lacks a DVI input and has a warranty of only one year. The HP has a three-year warranty and a DVI input.

For a full-featured 19-inch LCD:

14 Dell 1907FP, $390

A very good performer and easy to use. It can be rotated from landscape to portrait, adjusted for height, and has a DVI input along with a three-year warranty.

Best value in a 19-inch monitor; a CR Best Buy:

16 Westinghouse LCM-19V5, $300

A very good performer and very low priced. But it lacks a DVI cable. It has a warranty of only one year.

For Macintosh users who want a Mac display:

24 Apple 20-inch Cinema Display, $800

Designed for use with a Power Mac, this 20-inch model is the smallest Apple LCD. It offers a very wide viewing angle and wide shape, and a DVI input. But its video cable is not detachable, therefore it's inconvenient to repair if it breaks or malfunctions. It has free tech support for 90 days but only a one-year warranty. It's very costly, so it's primarily for Power Mac owners who want a large, very wide monitor that matches the styling of their computer.

Ratings

In performance order, within categories

Legend: Excellent ● | Very good ◕ | Good ○ | Fair ◑ | Poor ●

Key number	Brand & model	Price	Overall score (0–100)	Viewable image (in.)	Display quality	Ease of use	Wide viewing angle	Display rotates	Adjust height	3-year warranty
17-INCH LCD MONITORS										
1	**Samsung** SyncMaster 740T	$380	81	17	●	◕		●	●	●
2	**BenQ** FP72G+S	300	77	17	●	○				●
3	**Dell** 1707FP	320	74	17	◕	◕		●	●	●
4	**Eizo** FlexScan M1700	390	74	17	◕	○			●	●
5	**eMachines** E17T4 (CR Best Buy)	270	73	17	◕	◕	●			
6	**HP** L1706 (CR Best Buy)	250	73	17	◕	○				●
7	**LG** L1770HQ	350	73	17	◕	○				●
8	**ViewSonic** VP730b	400	72	17	◕	◕				
9	**Proview** PL713s	275	69	17	◕	○				
10	**NEC** MultiSync 1740CX	300	68	17	◕	○	●			●
11	**Envision** EN7600	280	67	17	◕	◕	●			
12	**NEC** MultiSync LCD1770NX	360	59	17	○	○			●	●
19-INCH LCD MONITORS										
13	**Planar** PX1910M	470	79	19	●	◕		●	●	●
14	**Dell** 1907FP	390	76	19	◕	◕		●	●	●
15	**HP** F1905	430	72	19	◕	◕	●		●	
16	**Westinghouse** LCM-19V5 (CR Best Buy)	300	72	19	◕	◕				
17	**Gateway** FPD1965	350	71	19	◕	◕				
18	**LG** L1932TQ	360	69	19	◕	◕				●
19	**Samsung** SyncMaster 970P	600	69	19	◕	○		●	●	●
20	**ViewSonic** VX922	430	69	19	◕	◕	●			
21	**Princeton** LCD1950	335	68	19	◕	◕				●
22	**KDS** K-9b	290	63	19	◕	○				
23	**Sony** SDM-HS95P	535	60	19	◕	○				
20-INCH LCD MONITORS										
24	**Apple** 20" Cinema Display	800	75	20	◕	◕	●			

Guide to the Ratings

Overall score is based on display quality, ease of use, and features. **Viewable image** is the viewable image size, in inches. **Display quality** covers image clarity, color accuracy, and contrast. It's based on the judgments of a panel who viewed text and photographs on each monitor, as well as lab measurements. **Ease of use** includes readability of buttons and other controls, clarity of onscreen control menus, and the ability to tilt the monitor on its base. **Features** columns list **wide viewing angle,** indicating models that can be viewed clearly from positions at least 45 degrees off the centerline; a **display** that **rotates** from landscape to portrait orientation and that **adjusts for height**; and a **three-year warranty. Price** is approximate retail. *Based on tests posted to ConsumerReports.org in June 2006, with updated prices and availability.*

CR Quick Recommendations

MP3 players

Like most digital devices, MP3 players perform very well at their key task. As the Ratings show, many MP3 players can produce near-audio-CD-quality sound out of the headphone jack, and the others were nearly as good. The headphones supplied with the players were a bit better on some models than others, though even the worst performed respectably.

Flash-memory players offer the smallest, lightest, and most affordable way to enjoy MP3 music on the go, and can typically run much longer than their hard-drive cousins on a single charge. But hard-disk players have much greater storage capacity, with larger LCD displays and controls. So-called microdrive players offer an appealing compromise between price and capacity, but perhaps not for long. Flash-memory-player capacities are steadily advancing into microdrive territory.

A growing number of players now have color displays. Most models allow you to display photos and other images, often in slideshow fashion and sometimes with the ability to listen to music as you do so. And an increasing proportion of color-display models also allow you to watch videos.

All players accept music you already own on CD, which you convert into digital music files and transfer to the player using supplied software. All the players we've chosen can play copy-protected music purchased from online stores.

Many tested models have similar models that differ from the test unit mainly in capacity; consider these if the tested unit is larger (and pricier) or smaller than you need.

QUICK PICKS

If low price, light weight, and small size are paramount:

2 **Cowon iAudio U3 (2 GB), $180**
4 **Apple iPod Nano (2 GB), $200**
8 **RCA Lyra RD2217 (1 GB), $125**
13 **SanDisk Sansa m240 (1 GB), $85**

The Cowon iAudio U3 and Apple iPod Nano combine fine performance and high capacity, albeit at a relatively high price. In their 2-GB versions, these players hold about 500 songs—enough variety for any long weekend. There's also a 4-GB Nano for $50 more. (A newer player that isn't in the Ratings, the Sansa e270, $270, has a 6-GB capacity and performed well in our initial tests, and more high-capacity flash players are expected from other manufacturers.) The Cowon includes an FM radio (from which you can record programs), a built-in microphone, and a line input for recording from other sources. It's also one of the few flash units that plays video. But it doesn't work with Macintosh computers. The slightly bigger—but much thinner—Nano lacks these bells and whistles, but provides seamless access to one of the biggest legal sources for online music: the 2 million-song iTunes store. It adds volume-leveling, plus a volume limiter to protect your hearing. For both players, the AC charger is optional equipment. The Cowon's costs $10; the Nano's $30.

The more-affordable RCA Lyra RD2217 and SanDisk Sansa m240 lack color displays and hold half the songs, but provide lots of features for the buck. The sports-oriented RCA has a stopwatch, and calorie and pulse-rate modes. It also has a relatively long playback time and an FM radio. The SanDisk also has an FM radio and stopwatch, plus a built-in microphone for personal memos. But it won't work with Macs. Both use standard batteries.

For fairly high capacity in a compact size:

25 **Creative Zen Micro Photo (8 GB) $225**
26 **RCA Lyra RD2765 (5 GB), $175**

These models are larger than flash-memory players, though they still fit comfortably in your palm. And they hold many more songs than most flash players. Both have color displays and show slideshows, though neither allows you to play accompanying music. The 8-GB Creative holds about 2,000 songs and features an FM radio, built-in microphone, and volume-leveling playback capability. But it doesn't work with Macs and the AC charger is a $40 option. The less expensive 5-GB RCA is similarly sized, but has fewer features and holds 1,250 songs.

For the best combination of huge capacity and a fairly low price:

32 **iRiver H10 (20 GB), $200**
34 **Creative Zen Vision M (30 GB), $300**
36 **Creative Zen Sleek Photo (20 GB), $200**
37 **Apple iPod (30 GB), $300**

While these models are larger and heavier than flash-memory and microdrive players, they can hold more music—from 2,500 to 15,000 songs, depending on the model. The Apple iPod (30 GB) should be the first choice for most people in a high-capacity MP3 player, given its palm-friendly dimensions. Video and photo quality was among the best of any model we tested. Like the Nano, it includes a volume leveler and limiter. Some quibbles: As with the Nano, the charger is a $30 option. It also lacks the proprietary cable ($20) needed for connecting the player to a TV set to view videos or photos on a larger screen.

Those who need a player with a radio or voice recorder must turn to other brands, some of which offer models that cost a little less than the iPod. The iRiver H10 (20 GB) offers an FM radio (from which you can record programs) and built-in microphone. The Creative Zen Vision M (30 GB) packs most of the features of the similarly priced iPod, including video playback and volume leveling, and adds an FM Radio (from which you can record programs), built-in microphone, and line output. Video quality was as good as the iPod, though there's not as much top-tier content to download. The less expensive—and less capacious—Creative Zen Sleek Photo (20 GB) has volume leveling but lacks video. All three models are thicker than the iPod and don't work with Macs.

MP3 PLAYERS

Ratings

Excellent ● Very good ◒ Good ○ Fair ◓ Poor ●

In performance order, within categories.

Key number	Brand & model	Price	Overall score (0–100; P F G VG E)	Ease of use	Headphone quality	Audio quality	Damage resistance	Picture quality	Audio playback time (hr.)	Width (in.)	Height (in.)	Depth (in.)	Weight (oz.)	Audio playback formats	Plays online music	Mac compatible	Color display	Video playback	Plays online video	Slideshow capability	FM radio	Built-in microphone	Firmware upgradeable
	FLASH-MEMORY MP3 PLAYERS (128 MB TO 4 GB)																						
1	**iRiver** U10 (1 GB)	$200	72	Very good	Very good	Excellent	Excellent	Very good	28	2.7	1.7	0.7	2.4	MP3, WMA, WMA-DRM, OGG	•		•	•			•	•	•
2	**Cowon** iAudio U3 (2 GB)	180	70	Very good	Very good	Excellent	Excellent	Good	18	1.3	2.8	0.7	1.3	MP3, WMA, WMA-DRM, OGG, FLAC, WAV	•		•	•			•	•	•
3	**Samsung** YP-T8Z (1 GB)	175	69	Very good	Good	Excellent	Excellent	Good	17	1.8	3.3	0.6	2	MP3, WMA, WMA-DRM, ASF, OGG	•		•	•			•	•	•
4	**Apple** iPod Nano (2 GB)	200	66	Very good	Very good	Excellent	Very good	Good	15	1.6	3.6	0.3	1.6	MP3, iTunes AAC, iTunes AAC-DRM, WAV, AA, AIFF, Apple Lossless	•	•	•			•			•
5	**iRiver** T10 (1 GB)	155	66	Good	Good	Excellent	Excellent	NA	39	3.4	1.6	1.2	2.6	MP3, WMA, WMA-DRM, OGG, ASF	•		•				•	•	•
6	**iRiver** iFP-799 (1 GB)	130	65	Good	Good	Very good	Very good	NA	34	3.4	1.4	1.1	2.2	MP3, WMA, OGG, ASF	•	•					•	•	•
7	**iRiver** T30 (1 GB)	130	64	Good	Very good	Excellent	Excellent	NA	15	2.5	1.3	0.9	1.3	MP3, WMA, WMA-DRM, OGG, AA	•							•	•
8	**RCA** Lyra RD2217 (1 GB)	125	64	Good	Good	Excellent	Excellent	NA	39	2.0	2.9	1.1	2.4	MP3, WMA, WMA-DRM, AA	•	•					•		•
9	**Samsung** YP-Z5 (2 GB)	200	63	Good	Very good	Excellent	Very good	Good	35	1.7	3.6	0.5	2.1	MP3, WMA, WMA-DRM, OGG	•		•			•			•
10	**Creative** Zen Nano Plus (1 GB)	70	62	Good	Good	Very good	Excellent	NA	13	2.6	1.4	0.6	1.2	MP3, WMA, WMA-DRM	•						•	•	•
11	**Oregon** Scientific MP121 (1 GB)	170	62	Very good	Very good	Excellent	Very good	NA	8	2.1	2.2	0.8	1.4	MP3, WMA, WAV		•					•		•
12	**Philips** SA178 (512 MB)	100	61	Good	Good	Excellent	Excellent	NA	13	3.2	1.2	0.6	1.3	MP3, WMA, WMA-DRM, WAV	•	•					•	•	•
13	**SanDisk** Sansa m240 (1 GB)	85	61	Very good	Good	Excellent	Very good	NA	15	3.1	1.4	1.0	1.4	MP3. WMA, WMA-DRM, AA	•						•	•	•
14	**Creative** MuVo TX FM (1 GB)	100	60	Good	Good	Excellent	Excellent	NA	14	3.0	1.5	0.6	1.5	MP3, WMA, WMA-DRM	•						•	•	•
15	**JVC** XA-MP101 (1 GB)	120	59	Good	Good	Excellent	Excellent	NA	13	2.0	2.0	0.6	1.4	MP3, WMA, WMA-DRM	•						•	•	•
16	**Samsung** YP-F1 Z (1 GB)	125	58	Very good	Good	Excellent	Excellent	NA	7	2.5	1.2	0.8	1.1	MP3, WMA, WMA-DRM, OGG, ASF	•						•	•	•
17	**Apple** iPod shuffle M9725LL/A (1 GB)	100	57	Good	Very good	Excellent	Very good	NA	16	1.0	3.4	0.4	0.8	MP3, iTunes AAC, iTunes AAC-DRM, WAV, AA, AIFF	•	•							•
18	**Dell** DJ Ditty (512 MB)	100	57	Good	Very good	Excellent	Excellent	NA	7	3.3	1.2	0.5	1.2	MP3, WMA, WMA-DRM, AA	•						•		•
19	**Sony** Walkman Bean NW-307 (1 GB)	125	57	Good	Very good	Excellent	Good	NA	52	2.7	1.0	1.5	1.6	MP3, ATRAC3, ATRAC3 Plus, ATRAC3-DRM	•						•		
20	**MobiBLU** DAH-1500i (1 GB)	130	56	Good	Very good	Excellent	Very good	NA	8	0.9	0.9	0.9	0.6	MP3, WMA, WMA-DRM	•	•					•	•	•
21	**SanDisk** Sansa e140 (1 GB)	85	56	Good	Good	Excellent	Excellent	NA	11	2.1	3.0	0.6	1.7	MP3, WMA, WMA-DRM, WAV, AA	•						•		•
22	**Sony** Network Walkman NW-E107 (1 GB)	95	56	Good	Good	Excellent	Very good	NA	41	2.3	2.3	0.8	1.4	MP3, ATRAC3, ATRAC3 Plus, ATRAC3-DRM	•								
23	**RiData** OLE 3000 (512 MB)	130	51	Good	Good	Excellent	Very good	NA	11	2.6	1.8	0.7	1.6	MP3, WMA, WMA-DRM, WAV	•						•	•	
24	**Bang** and Olufsen Beosound 2	460	45	Good	Very good	Excellent	Excellent	NA	8	2.9	2.9	0.9	3.1	MP3, WMA		•							•
	MICRODRIVE HARD-DISK MP3 PLAYERS (3 GB TO 8 GB)																						
25	**Creative** Zen Micro Photo (8 GB)	225	64	Good	Very good	Excellent	Very good	Good	16	2.0	3.3	0.7	3.8	MP3, WMA, WMA-DRM, WAV	•		•			•	•	•	•
26	**RCA** Lyra RD2765 (5 GB)	175	63	Very good	Very good	Excellent	Very good	Fair	11	2.0	3.4	0.7	2.9	MP3, WMA, WMA-DRM	•	•	•			•			•
27	**Archos** Gmini XS 100 (3 GB)	125	62	Very good	Good	Excellent	Very good	NA	11	1.7	3.6	0.6	2.7	MP3, WMA, WMA-DRM, WAV	•	•							•
28	**iRiver** H10 (6 GB)	270	61	Very good	Good	Very good	Very good	Fair	6	2.2	3.8	0.6	3.5	MP3, WMA, WMA-DRM, WAV	•		•			•	•	•	•
29	**Creative** Zen Micro (6 GB)	200	58	Good	Good	Excellent	Very good	NA	13	2.0	3.3	0.7	3.8	MP3, WMA, WMA-DRM	•						•	•	•
30	**Samsung** YH-820 (5 GB)	230	56	Good	Good	Excellent	Very good	Fair	9	2.0	3.5	0.6	3	MP3, WMA, WMA-DRM	•		•			•		•	•

Ratings (continued)

In performance order, within categories.

Excellent Very good Good Fair Poor

REFERENCE & RATINGS

HARD-DISK MP3 PLAYERS (10 GB TO 60 GB)

Key number	Brand & model	Price	Overall score	Ease of use	Headphone quality	Audio quality	Damage resistance	Picture quality	Audio playback time (hr.)	Width (in.)	Height (in.)	Depth (in.)	Weight (oz.)	Audio playback formats	Plays online music	Mac compatible	Color display	Video playback	Plays online video	Slideshow capability	FM radio	Built-in microphone	Firmware upgradeable
31	Cowon iAudio X5L (30 GB)	$300	68	◕	◕	⬤	◕	◑	30	2.4	4.1	1.0	6.6	MP3, WMA, OGG, FLAC, WAV, ASF			●	●			●	●	●
32	iRiver H10 (20 GB)	200	68	◕	◕	⬤	◕	◑	15	2.5	4.0	0.9	5.8	MP3, WMA, WMA-DRM, WAV	●		●			●	●	●	●
33	Cowon iAudio X5 (20 GB)	280	67	◕	◕	⬤	◕	◑	13	2.4	4.1	0.8	5.4	MP3, WMA, OGG, ASF, WAV, FLAC			●	●			●	●	●
34	Creative Zen Vision M (30 GB)	300	66	◕	○	⬤	◕	◕	18	2.4	4.1	0.8	5.6	MP3, WMA, WMA-DRM, WAV	●		●	●		●	●	●	●
35	Archos Gmini 402 Pocket Multimedia Center (20 GB)	340	65	◕	◕	⬤	◕	◕	12	4.2	2.4	0.7	5.6	MP3, WMA, WMA-DRM, WAV			●	●		●			●
36	Creative Zen Sleek Photo (20 GB)	200	65	○	◕	⬤	◕	◕	18	2.3	4.0	0.7	5.5	MP3, WMA, WMA-DRM, WAV	●		●			●	●	●	●
37	Apple iPod (30 GB)	300	63	◕	○	⬤	◕	◕	15	2.4	4.1	0.4	4.8	MP3, iTunes AAC, iTunes AAC-DRM, WAV, AA, AIFF, Apple Lossless	●	●	●	●	●	●			●
38	Creative Zen Sleek (20 GB)	250	63	◕	○	⬤	⬤	NA	18	2.4	4.0	0.7	5.6	MP3, WMA, WMA-DRM, WAV	●						●	●	●
39	Toshiba gigabeat MEGF20	210	63	◕	○	⬤	◑	○	19	2.5	4.2	0.7	5.3	MP3, WMA, WMA-DRM, WAV	●		●						●
40	Archos Gmini XS 202 (20 GB)	300	62	◕	○	⬤	◕	NA	16	2.3	3.0	0.8	4.2	MP3, WMA, WMA-DRM, WAV	●	●							●
41	Archos Gmini XS 202s (20 GB)	250	62	○	○	⬤	○	NA	16	2.3	3.0	1.1	4.2	MP3, WMA, WMA-DRM, WAV	●	●							●
42	Samsung YH-999 (20 GB)	340	62	○	○	⬤	◕	○	14	3.9	4.2	0.9	8	MP3, WMA, WMA-DRM, OGG, ASF	●		●	●		●	●	●	●
43	Philips HDD6330 (30 GB)	250	61	○	○	⬤	◕	○	17	2.5	4.1	0.7	5.4	MP3, WMA, WMA-DRM, WAV			●				●	●	●
44	Creative Zen Vision (30 GB)	400	59	◕	○	◕	○	○	15	4.9	2.9	0.9	8.5	MP3, WMA, WMA-DRM, WAV	●		●	●	●	●	●	●	●

Guide to the Ratings

The MP3 player market is dominated by three types of players: flash-memory, microdrive, and hard-disk. Flash-memory players are the smallest and lightest of the group. They're no bigger than a pack of gum and weigh no more than three ounces. They're solid-state, meaning no moving parts, and their storage capacities range from 128 megabytes up to six gigabytes (about 30 to 1,500 songs). Palm-sized microdrive players have tiny hard drives with a storage capacity of three to eight gigabytes (about 750 to 2,000 songs). They weigh about a quarter-pound. Hard-disk players are about the size of a deck of cards and have a storage capacity of 10 to 60 gigabytes (about 2,500 to 15,000 songs). Some hard-disk players with video capability have relatively larger displays, and as a result, tend to be the bulkiest players. You can expect a player can hold about 250 songs per gigabyte of memory. **Overall score,** as MP3 players, is based primarily on ease of use, headphone quality, audio quality, damage resistance and audio playback time. Video and picture quality are rated but not included in the overall score. **Ease of use** mainly covers player characteristics that aid in convenience, versatility, and portability. These primarily include navigation and scrolling features; the accessibility and readability of the controls; and the readability and breadth of the information in the display; size and weight; and ease of use while walking or jogging. Some features and capabilities considered include the presence of an FM radio, built-in microphone, upgradeable firmware, equalizer, data storage, software assessment, and the player's ability to be recognized as a hard drive by a computer without the installation of additional drivers. **Headphone quality** reflects judgments from a listening panel com-

paring the player and its supplied headphone to a test audio CD and a high-fidelity headphone. All uncompressed (audio CD or WAV) test music sources were ripped (encoded) to MP3 format (128, 192, and 256 kbps CBR rate) using a high-quality encoder. **Audio quality** reflects judgments from a listening panel comparing the player to a test audio CD, using the high-fidelity headphone for both. All uncompressed (audio CD or WAV) test music sources were ripped (encoded) to MP3 format (128, 192, and 256 kbps CBR rate) using a high quality encoder. **Damage resistance** mainly reflects drop-test results; scratch- and wipe-resistance results were also considered. **Picture quality** reflects judgments based mainly on viewing angle, display size, and clarity and color in different lighting conditions, using the JPEG format. **Audio playback time** reflects lab measurements of continuous playback time to the nearest hour, using a selection of music tracks encoded to MP3 format at a 128 kbps CBR rate; fully charged rechargeable batteries; backlight at the minimum setting; with included headphone; and volume set at a reasonable level. For players that can use standard batteries such as alkaline, expect a bit longer playback time. Our measurements should not be compared with those stated by the manufacturer, which may use different testing methods and criteria. **Dimensions** are measured to the nearest tenth, and listed the way the player would be oriented if you were viewing the screen. **Weight** is how much the player weighs in ounces, including batteries but not including accessories. For models with no internal memory, the memory card is included. **Price** is approximate retail. *Based on tests posted to ConsumerReports.org in July 2006.*

MP3 PLAYERS

Profiles Model-by-Model

FLASH-MEMORY PLAYERS (128 MB TO 4 GB)

1 iRiver U10 (1 GB) Very good overall. Very good video and picture quality. Video playback time measured five hours. Display measures 1.3x1.8 inches. Good recording quality via FM radio. Very good recording quality via built-in microphone. Has manual picture advance with simultaneous music. Has custom and presets equalizer, fade-in audio playback, text viewer, games, alarm clock, and multilingual menus. Can edit playlist but can't delete files on player. MTP compatible. No Mac support. Includes earbud-type headphone. Has nonremoveable battery that charges via computer USB2 port. AC charger not included. Similar: U10 (512 MB).

2 Cowon iAudio U3 (2 GB) Very good overall. Good video and picture quality. Video playback time measured eight hours. Display measures 0.7x0.9 inches. Excellent recording quality capable via line input. Fair recording quality via FM radio. Poor recording quality via built-in microphone. Has manual picture advance with simultaneous music. Has custom and presets equalizer, A-B repeat, channel balance, fade-in audio playback, text viewer, alarm clock, and multilingual menus. Can edit playlist and delete files on player. MTP compatible. No Mac support. Includes earbud-type headphone. Has nonremovable battery that charges via computer USB2 port. AC charger not included. Similar: iAudio U3 (1 GB).

3 Samsung YP-T8Z (1 GB) Very good overall. Fair video and good picture quality. Video playback time measured seven hours. Display measures 1.1x1.4 inches. Excellent recording quality via line input. Poor recording quality via FM radio. Good recording quality via built-in microphone. Has manual picture advance with simultaneous music. Has USB host mode, custom and presets equalizer, A-B repeat, text viewer, games, alarm clock, and multilingual menus. Can edit playlist and delete files on player. No Mac support. Includes earbud-type headphone. Has nonremovable battery. USB2 interface. Similar: YP-T8X (512 MB).

4 Apple iPod Nano (2 GB) Very good overall. Good picture quality. Has slideshow capability with simultaneous music. Has presets equalizer, volume limiter and leveling, contacts and calendar appointment application, text viewer, stopwatch, alarm clock, games, and multilingual menus. Can edit playlist but can't delete files on player. Includes earbud-type headphone. Has nonremoveable battery that charges via computer USB2 port. AC charger not included. Similar: iPod Nano (1 GB), iPod Nano (4 GB).

5 iRiver T10 (1 GB) Very good overall. Fair recording quality via FM radio. Very good recording quality via built-in microphone. Displays pictures in bitmap (BMP) format only. Has manual picture advance with simultaneous music. Has custom and presets equalizer, A-B repeat, alarm clock, and multilingual menus. Can edit playlist but can't delete files on player. No Mac support. Includes earbud-type headphone. Uses one AA battery. USB2 interface. Similar: T10 (512 MB).

6 iRiver iFP-799 (1 GB) Very good overall. Excellent recording quality via line input or built-in microphone. Fair recording quality via FM radio. Has custom and presets equalizer, A-B repeat, channel balance, fade-in audio playback, alarm clock, and multilingual menus. Can delete files but can't edit playlist on player. Includes earbud-type headphone. Uses one AA battery. USB2 interface. Similar: iFP-790 (256 MB), iFP-795 (512 MB).

7 iRiver T30 (1 GB) Very good overall. Excellent recording quality capable via line input. Good recording quality via built-in microphone. Has custom and presets equalizer, A-B repeat, alarm clock, and multilingual menus. Can't edit playlist or delete files on player. MTP compatible. No Mac support. Includes earbud-type headphone. Uses one AAA battery. USB2 interface.

8 RCA Lyra RD2217 (1 GB) Very good overall. Fair recording quality via FM radio. Has sports mode that includes a stopwatch, calorie and pulse rate modes—all novelty features not intended for use as medical equipment. Has presets equalizer, and multilingual menus. Can edit playlist but can't delete files on player. Includes earbud-type headphone with behind-the-ear hooks. Uses one AA battery. USB2 interface. Similar: Lyra RD2212 (256 MB), Lyra RD2215 (512 MB).

9 Samsung YP-Z5 (2 GB) Very good overall. Good picture quality. Has slideshow with simultaneous music. Has presets equalizer, and multilingual menus. Can't edit playlist or delete files on player. MTP compatible. No Mac support. Includes earbud-type headphone. Has nonremoveable battery that charges via computer USB2 port. AC charger not included. Similar: YP-Z5 (4 GB).

10 Creative Zen Nano Plus (1 GB) Very good overall. Fair recording quality capable via line input or FM radio. Good recording quality via built-in microphone. Has custom and presets equalizer, A-B repeat, and multilingual menus. Can delete files but can't edit on player. Doesn't list tracks. No Mac support. Includes earbud-type headphone. Uses one AAA battery. USB2 interface. Similar model: Zen Nano Plus (512 MB).

11 Oregon Scientific MP121 (1 GB) Very good overall. Currently doesn't play any copy-protected music purchased from an online music store. Has sports mode that includes pedometer and stopwatch features. These modes may not be intended to be used as medical equipment. Has presets equalizer, alarm clock, and multilingual menus. Can delete files but can't edit playlist on player. Includes earbud and earplug-type headphones. Has nonremoveable battery that charges via computer USB2 port. AC charger not included.

12 Philips SA178 (512 MB) Very good overall. Fair recording quality via FM radio. Good recording quality via built-in microphone. Direct connect to computer USB Port. Has custom and presets equalizer, A-B repeat, and multilingual menus. Can edit playlist but can't delete files on player. Includes earbud-type headphone. Has nonremoveable battery that charges via computer USB2 port. AC charger not included.

13 SanDisk Sansa m240 (1 GB) Very good overall. Fair recording quality via built-in microphone. Has custom and presets equalizer, A-B repeat, stopwatch, multilingual menus. Can edit playlist but can't delete files on player. No Mac support. Includes earbud-type headphone. Uses one AAA battery. USB2 interface. Similar: Sansa m230 (512 MB), Sansa m250 (2 GB).

14 Creative MuVo TX FM (1 GB) Good overall. Poor recording quality via FM radio. Fair recording quality via built-in microphone. Direct connect to computer USB port. Doesn't list tracks. Has custom and presets equalizer, A-B repeat, and multilingual menus. Can edit playlist but can't delete files on player. No Mac support. Includes earbud-type headphone. Uses one AAA battery. USB2 interface. Similar models: MuVo TX FM (128 MB), MuVo TX FM (256 MB), MuVo TX FM (512 MB).

15 JVC XA-MP101 (1 GB) Good overall. Fair recording quality via FM radio. Good recording quality via built-in microphone. Has line output, custom and presets equal-

Profiles Model-by-Model (continued)

izer, and multilingual menus. Can edit playlist but can't delete files on player. No Mac support. Includes earbud-type headphone. Uses one AAA battery. USB2 interface. Similar: XA-MP51 (512 MB).

16 Samsung YP-F1 Z (1 GB) Good overall. Fair recording quality via FM radio or built-in microphone. Has custom and presets equalizer, A-B repeat, multilingual menus. Can edit playlist and delete files on player. Lacks lock control. No Mac support. Includes earbud-type headphone. Has nonremovable battery that charges via computer USB2 port. AC charger not included. Similar: YP-F1 V (256 MB), YP-F1 X (512 MB).

17 Apple iPod shuffle M9725LL/A (1 GB) Good overall. Direct connect to computer USB port. Lacks display. No equalizer. Can't edit playlist or delete files on player. Includes earbud-type headphone. Has nonremoveable battery that charges via computer USB2 port. AC charger not included. Similar: iPod Shuffle M9724LL/A (512 MB).

18 Dell DJ Ditty (512 MB) Good overall. Direct connect to computer USB Port. Has presets equalizer, A-B repeat, and multilingual menus. Can't edit playlist or delete files on player. No Mac support. Includes earbud-type headphone. Has nonremovable battery that charges via computer USB2 port. AC charger not included.

19 Sony Walkman Bean NW-307 (1 GB) Good overall. Direct connect to computer USB port. Has volume limiter, custom and presets equalizer, and A-B repeat. Can't edit playlist or delete files on player. Firmware not upgradeable. No Mac support. Includes earbud-type headphone. Has nonremoveable battery that charges via computer USB1.1 port. AC charger not included. Similar: Walkman Bean NW-305 (512 MB).

20 MobiBLU DAH-1500i (1 GB) Good overall. Fair recording quality via FM radio. Good recording quality via built-in microphone. Has custom and presets equalizer, A-B repeat, fade-in audio playback, and multilingual menus. Can edit playlist and delete files on player. Includes earbud-type headphone. Has nonremovable battery that charges via computer USB2 port. AC charger not included. Similar: DAH-1500i (512 MB).

21 SanDisk Sansa e140 (1 GB) Good overall. Has custom and presets equalizer, A-B repeat, stopwatch, multilingual menus. Can't edit playlist or delete files on player. No Mac support. Includes earbud-type headphone. Uses one AAA battery. USB2

interface. Similar: Sansa e130 (512 MB).

22 Sony Network Walkman NW-E107 (1 GB) Good overall. Has volume limiter, custom equalizer, and A-B repeat. Can't edit playlist or delete files on player. Firmware not upgradeable. No Mac support. Includes earbud-type headphone. Uses one AAA battery. USB1.1 interface. Similar: Psyc Network Walkman NW-E103PS (256 MB), Psyc Network Walkman NW-E105PS (512 MB).

23 RiData OLE 3000 (512 MB) Good overall. Good recording quality capable via line input. Fair recording quality via FM radio. Very good recording quality using built-in microphone. Has presets equalizer, A-B repeat, and multilingual menus. Can edit playlist (but can't delete files) on player. Firmware not upgradeable. No Mac support. Includes earbud-type headphone. Uses one AAA battery. USB2 interface. Similar: OLE 3000 (128 MB), OLE 3000 (256 MB).

24 Bang and Olufsen Beosound 2 Good overall. Currently doesn't play any copy-protected music purchased from an online music store. Includes docking station. Memory card is required, but not included. No data storage capability. Lacks display, equalizer, and most play modes. Can't edit playlist or delete files on player. Includes behind the ear hooks, earbud-type headphone. Has nonremovable battery. USB2 interface.

MICRODRIVE HARD-DISK PLAYERS (3 GB TO 8 GB)

25 Creative Zen Micro Photo (8 GB) Very good overall. Good picture quality. Poor recording quality via FM radio. Good recording quality via built-in microphone. Has slideshow capability without simultaneous music. Has custom and presets equalizer, volume leveling, contacts and calendar appointment application, alarm clock, and multilingual menus. Can edit playlist and delete files on player. No Mac support. Includes earbud-type headphone. Player charges via computer USB2 port. AC charger not included. Removable rechargeable battery costs about $40 to replace.

26 RCA Lyra RD2765 (5 GB) Very good overall. Fair picture quality. Has slideshow capability without simultaneous music. Has custom and presets equalizer. Can edit playlist and delete files on player. MTP compatible. Includes earbud-type headphone. Nonremoveable battery. USB2 interface.

27 Archos Gmini XS 100 (3 GB) Very

good overall. Has custom and presets equalizer, channel balance, virtual keyboard, and multilingual menus. Can edit playlist and delete files on player. Includes earbud-type headphone with a volume control. Nonremoveable battery charges via computer USB2 port. AC charger not included.

28 iRiver H10 (6 GB) Very good overall. Fair picture quality. Fair recording quality via FM radio. Excellent recording quality via built-in microphone. Has slideshow capability with simultaneous music. Has custom and presets equalizer, fade-in audio playback, text viewer, multilingual menus. Can edit playlist but can't delete files on player. No Mac support. Includes earbud-type headphone. Removable rechargeable battery costs about $40 to replace. USB2 interface. Similar model: H10 (5 GB).

29 Creative Zen Micro (6 GB) Good overall. Fair recording quality via FM radio. Good recording quality via built-in microphone. Has custom and presets equalizer, volume leveling, contacts and calendar appointment application, alarm clock, and multilingual menus. Can edit playlist and delete files on player. No Mac support. Includes earbud-type headphone. Player charges via computer USB2 port. AC charger not included. Removable rechargeable battery costs about $40 to replace. Similar: Zen Micro (4 GB), Zen Micro (5 GB).

30 Samsung YH-820 (5 GB) Good overall. Fair picture quality. Excellent recording quality capable via line input. Fair recording quality via built-in microphone. Has slideshow capability with simultaneous music. Has presets equalizer, A-B repeat, fade-in/out audio playback, and multilingual menus. Can edit playlist but can't delete files on player. No Mac support. Includes earbud-type headphone. Has nonremovable battery. USB2 interface.

HARD-DISK MP3 PLAYERS (10 GB TO 60 GB)

31 Cowon iAudio X5L (30 GB) Very good overall. Currently doesn't play any copy-protected music purchased from an online music store. Fair video and picture quality. Video playback time measured eighteen hours. Display measures 1.1x1.4 inches. Excellent recording quality capable via line input. Good recording quality via FM radio. Very good recording quality via built-in microphone. Has manual picture advance without simultaneous music. Has USB host mode, line output, custom and presets equalizer, A-B repeat, channel balance,

(continued)

MP3 PLAYERS

fade-in audio playback, text viewer, alarm clock, multilingual menus. Can edit playlist but can't delete files on player. No Mac support. Includes earbud-type headphone. Has nonremovable battery. USB2 interface.

32 iRiver H10 (20 GB) Very good overall. Fair picture quality. Fair recording quality via FM radio. Excellent recording quality via built-in microphone. Has slideshow capability with simultaneous music. Has custom and presets equalizer, fade-in audio playback, text viewer, and multilingual menus. Can edit playlist but can't delete files on player. No Mac support. Includes earbud-type headphone. Has nonremovable battery. USB2 interface.

33 Cowon iAudio X5 (20 GB) Very good overall. Currently doesn't play any copy-protected music purchased from online stores. Fair video and picture quality. Video playback time measured eight hours. Display measures 1.1x1.4 inches. Excellent recording quality capable via line input. Good recording quality via FM radio. Very good recording quality via built-in microphone. Has manual picture advance without simultaneous music. Has USB host mode, line output, custom and presets equalizer, A-B repeat, channel balance, fade-in audio playback, text viewer, alarm clock, multilingual menus. Can edit playlist but can't delete files on player. No Mac support. Includes earbud-type headphone. Has nonremoveable battery. USB2 interface. Similar: iAudio X5 (30 GB).

34 Creative Zen Vision M (30 GB) Very good overall. Very good video and picture quality. Video playback time measured five hours. Display measures 1.5x2.0 inches. Very good recording quality via FM radio. Good recording quality via built-in microphone. Can view video or images on a TV. Has slideshow with simultaneous music. Has line output, custom and presets equalizer, volume leveling, contacts and calendar appointment application, alarm clock, and multilingual menus. MTP compatible. Can edit playlist and delete files on player. No Mac support. Inludes earbud-type headphone. Has nonremovable battery. USB2 interface.

35 Archos Gmini 402 Pocket Multimedia Center (20 GB) Very good overall. Good video and picture quality. Video playback time measured five hours. Display measures 1.4x1.7 inches. Excellent recording quality capable via line input. Very good recording quality via built-in microphone. Can view video or images on a TV. Has slideshow capability without simultaneous music. Has USB host mode, line output, custom equalizer, channel balance, virtual keyboard, games, multilingual menus. Can edit playlist and delete files on player. Includes earbud-type headphone with a volume control. Has nonremoveable battery. USB2 interface.

36 Creative Zen Sleek Photo (20 GB) Very good overall. Very good picture quality. Good recording quality via FM radio or built-in microphone. Has slideshow without simultaneous music. Has custom and presets equalizer, contacts and calendar appointment application, alarm clock, d multilingual menus. Can edit playlist and delete files on player. MTP compatible. No Mac support. Includes earbud-type headphone. Has nonremovable battery. USB2 interface.

37 Apple iPod (30 GB) Very good overall. Very good video and picture quality. Video playback time measured three hours. Display measures 1.5x2.0 inches. Has slideshow capability with simultaneous music. Has presets equalizer, volume limiter and leveling, contacts and calendar appointment application, text viewer, games, alarm clock, stopwatch, and multilingual menus. Can edit playlist but can't delete files on player. Includes earbud-type headphone. Has nonremovable battery that charges via computer USB2 port. AC charger not included. Can view video or images on a TV with optional AV cable ($19). To access video content, Windows users need QuickTime Pro software ($30).

38 Creative Zen Sleek (20 GB) Very good overall. Fair recording quality via FM radio or built-in microphone. Has custom and presets equalizer, volume leveling, contacts and calendar appointment application, text viewer, alarm clock, and multilingual menus. Can edit playlist and delete files on player. No Mac support. Includes earbud-type headphone. Has nonremovable battery. USB2 interface.

39 Toshiba gigabeat MEGF20 (20 GB) Very good overall. Good picture quality. Has slideshow capability with simultaneous music. Has USB host mode, line output, docking cradle, custom and presets equalizer, and multilingual menus. Can edit playlist and delete files on player. Firmware not upgradeable. No Mac support. Includes earbud-type headphone. Has nonremovable battery. USB2 interface. Similar: gigabeat MEGF10 (10 GB), gigabeat MEGF40 (40 GB), gigabeat MEGF60 (60 GB).

40 Archos Gmini XS 202 (20 GB) Very good overall. Has custom and presets equalizer, channel balance, virtual keyboard, and multilingual menus. Can edit playlist and delete files on player. Includes earbud-type headphone with a volume control. Has nonremoveable battery. USB2 interface.

41 Archos Gmini XS 202s (20 GB) Very good overall. Has custom and presets equalizer, channel balance, virtual keyboard, and multilingual menus. Can edit playlist and delete files on player. MTP compatible. Includes earbud-type headphone with a volume control. Has nonremovable battery. USB2 interface.

42 Samsung YH-999 (20 GB) Very good overall. Fair video and good picture quality. Video playback time measured six hours. Display measures 2.1x2.8 inches. Can view video or images on a TV. Has slideshow capability with simultaneous music. Wired remote control included. Has built-in speakers, line output, presets equalizer, and multilingual menus. Can edit playlist but can't delete files on player. MTP compatible. No Mac support. Includes earbud-type headphone. Has nonremovable battery. USB2 interface.

43 Philips HDD6330 (30 GB) Very good overall. Good picture quality. Very good recording quality via FM radio. Good recording quality via built-in microphone. Can view images on a TV with optional accessory. Has slideshow with simultaneous music. Has custom and presets equalizer, and multilingual menus. Can edit playlist but can't delete files on player. MTP compatible. No Mac support. Includes earplug-type headphone. Has nonremovable battery. USB2 interface.

44 Creative Zen Vision (30 GB) Good overall. Good video and picture quality. Video playback time measured four hours. Display measures 2.3x3.0 inches. Poor recording quality via FM radio. Fair recording quality via built-in microphone. Can view video or images on a TV. Has slideshow capability with simultaneous music. Has built-in speaker, line output, custom and presets equalizer, volume leveling, contacts and calendar appointment application, text viewer, alarm clock, and multilingual menus. Can copy files directly from a CompactFlash card though can't play music files from the card. Can edit playlist and delete files on player. No Mac support. Includes earbud-type headphone. Removable rechargeable battery costs about $40 to replace. USB2 interface.

CR Quick Recommendations

PDAs

Finding the best PDA for your needs also means weighing price and other considerations.

QUICK PICKS

For a basic organizer at a good price:

2 Palm Tungsten E2, $200
5 Palm Z22, $100
7 Dell Axim X51 (416 MHz), $240

The Palm Tungsten E2 and the Dell Axim X51 (416 MHz) are well priced yet offer plenty. Both have Bluetooth capability and let you view pictures, listen to music, and see daily tasks at a glance. Both models retain all of your data automatically in non-volatile memory, even when the battery has drained completely. The Dell Axim X51 series includes a task-switcher program that lets you manage multiple tasks better than other Pocket PCs, and it supports multiple memory cards. The Palm Z22 is low priced and fine for to-do lists and contacts.

For a full-featured Palm OS unit:

1 Palm LifeDrive, $400
3 Palm TIX, $275

The Palm LifeDrive is the closest thing we've seen to a "laptop replacement" in a PDA. It has an internal 3.7-GB hard drive and applications that let you view and store photos, listen to music, manage e-mail, and edit documents and spreadsheets. You can also access the hard drive via a desktop computer. Like the LifeDrive, the Palm TIX has both Bluetooth and Wi-Fi capability. It also has 115 MB of user memory, more than enough to store your favorite applications and data.

For a Windows look and feel in a PDA:

8 Dell Axim X51v, $400

The Dell Axim X51v is similar to the Dell Axim X51 (416 MHz) but has a faster processor, more nonvolatile memory, and a larger display that is very readable, even in bright sunlight. It also has both Wi-Fi and Bluetooth capability.

For a portable navigation system:

6 Garmin iQue 3200, $370
10 Garmin iQue M3, $500

The GPS-equipped Garmin iQue 3200 is similar to the previously tested Garmin iQue 3600. It's as easy to use and has better battery life, but has a smaller display and lacks a jog dial. The Garmin iQue M3 is the only Pocket PC–based PDA we've tested with GPS capability. You'll need a Windows PC with a DVD ROM drive and your own copy of Microsoft Outlook to synchronize this PDA.

Ratings

In performance order, within categories.

Excellent ● · Very good ◒ · Good ○ · Fair ◖ · Poor ●

Key number	Brand & model	Price	Overall score (0-100)	Ease of use	Battery life	Display	Convenience	In sync	Pocket size	Memory (MB)	Expansion card	Replaceable battery	Wireless connectivity	Display size (in.)	Office software	MP3 player
PALM OS MODELS																
1	**Palm** LifeDrive	$400	70	◒	○	◒	●	●		65	●		●	3.8	●	●
2	**Palm** Tungsten E2	200	62	◒	○	○	◒	◒	●	30	●		●	3	●	●
3	**Palm** TIX	275	60	◒	○	◒	○	◒		115	●		●	3.8	●	●
4	**Garmin** iQue 3600	450	54	◒	◖	◒	○	○		23	●			3.7	●	●
5	**Palm** Z22	100	54	○	◒	○	○	○	●	25				2.4		
6	**Garmin** iQue 3200	370	53	○	○	○	○	○		24	●			3.0	●	●
POCKET PC MODELS																
7	**Dell** Axim X51 (416 MHz)	240	68	◒	◒	○	●	◒		51	●	●	●	3.6	●	●
8	**Dell** Axim X51v	400	68	◒	◒	◒	●	◒		50	●	●	●	3.7	●	●
9	**Hewlett-Packard** iPAQ rx1950	300	66	○	◒	◒	●	◒	●	24	●	●	●	3.5	●	●
10	**Garmin** iQue M3	500	58	○	◒	○	○	◒		32	●			3.5	●	●

Guide to the Ratings

Overall score reflects evaluations of the PDA's ease of use, battery life, display, convenience, and the usefulness of the included desktop synchronization, e-mail, word-processing and spreadsheet software. **Ease of use** includes judgments of ergonomic factors—how well buttons and dials are integrated, shape and weight, display resolution-how easy it is to navigate from task to task, and the usability of the phone list, appointment book, to-do list, and memo pad. **Battery life** tracks fully charged batteries with the PDA turned on and active. The best models ran for 15 hours or longer. **Display** tests assess screen readability in low and normal room light, and in bright sunlight. **Convenience** includes bundled software, expansion capabilities, fit for shirt pockets, and other factors. **In sync** indicates how easily the PDA can be synchronized with a computer. **Price** is approximate retail. *Based on tests posted on ConsumerReports.org in December 2005, with updated prices and availability.*

PDAS

Profiles Model-by-Model

PALM OS MODELS

1 Palm LifeDrive Very good. A worthy laptop replacement for travelers. Combines the ease of use of Palm OS with the drag-and-drop convenience of Pocket PC. Easily readable display. Overall design better than most, and basic organizer functions easy to use. Has picture viewer, expense tracker, eBook Reader, and LED alarm. Can record voice memos. But too bulky to fit in a shirt pocket. Doesn't include backup program. New e-mail program is less reliable than previous versions. 3.7GB hard drive for storage. 6.8 oz.

2 Palm Tungsten E2 Very good. Overall design better than most, and basic organizer functions easy to use. All memory is nonvolatile, which prevents data loss even if battery dies. Fits easily in a shirt pocket. Has picture viewer, expense tracker, and eBook Reader. Doesn't include backup program. 26 MB flash memory for storage. 4.7 oz.

3 Palm TIX Very good overall. Has picture viewer. Expense tracker software included. eBook Reader included. Easily readable display. Overall design better than most. Basic organizer functions easy to use. No backup program included. Too bulky to fit in a shirt pocket. 5.25 oz.

4 Garmin iQue 3600 A good organizer with GPS capability. Well-conceived design, with large, easily readable display. Basic organizer functions easy to use, and user interface better than most. Has handy jog dial, eBook reader, and LED and vibrating alarms. Can record voice memos. But lacks e-mail and backup software. Not much battery life for GPS functionality. Too bulky to fit in a shirt pocket. 5.8 oz.

5 Palm Z22 Good overall. Has picture viewer. Expense tracker software included. eBook Reader included. Fits in a shirt pocket. Overall design better than most. Basic organizer functions easy to use. No backup program included. No e-mail program. 3.4 oz.

6 Garmin iQue 3200 Good overall. A good overall organizer with GPS capability. eBook Reader included. Has LED and vibrating alarms. Better battery life than the iQue 3600, and includes an e-mail program. Overall design better than most. Basic organizer functions easy to use. No backup program included. Too bulky to fit in a shirt pocket. 5.9 oz.

POCKET PC MODELS

7 Dell Axim X51 (416 MHz) Very good overall. A fine choice if you want to add peripherals. Has printed manual. Can record voice memos. Has picture viewer. Has LED alarm. User interface better than most. Basic organizer functions easy to use. Too bulky to fit in a shirt pocket. 5.7 oz. 76-MB flash memory for storage. Similar model: Axim X51 (520 MHz).

8 Dell Axim X51v Very good overall. A fine choice if you want to add peripherals. Has printed manual. Can record voice memos. Has picture viewer. Has LED alarm. Easily readable display. Easily readable in bright sunlight. User interface better than most. Basic organizer functions easy to use. Too bulky to fit in a shirt pocket. 6 oz. 195 MB-flash memory for storage.

9 Hewlett-Packard iPAQ rx1950 Very good overall. Has printed manual. Can record voice memos. Has picture viewer. Has LED alarm. Easily readable display. Fits in a shirt pocket. User interface better than most. Basic organizer functions easy to use. No backup program included. 4.6 oz. 35-MB flash memory for storage.

10 Garmin iQue M3 Good overall. A good overall organizer with GPS capability. Can record voice memos. Has picture viewer. Has LED alarm. User interface better than most. No backup program included. Software comes on DVD with PDA. CD version must be ordered separately. Requires separate purchase of MS Outlook to sync with PC. Too bulky to fit in a shirt pocket. 5.8 oz. 2-MB flash memory for storage. Similar model: iQue M5.

CR Quick Recommendations

Printers, all-in-one

If all you do is print, you can save money and space by purchasing a dedicated printer. But if there's any chance you might want to copy or scan, it's worth investigating an all-in-one. While most models are bigger than the typical new stand-alone printer, they take up less space and cost less than a separate printer, scanner, and copier. Having to hook up only one device to your computer simplifies setup as well. An all-in-one's scanning function should be fine for print originals. Some can also handle basic film and slide scanning, though for top quality we recommend a separate scanner. The copying function is fine for casual use. Some all-in-ones add fax, phone, and answering functions. As the Ratings show, paying more for a printer doesn't necessarily mean you'll get better photos. And don't consider only the purchase price of the printer itself. Per-print costs can make a cheaper model more expensive in the long run than a higher-priced printer with low per-copy costs.

QUICK PICKS
Best choices among all-in-one inkjets:

1 Canon Pixma MP800, $280
5 Canon Pixma MP450, $150

12 Epson CX3810, $90

The Canon Pixma MP800 printed excellent photos and text and was among the fastest we tested, printing an 8x10 in 2 minutes, for $1.25. The other Canon did almost as well, and its cost for an 8x10 was $1.05. Both have an LCD viewer, card reader, and PictBridge; the MP800 adds film-scanning. The Epson is low-priced, and it has fine photo and text quality. But it's slow (9 minutes for an 8x10) and lacks an LCD, card reader, and PictBridge. You can print only from a computer.

Ratings

In performance order, within categories.

Ratings key: Excellent ● / Very good ◕ / Good ○ / Fair ◖ / Poor ●

Key number	Brand & model	Price	Overall score	Text quality	Text speed (ppm)	Text cost (cents)	Photo quality	8x10 photo time (min.)	8x10 photo cost ($)	Graphics quality	Copy quality	Scan quality	Fax function	LCD viewer	Memory-card support	Individual color tanks	PictBridge support	Wireless connectivity
INKJET MODELS																		
1	**Canon** Pixma MP800	$280	74	●	11	4	●	2	1.25	◐	◐	○		•	•	•	•	•
2	**Canon** Pixma MP950	430	74	●	9	4	◐	2	1.05	◐	◐	◐		•	•	•	•	•
3	**Epson** Stylus Photo RX700	380	74	◐	3	7.5	●	3	0.90	◐	◐	◐		•	•	•	•	
4	**Hewlett-Packard** Photosmart 3210	270	71	●	6	3	◐	4	0.95	◐	◐	◐	•	•	•		•	•
5	**Canon** Pixma MP450	150	65	●	6	6	◐	3	1.05	◐	◐	○			•	•	•	
6	**Hewlett-Packard** Photosmart 2575	180	65	●	6	6	◐	6	1.25	●	○	○			•		•	•
7	**Epson** CX7800	170	63	◐	2	4.5	◐	6	0.95	◐	○	○			•	•	•	
8	**Dell** Photo All-In-One 964	200	62	◐	5	5	○	3	1.15	◐	○	○			•		•	
9	**Hewlett-Packard** PSC 1510	100	57	◐	4	3.5	○	6	1.45	○	○	◖				•	•	
10	**Lexmark** Photo Perfection All-in-one P4350	130	57	○	6	6	○	5	1.40	◐	○	○	•		•	•		
11	**Dell** Photo All-In-One 944	140	56	◐	8	5	○	5	1.15	◐	○	○			•		•	
12	**Epson** CX3810	90	53	●	3	4.5	◐	9	0.95	◐	○	○				•		
13	**Lexmark** Easy Compact All-in-one X2350	70	52	○	2	6.5	○	5	1.20	○	◖	◐						
LASER MODELS																		
14	**Brother** MFC-7420	300	69	●	15	2	NA	NA	NA	○	○	○	•			•		
15	**Brother** DCP-7020	200	66	●	13	1.5	NA	NA	NA	○	○	○				•		
16	**Samsung** SCX-4521F	250	66	●	13	3	NA	NA	NA	◐	○	○	•			•		•

Guide to the Ratings

Overall score is based on speed and quality of print, scan, and copy functions, plus ease of use. **Text quality** is an assessment of clarity and crispness of black text. **Text speed** measures pages per minute (ppm) for a five-page document at default settings. **Text cost** is for one black-text page (ink or toner plus plain paper) or one 8x10-inch color photo (ink and glossy 8½x11-inch paper). A borderless 4x6-inch print would cost about one-third as much. **Photo quality** reflects a color snapshot's appearance. 8x10-photo time measures, to the nearest half-minute, the time to print an 8x10-inch color photo at the best-quality setting.

Graphics quality assesses output such as Web pages, greeting cards, and charts; for laser models, we tested with black-and-white graphics. **Copy quality** is for photos, graphics, and text. **Scan quality** is for color photos, graphics, and text scanned at each model's default settings and judged on a high-quality monitor; scores can't be compared with those of the flatbed scanners, which were tested differently. **Price** is approximate retail. All tested models work with Windows XP and 2000; all but the Dell (8, 11) support Windows ME and 98. Most support Macs. *Based on tests posted to ConsumerReports.org in July 2006.*

PRINTERS, ALL-IN-ONE

Profiles Model-by-Model

INKJET MODELS

1 Canon Pixma MP800 Very good, with excellent text and photos. Fast text printing. Can scan negatives and slides. Space required (HWD): 14.2x18.5x22.4 in.

2 Canon Pixma MP950 Very good, with excellent text and very good photos. Can scan negatives and slides. Space required (HWD): 13.8x18.1x21.3 in.

3 Epson Stylus Photo RX700 Very good, with excellent photos and very good text, but slow for text. Can scan negatives and slides. Space required (HWD): 14x17.3x23.6 in.

4 Hewlett-Packard Photosmart 3210 Very good, with excellent text and very good photos. Low-cost text printing. Can scan negatives and slides. Supports Ethernet connectivity. Space required (HWD): 8.3x18.1x20.1 in.

5 Canon Pixma MP450 Very good, with excellent text and very good photos. Space required (HWD): 13.8x17.1x21.3 in.

6 Hewlett-Packard Photosmart 2575 Very good, with excellent text and very good photos. Compact for a multifunction printer. Supports Ethernet connectivity. Space required (HWD): 6.5x17.3x18.9 in.

7 Epson CX7800 Very good text and photos, but slow for text. Can scan negatives and slides. Space required (HWD): 14x17.3x23.6 in.

8 Dell Photo All-In-One 964 Very good text and good photos. Supports only Windows XP and 2000. Noisy. Space required (HWD): 10.2x17.7x21.3 in.

9 Hewlett-Packard PSC 1510 Very good text and good photos. Compact for a multifunction printer. Space required (HWD): 6.3x17.3x22.4 in.

10 Lexmark Photo Perfection All-in-one P4350 Good text and good photos. Noisy. Space required (HWD): 12.6x16.6x22 in.

11 Dell Photo All-In-One 944 Very good text and good photos. Supports only Windows XP and 2000. Noisy. Space required (HWD): 12.6x17.1x19.7 in.

12 Epson CX3810 Excellent text and very good photos, but slow for text. Space required (HWD): 13x16.3x21.7in.

13 Lexmark Easy Compact All-in-one X2350 Good text and good photos, but slow for text. Uses only one tri-color ink cartridge, which mixes color inks to produce a grayish black. Noisy. Space required (HWD): 13.4x14.8x22 in,

LASER MODELS

14 Brother MFC-7420 Very good, with excellent and fast text printing. Noisy. Space required (HWD): 11.4x16.5x17.3 in.

15 Brother DCP-7020 Very good, with excellent and fast text printing. Noisy. Space required (HWD): 11.4x16.5x17.3 in.

16 Samsung SCX-4521F Very good, with excellent and fast text printing.

Expert • Independent • Nonprofit

CR Quick Recommendations

Printers, regular

Standard inkjets are the best all-purpose printers for most consumers who want to print both text and color photos. They offer versatility, top print quality, and low-cost enlargements. They can print almost anything, including photos 8x10 inches or larger, text, and graphics such as greeting cards. You can use various types and sizes of paper, from business cards to banners.

Quality is another plus. The photos from the best inkjets are as good as those you get from a photofinisher. Larger prints also typically cost less than you'd pay a photo-finisher–about $1 to $1.50 for an 8x10-inch photo, compared with $2 to $4 for professional processing. But inkjets aren't renowned for speed, so it could take a while to print a number of 8x10s.

Don't print photos or color graphics? Traditional black-and-white laser printers can't be beat for fast text printing at a good cost, especially if you print reams of black-and-white text documents.

As the Ratings show, paying more for a printer doesn't necessarily mean you'll get better photos. And don't consider only the purchase price of the printer itself. Per-print costs can make a cheaper model more expensive in the long run than a higher-priced printer with low per-copy costs.

QUICK PICKS
The best all-around inkjets:

2 Canon Pixma iP5200, $150
5 Epson Stylus Photo R340, $175

The Canon stands out for quality, low print costs, and speed. Photos and text were excellent; costs were $1.05 for an 8x10 print, 35 cents for a 4x6 print, and 3 cents for a text page. It printed an 8x10 in a minute and a half and text at 8 pages per minute. It has a second paper tray, which you can use for 4x6 paper. It is PictBridge-enabled but has no card reader or LCD viewer. A sibling, the iP5200R, adds Wi-Fi, allowing wireless links to compatible computers and cameras, along with Ethernet for easy networking. It costs $225. The Epson produced very good photos and text but was much slower than the Canon, with speeds of 4 minutes for an 8x10 and 2 ppm for text. Print costs were comparable to the Canon's. It has an LCD viewer and card reader as well as PictBridge, but only one paper tray.

A bit slower but lower-priced:

3 Canon Pixma iP4200, $100

This model performed much like the newer iP5200, above, and has the same features. The main difference is slightly slower speed for photos: 3 minutes to print an 8x10.

Ratings

	Excellent	Very good	Good	Fair	Poor
	●	◕	○	◑	⬤

In performance order.

Key number	Brand & model	Price	Overall score (0–100, P F G VG E)	Text quality	Text speed (ppm)	Text cost (cents)	Photo quality	8x10 photo time (min.)	8x10 photo cost ($)	4x6 photo cost ($)	Graphics quality	LCD viewer	Memory-card support	Individual color tanks	PictBridge support	Wireless connectivity
INKJET MODELS																
1	**Canon** Pixma iP5200R	$215	88	●	10	4	●	1.5	1.05	0.35	●			•	•	•
2	**Canon** Pixma iP5200	150	87	●	10	4	●	1.5	1.05	0.35	●			•	•	
3	**Canon** Pixma iP4200	100	83	●	8	4	●	3	1.05	0.35	●			•	•	
4	**Canon** Pixma iP6600D	195	82	○	4	55	◑	1.5	1.05	0.35	○	•	•	•	•	•
5	**Epson** Stylus Photo R340	175	77	◑	2	35	◑	4	1.00	0.35	◑	•	•	•	•	
6	**Hewlett-Packard** PhotoSmart 8250	170	73	◑	4	25	◑	2.5	0.90	0.30	◑	•	•	•	•	
7	**Canon** Pixma iP6220D	145	72	◑	2	12	◑	4	1.40	0.45	◑	•	•		•	•
8	**Epson** Stylus C88	80	72	◑	5	4	◑	5.5	0.90	0.30	◑			•		
9	**Epson** Stylus Photo R320	180	72	◑	2	35	◑	4	1.00	0.35	◑	•	•	•	•	
10	**Epson** Stylus Photo R220	100	71	○	2	35	◑	3.5	0.85	0.30	◑			•	•	
11	**Canon** Pixma iP6210D	95	70	◑	2	12	◑	4	1.40	0.45	◑	•	•		•	
12	**Hewlett-Packard** Deskjet 5940	90	69	◑	6	55	○	5.5	1.30	0.45	◑			•		
13	**Hewlett-Packard** Photosmart 8050 Photo Printer	130	69	◑	7	5	◑	5.5	1.30	0.45	◑	•	•		•	
14	**Hewlett-Packard** Deskjet 3940	50	59	◑	2	12	○	11.5	1.00	0.35	◑					

PRINTERS, REGULAR

Guide to the Ratings

Overall score, for full-size printers, is based primarily on print quality and speed for printing text and color photos. **Text quality indicates** how crisply and clearly a printer produced black text in a variety of faces, sizes, and styles. Models with higher scores produce more uniform type, with sharper edges and smoother curves. **Text speed** is our calculation of the printer's typical output in pages per minute (ppm) for a three-page document. Speeds generally range from 2 to 9 ppm. **Text cost** is the estimated cost of black ink and paper, in cents, to produce a single text page. **Photo quality** is our assessment of the appearance of each photo. Models with higher scores produce more natural-looking photos, with smoother changes in shading and fewer problems with banding. **8x10 photo time,** to the nearest half minute, is our measurement of how long it took each full-size printer to output an 8x10 color print, at the printer's best setting, using a 2.8-GHz PC with 496 megabytes of RAM. **8x10 photo cost** is the estimated cost of the color ink and glossy photo paper needed to produce an 8x10 photo. **4x6 photo cost** is the estimated cost of the color ink or ribbon (for dye-sublimation models) and glossy photo paper needed to produce a 4x6 photo. **Graphics quality** is our assessment of the appearance of color graphics produced by the printer. Models with higher scores produce graphics whose colors are brighter, more uniform, and less prone to band or bleed into one another on the page. **Price** is approximate retail. *Based on tests posted to ConsumerReports.org in July 2006.*

Profiles Model-by-Model

INKJET MODELS

1 Canon Pixma iP5200R Excellent-quality photos and text, with fast photo and text printing. Has second paper tray. Supports Ethernet connectivity. Space required (HWD): 14x17x22 in.

2 Canon Pixma iP5200 Excellent-quality photos and text, with fast photo and text printing. Has second paper tray. Space required (HWD): 14x17x22 in.

3 Canon Pixma iP4200 Excellent-quality photos and text. Has second paper tray. Space required (HWD): 14x16x21 in.

4 Canon Pixma iP6600D Very good, with fast photo printing. Has second paper tray. Space required (HWD): 14x17x23 in.

5 Epson Stylus Photo R340 Very good-quality photos and text, but text printing is slow. Includes accessory for printing directly onto printable CDs and DVDs. Space required (HWD): 14x19x24 in.

6 Hewlett-Packard PhotoSmart 8250 Very good-quality photos and text. Has separate paper tray for 4x6-in. photo paper. Space required (HWD): 6x17x20 in.

7 Canon Pixma iP6220D Very good-quality photos and text, but text printing is slow with high per-page costs. Noisy. Space required (HWD): 13x17x22 in.

8 Epson Stylus C88 Very good-quality photos and text. Space required (HWD): 14x18x22 in.

9 Epson Stylus Photo R320 Very good-quality photos and text, but text printing is slow. Includes accessory for printing directly onto printable CDs and DVDs. Space required (HWD): 14x19x20 in.

10 Epson Stylus Photo R220 Very good-quality photos, but text printing is slow. Includes accessory for printing directly onto printable CDs and DVDs. Space required (HWD): 11x17x19 in.

11 Canon Pixma iP6210D Very good-quality photos and text, but text printing is slow with high per-page costs. Noisy. Space required (HWD): 14x17x22 in.

12 Hewlett-Packard Deskjet 5940 Very good-quality text. Space required (HWD): 6x18x19 in.

13 Hewlett-Packard Photosmart 8050 Photo Printer Very good-quality photos and text. Has separate paper tray for 4x6-in. photo paper. Space required (HWD): 6x18x19 in.

14 Hewlett-Packard Deskjet 3940 Very good-quality text, but slow for printing photos. Text printing is slow, with high per-page costs. Space required (HWD): 5x16x14 in.

CR Quick Recommendations

Printers, snapshot

There are three reasons to choose a snapshot printer over a full-sized inkjet printer: convenience, speed, and portability. Ease of use is unequaled—this is as close to one-touch printing as you can get. Getting images to print is also a snap. You simply connect the printer to a PictBridge-enabled camera with a USB cable, choose a shot, and click Print on the camera's display. Speed is a plus; most snapshot printers can print a 4x6-inch photo in less than 2 minutes. (Dye-sub models are usually faster than inkjets.) And then there's portability. Small and lightweight (3 to 7 pounds), these printers are easily toted on trips or to parties.

But you do sacrifice versatility. Snapshot printers can't print large photos, text, or graphics. If you want one device that can handle all of your printing, stick with a full-sized inkjet.

As the Ratings show, paying more for a printer doesn't necessarily mean you'll get better photos. And don't consider only the purchase price of the printer itself. Per-print costs can make a cheaper model more expensive in the long run than a higher-priced printer with low per-copy costs.

QUICK PICKS

For the best quality and value:

7 Canon Selphy CP710, $140

9 Hewlett-Packard PhotoSmart 335 GoGo Photo Printer, $130

13 Epson PictureMate Express Edition, $130

All three models are strong performers. Photos from the HP inkjet were a bit sharper and richer than those of the Canon dye-sub and Epson inkjet. The Canon printed a 4x6 in 90 seconds; the HP and Epson in less than 2 minutes. Photo costs were 23 cents for the Epson, 30 cents for the HP, and 28 cents for the Canon. All three are PictBridge-enabled and have a card slot; the HP and Canon have an LCD viewer. The Canon is small and can run on a battery ($80). If you'll print only from the camera and don't need a card slot, consider the Canon Selphy CP510, similar to the CP710 but only $90.

Tops if you don't print many photos:

5 Samsung SPP-2040, $100

The Samsung dye-sub printer produced very good photos in 70 seconds, but its per-photo cost was high at 42 cents. If you don't print a lot, the quality and speed might be worth the cost. The SPP-2020, $80, offers comparable performance but lacks the card slot and LCD viewer of the SPP-2040. Both are PictBridge-enabled.

Great for portable use:

2 Canon Selphy CP600, $200

This printer includes a battery—a costly option for other models—and it's among the smallest and lightest models. It's as good as its brandmates (mentioned above) for photo quality and costs, but is faster, printing a 4x6 in just over 1 minute. It's PictBridge-enabled but has no card slot or viewer.

Ratings

Excellent ◉ Very good ◕ Good ○ Fair ◑ Poor ●

In performance order.

Key number	Brand & model	Price	Overall score (0–100)	Photo quality	4x6 photo time (min.)	4x6 photo cost ($)	Printing method	LCD viewer	Memory-card support	PictBridge support	Wireless connectivity
1	**Hewlett-Packard** PhotoSmart 475 GoGo Photo Printer	$250	67	◑	2	.30	Inkjet	●	●	●	●
2	**Canon** Selphy CP600	200	66	○	1.25	.28	Dye-sub			●	●
3	**Hewlett-Packard** PhotoSmart 425 GoGo Photo Printer	280	65	◑	2	.30	Inkjet	●		●	●
4	**Hewlett-Packard** PhotoSmart 428 GoGo Photo Printer	300	65	◑	2	.29	Inkjet	●		●	●
5	**Samsung** SPP-2040	100	65	◑	1.25	.42	Dye-sub	●	●	●	
6	**Hewlett-Packard** PhotoSmart 385 GoGo Photo Printer	170	63	◑	2	.30	Inkjet	●	●	●	●
7	**Canon** Selphy CP710	140	62	○	1.5	.28	Dye-sub	●	●	●	
8	**Canon** Selphy DS810	150	62	○	2	.60	Inkjet		●	●	
9	**Hewlett-Packard** PhotoSmart 335 GoGo Photo Printer	130	62	◑	2	.30	Inkjet	●	●	●	
10	**Samsung** SPP-2020	80	62	◑	1.25	.42	Dye-sub			●	
11	**Canon** Selphy CP510	90	60	○	1.5	.28	Dye-sub			●	
12	**Epson** PictureMate Deluxe Viewer Finder	200	59	○	1.5	.23	Inkjet	●	●	●	
13	**Epson** PictureMate Express Edition	130	58	○	1.75	.23	Inkjet		●	●	
14	**Sony** PictureStation DPP-FP50	150	58	○	1	.40	Dye-sub		●	●	
15	**Kodak** EasyShare Photo Printer 500	190	56	○	1.5	.29	Dye-sub	●	●	●	
16	**Kodak** EasyShare Printer Dock Plus Series 3	160	56	○	1.5	.29	Dye-sub		●	●	
17	**Kodak** EasyShare Printer Dock Plus	180	55	○	1.5	.29	Dye-sub	●	●	●	

(continued)

PRINTERS, SNAPSHOT

Ratings (continued)

Excellent	Very good	Good	Fair	Poor
●	◒	○	◔	●

Key number	Brand & model	Price	Overall score (P F G VG E)	Photo quality	4x6 photo time (min.)	4x6 photo cost ($)	Printing method	LCD viewer	Memory-card support	PictBridge support	Wireless connectivity
18	**Olympus** P-11 Digital Photo Printer	$140	54	○	0.75	.39	Dye-sub			●	
19	**Lexmark** P450 Photo Printer	200	44	◔	2.75	.42	Inkjet	●	●	●	●
20	**Kodak** EasyShare Photo Printer 300	100	37	◔	1.75	.29	Dye-sub			●	
21	**Kodak** EasyShare Printer Dock	135	37	◔	1.75	.29	Dye-sub			●	
22	**Kodak** EasyShare Printer Dock Series 3	150	37	◔	1.75	.29	Dye-sub			●	

Guide to the Ratings

Overall score is based on speed, photo quality, and ease of use. **Photo quality** is our assessment of the appearance of each photo. Models with higher scores produce more natural-looking photos, with smoother changes in shading and fewer problems with banding. **4x6 photo time** is our measurement, to the nearest half-minute, of how long it took each snapshot printer to output a 4x6 borderless photo directly from a digital camera. **4x6 photo cost** is the estimated cost of the color ink or ribbon (for dye-sublimation models) and glossy photo paper needed to produce a 4x6 photo. **Printing method** indicates which technology a printer uses to create an image onto paper or other media. Most printers use inkjet technology, though many snapshot printers use dye-sublimation. Printers intended primarily for text use laser technology. **LCD viewer** indicates whether the printer has a built-in LCD screen for viewing and editing images from a memory card. The screen is small, usually only 1 to 3.5 inches, and editing capability is very limited. **Price** is approximate retail. *Based on tests posted on ConsumerReports.org in July 2006.*

Profiles Model-by-Model

1 Hewlett-Packard PhotoSmart 475 GoGo Photo Printer Very good photos. Includes 1.2-GB internal memory, to which photos can be stored. Can also print 5x7 photos. Composite-video output permits use of TV as image viewer. Space required (HWD): 8x10x12 in.

2 Canon Selphy CP600 Good and fast photos, but noisy. Space required (HWD): 2x7x16 in.

3 Hewlett-Packard PhotoSmart 425 GoGo Photo Printer Very good photos. Comes with an HP Photosmart M417 camera, which docks on top of printer. Composite-video output permits use of TV as image viewer. Space required (HWD): 7x9x11 in.

4 Hewlett-Packard PhotoSmart 428 GoGo Photo Printer Very good photos. Comes with an HP Photosmart M517 camera, which docks on top of printer. Composite-video output permits use of TV as image viewer. Space required (HWD): 7x9x11 in.

5 Samsung SPP-2040 Very good and fast photos, but high cost per print. Noisy. Space required (HWD): 4x7x16 in.

6 Hewlett-Packard PhotoSmart 385 GoGo Photo Printer Very good photos. Space required (HWD): 7x9x11 in.

7 Canon Selphy CP710 Good photos, but noisy. Has built-in, retracting PictBridge cable. Space required (HWD): 3x7x16 in.

8 Canon Selphy DS810 Good photos, but with high cost per print. Space required (HWD): 6x9x16 in.

9 Hewlett-Packard PhotoSmart 335 GoGo Photo Printer Very good photos. Space required (HWD): 7x9x11 in.

10 Samsung SPP-2020 Very good and fast photos, but high cost per print. Noisy. Space required (HWD): 3x7x16 in.

11 Canon Selphy CP510 Good photos, but noisy. Has built-in, retracting PictBridge cable. Space required (HWD): 3x7x16 in.

12 Epson PictureMate Deluxe Viewer Finder Good photos, with low cost per print. Pigment-based color and black inks. Space required (HWD): 9x11x14 in.

13 Epson PictureMate Express Edition Good photos, with low cost per print. Pigment-based color and black inks. Space required (HWD): 7x11x14 in.

14 Sony PictureStation DPP-FP50 Good and fast photos, but high cost per print. Composite-video output permits use of TV as image viewer. Noisy. Space required (HWD): 3x7x17 in.

15 Kodak EasyShare Photo Printer 500 Good photos, but noisy. Space required (HWD): 5x7x17 in.

16 Kodak EasyShare Printer Dock Plus Series 3 Good photos, but noisy. Composite-video output permits use of TV as image viewer. Space required (HWD): 3x7x17 in.

17 Kodak EasyShare Printer Dock Plus Good photos, but noisy. Composite-video output permits use of TV as image viewer. Space required (HWD): 3x7x17 in.

18 Olympus P-11 Digital Photo Printer Good and fast photos, but high cost per print. Clips away outer 20 percent of image when printing from computer. Noisy. Space required (HWD): 8x7x8 in.

19 Lexmark P450 Photo Printer Fair photos, with high cost per print. Has a built-in CD burner. Composite-video output permits use of TV as image viewer. Lacks USB support; can print only from PictBridge cable or removable media. Noisy. Space required (HWD): 8x11x15 in.

20 Kodak EasyShare Photo Printer 300 Fair photos. Noisy. Space required (HWD): 3x7x17 in.

21 Kodak EasyShare Printer Dock Fair photos. Noisy. Space required (HWD): 3x7x17 in.

22 Kodak EasyShare Printer Dock Series 3 Fair photos. Noisy. Space required (HWD): 3x8x17 in.

CR Quick Recommendations

Scanners

Any scanner judged very good for photo and text quality should be fine for general-purpose use. Models with higher resolution generally did better scanning transparent material. Most will work with Macintosh as well as Windows computers, but there are some exceptions, noted in the Ratings.

QUICK PICKS

For the fastest scans:

1 **Epson Perfection 3590 Photo, $150**

2 **HP Scanjet 4890, $200**

These two models were the fastest of the scanners we tested, and they produced high-quality scans of photos and text. The HP was better at scanning film and slides. It's the only tested scanner that can accommodate transparent originals larger than 35 mm—up to 8x10 inches, in this case. It also has a wide range of settings that let you optimize each scan, though you can get fine results from its default

settings if you don't want to fine-tune the settings. The Epson is a top choice for use with photos and text, but stick with the HP for scanning film or slides.

Best values for typical use; both are CR Best Buys:

4 **Canon CanoScan 4200F, $100**

8 **Epson Perfection 3490 Photo, $100**

The Canon and the Epson offer the best combination of speed, quality, and low price. They're among the many capable models to consider for everyday scans of photographs and text.

Ratings

In performance order.

	Excellent	Very good	Good	Fair	Poor
	●	◓	○	◒	●

Key number	Brand & model	Price	Overall score (P F G VG E)	Quality — Photos and text	Quality — Film/slide	Speed	Ease of use	Resolution (dpi)	Mac support
1	**Epson** Perfection 3590 Photo	$150	73	◓	◒	●	◓	3200	●
2	**HP** Scanjet 4890	200	72	◓	◓	●	○	4800	●
3	**Canon** CanoScan 8400F	150	70	◓	①	◓	◓	3200	●
4	**Canon** CanoScan 4200F	100	67	◓	①	◓	○	3200	
5	**Visioneer** OneTouch 9320 USB	120	66	◓	①	○	◓	3200	
6	**Epson** Perfection 4490 Photo	250	65	◓	○	◓	◓	4800	●
7	**HP** Scanjet 4850	150	65	◓	◓	◓	◓	4800	●
8	**Epson** Perfection 3490 Photo	100	64	◓	○	◓	◓	3200	●
9	**Canon** CanoScan LiDE 500F	130	63	◓	○	◓	◓	2400	●
10	**Microtek** ScanMaker i320	100	62	○	①	◓	◓	3200	●
11	**HP** Scanjet 4370	100	59	○	○	◓	◓	3600	●
12	**Visioneer** OneTouch 9420	120	58	○	◓	○	◓	4800	
13	**Microtek** ScanMaker s400	150	57	◓	①	◒	◓	4800	●

Items 4 and 8 are marked **CR BEST BUY**.

① We do not have test results for film scans on these models.

Guide to the Ratings

Overall score is based on quality of photo and text scans, speed, ease of use, and useful features (not shown). **Quality** received the greatest weight in the Ratings. It measures how faithfully the scanner reproduced a color photo and black-and-white images. Using the software included with each unit, we scanned images at the appropriate resolution and printed them on a high-quality inkjet printer. **Speed** measures how quickly each model scanned 8x10-inch color and black-and-white photos at both 150- and 300-dpi resolution. **Ease of use** is for scanning printed originals. **Resolution**, in dots per inch (dpi), lists the scanner's maximum optical resolution. As with color-bit depth, the scanner's ability to differentiate among gradations of light and dark matters only if you scan film and slides. **Price** is approximate retail. *Based on tests posted on ConsumerReports.org in May 2006, with updated prices and availability.*

CR Quick Recommendations

Antispam software

In addition to performance differences, the Ratings show some important features. Those include integration that will usually add a toolbar to popular e-mail programs so that you can block or approve senders simply by clicking on e-mail from them. Integrated programs also often automatically add your address-book contacts to a list of "good" senders.

All of the add-ons in the table are compatible with Windows XP, but not with Mac OS 9 or OS X. Some programs are loaded with features, but those don't always translate into better blocking.

QUICK PICKS

If you use an older version of Microsoft Outlook or Apple Mail:

1   **Microsoft Outlook 2003, $100**
2   **Apple OS 10.4.6 Mail, $130**

Microsoft was one of the top two performers for identifying spam while not confusing good mail with spam. You can either block all images, allow them manually, or allow them from designated senders only. With Apple, you can also block Web bugs and HTML in spam.

For a free add-on spam blocker:

3   **Trend Micro Anti-Spam Pilot, free download**

The best performer in our delivery and detection tests, Trend Micro's antispam program is also free. It's not as feature-rich as other programs, but ultimately all those extra features don't matter. The stand-alone version is better overall than the one included with the $50 suite. Stick to the free version unless you need the other programs in the suite.

If you use an e-mail program other than Outlook or Outlook Express:

4   **Allume Systems SpamCatcher, $30**

The most feature-rich among top-performing add-ons, Allume also works with POP3 e-mail programs other than Outlook, including Eudora. Be careful training this program; its performance decreased slightly after training in our tests.

Ratings

In performance order, within categories.

Legend: Excellent ◉ Very good ◑ Good ○ Fair ◕ Poor ●

Key number	Product	Price	Annual fee	Overall score (0–100)	Delivers valid e-mail	Detects spam	Features	Ease of setup and use	Integrates w/mailer	Learns	Online collaboration	Rules-based filter	Also in suite
	E-MAIL PROGRAMS *Sometimes bundled with new computers; filter spam without additional software.*												
1	**Microsoft** Outlook 2003	$100	None	87	◉	◉	◑	◉	●				●
2	**Apple** OS 10.4.6 Mail	130	None	83	◑	◉	○	◑	●	●			●
	ADD-ONS *Used in conjunction with an e-mail program to recognize and filter spam.*												
3	**Trend Micro** Anti-Spam Pilot (stand-alone version)	Free	None	95	◉	◉	○	◑	●				
4	**Allume Systems** SpamCatcher	30	$10	85	◉	◉	◑	○	●	●	●	●	
5	**Cloudmark** Desktop	40	40	81	◑	◉	◑	○	●	●	●		
6	**Trend Micro** Anti-Spam (suite version)	50	25	76	◑	◉	○	○	●			●	●
7	**PC Tools** Spam Monitor	30	20	71	◉	○	○	○	●			●	
8	**BitDefender** SpamDeny	20	15	56	◑	◉	◑	◕	●			●	●
9	**McAfee** SpamKiller	40	30	51	○	○	○	◕				●	●
10	**Symantec** Norton Anti-Spam (suite version)	70	40	48	◑	●	◑	○	●	●		●	●
11	**Sunbelt Software** iHateSpam	20	10	11	●	◉	◉	◑	●	●	●	●	●
12	**Blue Squirrel** Spam Sleuth Pro	30	None	10	○	●	◑	◕				●	
13	**CA/eTrust** Anti-Spam	30	20	10	●	◉	○	○	●	●			

Guide to the Ratings

Overall score is based on the ability to recognize valid e-mail and spam. **Delivers valid e-mail** indicates how well a product correctly identified e-mail that wasn't spam; excellent products correctly identified more than 95 percent. Poor ones misidentified at least 20 percent. **Detects spam** indicates how well each product correctly identified spam. A product that **integrates with mailer** blends its own controls with those of the e-mail program. One that **learns** identifies patterns in your e-mail, if you tell the software which messages are spam and which are not. With **online collaboration**, a product checks each message against a "live" online database of reported spam messages to improve accuracy. **Rules-based filters** detect known attributes, such as whether it contains a suspicious link. **Also in suite** means similar software is available in the manufacturer's security software suite. All products let you add "friendly" and "unfriendly" senders to the filter (either automatically or manually). **Price** is for the retail, boxed version. Some products are available via download, with a free trial period of at least 15 days. (Most will mail a CD for a few dollars.) *Based on tests published in September 2006 CONSUMER REPORTS.*

CR Quick Recommendations

Antispyware software

If you surf the Web often but have not checked your PC for spyware, download a free product such as Spybot and remove whatever spyware may have accumulated.

We recommend that you use two antispyware programs to provide extra protection. You should enable the real-time protection, which monitors activities in the background without you having to intervene, but enable it for only one antispyware program at a time.

Obtain software only from the official sites listed because similar software offered at other sites may actually be spyware. Because it's available only as part of a suite, we didn't recommend F-Secure as a Quick Pick. All of the products we tested are compatible with Windows XP, but not with Mac OS 9 or OS X.

QUICK PICKS

For an excellent, feature-rich antispyware program:

2 Webroot Spy Sweeper 4.5, $25

With excellent ratings for both features and spyware-blocking capabilities, Webroot blocked almost all of the start-up changes we threw at it in our spyware tests. Unusual among the products we tested, its firewall detects suspicious outgoing communications. When spyware is detected, Webroot tells you more about what type it is and what it can do.

For excellent antispyware with an easy-to-use interface:

3 PC Tools Spyware Doctor 3.8, $30

This provides excellent blocking and a simple, clean interface with a hierarchical set of options that summarizes each feature so that you can understand it. It's also the only stand-alone program with anti-phishing protection, which prevents access to malicious Web sites.

For a free complement to your main antispyware:

6 Spybot Search and Destroy 1.4, free download

This is very good at detecting spyware behavior and is easy to use. For a free program, it's a rich offering, with the ability to schedule hard-drive scans and to quarantine suspected spyware. It also includes a file shredder.

Ratings

In performance order.

Excellent ● | Very good ◒ | Good ○ | Fair ◐ | Poor ●

Key number	Product	Price	Annual fee	Official site	Overall score (P F G VG E 0–100)	Blocking	Features	Ease of use	Protects browser	Protects start-up	Describes spyware	Also in suite
1	**F-Secure** Anti-Spyware 2006 ⑴	$60	$50	f-secure.com	89	●	●	◒	•	•	•	•
2	**Webroot** Spy Sweeper 4.5	25	20	webroot.com	89	●	●	◒	•	•		•
3	**PC Tools** Spyware Doctor 3.8	30	20	pctools.com	88	●	◒	◒	•	•		
4	**Trend Micro** Anti-Spyware 3	30	30	trendmicro.com	85	●	●	○	•	•		•
5	**Lavasoft** Ad-Aware SE Plus 1.06	30	10	lavasoft.de	79	◒	◒	◒	•		•	
6	**Spybot** Search and Destroy 1.4 ⑴	Free	None	spybot.info	77	◒	◒	◒	•	•	•	
7	**Zone Labs** Zone Alarm Anti-Spyware 6.5	30	20	zonealarm.com	76	○	●	◒	•	•	•	•
8	**Sunbelt Software** CounterSpy	20	10	sunbeltsoftware.com	70	○	◒	◒	•	•		
9	**CA/eTrust** Pest Patrol	30	20	pestpatrol.com	67	○	○	◒		•	•	•
10	**BitDefender** Antispyware 9 ⑴	30	22	bitdefender.com	51	◐	◒	○	•		•	•
11	**McAfee** AntiSpyware 2006	30	30	http://us.mcafee.com	44	●	◒	◒	•		•	•
12	**Microsoft** Windows Defender (beta 1) ⑴	Free	None	microsoft.com	43	●	○	●			•	•

⑴ Available only by download.

Guide to the Ratings

Overall score combines blocking, features, and ease of use. **Blocking** shows how completely the product detected a number of different spyware behaviors and blocked or removed the initiator. **Features** includes auto update and real-time protection. **Ease of use** indicates how intuitive the interface is and how easy it is to perform common functions. **Protects browser** means spyware is prevented from changing your home page and redirecting Web searches. **Protects start-up** shows which products detect and stop spyware from starting automatically at boot-up. **Describes spyware** provides extra guidance to help decide whether to remove a detected item. **Also in suite** means similar software is available in the manufacturer's security suite. **Price** is for the retail, boxed version; downloads are usually available. All except Trend Micro (4) let you set computer scans for a specific time. All let you selectively restore programs removed as spyware. *Based on tests published in September 2006 CONSUMER REPORTS.*

SOFTWARE, ANTIVIRUS

CR Quick Recommendations

Antivirus software

Properly updated, all rated products detect viruses that have been circulating for more than a few days, but may not detect new ones until remedies are distributed. That can take days. Only Norton (5) is compatible with Mac OS.

All the programs have a trial version you can download, real-time protection, and scan-on-demand. All scan e-mail attachments; automatically scan new files; automatically update for detection of new viruses; and are easy disabled to allow installation of new software.

QUICK PICKS
For excellent detection at a low price:

1 **BitDefender Standard, $30 (download only)**
2 **Zone Labs ZoneAlarm Antivirus, $30**

Both scored excellent in our detection tests, including recognition of viruses they had never seen. Both let you schedule scans. BitDefender scans instant messages. Zone Labs has a full-featured firewall and scans within Zip files.

For both detection and ease of use:

3 **Kaspersky Labs Anti-Virus Personal, $50**

Kaspersky was very good at overall detection, and its features and ease of use both rated excellent. It scans within Zip files by default. It was excellent at recognizing newly discovered viruses, but only fair at our toughest test—recognizing those it had never seen before.

For good protection that's free:

8 **Alwil Avast! Antivirus, free download**

With good detection, ease of use, and scanning speed, and very good features, this free program is useful for protecting multiple computers on a tight budget.

Ratings

In performance order.

Excellent ● | Very good ◓ | Good ○ | Fair ◑ | Poor ●

Key number	Product	Price	Annual fee	Overall score (0–100, P F G VG E)	Detection	Features	Ease of use	Speed	Scheduled scan	IM scan	Firewall	Also in suite
1	**BitDefender** Standard [1]	$30	$20	87	●	◓	◓	●	•	•		•
2	**Zone Labs** ZoneAlarm Antivirus	30	20	85	●	○	◓	◓	•		•	•
3	**Kaspersky Labs** Anti-Virus Personal	50	35	82	◓	●	●	◓	•		•	•
4	**Norton** Antivirus	40	30	80	◓	◓	◓	◑	•	•	•	•
5	**Norton** Antivirus for Macintosh	50	15	80	◓	◓	○	◓	•		•	•
6	**McAfee** ViruScan	40	35	77	◓	◓	◓	◓	•		•	•
7	**Trend Micro** PC-cillin Internet Security	50	25	75	○	◓	●	◓	•		•	•
8	**Alwil** Avast! Antivirus [1]	Free	None	68	○	◓	○	○	•	•		
9	**F-Secure** Anti-Virus [1]	40	40	66	○	○	◓	○	•			•
10	**Panda Software** Titanium AV [2]	40	50	64	○	◓	◓	◓	•	•		•
11	**CA/eTrust** EZ Antivirus [2]	30	20	57	○	◓	◓	○	•			
12	**PC Tools** AntiVirus [1]	30	20	41	●	◑	○	◓	•			

[1] Available only by download. [2] Boxed price; download price is $10 more.

Guide to the Ratings

Overall score is based primarily on detection, plus the other test results. **Detection** is how well the product detects new viruses without falsely identifying benign files as viruses. **Features** indicates how many useful features are included. **Ease of use** indicates how easy the product is to use. **Speed** is how quickly the product scans a typical hard drive. **Scheduled scan** means you can set up automatic scans. **IM scan** shows whether the product scans instant messages. **Firewall** indicates whether there are features to block hackers. **Also in suite** means that the same, or similar, software is available in the manufacturer's security software suite. **Price** is for the retail, boxed version; downloads are usually available. **Annual fee** is for protection after the first year. *Based on tests published in September 2006 CONSUMER REPORTS.*

BRAND LOCATOR

Manufacturer contacts

Name	Phone number	Web address
ACD Systems	866-244-2237	www.acdsystems.com
Adobe	800-833-6687	www.adobe.com
Akai	800-726-4405	www.akaiusa.com
AMD	800-222-9323	www.amd.com
America Online	800-827-6364	www.aol.com
Apex Digital	866-930-1236	www.apexdigitalinc.com
Apple	800-692-7753	www.apple.com
Asus	888-678-3688	usa.asus.com
ArcSoft	510-440-9901	www.arcsoft.com
AT&T	800-222-3111	www.att.com
Audiovox	800-229-1235	www.audiovox.com
Brother	800-276-7746	www.brother-usa.com
Canon	800-385-2155	www.usa.canon.com
Casio	800-706-2534	www.casio.com
Cingular	888-331-6651	www.cingular.com
Compaq	800-752-0900	www.compaq.com
Corel	800-772-6735	www.corel.com
CTX	877-688-3288	www.ctxintl.com
Dell	800-624-9896	www.dell.com
Disney Interactive	800-328-0368	disney.go.com/disneyinteractive
DirecTV	800-4944388	www.directv.com
DirecWay	866-347-3292	www.direcway.com
Dish Network	888-825-2557	www.dishnetwork.com
EarthLink	800-327-8454	www.earthlink.net
Emachines	408-273-0888	www.E4me.com
Envision	888-838-6388	www.envisionmonitor.com
Epson	800-463-7766	www.epson.com
Ericsson	866-766-9374	www.sonyericsson.com
Fisher	818-998-7322	www.fisherav.com
Franklin	800-266-5626	www.franklin.com
Fujifilm	800-800-3854	www.fujifilm.com
Fujitsu	800-838-5487	www.fujitsupc.com
Gateway	800-369-1409	www.gateway.com
Garmin	800-800-1020	www.garmin.com
Hewlett-Packard	800-752-0900	www.hp.com
Hitachi	800-448-2244	www.hitachi.us
IBM	800-426-4968	www.ibm.com

Manufacturer contacts (continued)

Name	Phone number	Web address
Inkjetsinc	800-275-2410	www.inkjetsinc.com
Intel	800-628-8686	www.intel.com
Iomega	888-516-8467	www.iomega.com
GE	800-720-2094	www.home-electronics.net
JVC	800-252-5722	www.jvc.com
KDS	800-283-1311	www.kdsusa.com
Kodak	800-235-6325	www.kodak.com
Konica	800-285-6422	www.konicaminolta.us
Kyocera	800-421-5735	www.kyoceraimaging.com
LearningCo.com	800-395-0277	www.learningco.com
Lexmark	888-539-6275	www.lexmark.com
LG	800-243-0000	us.lge.com
Lotus	800-465-6887	www.lotus.com
Lucent	866-237-4448	www.lucent.com
Microsoft	800-426-9400	www.microsoft.com
Microtek	310-687-5940	www.microtekusa.com
Minolta	800-285-6422	www.minoltausa.com
Mintek	866-709-9500	www.mintekdigital.com
Motorola	800-353-2729	www.motorola.com
Network Associates (McAfee VirusScan)	800-338-8754	www.mcafee.com
NEC	800-338-9549	www.nec.com
Nextel	800-639-6111	www.nextel.com
Nikon	800-645-6689	www.nikonusa.com
Nintendo	800-255-3700	www.nintendo.com
Nokia	888-665-4228	www.nokiausa.com
Olympus	888-553-4448	www.olympusamerica.com
Palm	800-881-7256	www.palm.com/us
Panasonic	800-742-8086	www.panasonic.com
Pentax	800-877-0155	www.pentaximaging.com
Philips	888-744-5477	www.philipsusa.com
SBC Prodigy	866-722-9246	myhome.prodigy.net
RadioShack	800-843-7422	www.radioshack.com
RCA	800-336-1900	www.rca.com
ReplayTV	866-286-3662	www.replaytv.com
Riverdeep	888-242-6747	www.riverdeep.com
Samsung	800-627-4368	www.samsung.com
Sanyo	800-877-5032	www.sanyousa.com
Sega	800-872-7342	www.sega.com
Sharp	800-237-4277	www.sharpusa.com
Siemens	888-777-0211	www.icm.siemens.com
Sierra	310-649-8033	www.sierra.com
Sony	877-865-7669	www.sonystyle.com
Sprint PCS	800-777-4681	www.sprintpcs.com
Symantec (Norton AntiVirus)	800-441-7234	www.symantec.com
TiVo	877-289-8486	www.tivo.com
T-Mobile	800-866-2453	www.t-mobile.com
Toshiba	800-631-3811	www.toshiba.com
Uniden	800-297-1023	www.uniden.com
Verizon Wireless	800-922-0204	www.verizonwireless.com
ViewSonic	800-688-6688	www.viewsonic.com
Visioneer	925-251-6398	www.visioneer.com
Vtech	800-595-9511	www.vtech.com
WinBook	800-254-7806	www.winbook.com
Zone Labs	415-633-4500	www.zonealarm.com

BRAND LOCATOR

Expert • Independent • Nonprofit

GLOSSARY

With advice on choosing and using electronics products

A

AAC Advanced Audio Coding, a form of digital music compression using the MPEG-4 standard that improves on the common MP3 compression used for transferring music over the Internet and to portable devices. AAC is licensed by Dolby Labs and popularized by Apple Computer's iTunes music sales service.

Access The ability to connect to the Internet. Also, to store or retrieve data from a storage device such as a disk or from a database. Sometimes access is restricted by an authentication scheme, such as a password.

Accessibility The degree to which hardware or software is designed to allow persons with disabilities to use a computer. Windowed operating systems have many accessibility features, such as the ability to enlarge fonts, icons, and menus, and to use alternate Human Interface Devices (HIDs).

Active-matrix display A high-quality, flat-panel display in which a separate transistor switch is used for each pixel, allowing viewing from wider angles. Most color LCDs are active-matrix displays. Commonly listed as "TFT LCD." Compare with "passive matrix display."

Additional connectors, camcorders All camcorders have audio and composite-video output, which let you monitor during recording or playback. Other connectors include stereo-audio, headphone, and S-video outputs and a microphone input. Edit-control signal inputs (including LANC, JLIP, and Control-L) are for use with editing equipment or a suitable VCR. A FireWire (IEEE-1394) port lets you connect to a computer or digital camcorder. And for camcorders that let you capture still images, a USB or FireWire port lets you transfer saved images to a computer.

Additional disc formats In addition to playing DVD-video discs, DVD players can handle audio CDs. (Some can also play video CDs, a format that's popular overseas.) Other disc formats that some players support include CD-R and CD-RW (the audio discs you record yourself, using other equipment); MP3 on CDs; HDCD; DVD-Audio and Super Audio CD (SACD), two audio-centric formats intended to succeed CD audio; and the DVD-RAM, DVD+R, DVD-R, DVD+RW, and DVD-RW writable formats.

Add-on (or add-in) A computer component that can be attached to a larger device by a simple process such as plugging it into a socket.

Adjustable color temperature Also known as "color warmth adjustment" or "white balance," a TV's adjustable color temperature setting that, when present, lets you vary the overall color tone of the picture between cooler (bluish) and warmer (reddish).

Advanced playback controls Most phone answerers can skip to the next message, back to a previous one, or repeat a message. Some also have more advanced conveniences such as fast playback, slow playback (say, to slow down a part of the message to understand a phone number), and rewind (to go back to a certain part of a message).

Adware software displays advertising when it is active. Usually synonymous with spyware, adware may be installed on a PC along with desired (often free) software, in order to generate sales or advertising revenue for the software provider. Rarely, the user has an opportunity to "opt out" of the adware while continuing to use the desired software.

All-in-one A desktop-computer design with all required parts built in—display, hard drive, optical drive, and speakers. Apple's iMac is one example. Multifunction printers—which scan, copy, and sometimes fax as well as print—are also called all-in-ones.

Analog A representation of a continuous measurement of some function. A common example is the commercial AM/FM radio, where sound is converted to a varying voltage that is transmitted via radio waves and converted from voltage to sound on the other end.

Analog input lets a camcorder record analog audio and video from other devices, such as a VCR or another camcorder. This feature can drive up the price of a digital camcorder, since a unit must also have additional circuitry to convert analog signals to digital.

Announce-only mode For phones with an answerer, this mode lets you set the unit to play a greeting without giving callers the option to leave a message.

Answerer mailboxes Some answering machines have mailboxes that let you separate business from personal calls or set up boxes for different members of the household.

Answering machine, cordless phones Cordless phones of all types are available with a built-in answering machine that has digital message storage, typically 15 to 20 minutes. Desirable features include a digital message-counter display, the ability to repeat or skip a message, and, for large households or for separating personal and business messages, several mailboxes. May be referred to as ITAD (integrated telephone answering device).

Antenna/cable input Also called RF or VHF/UHF, the most basic connection through which a TV can receive the signal it displays. It's the easiest to use since it's the only connection available on every TV that carries both sound and picture. A newer connection available on many digital (HD/ED/SD) sets, HDMI (see "HDMI") also carries both signals. The other video inputs—chiefly composite-video, S-video, and component-video—accept only the picture, requiring the use of separate audio inputs to receive the sound. Those other inputs, however, offer incremental improvements in quality.

Antivirus program A program designed to detect, remove, and protect against computer viruses, worms, and Trojan horses. Antivirus programs must be updated regularly to maintain protection against new threats.

Any-key answerer The ability to answer an incoming phone call by pressing any key (except "off").

Aperture modes The number or range of settings for a digital camera's aperture, which is the opening in the lens that controls how much light hits the camera's image sensor. Apertures are stated as f-stops or f-numbers (for example, f/8). The smallest number in this range is the most important: The smaller that number, the larger the maximum aperture, and the less light the camera requires to take a picture.

Aperture range The minimum and maximum aperture (lens opening) range for wide and telephoto shots.

Application programs have a particular function. Typical examples are word processors, spreadsheets, and games. For a PDA (as with personal computers), these are the software programs included. Contacts/address book, calendar/date book, to-do list/tasks, and memo pad/notes are standard on every unit.

Aspect ratio The aspect ratio is the proportion of a TV screen's width to its height. Standard TV screens have an aspect ratio of 4:3, giving them a squarish shape that is 4 units wide for every 3 units high. Wide-screen TVs typically have a 16:9 aspect ratio, giving them a wider screen that better resembles the screen in a movie theater. (Some LCD TVs have a 15:9 aspect ratio that differs slightly, but they're often not identified as such.) Wide-screen TVs can use the full screen to more fully display HDTV broadcasts and recorded movies. When displayed on a standard screen, such images must be framed at the top and bottom with black bars in order to maintain the wide-screen aspect ratio. Conversely, regular TV programming displayed on a wide screen has black bars on both sides.

Athlon A family of microprocessors from AMD that competes with Intel's Pentium series and has similar performance.

ATSC Advanced Television Systems Committee, an international, nonprofit organization developing voluntary standards for digital television. In the United States, digital off-air tuners such as those in HDTVs receive content transmitted in ATSC formats. These formats include 480p, 720p, and 1080i. An ATSC tuner refers to one capable of accepting HD (720p, 1080i, or 1080p) and 480p signals.

Audible message alert An answerer alert, typically in the form of a beep, that proves handy if you often forget to look at the answerer to see if you have new messages.

Audio dynamic range control This DVD-player feature, useful for late-night viewing, keeps explosions and other loud sound effects from sounding too loud, while it makes whispers loud enough to be heard.

Audio outputs Audio outputs, found on many TVs, let you relay the set's audio signal to a receiver or external, powered speakers—a must if you desire top-quality sound. Fixed-audio outputs, true to their name, have a fixed output level; you might prefer them if you will use a receiver to control the TV's volume. With variable-audio outputs, the sound level you'll hear from your sound system or external speakers rises and falls with any adjustment of the TV's volume control.

Audio playback formats The audio formats an MP3 player will recognize and be able to play. Even when a format isn't supported, most players come with music-management software that lets you convert or "rip" the file into a format the player can play. Some formats can also be copy-protected. Examples include AAC and WMA on songs downloaded from online music sites. These may have the suffix "-DRM," and may be referred to, for instance, as secure WMA.

Audio recording With digital cameras, this feature lets you record a short sound bite with each image—say, to make notes for future reference. May also permit the recording of sound with any mini-movie feature.

Audio tone controls Found on nearly all TVs equipped with built-in speakers, a control for adjusting treble and bass.

Auto channel setup Useful when you connect your TV set for the first time, this common feature scans all the channels you receive and sets up the TV to access only the ones with programming, so you don't have to program the channels yourself. Once they're set up, your remote will skip the blank channels when you scroll up or down channels.

Auto fleshtone correction A TV feature you can set to adjust color balance automatically to make flesh tones look more natural.

Auto focus Automatically brings a camera's subject into sharp focus. Some models offer manual focus in addition to auto focus.

Auto power-off Shuts off a TV after a preset (and often adjustable) period during which the screen image is stationary, intended to prevent screen burn-in.

Auto talk Also referred to as auto answer, this cordless-phone feature allows you to lift the handset off its base for an incoming call and start talking without having to press a button. On some phones this is automatic; for others, it is a selectable feature.

Auto volume leveler Found on some TV sets, the auto volume leveler compensates for changes in the audio signal that you'd hear as a jump in volume. With this somewhat-helpful feature, there are fewer fluctuations in sound level as you switch between channels and view commercials, which are frequently louder than regular programming.

AV input On a camcorder or video recorder, these let you record sound or images from another camcorder or a VCR. On a TV, these let you view images from sources other than the built-in tuner.

Available memory, PDAs The amount of usable internal memory in a PDA that is available for new uses—such as appointments, addresses, and applications—when the model is new. For memory-intensive applications, such as MP3-playing and picture-taking, most new PDAs support the use of external memory cards to store music, image, and video files.

B

Back up To copy data or other content onto a computer's removable disk, second hard drive, or another storage medium, to prevent loss should the original become damaged.

Backlight A PDA feature, found in units with a monochrome screen, that lets you view the display better under low-light conditions. Using the backlight, however, will cause the unit's battery to run down more rapidly.

Backlight compensation When the light behind a camcorder's subject is brighter than the light on your subject, the subject ordinarily will appear silhouetted. Backlight compensation slightly increases the exposure to make the subject more visible.

Backlit keypad A cordless-phone keypad that glows in the dark or when you press a key.

Backward compatibility The ability of a new computer product to work properly with other products that use older technology.

Bandwidth In digital systems, the maximum speed of a data link in bits per second (bps), thousands of bps (kbps), or millions of bits per second (megabits per second, or Mbps). Ethernet has a bandwidth of 10 to 1,000 Mbps; WiFi wireless, between 11 and 54 Mbps. Cable-modem downloads are 1 to 5 Mbps, consumer-grade DSL is 768 to 1,500 kbps, and a V.90 or V.92 modem connection has a bandwidth of up to 53.3 kbps.

Base keypad Also referred to as a cordless phone's dual or second keypad, a keypad on the base that supplements the one on the handset. It can be handy for navigating menu-driven systems because you don't have to take the phone away from your ear to punch the keys. When it's used with the speakerphone, you can make a call from the base hands-free.

Base speakerphone A base speakerphone offers a hands-free way to converse or wait on hold and lets others chime in as well, and lets you answer a call without the handset. When it's used with a base keypad, you can make a call from the base and have a hands-free conversation.

Battery backup Protects cordless-phone memory (stored phone numbers) during power outages or when the phone is unplugged. On an answerer, this feature can save greetings and messages.

Battery holder A compartment in a cordless phone's base that can charge a spare handset battery pack or to hold alkaline batteries for power backup. The spare handset battery is usually not included. The handset battery pack or alkaline batteries sometimes can be used as the base power backup, enabling the phone to work if you lose household AC power.

Bay A position in a computer case to mount a device, such as a hard drive or DVD writer.

Bidirectional With computers, capable of transferring information in both directions.

BIOS Basic Input/Output System, the fundamental instructions by which a computer communicates with various peripheral devices. The BIOS usually resides in a firmware chip on the motherboard, allowing the computer to boot. A "flash" BIOS can be updated by overwriting its contents with new instructions from a file.

Bit Short for binary digit and abbreviated as "b," it's the smallest piece of data recognizable by a computer.

Black-level adjustment On TVs, this is commonly labeled "brightness." This feature lets you make adjustments to the intensity of black in the picture from a DVD. When the black is too deep, details in dark areas of images may be obscured; when black isn't deep enough, dark areas of images will be too bright.

Bluetooth A short-range (35-foot) wireless-data

protocol that can link compatible devices in a secure connection, using the 2.5-GHz radio-frequency band, with transfer speeds of up to 720 kbps. Examples are computer-to-printer, PDA-to-computer, and headset-to-telephone.

Board A thin, usually rectangular card on which various electronic components are mounted and interconnected.

Bookmark An easy way to access frequently visited Web sites; the user saves Web-page URLs to a list (called either Bookmarks or Favorites) through a drop-down menu in the browser.

Boot To bring a computer into operation. This normally includes loading part or all of the computer's operating system into main memory from a storage device.

bps Bits per second, a measure of data-transfer throughput. Rates are usually expressed with the prefixes k- for kilo-, M- for mega-, or G for giga-.

Broadband As commonly used, a connection to the Internet that has a receiving bandwidth greater than that of dial-up or ISDN service, about 128 kbps. (The FCC defines broadband as "256 kbps in at least one direction.") Common broadband connections are cable-modem, DSL, and satellite. Broadband makes streaming audio and video practical.

Buffer A computer memory area used to hold data temporarily while it is being transferred from one location or device to another or waiting to be processed. Buffers are essential for the efficient operation of the CPU and are often used in graphics processors, CD-ROM drives, printer drivers, and other input/output devices to compensate for differences in processing speed.

Bug An error in a computer program that prevents proper operation.

Built-in digital tuner, TVs Includes a tuner that can decode digital TV signals received off-air (ATSC broadcasts) or via cable or satellite. An HD set with such a tuner may be referred to as an "integrated HDTV." A TV that requires you to connect an external tuner (in a cable box, satellite receiver, or set-top box) is called a TV "monitor"—as in "HDTV monitor"—or labeled with the word "ready," as in "HD-ready."

Built-in fax modem, printers Refers to a multi-function printer that comes with a modem, which lets you send and receive faxes without using the host computer's own faxing capability.

Built-in light On a camcorder, it provides illumination for close-ups when the image would otherwise be too dark. It's no substitute, however, for a well-lit room.

Built-in microphone Useful for recording interviews, lectures, etc., onto an MP3 player or other recording device.

Built-in multichannel audio decoder output For a DVD player with built-in decoding of Dolby Digital or DTS multichannel audio (necessary for full enjoyment of multichannel audio soundtracks if your receiver lacks this capability), the ability to

connect speakers and a subwoofer directly to the DVD player.

Bundle The software that comes preloaded with many personal computers. This typically includes a word processor, financial program, encyclopedia, productivity suite, and assorted games. Also, the combination of a PC and peripheral devices such as a monitor, printer, scanner, or accessories, usually as a sales incentive.

Burner An optical disk drive that can save data or program content. Also called a CD or DVD writer.

Burst mode Lets you take multiple, rapid-fire shots with one touch of a camcorder's or digital camera's shutter button; useful when you're shooting a subject in motion. The number of shots that can be taken in burst mode varies from camera to camera. Burst mode may not be available in a camera's highest-resolution mode. Also called "continuous shooting" or "rapid-fire shots."

Bus A pathway that connects devices inside a computer, usually the CPU and memory, or a peripheral such as an adapter card. Common bus designs include PCI and CardBus.

Byte The basic computer-storage unit, abbreviated as "B," needed to store a single character, nominally 8 bits.

C

CableCard For digital-cable-ready (DCR) TVs, this credit-card-sized card must be inserted into a slot on the set in order for you to receive digital-cable programming without the need for a cable box. (You typically rent the card from your cable operator for a few dollars a month.) Current DCR TVs are one-way, so they don't provide an interactive program guide, video on demand, or pay-per-view ordering via the remote control. For those features, you'll still need a cable box. Two-way DCR TVs are expected to be out soon.

Cable modem A means of providing high-speed Internet service through a TV cable.

Cable/satellite box control A recording device's ability to change channels automatically on a cable box or satellite receiver—needed to record programs from several channels when time-shift recording from either satellite or cable systems that use cable boxes.

Cache memory is dedicated to improving a computer's performance. It accomplishes this by setting aside part of main memory, using driver software, or employing special high-speed memory.

Call screening An answering-machine feature. It allows you to listen to the caller over the speaker while the caller's message is being recorded, so you can decide whether to answer the call.

Caller ID Caller ID with a three-line display shows the name and phone number of a caller and the date and time of the call, provided you subscribe to Caller ID services. Some models have an additional display line that shows on which line—say, line 1 or line 2—the call came in, or indicators such as battery strength or voice mail. If you have Caller ID

with Call Waiting and are already on the phone, the phone displays the name and number of the second caller. A phone with distinctive-ring capability also lets you hear who is calling by associating the calling number with a specific ring tone. Some are visual, so you can tell who's calling by the handset display or the antenna flashing a particular color.

Caller ID memory locations Provided you subscribe to Caller ID services, the maximum number of Caller ID memory locations the phone can store for the most recent incoming phone numbers, along with associated names and information such as the date and time of a call.

Caller IQ Also referred to as Viewer IQ, or Info IQ, this cordless-phone feature is compatible with a service from openLCR (*www.openlcr.com*). The service claims to offer low-cost routing for reducing your phone bills. Among other features, it also handles date and time settings, and information updates shown on your phone's display, such as weather forecasts and stock quotes.

Camera connections Input or output connections for data transfer, power, image display (on a video monitor), or addition of an external flash unit.

Can-Spam Act An effort in 2004 by the U.S. Congress to curb the proliferation of e-mail "spam" by mandating labeling and opt-out provisions. It has thus far failed to accomplish its purpose, probably because most spammers are outlaws, and many are based offshore.

Capacity provided The total memory that comes with an MP3 player, combining memory built into the unit plus any external media supplied with the unit.

Card An electronic circuit board that serves a particular function, such as memory or graphics; in a PC, cards are usually plugged into a bus connector on the motherboard.

Carpal Tunnel Syndrome A painful, potentially debilitating injury that can arise from heavy keyboard use. Symptoms may include weakness, numbness, tingling, and burning in the hands and fingers.

CCD pixels Light from a camcorder's subject is focused by the lens onto a charge-coupled device (CCD), a sensor that converts light into minute blocks of information, called pixels. A CCD's light-sensitive area is typically composed of 250,000 pixels or more. A higher number of active pixels generally means a sharper picture but less sensitivity to light.

CCD size A charge-coupled device (CCD) converts light into minute blocks of information, called pixels, to form the images stored on a camcorder. Almost all CCDs measure ¼-inch diagonally. A few are larger; the additional size generally produces more light sensitivity. Some high-end camcorders have more than one CCD.

CD, or Compact Disc A 5-inch, aluminum-coated polycarbonate plastic disc with embedded digital data, read by focusing a laser beam on the data tracks and sensing its reflection. CDs can carry about 650 megabytes (MB) of digital information, which can be entertainment, such as music or motion video, or computer data.

CD-R CD-Recordable, a disc that can be recorded, once only, in a CD writer.

CD-R and **CD-RW, digital cameras** A few cameras use small-size versions of these optical discs to store images. The discs are about 3 inches in diameter, hold 165 MB of data, and can be read in a computer's CD drive.

CD-R and **CD-RW** Disc format that allows discs to be recorded either once only (CD-R) or repeatedly (CD-RW) in a CD writer.

CD-ROM Compact Disc-Read Only Memory, a 5-inch disc holding data or software; also, the drive that retrieves digital data from the disc.

CD writer A drive that lets you record to or copy CD-ROM discs. With the right software, you can also record to or copy audio and video CDs. CD writers and blank media have dropped in price significantly over the past few years, and are now virtually standard in PCs.

Celeron A processor series from Intel that is slower and less costly than its Pentium counterpart, used in lower-priced PCs.

Center-channel audio input An input, found in some TVs, that accepts the center-channel portion (mostly comprising dialog) of a multichannel audio soundtrack for output through the set's built-in speakers, as opposed to an external center-channel speaker.

Centrino Intel's motherboard chipset design for laptop PCs that uses the Pentium M processor and emphasizes long battery life and wireless networking. The Pentium M processor has a reduced clock speed to save power but is designed to have as high performance as more power-hungry Pentiums.

Chain dialing, cordless phones A useful feature for those who often use calling cards or have to key in an authorization code, it lets you access a previously programmed number in your phone book or a speed-dial memory location and dial the number while you're on a phone call. This way you can make calls that require a sequence of separate numbers, such as a calling-card number used for a frequently called long-distance number or, say, an authorization code.

Channel block-out A TV parental-control feature that can block specific channels altogether, as opposed to the program-specific V-chip, and may also prevent or otherwise limit use of the audio/video inputs to which video-game consoles are connected.

Channel labels With this common TV feature, you can enter a channel's name into an onscreen display. As you surf, you can then quickly identify the channel.

Channel-guide menu A TV feature, such as Guide Plus, that displays program listings. The set receives program information while off but still in "standby."

Chapter preview Movies on DVD are divided into "chapters." This feature helps you find the scene you are looking for by playing the first few seconds

of each chapter or—with the related chapter gallery—showing the first scene of each chapter. This, in effect, lets you visually scan the disc.

Chat Internet term for any site or service that allows real-time communication between two or more users, using text, graphics, voice, and video or a combination. Participants often refer to the interface as a "chat room."

Chip An integrated circuit such as those commonly used for a PC's microprocessor and memory systems. It is composed of a small, rectangular slice of semiconductor material, encased in a larger rectangular carrier with electrical connections.

Clock In a PC, a circuit that regulates all processes by synchronizing them to a defined frequency. In a TV, its internal time-keeper, primarily for use with the set's alarm ("on") timer.

Clock speed The rate at which a computer's CPU clock operates, measured in megahertz (MHz) or gigahertz (GHz). In theory, the faster the clock speed, the faster the CPU will perform its operations. Most new PCs now work at clock speeds ranging from about 1 GHz to nearly 4 GHz.

Closed caption on mute With this feature, your TV's screen will automatically display captions whenever you mute the sound. Otherwise, you typically would have to press several buttons to mute the sound and view closed captions.

Closed captioning Closed captioning displays the dialog and other sounds in text across the bottom of the screen. It is particularly useful for the hearing-impaired.

Coaxial cable A type of telecommunications link with a wider bandwidth than conventional phone lines. It is also used for cable TV.

Coaxial digital-audio out, DVD players Digital-audio output is important only if you plan to pipe the signal from the DVD player into a home-theater system that has a digital receiver. When choosing your DVD player, consider the models that have the outputs to match the inputs on your digital receiver or external, digital decoder. All DVD players have digital audio outputs—coaxial, optical, or both.

Code (1) A set of instructions, written by a programmer, that tells a computer what to do; (2) to write a program; or (3) one or more characters that perform a specific function, such as a control code.

Cold boot To start or restart a computer from the power-off condition, or via a reset button.

Color display, MP3 players This is typically a backlit liquid crystal display (LCD). Some displays instead use organic light-emitting diodes (OLEDs). Virtually all players with a color display can show pictures taken with your digital camera.

Color display, PDAs PDA screens have either a color display capable of as many as 64,000 colors or a black-and-white display capable of multiple shades of gray. While a color screen offers rich detail, it will drain the batteries faster than a

monochrome one. The quality of a color display (for example, detail and sharpness) is most affected by its contrast ratio; the greater the ratio, the better the display.

Command An instruction, usually entered directly from a computer's keyboard or a pointing device, that is designed to bring about an action.

Commercial skip Useful to channel surfers and anyone averse to commercials, the commercial-skip function lets you jump temporarily to another channel, in 30-second increments, for a duration you select.

CompactFlash CompactFlash (CF) memory cards are about the size of a matchbook. Most digital cameras equipped with a type-II CF slot can also accept the high-capacity IBM Microdrive cards.

Compatible operating system, printers An operating system is the underlying program that manages a computer's applications. Most computers use a version of the Windows or Macintosh operating system. The type of computer a printer can serve also depends on its interfaces, or ports. All printers have a universal serial bus (USB) port, which makes them compatible with newer Windows or Macintosh computers. Some have USB2, a higher-speed port found on the latest computers. Some have an IEEE 1284-compliant parallel port, which lets them work with older Windows machines. (IEEE 1284 refers to the timing specifications of the electronics and the design properties of the cable used.) All of these printers lack a serial port, which means they won't work with older Macs.

Component-video input Component-video input uses three jacks that separate the video signal into three parts: two for color and one for luminance. This provides slightly better quality than an S-video connection, most evident in color fidelity. It can be used only with a DVD player, digital-cable box, or other equipment that has component-video output. On some products, it may also be used for progressive-scan and HD signals.

Component-video output Nearly all DVD players offer component-video output. Technically superior even to an S-video connection, a component-video connection can provide a picture with better color accuracy.

Composite-video inputs Composite-video inputs are the most common type of video inputs found on TVs. These carry only the video signal, providing better picture quality than RF (often labeled as "VHF/UHF" on your TV). These are often used to connect a VCR or cable box. Many sets have front-panel composite-video inputs, which let you make temporary connections to camcorders, game consoles, digital cameras, and other devices with composite-video output.

Composite-video output All devices that output a video signal offer composite-video output at a minimum. A composite-video connection between the playback device and the TV provides a picture with less detail and more color artifacts than you're likely to get using an S-video connection. A component-video connection is necessary for optimal picture quality from a progressive-scan player used with a digital TV.

Computer link for stills For camcorders that have still-image-capture capability, a USB or serial port is used to transfer saved still images to a computer.

Computer monitor option The ability of some flat-panel TVs, notably LCD models, to double as a computer monitor, having the required inputs for a computer connection. Some models, notably HD sets, may accept computer signals through their Digital Visual Interface (DVI) input if compatible. A standard VGA connection, however, is the surest guarantee of dual-use potential.

Conferencing Also referred to as three-way conferencing. For some single-line phones, allows conversation among an outside party, the handset, and base speakerphone. For some two-line phones, you can conference two callers in a three-way conversation. Some two-line phones with a base speakerphone can support four-way conferencing. For multiple-handset-capable phones, conferencing can take place among the handsets and an outside party.

Configuration The way various components of a system (such as a computer) are linked. This refers not only to the way the hardware is physically connected but also to how the software is set up to govern the system and its parts; also, the setup and operating parameters of a software program.

Convergence For CRT-based projection sets, convergence is periodically necessary to align the three CRTs for a sharp, accurate image. It's recommended that you do so when the TV is first set up and whenever you move the set. Convergence capability can be automatic, manual, or both. Automatic convergence provides a one-touch adjustment. It's much more convenient than manual convergence alone, which can require many time-consuming adjustments. Having both automatic and manual convergence lets you manually fine-tune the CRTs' alignment after following the automatic procedure.

Conversation recording A feature that, in some phones with answerers, lets you record a two-way conversation.

CPU Central processing unit, the part of a computer that controls and performs all processing activities. It consists of the ALU (arithmetic logic unit), control unit, and main memory.

Crash An uncontrolled shutdown of one task or the entire computer.

CRT Cathode-ray tube, the familiar picture tube used to create a TV picture since the advent of television. Despite the growing popularity of other technologies such as LCD, plasma, and DLP, CRT TVs represent a mature technology with proven reliability and long life. The best sets have top-notch picture quality, with excellent detail, color, and contrast, plus no limit on viewing angle. CRTs are also used in some rear-projection TVs, in which case the TV contains three CRTs—one each for red, green, and blue—making the cabinet relatively big and heavy. Three beams converge on the inside of the screen to form an image. You must periodically align the CRTs, using the TV's controls, to ensure a sharp image.

Cryptography The science of encrypting a data message for transmission such that an eavesdropper cannot discover its content, but that the intended recipient can decrypt it using a string of characters called a "key." The length of the required key determines how secure the message is.

Cursor A symbol that marks the current position on the screen and moves as the position changes. It is most often a single underline, a vertical line, or a block the size of one character. It may be either steady or blinking.

Cursor-control keys A special group of keys on a keyboard or keypad (designated by arrows pointing up, down, left, and right) that perform cursor-movement functions.

Custom bookmark Should you want to view a DVD scene again later, this feature lets you mark a spot on the disc to which you can later return.

Cyberspace First used by William Gibson in the novel "Neuromancer" to refer to a futuristic computer network into which people plugged their brains and interacted with it. It has come to refer to the interconnection of computers known as the Internet.

D

D/A converter sampling rate With respect to video, most standard DVD players use a 10-bit/27-MHz digital-to-analog converter. Progressive-scan DVD players use a 10- or 12-bit/54-MHz digital-to-analog converter.

Data An item or collection of items of information to be processed, displayed, or stored. Data can be text, numbers, binary code, images, sounds, or any combination.

Data file A collection of information to be used as input to a program for processing, display, or any other useful purpose.

Data storage The ability of an MP3 player to store files other than digital-audio files, including text, image, and video files.

Database A collection of data, organized for retrieval, on a specific topic or for a designated purpose.

DCR See "Digital-cable-ready."

Decoder A circuit that converts a TV signal's information into another set of information. In video, it usually decompresses the information to convert it into a playable form.

Dedicated line A telephone line used solely for data or fax services.

Default A value that is automatically assigned to a setting when no other value is entered. A default password, such as "secret," should be changed to ensure security.

Delay between shots The time, in seconds, it takes a digital camera to ready itself for another picture when shooting in normal (nonburst) mode, at the camera's highest-resolution, lowest-

compression, JPEG setting. Also called lag time or maximum-recycle time.

Desktop In a window-based user interface, the bottom-level window you see when no program window is open. The desktop can be set up as a user prefers, with icons allowing easy launching of often-used programs and documents.

Desktop computer A PC featuring the traditional full-size case, monitor, and keyboard designed to be used in a stationary, "desk-centered" environment.

Dialog box A window that appears on a computer's screen to convey a message (such as a warning or error) or to request input (such as a choice of alternatives or a confirmation of some action).

Dialog enhancer If you're having trouble hearing dialog in a movie, this feature helps dialog stand out from other noises in the soundtrack.

Dial-up line A communications line that connects through the telephone system, usually by dialing touch-tones.

Digital Characterized by the representation of data as numbers; computers, for example, are digital.

Digital-audio output, TVs A TV with a built-in digital tuner often comes with either a coaxial or optical digital-audio output to let you route the Dolby Digital or DTS multichannel soundtrack to a receiver for decoding. The receiver thus splits apart the soundtrack for distribution to various speakers in the room. This output must match the input of the receiver.

Digital-cable-ready Digital-cable-ready (DCR, or plug-and-play) TVs are a new type of integrated HDTV. They can not only get broadcast HD by antenna but also receive digital-cable programming without using a box. For digital-cable programming, including HD fare, you insert a CableCard into a slot on the set. Many of the integrated HDTVs coming out now are DCR models, and they typically cost more than other HDTVs. In addition, while the first-generation of DCR TVs can receive digital-cable signals without a cable box, they're only one-way— you'll lose the two-way features: interactive program guide, video on demand, and scheduling of pay-per-view events via the remote control. Two-way DCR TVs are expected to be out soon.

Digital camcorder DV in Also known as FireWire, iLink, and IEEE 1394. For video recorders, the ability to accept audio/video input (for recording) from a digital camcorder's DV (digital-video) output. See "FireWire input."

Digital camera or **digicam** A photographic still-image recording device that uses an electronic sensor and memory system instead of film to record and store images as data files. The images can be subsequently transferred to a computer for long-term storage, editing, inclusion in documents, or sent to others over the Internet. Some digicams can take short, low-resolution motion-video clips.

Digital effects Permits special camcorder effects beyond the usual, analog effects such as fading.

Examples include cross-fades, wipes, overlaps, bounces, and cross-dissolves. Found on both analog and digital camcorders.

Digital output type Important only if you plan to pipe the signal from a DVD player into a home-theater system that has a digital receiver. When choosing your DVD player, consider the models that have the outputs to match the inputs on your digital receiver or external, digital decoder. All DVD players have digital audio outputs—coaxial, optical, or both.

Digital security A built-in cordless-phone security feature in which digital verification between the base and handset prevents your dial tone from being intercepted and used to make calls.

Digital still capable Some camcorders can take snapshots, much like a digital camera (though not necessarily of the same quality). The camcorder can then be plugged into a computer, and the images downloaded from the memory. Using a removable memory card (such as Memory Stick, CompactFlash, MultiMedia Card, or SmartMedia), you can transfer stills to a computer without having to connect the camcorder, but you need proper card-reader hardware.

Digital-video input This input is found on some computers and increasingly on digital (HD/ED/SD) TVs. Found in the form of DVI, HDMI, or FireWire (see "DVI," "HDMI," and "FireWire"), it provides a high-quality digital connection for video while potentially allowing the content providers to control your ability to record the content.

Digital video recorder (DVR) Another name for a hard-drive recorder, the term originated years ago with TiVo and ReplayTV models. A DVR is a video recorder that stores recordings on a computer-style hard drive. Standard DVR features include pausing a "live" TV program when viewing is interrupted, and recording one program while playing back another. Variations include stand-alone models designed to work with an onscreen programming service and combination models that include a DVD recorder.

Digital Visual Interface See "DVI."

Digital zoom Magnifies the central portion of a digital camera's or camcorder's image by interspersing additional pixels among those captured by the image sensor. This makes the image larger but does not add detail or improve sharpness. You could get the same effect by trimming or cropping the full image later, on the computer. Always use the maximum optical zoom before resorting to digital zoom.

Digital8 (D8) A camcorder format that uses 8mm or Hi8 tape to record images digitally. Many models can also read 8mm and Hi8 recordings. Tapes generally offer a shorter recording time than most other formats.

Digitize To convert an analog signal to digital format.

Digitizer A device that converts an analog signal (such as video or sound) into a series of digital values.

Disc capacity DVD changers range in capacity from two discs to several hundred. (The larger, "jukebox" changers may suit you if you'd like to store your entire CD collection in the player.)

Disc formats, DVD players In addition to playing DVD-video discs, DVD players can handle audio CDs. (Some can also play video CDs, a format that's popular overseas.) Other disc formats that some players support include CD-R and CD-RW (the audio discs you record yourself, using other equipment); MP3 on CDs; HDCD; DVD-Audio and Super Audio CD (SACD), two audio-centric formats intended to succeed audio CDs; and writable formats such as DVD-R, DVD-RW, and DVD+RW. Some discs may not play on a particular player for one reason or another.

Diskette A small, portable plastic-encased flexible (floppy) disk used as a magnetic data storage medium. Data are recorded as magnetic signals arranged in a series of circular tracks. Most diskettes hold 1.44 megabytes of data, a small capacity by today's standards.

Display Any electronic device that visually conveys information or images, usually graphically. A computer's display is often called a monitor.

Display size A PDA-screen measurement that, as with computer monitors, is made diagonally, in inches.

Display type, MP3 players Most players have a liquid crystal display (LCD) screen, often backlit, that lets you view song title, track number, amount of memory remaining, battery life, and other functions. Display size and shape vary, including shapes such as square, rectangular, or oval. Displays are usually liquid crystal display (LCD) monochrome or color. Another type of display uses organic light-emitting diodes (OLEDs).

Display type, PDAs Screens come with either color or black-and-white (four shades of gray) screen displays. Color screens offer more detail but also tend to drain the batteries more quickly than monochrome.

DLP Digital light processing, a form of projection-TV technology that creates images using a chip with millions of tiny swiveling mirrors. Most rear-projection DLP sets currently employ one chip and a rotating color wheel, which may cause occasional annoying flashes of color visible to some viewers—what's called the rainbow effect. Some front projectors have three chips, which alleviates the problem.

Dock On Apple's Mac OS X desktop, an icon-filled bar for launching and switching between applications.

Docking station A rectangular platform with a connector and a power supply for a laptop or handheld computer. It connects with a CRT monitor, printer, and other peripherals to, essentially, turn a laptop computer into a desktop computer.

Documentation Material that comes with a software package or a computer system and offers directions for setup and operation, features, capabilities, and troubleshooting advice. More and more often, paper documentation is being

replaced by "online" help, files installed on the PC's hard disk, a CD-ROM, or the Internet.

Dolby Digital (AC-3) All DVD players can extract the typically six-channel Dolby Digital soundtrack from a DVD-video disc. To hear all the channels discretely, however, requires that either the player or a digital receiver to which it's connected have a built-in multichannel audio decoder—or that you have a separate decoder connected between the DVD player and the receiver. It also demands a full multispeaker home-theater system. If you don't have all that equipment, the soundtrack can be "downmixed" to two channels with no loss of key audio information.

Dolby Pro Logic An analog audio-encoding format that, when output by the DVD player and decoded by a sound system, splits the signal into four: left and right front, center channel (for dialog), and one limited-range surround channel carried by two rear speakers. Audio encoded in this way is found on most recorded VHS movies, all DVDs, many movies on TV, and some TV-show soundtracks.

Domain name A structured, alphabetic name, such as ConsumerReports.org, for a location on the Internet. These names are aliases for numeric IP addresses and are leased from an Internet naming authority by the domain-name owner.

Dongle Any small peripheral device connected to a computer by a short cord and plug.

DOS Disk operating system, a set of programs that activates the computer and allows the user or other programs to perform simple functions; the term is used synonymously with MS- or PC-DOS, early operating systems used in personal computers in the 1970s and 1980s. A simple command-line DOS was built into Windows 95 and later versions; it can be invoked if needed.

Dot-com An Internet-based business or service, especially one new to the market.

Double-click A quick double-press of the left button on a computer mouse (or the typical Mac mouse's single button) to activate a file or icon.

Download To transfer a copy of a file from a host (server) computer to a client computer, a term frequently used to describe the process of transferring a file or data from the Internet to a computer's hard drive. The other way, it's an upload.

dpi Dots per inch, a common measure of the resolution of an image file, or the image-handling capability of a printer, scanner, or display. In theory, the higher the dpi, the better the image quality. But the unaided human eye cannot distinguish differences beyond about 200 dpi.

DPOF With digital cameras, digital print-order format lets you store information on the camera's memory card that indicates how many prints to make of each image. It's intended for use when having prints made at a digital photo kiosk or when printing images on certain inkjet printers.

Draft mode A faster, ink-saving printing mode for inkjet printers, and a toner-saving mode for laser printers.

Drag and drop Using a computer's mouse, this refers to the way you move objects onscreen, and by reference, among the storage devices, in a graphical operating system such as Windows or Mac OS. You click on an item, which represents a folder or file, and drag it while holding the mouse button; you then release the button where you want to place the item.

Drive A unit that writes data to or reads data from a storage medium, such as a tape or disk.

Driver A program that controls some component of a computer system, such as a monitor, disk drive, or printer.

DRM Digital rights management, any scheme used to prevent the unauthorized use or dissemination of copyrighted, file-based content, such as music, video, or software. DRM often makes use of data encryption in combination with a software or hardware decoder that performs user authentication at the point of content use. Hackers, however, are often able to "crack" DRM schemes and provide programs over the Internet to allow other users to circumvent DRM protections. DRM is controversial among privacy advocates because some schemes use centralized management of rights.

DSL Digital Subscriber Line, which provides high-speed Internet access through existing phone lines without affecting normal phone operation.

DTS audio Digital Theater Systems, a multichannel sound format used in some movies. It's a useful extra that ensures you can hear multichannel sound from virtually any movie—provided you have the necessary speakers and that the DVD player or connected digital receiver has a multichannel DTS decoder; a separate DTS decoder can also be connected between the player and the receiver. While all DVD players support Dolby Digital surround sound, many models also support DTS.

Dual antenna inputs With two antenna inputs, you can easily switch between two antenna signals using your remote control. This capability can be handy if you use, for example, both a roof antenna and a cable hookup, or in order to take full advantage of dual-tuner picture-in-picture (PIP).

Dual-band Some cordless-phone models have dual-band transmission, which—between the base and handset—wirelessly transmit within one frequency band and receive on the other. Some 2.4-GHz models have dual-band (2.4-GHz/900-MHz) transmission, and some 5.8-GHz models have dual-band (5.8-GHz/2.4-GHz or 5.8-GHz/900-MHz) transmission.

Dual-core processor See "Multi-core processor."

Dual-sided printing This capability is also known as double-sided or two-sided printing. Some printer models can print on both sides of a page automatically, typically more slowly than when printing on one side of a page. With most others, you can print the odd-numbered pages first, then manually flip the document over to print the even-numbered pages.

Duron A processor family from AMD that is generally slower and less costly than its Athlon counterpart. It is used in lower-priced PCs.

Duty cycle For printers, the monthly volume—in number of pages—that the manufacturer recommends for optimal use.

DVD Digital versatile disk or digital video disk, an optical digital-storage medium the same size as a CD, but with at least four times the capacity. DVDs were originally used for consumer distribution of movies and were adapted for computer use. There are drives with write-once (DVD-R and DVD+R) and re-writable (DVD-RW, DVD+RW, and DVD-RAM) capabilities.

DVD-Audio This is one of two relatively new, competing music formats. DVD-Audio discs encode the music so that it can be output in either two or up to six channels. Both this and the other competing format, Super Audio CD (SACD), claim to offer better sound quality than CDs can deliver. Note that while program material formatted in DVD-Audio will only play on DVD players that specify DVD-Audio capability, DVD-Audio discs may also contain a Dolby Digital or DTS version of the program material that will play on any DVD player.

DVD-R A write-once DVD format. Certain camcorders record in this format onto a disc measuring a little over 3 inches (8cm) in diameter. Discs can be played on most DVD players.

DVD-RAM A rewritable DVD format supported by some DVD recorders. Certain DVD-RAM camcorders record onto discs measuring a little over 3 inches (8cm) in diameter, in MPEG-2 format, the same technology used for commercial DVD. Discs, however, cannot be played on most DVD players.

DV input See "FireWire input."

DVD recorder A device that records video to a DVD. It may be a stand-alone recorder or one integrated with a DVR or VCR in a combination model.

DVI Digital visual interface, a relatively new form of connection standard supported by some set-top boxes, computers, computer monitors, and high-definition TVs; DVI input in the displays matches a corresponding output in some computers and digital TV tuners. Like HDMI, it potentially allows content providers to control your ability to record the content. Unlike HDMI, DVI requires a separate audio cable to carry the audio signals.

DVI output, DVD players Has digital visual interface (DVI) output for direct digital video connection to digital TVs with DVI input. Can output 480p, 720p, and 1080i video signals, although signals upconverted from 480i or 480p to 720p, 1080i, or 1080p do not produce a true HD picture.

E

EBook reader PDA software that, when installed, lets you read electronic books. Generally, you have to purchase the eBooks separately and download them to your PDA.

ED-ready Also referred to as an EDTV monitor, a TV (typically flat-panel) that requires you to connect an external tuner that can decode digital signals for display. The category EDTV (for enhanced-definition TV) lies between high-definition and standard-definition in terms of resolution and, generally, picture quality. Overall, ED sets can display smooth, pleasing images such as those from a progressive-scan DVD player. When connected to an HD tuner, some ED sets down-convert HD signals to display a less-detailed version of HD images.

EDTV A TV (typically flat-panel) that includes a built-in tuner for digital off-air signals for display. The category EDTV lies between high-definition and standard-definition in terms of resolution and, generally, picture quality. The best ED sets can display very good or excellent picture quality from a progressive-scan DVD player. When connected to an HD tuner, some ED sets can downconvert HD signals to display a less-detailed version of HD images.

Edit search Allows you to search for specific footage on a camcorder's recording; it can be very helpful when editing.

Editor A program that lets you create or make changes in a document. A word processor is an advanced type of editor, with special features such as word-wrap, headers/footers, and print attributes (boldface, underline, italics).

EFT Electronic funds transfer, a system commonly used by banks and other money handlers that involves secure, computer-controlled money transfers between accounts.

Electronic commerce Shopping through electronic catalogs and making purchases using the Internet.

eMac Apple Computer's value-priced Macintosh desktop computer series, with an all-in-one case and a built-in CRT screen.

E-mail or **email** Electronic mail lets you send and receive personal messages, including those with attached files such as text or graphics, through the Internet, an online service, a BBS, a network, or other system.

Encryption A process applied to a data file to render its contents unreadable to a non-authorized user or computer system. Reading an encrypted file requires a software "key" that is available only to an authenticated user.

End user The final person or business to make use of a product or service. This is generally you, the consumer.

Energy Star A label, on many kinds of appliances, that designates compliance with energy-efficiency goals developed by the U.S. Environmental Protection Agency. In order to qualify for certification, a device must typically power down to no more than about 10 percent of normal power consumption after a period of inactivity.

Entertainment PC, or **EPC** A form of media-center PC designed to fit into a home entertainment system as a source component. EPCs have a remote control, a quiet cooling system, and one or more TV tuners, allowing use as a DVR. They can also be used for normal computer tasks, such as Web access and e-mail, controlled by a wireless keyboard and mouse. When attached to a home network, they can share content with other devices, such as media receivers.

Envelope capacity The number of standard-weight, business-size (#10) envelopes that a printer with an envelope-input tray can accommodate.

Envelope input This can be an input tray or slot that holds a small stack of envelopes in a printer, though it doesn't have to be dedicated to envelopes. It can also be a manual, single-feed envelope slot.

Equalizer Most MP3 players have an equalizer, which lets the listener adjust the sound in various ways. Separate bass and treble controls or adjustable equalizers found on players give you the most control over tone. Presets (also referred to as DSP modes) are settings such as Jazz, Rock, Pop, Classic, Rap, or Normal "mixes" that you may or may not like. Some players simply have a bass-boost control, not considered an equalizer.

Ergonomic Designed with the needs and comfort of the user in mind.

Ethernet The most common type of local area network (LAN) protocol used to connect personal computers to each other, or to a router or other devices on a network.

EULA End-user license agreement. A legal instrument, accompanying most software, that states the terms under which the company is allowing its use by the consumer. An EULA is typically written in virtually incomprehensible legal jargon, but must often be agreed to by clicking an on-screen "I Agree" button before one can use the software.

Expansion card, PDAs Most PDAs come with expansion slots for flash memory, a modem, or another device. The most common expansion option for PDAs is through a connector that accommodates either a MultiMedia Card (or Secure Digital card), Memory Stick, or CompactFlash card. A few models offer more than one type of expansion.

Expansion memory format, MP3 players The format for the removable-memory medium used in a standard-capacity player: Most are external cards (some the size of a matchbook) that install into the player. Among the most common are CompactFlash, MultiMedia Card, Secure Digital, and SmartMedia. In addition, some players use a proprietary memory format, such as Sony's MagicGate Memory Stick (a copy-protected version of Sony's existing Memory Stick media). Such formats may work only on products of the brand for which they're designed—a disadvantage if you want to swap memory media with another brand of handheld device. (You must get the correct type of storage for your player; check with the manufacturer or retailer if you're uncertain.) Some hard-drive players have removable memory media for transferring files; however, you cannot play music directly from the card.

Expansion slot A position in a computer for adding an expansion board or card. Desktop PCs usually have at least two free PCI expansion slots. Laptops use PC cards for expansion.

Export To transfer from the file format currently in use to another one.

Exposure compensation, digital cameras Allows for minor adjustments to the automatic-exposure settings. When a scene has high contrast, as in a backlit scene, automatic exposure may not achieve the effect you want. It helps to be able to alter the settings so that the subject of a photo does not appear too dark or too light.

External bay In a desktop computer, a front-mounted drive bay that allows physical access.

External drive A storage device that is physically separate from the computer. Such drives often have their own power supply and attach to the computer through a FireWire port, SCSI port, or a laptop computer's PC card.

F

F connector A type of coaxial connector, most frequently used to connect cable, antenna, or satellite television signals to components such as TVs, VCRs, and PC tuner cards. Receivers and minisystems may also have F connectors to connect to FM antennas.

FAQ A list of frequently asked questions and their answers, meant to help users of a product or service understand its features and operation, and perform simple troubleshooting.

Fatal error The cause of premature termination of processing, often as a crash. Fatal errors can occur as a result of read/write errors, program bugs, system conflicts, and hardware defects. Some errors crash only one application; others require that you restart the computer.

File A collection of related records. Computer data and documents are normally stored as files.

File extension An identifier of the type or purpose of a file, usually written as one to three letters following the file name and separated from it by a period. For example, the file My Letter.doc might be a text document, while Numbers.dat could be a data file. File extensions are used by Windows to determine what program to use to open a file, and are hidden by default if Windows has registered a program for the extension.

File name The unique identification given to a program or data file for storage. File names were once limited to eight characters (plus a three-character extension) in older operating systems like DOS. Newer operating systems such as Windows and Mac OS allow much longer file names.

File-sharing One of the common uses for a network. Files can be designated as shared by their owners on one PC, and accessed by other authorized users in the same network work group, or over the Internet through peer-to-peer protocols.

File-swapping An Internet activity, popularized by free, peer-to-peer services such as BitTorrent and eDonkey, with which users can search for files of interest and download them from designated shared folders on a network of thousands of other users' computers. File-swapping has been criticized because users often trade files containing copyrighted material.

Film mode See "3:2-pulldown compensation."

Firewall A network gateway (software or hardware) that filters data requests, rejecting those that lack the necessary security clearance. Firewalls were originally used to protect corporate, government, or institutional networks from unauthorized access; they now also help keep individuals' home computers safe from intruders on the Internet.

FireWire input Also known as IEEE-1394, iLink, and DV input, an all-digital means of relating audio as well as video digitally from, say, a digital camcorder to a computer or DVD recorder. It's found on some computers, DVD recorders, D-VHS decks, digital set-top boxes, and high-definition TVs. Among TVs, it is less common than HDMI and DVI inputs. Like both of those inputs, it supports copy-protection schemes.

FireWire port Now found on virtually all digital camcorders, this feature (also known as a IEEE 1394, DV, or iLink connection) lets you transfer video data to a computer or another digital camcorder with little or no loss of quality. The other device, however, must also have an FireWire connection, and only some new computers are so equipped. It includes audio and control signals. It is bidirectional for recordings could be sent to your camcorder from the computer.

Firmware-upgradable, MP3 players The firmware—the player's built-in operating instructions—can be upgraded so the player does not become obsolete. Upgrades can add or enhance features, fix "bugs," and add support for other audio formats and operating systems. Check the manufacturer's and music-management software developers' Web sites for upgrades.

Flash, cordless phones A button to answer call waiting.

Flash animation A programming platform commonly used for embedding animation in Web pages. Flash "movies" are relatively small, allowing them to download quickly on slow dialup connections. Playing one requires a plug-in for your browser software.

Flash memory A low-cost, high-density, erasable memory chip that holds its data without power. It's used in computers and peripheral devices to hold settings and allow easy BIOS updating, and is packaged in plug-in cards to act as data storage in small portable devices such as digital cameras.

Flash modes, digital cameras Like film cameras, most digital cameras have a built-in flash for shooting indoors or in other low-light conditions. Many cameras have an automatic-flash mode, which automatically fires the flash when more light is needed. The flashes built into most digital cameras have fairly limited range (up to 10 to 13 feet on most models), compared with external flash units, which can be much more powerful. A camera with an external "flash sync" or "hot shoe" will usually have a built-in flash as well.

Flat-panel display A thin display screen

employing one of several technologies, usually LCD or plasma. Flat-panel displays are commonly used on portable devices to reduce size and weight, and are rapidly increasing in popularity as desktop-monitor replacements. They're also used in newer costly TVs.

Flat screen Indicates whether the set has a flat screen. (It refers to flat-front picture tubes on conventional TVs, not to be confused with flat-panel LCD or plasma models.) While a flat screen looks sleek and shows fewer reflections than a curved screen, it doesn't guarantee better picture quality.

Flexible LCD angle A camcorder's LCD monitor with this feature is adjustable so you can angle it, making it easy to view while you record.

Floppy disk See "Diskette."

FM recording, MP3 players For a player that has an FM radio; can record from an FM radio station onto the player without the use of a microphone.

FM transmitter, MP3 players A built-in FM transmitter that lets the player wirelessly transmit your music and play on an FM radio station.

Folder The Windows and Mac OS name for a disk directory.

Font In word processing, a typeface enhancement such as bold or script. The term also is often used to refer to a typeface such as Arial, Times Roman, or Courier.

Footer A special message or identification placed at the bottom of a document page.

Footprint The space on a floor or table occupied by a piece of hardware.

Format To initialize a data-storage medium; to lay out in a specific pattern, such as a screen or report format; or the layout or pattern itself.

Format, camcorders Format is based on the type of recording tape or disc that a camcorder uses and whether the model records in analog or digital mode. Currently, there are at least nine formats: Hi8, MiniDV, MicroMV, Digital8 (D8), VHS, VHS-C, S-VHS-C, DVD-RAM, and DVD-R. Key differences among those formats include picture quality, size of camcorder, and compatibility with a VCR or DVD player.

Formats supported, MP3 players The formats (such as MP3, WMA, and AAC) that the bundled music-management software can convert to a format compatible with the player.

Forum An information exchange, usually found on the Internet, that is confined to a single topic or area of interest.

FPS See "Frame rate."

Frame advance Allows you to advance DVD playback frame-by-frame, instead of at normal play speed.

Frame rate Expressed in FPS (frames-per-second), the rate at which a display of moving graphical images is updated. Motion-picture film runs at 24

FPS, the minimum considered to be essentially jitter-free. Television in North America operates at about 30 FPS. Computer-generated graphics, such as from games, can run at much higher rates, limited by the graphics processor. Avid gamers look for rates of 50 FPS or higher, producing more-realistic motion.

Freeware Software that is distributed, mostly via the Internet, essentially without charge to interested users.

Freeze frame A DVD-player feature that allows you to pause playback on your screen.

Frequency Cordless phones transmit their signals between the base and handset wirelessly in the 900-MHz, 2.4-GHz, and/or 5.8-GHz frequency bands.

Front-firing speakers, TVs Found on most sets, these are built into the front of the TV set. Such speakers provide direct sound to the viewer, desirable if you plan to put the TV in a wall unit—a placement that can make side-firing speakers sound muffled.

Front-panel A/V inputs These are handy if you want to connect a camcorder or video game to the TV without having to reach around to the rear of the set. On some TVs, they may be on the side.

Front-projection A display system where the image is beamed from a projector onto the front of a projection screen. You view the same side of the screen that faces the projector.

FTP File Transfer Protocol, an Internet protocol that lets you transfer files between your computer and an FTP site. "Anonymous" FTP allows a user to retrieve files without having to establish a user ID and password.

Full auto switch A camcorder feature that essentially lets you point and shoot. The camcorder automatically adjusts the color balance, shutter speed, focus, and aperture (also called the "iris" or f-stop with camcorders).

G3, G4, G5 Families of PowerPC microprocessors from IBM (originally from Motorola), used in Apple Macintosh computers. The G5 features speeds up to 2.5 GHz.

Game controller Originally limited to knobs and joysticks, such devices now include driving simulators, cockpit simulators, movement sensors, and the entire class of human interface devices (HIDs).

Game port A 15-pin serial port used for attaching joysticks or other game controllers, along with MIDI music devices, to a computer. Game ports can handle a pair of controllers and may come as part of an original system or be supplied on sound boards. They are becoming less common on new PCs, supplanted by newer interfaces like USB.

Game timer A parental-control feature that limits the number of minutes an input will accept signals from a gaming system such as Xbox or PlayStation.

GB See gigabyte.

GIF (jiff) Graphics Interchange Format, a lossless, compressed file format for image bitmaps created by the CompuServe online service to reduce download time.

Gigabyte Literally, a billion, 10^9, or 1,000,000,000 bytes. Also commonly used to mean 1,024 megabytes, equal to 2^{30}, or 1,073,741,824 bytes.

Glitch A nonreproducible problem in a system. Glitches often result from voltage fluctuations, static discharges, and data-transmission errors.

Graphics Special characters or drawings such as graphs, charts, and picture-like renderings of various objects or entire scenes.

Graphics card or **adapter** In a computer, an expansion card or built-in circuitry that provides the memory and graphics coprocessor necessary to produce text and graphics displays; along with the monitor, it determines the resolution and colors that can be displayed.

Graphics processor, or GPU On a computer's graphics adapter, a set of chips that has built-in firmware, processing capabilities, and adequate memory (usually 32 to 128 MB) to relieve the CPU of much of the burden of processing graphics.

Guide Plus+ Found on a limited number of sets, TV Guide Plus+ receives onscreen program information. Versions such as Guide Plus+ Gold offer more features, such as VCR recording control.

Hacker A nonprofessional computer whiz, usually one who tries to gain unlawful access to a computer system or alters programs to allow unlicensed usage.

Handheld Shorthand for any computing device that is operated while held in the hand.

Handset memory dialing locations The number of phone numbers and names, for phones with an LCD display, that you can program into a handset's memory to make calls with only a few button presses.

Handset speakerphone A handset speakerphone offers a hands-free way to converse or wait on hold and lets others chime in as well, conveniently, anywhere in the house as long as you stay within a few feet of the handset.

Handset-to-handset talk Most multiple-handset-capable phones allow conversation handset-to-handset, or among handsets for conferencing. For some phones, the handsets have to be within range of the base, while others allow a direct link among handsets so you can take them with you to use like a walkie-talkie. Also referred to as handset-to-handset intercom.

Handset volume control Found on all cordless-phone handsets, this lets you adjust the volume of the voice in the handset's earpiece.

Hard disk, or **hard drive** A magnetic data storage

system using one or more rigid platters sealed in a dustproof housing and spun at several thousand RPM. Data are recorded as magnetic signals arranged in a pattern of concentric circles on the surfaces. Typical storage capacities range from about 30 to 300 gigabytes.

Hard-drive recognition, MP3 players Computers with newer operating systems, such as Windows XP, can recognize an MP3 player as a hard or removable drive when you plug it in. Some players require you to install software before they can be recognized as hard drives. You may also have to upgrade software if your computer has an older or less-common operating system. These situations make the player less convenient for shuttling files from one PC to another.

Hard-drive recorder See "Digital video recorder."

Hard-drive recording times (min./max., hrs.) For a DVD recorder with a built-in hard drive, the minimum and maximum hours of content that may be recorded onto the drive using, respectively, the least and most compression.

Hardware The electronic equipment that makes up a system. In a computer system, hardware includes the CPU, monitor, printer, circuit boards, drives, cables, etc. It does not include data or computer programs, which are software.

Hardwired Connected with a nondetachable cable; permanently wired.

HDMI High-Definition Multimedia Interface. A relatively new form of digital audio/video input in some high-definition TVs, it matches a corresponding output in some DVD players and digital TV tuners. Like DVI and FireWire, it potentially allows content providers to control your ability to record the content. Unlike DVI and FireWire, HDMI carries audio, video, and control signals on the same cable.

HDMI output, DVD players Has High-Definition Multimedia Interface (HDMI) output for direct digital audio and video connection to digital TVs with HDMI input. Can output 480p, 720p, and 1080i video signals, although signals upconverted from 480i or 480p to 720p or 1080i do not produce a true HD picture.

HD-ready HD-ready TVs, also known as HDTV monitors, lack a high-definition receiver (tuner) and require an external device to decode the HD signals displayed on the TV. Sources for HD signals include HD-capable satellite receivers, over-the-air digital TV (DTV) receivers, and HD-capable digital-cable boxes. Those devices connect to the TV's HD component-video, HDMI, DVI, or FireWire input. An integrated HDTV set has a built-in DTV receiver/decoder and typically costs more.

HDTV An HDTV set is capable of displaying high-definition TV signals and has a built-in receiver (tuner) to decode the HD signals displayed on the TV. Note that the included tuner will decode digital TV (DTV) signals from sources such as off-air (broadcast) signals, cable, or satellite. HDTVs that can decode digital-cable signals are called digital-cable-ready. Some HD-capable cable boxes and satellite receivers also include a tuner to decode off-air DTV.

Header A special message or identification that is placed at the top of a document page; also, the information, sometimes hidden at the top of an e-mail message, that lists each computer the message passed from sender to recipient, along with the date and time.

Headphone out, camcorders An output for connecting a pair of headphones to a camcorder.

Headphone type The type of headphone or earphone included with an MP3 player. Some can fold up or permit volume control.

Headset jack, cordless phones Lets you plug a headset into the phone. Many cordless phones have a handset headset jack plus a belt clip (headset usually sold separately), allowing hands-free conversation anywhere in the house. Useful for, say, a home office, some have a base headset jack, allowing long or many hands-free conversations without the need to be concerned about the handset's battery life.

Hertz, or **Hz** A measure of frequency, being the number of cycles per second.

Hi8 A camcorder format that uses a specific tape about the size of an audiocassette. Most Hi8 models can also operate in 8mm format.

Hibernation A shutdown mode in many PCs and most laptops that saves the current state of the machine and all its running processes on the hard drive for quick restoration on demand. It's also called suspend-to-disk.

High-resolution Showing great detail; the higher the resolution of a TV, computer monitor or printer, the greater the detail of a drawing or image it is able to reproduce.

Home page The page in a Web site usually visited first; it contains links to other pages on the site or to other sites. The home page is automatically selected when you type a Web address ending in ".com," ".org," or another common domain suffix.

Horizontal resolution A technical specification that offers a rough guide to picture quality of camcorders and video displays. This indicates the maximum number of displayed vertical lines that can be counted horizontally across the screen. The closer they can get before blurring, the more lines of horizontal resolution there are. Most analog sets 27 inches and larger have roughly the same horizontal resolution. Higher horizontal resolution (a higher line count) is said to provide a better picture, but this claim is not necessarily true. Some TVs with a lower line count but higher contrast, for example, can actually provide a picture that looks sharper.

Host computer A computer that serves as a source for data and information retrieval for client computers, usually networked PCs.

Hotkey A key or combination of keys that, when pressed, take priority in causing an action to take place. Typical uses for hotkeys include initiating menu options or interrupting an ongoing process.

HTML Hypertext markup language, the standard

language for creating pages on the World Wide Web. Even if you do not understand HTML, you can create it with Web-page authoring programs, popular word-processors, or basic step-by-step instructions at certain Web sites to build pages.

http Hypertext transfer protocol, a protocol developed for exchange of hypertext documents across the Internet. All Web addresses begin with http://, which a browser will automatically insert for you.

Hub A multiport device that connects several computers together into a wired network, without performing any data-management functions. A "switched" hub adds the ability to prevent data "collisions," increasing overall speed.

Hyperlink Within a hypertext document, a clickable object that retrieves another location within the document or anywhere else on the Web. These can be either graphics or text; text links are usually blue and underlined.

Hypertext A method of linking information within and between text or other files. The linked data may be almost anything from text to graphics to programs. The Internet's World Wide Web is an ad-hoc collection of linked hypertext documents.

I

I/O Input/output, referring to an electronic device's transfer of digital data or analog signals.

Icon A small graphical image that appears on a graphical user interface such as a computer's desktop in a Windows or Mac system. These normally represent a specific file or program or cause a desired action to occur when clicked with a mouse.

IDE Integrated Drive Electronics, a hard-disk interface technology.

IEEE A standards organization that publishes computer-industry-defined standards for hardware, software, and data communications. IEEE 1394 is the standard for the FireWire interface, and IEEE 802.11 is the standard for Wi-Fi wireless networking.

Illuminated remote Some remote controls offer illuminated buttons for easier operation in a dimly lit room.

Image stabilization A feature that automatically reduces the shakes in a scene caused by holding a camcorder. It's also called digital image stabilization (DIS), electronic image stabilization (EIS), picture stabilizer, or steady shot. Using a tripod is the surest way to get a steady image.

Import To transfer data from another file into the one currently in use.

In-camera editing All but universal, this digital-camera feature lets you decide to keep or erase pictures you've taken. You can review the pictures on the LCD display and delete those you don't want, which will free up memory for more pictures.

In-home warranty A warranty under which a technician comes to your home to either retrieve or diagnose and service the set when you have a problem—of particular importance with heavy (especially projection) or wall-mounted sets.

Incompatible Unable to work with, usually referring to a program that can't be run under a different operating system than that for which it was created, or a device not supported by a computer's hardware or BIOS.

Individual color tanks Some printers use a separate tank for each color. Others have tri-color cartridges with three colors in one. A printer with individual tanks lets you replace only the color that runs out rather than tossing out a tri-color cartridge that may have some ink left.

Initialize To set up, prepare, or start from the beginning. Initializing a disk deletes any data on it and makes it ready for use by a system.

Inkjet printer A printer that uses tiny jets or droplets of charged ink particles, projected from a set of nozzles, to create images, usually of high quality. Inkjets are currently the most popular printers for home use and are the most economical way to produce high-quality full-color printouts.

Installed memory, printers Measured in megabytes (MB), the amount of memory installed—not an important consideration for most home users. While inkjet printers themselves contain varying amounts of installed memory, they mainly use a computer's microprocessor and memory to process data.

Instant messaging, or IM An online system, usually proprietary, that lets you hold a private, real-time text-based conversation between two users. Messaging among more than two users is usually referred to as chat, though it may use the same system. Some IM systems allow voice, image or video messaging.

Instruction In the computer world, a command to the CPU to carry out an operation.

Interactive electronic program guide An onscreen guide to upcoming TV programming. Using your remote, you can switch channels, select programs to record (on models with recording capability), and—depending on the guide—search for upcoming material.

Integrated amplifier A few DVD players have built-in amplifiers; connected to speakers, such models can amplify signals from the player and any other components of a home-theater system.

Integrated camera, PDAs Some PDAs include a camera that lets you take photos for viewing or attachment to e-mails. Resolution is typically much lower than that of standard digital cameras.

Integrated keyboard, PDAs A few PDAs include a small keyboard that you can use instead of an onscreen "soft keyboard" representation or the PDA's handwriting-recognition software.

Integrated receiver A few DVD players have built-in AM/FM tuners, amplifier, and auxiliary inputs; connected to speakers, such models can amplify signals from the player and any other components of a home-theater system.

Interactive Able to respond to a user's wishes. Interactive software usually refers to a multimedia presentation that the user controls, moving at a speed and in a direction specified by the user.

Interface The connection between two components such as the PC and a printer; also, to connect two components together.

Interface type, MP3 players The connection type required on your computer to interface (usually via a cable and/or interface module) with an MP3 player, or its memory-card adapter. Most players use Universal Serial Bus (USB 2.0). Some have FireWire (also known as IEEE-1394, or iLink). Some players have both FireWire and USB. FireWire allows faster file transfers than USB.

Interlaced A video display (usually a TV) in which odd and even scan lines are displayed on alternate cycles. Compared to progressive scan, interlaced signals require less processing but can produce flicker. Conventional standard-definition televisions use an interlaced display.

Internal bay A drive bay inside a computer that does not permit physical access from the outside; these often hold a hard drive.

Internal drive A drive housed within the computer's case. Such drives normally derive power from the computer's power supply.

Internal dubbing On DVD recorders that include a built-in hard drive or VCR, the ability to copy recorded content internally from one medium to another.

Internal memory, MP3 players Also called onboard or built-in memory, the amount of internal memory that comes with the player for storing music. Some MP3 players have additional memory slots into which removable media such as CompactFlash, MultiMedia, Secure Digital, and SmartMedia cards can be inserted.

Internet A "super" network consisting of a collection of many commercial, academic, and governmental networks throughout the world. Public access to the Internet, now used by millions of people, is obtained through a contract with an Internet service provider (ISP).

Internet gateway A device or computer that provides the connection and protocols to link a single computer or network to the Internet.

Intranet An "Internetlike" hyperlinked information-exchange system established within an organization or institution, for its own purposes, protected from unauthorized public access.

IP or **IP address** Internet protocol address, a means of referring to locations on the Internet. Composed of a series of four numbers from 0 through 255, separated by decimal points. All machines on the Internet have one, often assigned by the ISP at connection time. An extended version of IP, called IPv6, has more digits, allowing for future use to address many more Internet-connected devices, even down to the level of specific controls on an appliance.

IP telephony Use of an Internet connection to establish two-way voice communications between users, also called VoIP (Voice over Internet Protocol). It may use computer-to-computer, computer-to-phone, or phone-to-phone connections, depending on the telephony-service provider.

ISDN Integrated services digital network, a high-speed telephone line that is a faster but expensive alternative to traditional dial-up modems, and is available farther from the telephone office than DSL.

ISO equivalent Conventional camera film speed is rated using a standard from the International Standards Organization (ISO). The higher the ISO film speed, the more sensitive, or "faster," the film—meaning that less light is needed to take a picture. Although digital cameras don't use traditional film, the industry uses an ISO equivalency rating to describe their light sensitivity.

J

Java, or **JavaScript** A programming language that brings animation and interactivity to Web pages by embedding program code that is run on the client PC.

Jog/shuttle on unit A DVD player's jog control lets you advance or rewind just one frame at a time to find the exact spot you want, while a shuttle control lets you scan video segments at speeds from slow to fast.

Joystick A device used with computer games and other interactive programs to manually control the cursor, an object, or the action by moving a stick back and forth, right and left, or by the push of a "fire" button.

JPEG Joint Photographic Experts Group, an image-file format that allows for several levels of file compression from "lossless" (high quality, large file) to quite "lossy" (lower quality, small file), to suit different needs. Commonly used on Web pages or digital-camera files.

Justification The alignment of text or images in a document, usually to the left and/or right margins, or centered.

K

K, or **KB** Kilobyte, which is exactly 1,024 bytes but is usually thought of as 1,000 bytes. Sometimes incorrectly represented by a small k, which just represents the prefix kilo.

Karaoke available On some DVD players, lets you sing along with special karaoke DVDs. Discs provide backing music as the lyrics appear on the screen, so you can sing along with the music.

kb Kilobit.

Key A button on a computer's keyboard. Also, in a database, an item—usually a field within a record—that is used to uniquely identify the record.

Keyboard The typewriterlike panel used to enter and manipulate text or other data and enter instructions to direct the computer's operations.

Keypad A set of keys grouped together and performing a particular function. The most common keypads on a computer are the numeric and cursor controls.

Kilo- A prefix meaning 1,000. Because of the binary nature of computers, kilo is also used to refer to 1,024.

Kilobit Literally 1,000 bits, but usually used to mean 1,024 bits (2 to the 8th power).

Kilobyte Literally 1,000 bytes, but usually used to mean 1,024 bytes (2 to the 8th power).

L

LAN Local-area network, a system of two or more computers within an area (typically a building) that share some of the same resources, such as files, disks, printers, and software.

Landscape A page or screen orientation in which information is printed or displayed across the longer dimension.

Laptop computer A portable, battery-equipped computer with a flat-panel display screen, small enough to be used on a lap or small table. Also called notebook computers, some are complete systems offering advanced features nearly the equal of desktop PCs, along with wireless-networking capability.

Laser printer A fast, economical page printer that produces high-quality print and graphics. Only black-and-white laser printers have been affordable for consumers, though color models are dropping in price, and a few are now affordable.

Last channel recall Found on many sets, this feature lets you return to the previous channel you were watching with just a single button push on the remote. It will also let you switch back and forth easily between two channels.

Launch To load and run a program.

Layer indicator Certain DVDs have two layers of data for additional capacity; a dual-layer disc can typically hold about four hours of video. All DVD players are designed to play these discs, but not all have an indicator showing which layer of a dual-layer disc is playing.

LCD, TVs Liquid crystal display. Like plasma TVs, LCD sets are renowned for their slimness and light weight, making small models good candidates for wall-mounting or hanging below a cabinet. On a stand, they have a compact footprint that fits neatly on a kitchen counter or desk. Picture quality of the best LCD sets, usually high-definition (HD) models, is very good. But LCD panels generally haven't been as good as picture-tube or plasma TVs at displaying fast motion, deep black levels, and accurate colors. LCD technology is also used in some microdisplay projection TVs, which are slimmer than CRT-based models.

LCD size, camcorders A camcorder's LCD typically ranges from 2 to 4 inches, measured diagonally.

LCD size, digital cameras Most digital cameras

have a small LCD screen on the back so you can view images and decide which to keep. (You can use the LCD to help frame photos, but that's a sure way to run down the battery in a hurry.) Most LCD screens are too dim for viewing clearly in sunlight.

LCD viewer, printers Some printers have a built-in LCD screen for viewing and editing images from a memory card. The screen is small, usually only 1 to 2 inches, and editing capability is very limited.

LCoS Liquid crystal on silicon, a form of projection-TV technology that shares some attributes with DLP and LCD in its use of both tiny mirrors and liquid-crystal technology. The mirrors do not swivel as in DLP, but are formed by a layer of liquid-crystal pixels that can switch their reflectance.

LED Light-emitting diode, a small electrical component that produces light when a current is passed through it. LEDs have become more efficient and can now produce virtually any color of light. But the fluorescent lamps used to backlight LCDs are generally more efficient.

Lighted keypad Also referred to as backlit keypad. A cordless-phone keypad that either glows in the dark or lights up when you press a key, it makes the phone easier to use in low-light conditions.

Line input, MP3 players A digital, optical, or analog line input that lets you record from an external audio system to the player.

Line output, MP3 players A line output is intended to work best when the player is connected to an external audio system, with a fixed-level output and no effect when using the player's volume control.

Link See "hyperlink."

Linux A freely downloadable, user-supported open-source computer operating system, based on Unix. Linux is touted as an alternative to Windows but is more suited to certain business applications, such as Web servers.

List server One of thousands of Internet-connected computers running software that acts as a message-broadcasting service for members who sign up to a "mailing list." When any member sends an e-mail to the address of the list server, it goes out to all the other members.

Lists tracks On an MP3 player's display, the songs can be shown in the form of a list.

Lock control, MP3 players A button, switch, or setting through the player's menu system that lets you lock the controls of the player. Also referred to as Hold.

Low-battery indicator A visual or auditory signal that indicates a cordless phone's handset battery needs to be recharged.

Low recycle time, digital cameras A relatively low period of time that it takes a camera to process and store an image when shooting in normal (non-burst) mode, at the camera's lowest-resolution, highest-compression setting.

Lux rating Supposedly the minimum amount of light needed for a camcorder to produce a usable picture (the lower, the better). Because there is no agreed-upon standard, however, it's an imprecise way to compare light sensitivity.

Mac OS The windowed operating system of the Apple Macintosh computer family. Mac OS X (version 10) departs radically from earlier versions—it's Unix-based and has its user-interface modernized with an equivalent to the Windows taskbar called the "dock."

Macintosh, or **Mac** A computer family from Apple that was the first to use a mouse and icon-based operating system to make it user-friendly. Macintosh computers now include eMac, iMac, PowerMac, Mac Mini, iBook, and PowerBook.

Macro A series of commands that can be easily initiated, often by a solitary keystroke or simple combination of keys; also, a sequence of instructions embedded in a spreadsheet or other document that can be easily executed at will.

Macro, digital cameras A lens feature that lets you take close-up shots, usually within a foot or less; good for taking pictures of small objects such as a postage stamp or an insect.

Macro focus, camcorders This camcorder feature lets you focus on small objects from a close distance (say, less than 3 feet).

Mailboxes For cordless phones with an answerer, some models let you assign individual voice mailboxes for business and personal calls, or for each person who uses the phone.

Mailing list A list of subscribers to a topical information exchange that operates through e-mail. Most mailing list users refer to their group as "the list." The list server is the host software, residing on a server computer that manages the traffic for the list. A directory of more than 60,000 public lists is available at *www.lsoft.com/catalist.html.*

Main memory The data-storage area inside a computer that is directly accessible by the CPU; also called RAM, for random-access memory. Memory can range from as little as 1 MB to more than 8 GB.

Manual aperture Gives the digital-camera user more control over how much light hits the lens. Manual exposure compensation can serve the same function.

Manual controls, camcorders These let you override automatic settings and allow more control over your recording. May include aperture, color (white) balance, focus, and shutter speed. They're useful for situations in which conditions are less than ideal.

Manual controls, digital cameras Some cameras allow the user to set the aperture (f-stop) and/or shutter speed; used to override the automatic exposure settings when more control is needed.

Manual exposure, digital cameras Allows the user to control both the shutter speed and the aperture settings. Most digital cameras offer fully automatic exposure, often with an exposure-compensation option. While these options cover most situations, direct control of the shutter-speed setting is desirable when going for more specialized effects, such as a blurred image.

Manual exposure compensation Not to be confused with manual exposure, this allows for minor adjustments to a digital camera's automatic-exposure settings. When a scene has high contrast, automatic exposure may not achieve the effect you want. Being able to lighten or darken the scene is an important option.

Manual focus Digital cameras provide greater depth of field than cameras with longer focal-length lenses, such as 35mm or APS cameras; therefore, manual focusing will rarely be needed. Manual focus options vary. A few cameras provide a continuously adjustable manual focus ring; others, only a limited number of discrete focus distance settings.

Manual shutter The camera's shutter opens and closes when you take a shot, allowing light to hit the image sensor. Being able to control the speed of the shutter allows for more creative control over how motion is expressed in your pictures.

Manual white balance In a digital camera, this feature corrects for differences in lighting so that white objects remain white and colors appear the same as they do by eye. Most cameras have automatic white balance, which works well for most scenes. A manual white balance control lets the user set the proper lighting type when the automatic system errs.

Matrix An array or an ordered arrangement. For example, 63 dots might be arranged into a rectangular matrix, an array of nine rows and seven columns.

Maximum aperture The aperture is the opening in the lens that controls how much light hits a camera's image sensor; maximum aperture refers to the widest it will open. Apertures are stated in f-stops or f-numbers (for example, f/2). The smaller the f-stop number, the larger the aperture, and the less light the camera needs to take a picture. A maximum aperture of f/2.8 is typical for a digital camera.

Maximum focal length (35mm) When set to its maximum (longest) focal length, a digital-camera lens gives its narrowest, most telephoto-like angle of view. For comparison purposes, it is often given in terms of the 35mm camera lens focal length that would cover the same angle of view.

Maximum horizontal pixels The number of pixels along the longer (horizontal) dimension of the image when a digital camera is set to its highest resolution.

Maximum image quality An indication of the color intensity of a digital camera's images. The more bits a camera uses to indicate the intensity of the three colors for each pixel, the more precisely the pixel's color can be specified. Almost all digital cameras have 24-bit color depth (8 bits each for red, green, and blue, within each pixel) and are capable of reproducing millions of different colors.

Maximum number of still pictures The maximum number of still images that can fit on a tape, for a camcorder that can record still images.

Maximum shutter speed, camcorders Camcorders electronically adjust their light sensitivity in a way that models a film camera's shutter. All camcorders do this automatically; some also have a manual override capability. Shutter speed is measured in fractions of a second.

Maximum shutter speed, digital cameras The fastest shutter speed provided, often 1/1,000th of a second or less. Being able to control shutter speed lets you decide if a moving object will appear sharp or blurred in the image. A faster shutter speed lets you freeze faster action.

Maximum vertical pixels The number of pixels along the shorter (vertical) dimension of the image when a digital camera is set to its highest resolution.

Mb Megabit.

MB Megabyte.

Media The physical object, usually a disk or tape, upon which digital data or content is stored.

Media-card slot, printers On some printers, it's where you can insert a memory card from a digital camera. Once you've inserted the card into the slot, you can either print the card's files directly or download them to your computer.

Media player Generically, a program that decodes file- or Internet-based multimedia material into an audible and/or visual presentation. Examples are Windows Media Player, RealOne Player, and MusicMatch Jukebox.

Media receiver One of a family of devices that link a home entertainment system (TV and audio) to a PC via a home network. Operated by a remote control and a simple visual interface, the media receiver accesses multimedia files (music, pictures, and/or video content) stored on the PC and plays them through the entertainment system.

Meg Short for megabyte or megahertz.

Mega- A prefix literally meaning one million but, because of computers' binary nature, is used to refer to 1,048,576 (or 2 to the 20th power).

Megabit 1,024 kilobits, yielding 1,048,576 bits, usually considered a million.

Megabyte (MB) Literally, one million, 10^6, or 1,000,000 bytes. Also commonly used to mean 1,024 megabytes, equal to 2^{20}, or 1,048,576 bytes.

Megahertz 1 million hertz.

Megapixels (MP) This shows approximately how many million pixels a digital camera's image sensor has. As a rule, with more megapixels, you can make larger prints or enlarge parts of an image without losing detail or image quality.

Memory, PDAs The amount of usable internal memory, available for new uses—such as appointments, addresses, and applications—when

the handheld PDA model is new. With Palm OS units, for which a large body of third-party software exists, available memory is an important indicator of how much additional software you can easily install. With either Palm OS or Pocket PC, you can't rely on the manufacturer's advertised memory capacity to estimate how much room is left for new uses because it generally includes memory already in use by the operating system or included software.

Memory cards, printers If a printer has a built-in memory-card reader, this feature lets you print image files from a digital camera's memory card without using a computer. You can also download the files to a computer.

Memory-card slot, TVs Found in a few TVs, a slot that accepts memory cards for viewing still images from digital cameras. Inserting the camera's card typically results in better image quality than if you connect the camera to the TV's composite-video input. Some memory cards are specific to one or more specific manufacturers—such as Memory Stick slots in some Sony TVs. Other slots may accept CompactFlash, SmartMedia, MultiMedia Card, Secure Digital, and/or other media.

Memory-card support, printers Indicates whether the printer has a built-in memory-card reader. If so, this feature lets you print image files from a digital camera's memory card without using a computer. You can also download the files to a computer. Some printers have a slot for a PC-card adapter. You can then purchase the adapter for the type of memory card your camera uses.

Memory Stick A type of digital data storage card, introduced by Sony, that is smaller than a stick of chewing gum. A diskette-shaped adapter is also available for using Memory Stick cards in a computer or in some Sony cameras that use diskette storage. Memory Stick Pro has the same form factor as the original Memory Stick but with twice the number of connectors as the original.

Memory Stick with select function On a digital camera, this card provides higher capacity for other Memory Stick devices by providing two banks of 128 MB on a standard Memory Stick, which can be selected with a manually operated switch.

Menu A list of available options, often in a "drop-down" or "pull-down" list, that is typically hidden until activated via a mouse click.

Menu-access lock A parental-control feature that requires password access to call up a TV's menu, using which other restrictions could potentially be disabled.

Menu bar A bar across the top of a computer screen that presents the first level of options for a drop-down menu system.

Menu-driven A program or computer system that uses a series of menus to make it easier to use. The user selects the desired option by clicking on an entry with the mouse, typing the corresponding letter or number, or moving the cursor to the proper selection and hitting the Enter key. The program will then perform the chosen function.

MHz Megahertz.

Microdisplay An industry term sometimes used to describe rear-projection sets using LCD (liquid-crystal display), DLP (digital light processing), or LCoS (liquid crystal on silicon) chips and a bright lamp to create images. This space-saving "light-engine" technology makes microdisplays slimmer and lighter than CRT-based sets.

MicroMV Sony's relatively new camcorder-tape format, which uses cassettes smaller than MiniDVs.

Micron One-millionth of a meter, or one-thousandth of a millimeter.

Microphone input, camcorders A jack for an external microphone to improve sound quality and prevent picking up noise from the camcorder. It's an alternative to using the built-in mike.

Microprocessor The CPU of a personal computer, such as the Pentium 4 or Athlon XP. Micro-processors have an arithmetic logic unit to perform calculations and a control unit with limited memory to hold instructions.

Microsecond One-millionth of a second.

MIDI Musical instrument digital interface, standard for the exchange of information among various musical devices, including instruments, synthesizers, and computers that are MIDI-capable.

MiniDV Refers to a camcorder that uses a MiniDV tape (a little larger than a matchbox) to record images digitally. Tapes generally offer a shorter recording time than most other formats.

Minimovie, digital cameras Lets you create a short, low-frame-rate, low-resolution movie (on some models, with sound).

Minimum focal length (35mm) When set to its minimum (shortest) focal length, a digital-camera lens gives its widest angle of view. For comparison purposes, it is often given in terms of the 35mm camera lens focal length that would cover the same angle of view.

Minimum shutter speed The slowest shutter speed provided in a digital camera, often ½ or ¼ of a second or less. Being able to control shutter speed lets you decide if a moving object will appear sharp or blurred in the image.

Minitower and microtower cases Smaller versions of the tower case of some computers.

Mode A condition or set of conditions for operation. A printer may have modes for different print qualities, or a different port for different transmission speeds or protocols.

Modem (modulator/demodulator) Used to connect a digital device (computer) to a data communications channel (telephone line, cable or radio link). A modem is used to send a fax, to access e-mail, and to get online to the Internet. A modem intended to work with normal dial-up telephone lines has a top speed of nominally 56 kilobits per second (kbps). (DSL and cable models permit much higher speeds.)

Modular bay In a modular laptop computer, a device bay that accepts a device such as an optical disk drive, a diskette drive, a second battery, a back-up hard drive, or a memory-card reader.

Modular laptop A laptop PC that contains one or more modular bays allowing various drives or a battery to be inserted as desired, or removed to save travel weight.

Monitor The "face" of the computer, most often an LCD screen. Monitors are similar to TVs but usually do not have a tuner and so cannot directly receive television broadcast signals.

Motherboard The main board inside a PC into which a computer's memory, microprocessor, and other components are plugged.

Mouse A palm-size device that controls the cursor, an object on the screen, or other screen action by moving the device around on a flat surface. A small ball or optical sensor on the bottom of the mouse senses direction of the motion, transferring this action to the screen. One or more buttons are also used for additional control, such as clicking and dragging.

Mouse pad A thin, resilient pad used as a surface to support a computer mouse, providing a better "grip" for the ball than some desk surfaces.

Mouse pointer A type of cursor used by a computer mouse or other pointing device to indicate a specific screen location. The pointer may be any number of different shapes, but the most common types are the arrow and crosshair.

Movie mode This feature lets you record short video clips using your digital camera; some models record with sound, while others do not.

MP3 An encoding format (it stands for Moving Pictures Expert Group 1 Audio Layer 3) for compressed digital music files. It offers high quality with less than one-tenth the data rate of an uncompressed CD-music bitstream. The small files required for typical songs allow for fairly fast transfer over consumer-grade Internet connections, and have spawned a hobby of sharing music over the Internet, both within and in violation of copyright laws.

MPEG Motion Picture Experts Group, a modern-standard format for compression and storage of video files. MPEG-1 allows a full-length movie to be stored on a standard CD-ROM disc with a moderate amount of visual artifacts; MPEG-2 allows a full-length movie to be stored on a DVD-ROM with few visual artifacts.

MSRP The manufacturer's suggested retail price, generally higher than the price you will pay at the store for a given product.

Multi-angle Enables you to see DVD scenes from different camera angles, provided that the scenes are recorded that way on the disc.

Multicore processor A microprocessor that contains more than one processor "chip" on a single plug-in carrier unit, allowing computations to be split among the processors to increase overall throughput. Multi-core processing is most effective with an operating system and software that is specially designed for multiple processors.

Multifunction keyboard A computer keyboard that has additional keys to launch e-mail, the Internet, and selected applications, and to control computer functions such as the CD or DVD drive, sound volume, and sleep mode.

Multifunction printer An inkjet or laser printer that, in addition to printing, may serve as a fax machine, scanner, copier, and/or other device. Also called an all-in-one printer.

Multihandset capability, cordless phones Multiple-handset-capable phones support more than one handset with one base, so you can have several handsets around the house, each charging in a base, without the need for extra phone jacks. Additional handsets, including the charging cradle, are usually sold separately.

Multilingual menu, TVs A multilingual menu that presents the onscreen TV menu in a choice of languages, usually English, Spanish, and French.

Multilingual support, DVD players With this DVD-player feature, you can choose among various audio or subtitle languages from compatible DVDs.

Multimedia Generally, any computer system or application that incorporates two or more of graphics, text, audio, and video into an integrated presentation.

Multiple-disc player Most DVD players still hold only a single disc at a time. While that suffices for movies, a multiple-disc (or multidisc) player may be useful if you'll also use the unit as your primary CD player. These units accommodate discs using either a carousel- or drawer-type changer.

Multitasking A computer's ability to run more than one program or process at the same time—for example, printing a document while you're surfing the Web. The increasing power of 32-bit and 64-bit processors has made multitasking more efficient and popular.

N

Native resolution Applies to "fixed-pixel" display types such as LCD, DLP, plasma, and LCoS. It's expressed in horizontal by vertical pixels (for the picture elements making up a displayed image), or a 3- or 4-letter acronym may be used (VGA, SVGA, etc.). Incoming signals of higher or lower resolution must be down- or up-converted as necessary to match the set's native resolution.

Network Any system of two or more connected computers, along with their peripherals, organized to share files and other resources.

Network-ready Some printers can be used in a local-area network (LAN), a link of computers within a building; a home network is one example.

Newsgroup An informal information-sharing message board on the part of the Internet known as Usenet. It is accessed through a newsreader such as Outlook Express. Most are unmoderated and may contain material unsuitable for children.

NIC Network interface card, an expansion card used to connect a computer to a local-area network (LAN).

Night vision, camcorders This feature lets you record in very dim or dark situations, using invisible infrared light that is emitted from the camcorder. The picture is grainy and monochrome. It's also called zero lux, nightshot, IR filter, or infrared sensitive recording mode.

Noise Unwanted electrical or communication signals; interference.

Noise filter An electric device designed to reduce electrical noise on a data or AC line.

Noise level Measured in decibels one meter away (dBA), this tells you how noisy a printer is when in use. A typical noise level for an inkjet printer is 50 dBA. As a frame of reference, a soft whisper is about 20 dBA; a normal conversation, about 60 dBA.

Noninterlaced See "Progressive scan."

Notebook computer See "Laptop computer."

Number of discs, DVD players DVD changers range in capacity from two discs to several hundred. (The larger "jukebox" changers may suit you if you'd like to store your entire CD collection in the player.)

Numeric keypad A group of keys set aside for the entry of numeric data and the performance of simple arithmetic operations.

OCR Optical character recognition, a text-recognition program that converts scanned paper documents into a word-processing file format for storage, editing, and inclusion into other documents.

Off-air Broadcast TV, the way the nation invariably received television signals before the debuts of cable and satellite service. In addition to the standard analog TV signals transmitted via antenna for decades, digital broadcast TV signals (typically high-definition) are increasingly available as well.

Office suite A collection of office-oriented programs, sold as a single product. Examples are Microsoft Office, Corel WordPerfect Office, Lotus SmartSuite, and Sun StarOffice.

Offline Not currently accessible by the PC; a PC that is not networked.

One-touch dial A dedicated button or buttons on a cordless phone's handset or base that let you dial a phone number with the press of a single key. It's useful for, say, an emergency number or a number frequently called.

Online Connected to the Internet or to another computer via modem, cable, or satellite. Going online refers to using the Internet.

Online help A feature of many software programs that provides assistance in how to operate the program. You normally access it by hitting a key such as F1 or selecting a menu option.

Online music store, MP3 players If you plan to download copyright-protected music from an online music store, check to see that it supports the player you plan to buy. Some popular sites are iTunes, which supports Apple iPods, and Sony Connect, which supports Sony MP3 players. BuyMusic, Napster, Musicmatch, and Wal-Mart Music Downloads offer copyright-protected songs in the WMA format; players supported by these sites can be found on the Microsoft Web site.

Online service A collection of information databases and other offerings that can be accessed via a modem or the Internet. The various features range from reference material (encyclopedias and atlases) to current updates (weather and stocks) to interactive features with other users (bulletin boards and games). Popular services include America Online, CompuServe, and MSN.

Operating system and configuration requirements, MP3 players The minimum recommended operating system and configuration requirements for a player and its software package. If your computer has less than the minimum requirements, it may still work with the player, but make sure you can return the player in case it doesn't. Check the manufacturer's and music-management software application Web sites for availability of previously unsupported operating systems.

Operating-system type For a PDA, the control program that runs it. PDAs use either Pocket PC, Palm OS, or a proprietary operating system.

Optical cable Cable that contains very thin, flexible glass or plastic fibers through which information is carried using a modulated light beam. It's used in high-speed data communication links, newer telephone and cable-TV systems, and some digital surround-sound connections.

Optical digital-audio out, DVD players Digital-audio output is very useful for easily sending the multichannel audio signal from a DVD player into a home-theater system that has a digital receiver. When choosing your DVD player, consider the models that have the outputs to match the inputs on your digital receiver or external, digital decoder. All DVD players have digital audio outputs—coaxial, optical, or both.

Optical disk Generally refers to any disc read or written to by a laser or other light-emitting/sensing device.

Optical zoom, digital cameras and camcorders Magnifies the image using a real multifocal-length lens, whereas a digital zoom uses electronics to enlarge the center portion of the image using interpolation. Some cameras have both optical and digital zoom. The optical-zoom range is what really matters; image quality decreases the further one goes into the digital-zoom range.

Opt-out A means by which a consumer can indicate his or her disapproval of receiving offered solicitations or content delivery, especially via e-mail.

OS Operating System, the software that is necessary to control the basic operation of the computer. Examples are DOS, Windows, Mac OS,

and Linux. A computer's OS determines, to a large extent, the "look and feel" of the machine.

Outputs, TVs TVs may have one or more of several outputs. Many models have audio outputs, which let you pipe the set's sound to a sound system (to drive unpowered speakers) or directly to powered speakers. A few models also have a headphone jack in front. Higher-end models may additionally have various video outputs (of the antenna/cable, composite-video, S-video component, DVI, or HDMI types). These are useful if you want to route the set's video signal to another device, say, for recording.

Page/handset locator, cordless phones Also called one-way paging, a button on the base set you can press to send a beep tone to the handset so that a missing handset can be located.

Paint program An application that lets a user draw a graphical "bitmap" image directly by moving the pointing device.

PAL/SECAM-compatible In the U.S., TVs use the NTSC television format signal; however, PAL- or SECAM-format signals are used in most other countries. Sets equipped to handle PAL and SECAM signals in addition to NTSC may be useful if you want to receive or view foreign programming, or if you're using a VCR or camcorder of a different standard.

Palette The range of colors and shades that are displayable on a certain TV or monitor, or that are printable with a certain printer.

Parallel port A type of connection that transmits data one byte or data word at a time. Parallel-port connections were most frequently necessary between printers and IBM-compatible computers running Windows 95 or older versions of Windows. Most newer printers, however, support only faster USB connections.

Parental control With such frequently available features, you may keep a child from watching one or more channels that you select. On some sets it can also block the use of audio/video inputs, to which video games could be connected, or limit the time a game can be played. The V-chip (included in all TVs with screens 13 inches or larger) is also a parental-control feature.

Parental security A feature that lets parents "lock out" DVD content based on various criteria, such as a movie's title or rating.

Parts/labor warranty The length of time, expressed in months, that a product is covered by its manufacturer for defects or repairs.

Passive-matrix display An early flat-panel LCD display in which all transistors are outside the display area. Passive matrix displays lose brightness when not viewed from straight on, and they blur moving images. See also "Active-matrix display."

Password A series of characters used as a code to access a system, program, or file. A password should be chosen that is hard to guess, and not a common word.

PC Personal computer; sometimes used to denote any IBM-standard personal computer; also, a printed circuit.

PC card A credit-card-sized, plug-and-play module commonly used to attach expansion devices (such as memory, modems, and drives) to portable computers.

PC-compatible Used to indicate compatibility with Windows or IBM PCs, not Apple Macintosh.

PCI Peripheral component interconnect, a local bus design, popular on Pentium-based computers, that provides high-speed communications between various components and the processor.

PDA Personal digital assistant, a small, handheld computer that functions as a personal organizer, with a calendar/reminder, to-do list, notepad, and address/phone directory. Usually uses a stylus for input, though some have small keyboards. Some PDAs offer optional wireless access to such services as e-mail, Internet, or cellular phone service.

Peer-to-peer A network architecture in which data can flow directly among any of the nodes without the need for a computer to act as a server.

Pentium An Intel microprocessor employing a fast, 32-bit architecture (with a 64-bit internal bus) that makes extensive use of RISC (reduced instruction set computer) technology, employs internal memory caches, and can execute multiple independent instructions in the same clock cycle, giving it higher performance than its predecessors. The most recent series is the Pentium 4.

Peripheral Any hardware attachment to a computer, such as a keyboard, monitor, disk, or printer.

Phishing An illegal, e-mail-based scam in which the recipient is led to believe the sender is a legitimate company (often a financial institution), and is asked to provide (usually through a Web site link) personal information that allows the scammer to access their account and commit theft or other malicious activities. As of 2005, phishing attempts are rampant on the Internet, and Internet providers, software makers, and Internet authorities are working on various ways to combat it.

PictBridge support This feature allows direct printing (without the use of a computer) from any brand of digital camera to any brand of printer.

Picture-audio capability, MP3 players Some players have the ability to display pictures in conjunction with music, sometimes in slideshow fashion.

Picture presets Some TVs offer different picture settings, each designed to complement different programming, such as movies or sporting events.

Picture zoom One of the effects DVD players offer: the ability to zoom in on details in the picture.

PIM Personal information manager, a software application that organizes information on a day-to-day basis. PIMs routinely include features such

as a reminder calendar, notepad, address book, phone dialer, calculator, and alarm clock.

Pincushion effect A bowing-in on each side of the image on a CRT monitor screen, usually correctable with the monitor's controls. For CRT TVs, this requires special service-level adjustments. Flat-panel monitors do not have this effect.

PIP Many TV sets offer PIP (picture-in-picture), a feature that lets you watch two images at the same time on one screen: the first, full-size; the second, in a small box within the larger picture. A variant of this is POP (picture-outside-of-picture), with which the screen image is split evenly in two. TVs with dual-tuner PIP or POP can tune in to two channels simultaneously without the contribution of additional equipment. Those with only one tuner require a second, external tuner, such as a VCR, in order to use PIP. Some TVs can send the second channel's audio to a separate audio output.

Pixel, TVs, computer monitors Short for picture element, the smallest individually controllable unit of a visible image on a display. Often erroneously used to refer to the triad of dots on a CRT screen. On flat-panel (LCD, plasma) displays, there is always one pixel per triad of stripes, but there is no such mapping on a CRT monitor.

Plasma A plasma screen is made up of thousands of pixels containing gas that's converted into "plasma" by an electrical charge. The plasma causes phosphors to glow red, green, or blue, as dictated by a video signal. The result: a colorful display with high brightness and a wide viewing angle. Image quality may not be quite the equal of a very good picture-tube TV, especially with quickly moving images or dark scenes, but the better new plasma sets have narrowed the gap. Like CRT-based TVs, plasma sets are vulnerable to screen burn-in. Plasma sets run hot and consume more power than any other type of TV.

Platform The hardware architecture on which software applications run; the operating system or user interface under which the software application is intended to be used. Also, with digital cameras, the provided camera software's compatibility with a Windows-based PC, a Macintosh, or both.

Platform, MP3 players This refers to whether an MP3 player and its software are compatible with a Windows-based PC, a Macintosh computer, or both. Check the manufacturer and music-management software application Web sites for upgrades or new platforms supported.

Playback time, MP3 players Also referred to as battery life. This reflects our lab measurements of continuous playback time, to the nearest hour, using new alkaline or fully charged rechargeable battery (or batteries).

Play exchange For multidisc CD or DVD players, this feature (also called disc exchange) lets you remove or swap out one disc while another is playing.

Play modes Many MP3 players let you set a play mode so you can repeat one or all music tracks, or in a random order, also referred to as "shuffle" mode. Some players have A-B repeat, a way to set bookmarks, to repeat a section of the music track.

Plays online video, MP3 players An increasing number of players can now play TV shows, music videos, and short films that can be purchased from online stores. The videos are copy-protected by digital rights management (DRM) software. Some players with video capability, however, won't play copy-protected video.

Plug and play A standard for managing the installation of expansion cards and peripherals in modern PCs and operating systems. If both a PC and a device are plug-and-play compatible, the computer should handle the installation automatically.

Pointing device A hand-operated device used to move a pointer on the screen of a graphical user interface, selecting program objects, activating controls, or manipulating objects. A mouse is one type of pointing device.

POP, TVs Picture-Outside-of-Picture. See "PIP."

POP or **POP3** Post office protocol, an e-mail system that communicates between your primary mailbox in your own computer and the one at your access provider's site. POP mail is the usual protocol for incoming mail, while SMTP is used for outgoing.

Pop-up A message or window that appears on a computer screen, often in response to a user or program action. Pop-ups are also a common way to present advertising associated with Web sites. Pop-up ads that appear when you close a browser window are called "pop-under" ads.

Port A socket on a computer that's used to connect a peripheral such as a printer or modem.

Port expander or replicator A small module with connectors for attaching power, network, and several peripheral devices to a laptop computer via a single connection.

Portrait A page or screen orientation in which information is displayed or printed across the shorter dimension.

PowerMac A desktop Apple Macintosh computer that employs the PowerPC microprocessor.

PowerPC A fast, 32-bit chip that employs advanced RISC technology. It is used in Apple computers.

Power strip An AC electrical device that provides multiple outlets, usually having an on/off switch, a circuit breaker, and surge protection.

ppm Pages per minute, a measure of the speed of a printer.

Print head The part of a character printer (such as an inkjet) that moves across the paper to produce the characters or images.

Print server A small device that connects a printer directly to a network for shared use.

Prints from camera, printers This feature lets a printer receive images directly from a digital camera, either via a built-in memory-card reader or over a provided cable or via wireless technology, in which case the printer and camera communicate via infrared beam.

Privacy policy A legally binding statement by any entity (such as a Web site) that collects personal information from users, as to how that information will be used and protected from misuse or dissemination. It's often accompanied by a means for users to "opt out" of commercial use of their information.

Privileges, rights, or permissions Granted to a user by a system administrator, the set of operations that the user may perform on a system, such as the ability to access, change or delete files in certain directories, or change the configuration of the system. They are usually tied to a user's login ID.

Processor The "brain" of a computer or other "smart" device.

Productivity software Applications for the office, such as word-processor, spreadsheet, and database software.

Program A logical sequence of instructions designed to accomplish a specific task, written in such a way that it can be read and executed by a computer. Also, to construct a program.

Program file A file that contains a program. Program files may also be data files if they serve as the input or output for other programs.

Programmed recording Lets you program a camcorder to start recording at a specific time.

Progressive scan A video display mode used in computer monitors, DVDs, and DTV in which every scan line is displayed progressively, or in one pass. Compared to an interlaced display, a progressive-scan image, such as from a DVD player, can provide a smoother, more filmlike picture when used with compatible digital (such as high- and enhanced-definition) TVs. Nowadays, all computer monitors are progressively scanned.

Prompt A character, symbol, sound, or message sent to the screen to signal the user that the computer is ready for input; also, to issue a prompt.

Proportional spacing The characteristic of some print fonts (such as this text) in which narrow characters such as I and J use less space than wider ones such as M and W.

Proprietary Incompatible with others of the same type, not adhering to any specific industry standard; also, exclusively owned by a company or individual.

Public-domain software Programs that are neither owned nor copyrighted by anyone and are available to all who want them without restriction. These programs can usually be obtained for a small service fee.

Query A request for information from a computer database; also, to issue a query.

Quick review A camcorder feature that lets you

view the last few seconds of a scene without having to press a lot of buttons. It's handy for helping you decide if you need to reshoot a scene.

Quicktime A multimedia extension to the Macintosh operating system that can play sound or video content. A version is also available for Windows-based PCs.

QWERTY keyboard The traditional keyboard layout familiar to most typists and keyboard users. (It's named for the first six letters from the left on the top alphabet row.)

Radio buttons A set of on-screen options, only one of which is selectable at any one time. Once a selection is made (usually indicated by a dot or similar symbol), any previous choice is turned off (the dot is removed).

RAM Random-access memory, a read/write type of memory that permits the user to both read the information that is there and write data to it. This is the type of memory available to the user in most computers.

Random play, DVD players Lets you have a DVD unit randomly play different titles or chapters of a DVD (or tracks of a CD).

Random/repeat, MP3 players Many players let you set a play mode so you can repeat one or all music tracks, or in a random order, also referred to as "shuffle" mode.

Rapid-fire shots Also called continuous shooting or burst mode, this feature lets you take multiple digital-camera shots in quick succession with one touch of the shutter button; useful when shooting a subject in motion. The number of shots varies by camera and with resolution setting.

RealAudio or **RealMedia** Popular streaming audio (.ra) and video (.rm) file formats for the Web. Downloading the free RealPlayer plug-in applet turns your Web browser into an Internet radio/television.

Rear-projection TV A TV display system in which the image is beamed from a projector onto the rear of a projection screen. You view the opposite side of the screen from that which faces the projector.

Recording modes Like a digital camera, a digital video recorder can compress a recording so that it takes up less space on a hard drive or DVD, but at the expense of picture quality. Most recorders let you choose among several such recording modes. It's similar to choosing between SP and EP mode on a VCR. Here are three commonly available modes: **Fine mode:** Typically the highest quality mode, yielding picture quality nearly as good as that of a commercial-grade DVD. But it lets you store just one hour of video on a blank, 4.7-gigabyte DVD or the fewest hours of video on a hard drive. **SP mode:** Not as high in quality as fine, this lets you store two hours of video, enough capacity for most full-length movies, on a blank DVD. **EP mode:** The most space-conserving

mode, it lets you typically store six hours of video on a DVD or the most hours on a hard drive. The picture quality is comparable to the quality of EP mode for a run-of-the-mill VCR.

Recording time (min.), cordless phones Most answering machines store messages electronically. Recording time of 15 to 20 minutes is typical. In many cases, recording time may include not only incoming messages, but greetings, memos, and saved messages, so the total may be misleading. Most answerers maximize capacity by detecting pauses in a message and not storing them in memory.

Red-eye reduction With a digital camera, this reduces the chances that the pupils of your subject's eyes will appear red in flash photos. With red-eye reduction, the camera emits a burst of light just before the main flash, causing the pupils to contract. Most cameras with a flash have this feature. Image-editing software often offers red-eye correction as well.

Redial button Found on almost all cordless-phone models, this feature lets you automatically dial the last number called.

Refresh To continuously renew or update, as contents of volatile memory; to redraw information after alteration, such as a graphics image that is being edited.

Refresh rate The number of times each second that a CRT monitor redraws an image on the screen. A refresh rate below about 72 Hz can appear to "blink" because the image fades between refreshes.

Remote control A remote control is standard with nearly all TVs, and most do more than turn on the power and switch channels. Here's what's available: The familiar **standard remote** controls only the TV and can't operate any other component. A **unified remote** will operate other equipment of the same brand. The more common **universal remote,** the code-entry or learning type, will operate other brands and types of equipment; it requires you to input appropriate codes for your equipment. A **learning remote,** less frequently offered, can determine the codes of remotes belonging to other systems, so you don't have to look them up. Some remotes offer illuminated buttons for easier operation in dimly lit rooms.

Remote control, camcorders A remote control is handy for operating a camcorder from a distance (say, to let the user be in the picture). It's also useful in playback mode since all the buttons are readily at hand.

Remote control, digital cameras Lets you take a picture without touching the camera; an alternative to using a self-timer.

Remote control, MP3 players Some MP3 players include a wired or infrared remote control to access the player's function controls.

Remote handset For cordless phones with an answerer, this lets you listen to messages from the handset and may allow access to other answerer functions, such as recording your greeting.

Removable-media slot Found in a few TVs, a slot that accepts memory cards for viewing still images from digital cameras. Inserting the camera's card typically results in better image quality than if you connect the camera to the TV's composite-video input. Some memory cards are specific to one or more specific manufacturers—such as Memory Stick slots in some Sony TVs. Other slots may accept CompactFlash, SmartMedia, MultiMedia Card, Secure Digital, and/or other media.

Repeat play Allows you to repeat, from the beginning, an entire DVD—or a DVD's title or chapter—that is currently being played. The same feature can be used to repeat an entire CD or CD track.

Replaceable battery, camcorders All camcorders come with a rechargeable battery and an AC adapter. The adapter can recharge the battery or power the camcorder if an outlet is nearby, but generally not at the same time. Most models let you install a more-powerful battery than the original. Commonly used battery types are lithium-ion, nickel-cadmium, and nickel-metal hydride. A nickel-cadmium or nickel-metal hydride battery that's repeatedly recharged when not totally drained may lose the ability to recharge completely. A refresh switch on the adapter lets you fully drain the battery before recharging, to help maintain full running time.

Replaceable battery, digital cameras Some digital cameras use two or four AA batteries. Nonrechargeable batteries, such as alkaline and lithium, or rechargeable batteries, such as nickel-metal hydride (NiMH) or lithium-ion, may be used. Some cameras that use rechargeable batteries come with a charger and a set of rechargeable batteries.

Resolution Indicates the degree of detail that can be perceived—for example, in a displayed or printed image. The higher the resolution, the finer the detail.

Resolution, digital cameras A digital image is made up of hundreds of thousands or, more typically, millions of tiny dots called pixels. The resolution of a digital camera's sensor is the number of pixels horizontally multiplied by the number of pixels vertically. The more pixels the sensor has, the sharper and more detailed the picture. Resolution may range from 1280x960 pixels (1-megapixel models) to as much as 2560x1920 (5-megapixel models). While desirable, high resolution is expensive and requires much more memory per picture.

Resolution modes The number of levels, or modes, of resolution a digital camera offers.

Resume play Lets you stop playing a DVD and later resume playback from where you left off.

Reverse frame-by-frame Most DVD players let you view a movie frame-by-frame going forward. This feature lets you do so in reverse as well.

Reversible charging With this feature, a cordless-phone handset battery can charge in the charging cradle with the handset face up or down.

Ribbon cable A flat, multiwire cable design that is commonly used to connect devices, such as disk drives, within a computer.

ROM Read-only memory, storage that permits reading and use of data but no changes. ROMs are preprogrammed at the factory for a specific purpose and are found on many boards such as graphics and in many systems that automatically boot when they are turned on.

ROM BIOS A BIOS routine contained in a ROM chip, enabling a computer device to boot. The system BIOS on a PC's motherboard is one example; however, some components have their own ROM BIOS chips.

Rotatable lens A digital-camera lens that tilts up or down. Some can rotate nearly 360 degrees, letting you compose a self-portrait while viewing yourself on the LCD monitor.

RSI Repetitive strain injury, a disorder of the hands, arms, back, neck, and even eyes that can arise from very heavy computer use.

Run To execute a program.

#

SACD One of two relatively new, competing music formats. SACD (for Super Audio CD) discs contain a stereo (and possibly also a multichannel) version of the music content. Both this and the other competing format, DVD-Audio, also claim to offer better sound quality than CDs can deliver. Note that while SACD-formatted program material will only play on models that specify SACD capability, some "hybrid" SACD discs contain another version, in standard CD format, of the same program material. Such discs should be playable on any DVD or CD player.

SAP Secondary audio programming (SAP) reception, offered on many TV sets, is valuable for those who want to tune into the alternate sound versions sometimes available, such as a Spanish-language soundtrack or a specially designed audio track for the blind.

Scanner A peripheral device that digitally translates and then transfers photos, graphics, and/or text onto a computer's hard drive.

Screen dimmer or **saver, computers** An applet that produces a moving image on a CRT monitor screen to prevent ghost images from being burned into the phosphors by lingering, unattended displays. Modern monitors are better served by use of the power-saving standby mode.

Screen dimmer or **saver, DVD players** Over time, long-term pausing of movies or displaying the player's menu or logo may cause parts of those images to "burn" onto the screen. A screen dimmer helps stave off this effect by dimming the screen whenever the picture is motionless for a long period; a screen saver substitutes a moving image in the same situation.

Screen shape The screen shape, or aspect ratio, is the proportion of a TV screen's width to its height. Standard TV screens have an aspect ratio of 4:3, giving them a squarish shape that is 4 units wide for every 3 units high. Wide-screen TVs typically have a 16:9 aspect ratio, giving them a wider screen that better resembles the screen in a movie theater. (Some LCD TVs have a 15:9 aspect ratio that differs slightly, but they're often not identified as such.) Wide-screen TVs can use the full screen to display HDTV broadcasts and recorded movies. When displayed on a standard screen, such images must be framed at the top and bottom with black bars in order to maintain the wide-screen aspect ratio. Conversely, regular TV programming displayed on a wide screen has black bars on both sides. (Note that much programming actually differs from 4:3 or 16:9, often necessitating bars of some width.) Many sets have stretch and zoom modes to eliminate the bars and fit the image to the screen, albeit with some distortion.

Screen size (in.), TVs The size of the television's screen, measured diagonally in inches. In general, the larger the screen size, the farther away you need to sit for optimal picture quality. It's best to sit approximately 11 feet from a 36-inch set, 10 feet from a 32-inch set, and 8 feet from a 27-inch set. For HD (high-definition) sets, the distances can be halved.

Scroll bar A computer screen element consisting of a horizontal and/or vertical bar with a slider that moves within the bar, both to control scrolling and to indicate position in a document.

Scrolling channel preview Provides, on some higher-end TVs, thumbnail images of what's on other channels besides the one you're currently watching.

Secure Digital (SD) card The Secure Digital (SD) card is a highly secure stamp-sized flash-memory card that weighs approximately two grams.

Secure grip, digital cameras Denotes cameras designed with room for your fingers, so you can hold the camera steady and keep your fingers clear of the flash, lens, or auto-focus sensor. The grip is especially important on the smallest cameras, which by their nature, have little room for a handhold.

Secure site A Web site that uses encrypted pages that cannot be read by unauthorized persons such as hackers. Many commercial and financial Web sites have secure sections for exchange of personal information with customers.

Selectivity Your TV's ability to tune channels without interference from adjacent channels, important only if you use your TV, not a cable box or other device, for tuning.

Self-timer A digital camera's self-timer lets you take shots that include yourself. A countdown timer delays the shot by 10 seconds or more, giving you time to get within its field of view. A remote control provides the same function without the rush.

Sensitivity Your TV's ability to pick up relatively weak signals and still display a picture, important only if you receive off-air broadcasts far from transmitting antennas.

Sensor, digital cameras, camcorders The sensor

is the chip (CCD or CMOS) that records light falling on it as it travels through the digital camera's lens. It is the device that actually captures the image.

Serial port A type of computer connection that transfers data one bit at a time. Serial ports are commonly used by older input/output devices.

Server A computer in a network, the resources of which are shared by part or all of the other users.

Set-top box Also referred to as an external tuner or, for digital types, a receiver/decoder, it's a small box that converts incoming TV signals into a signal that a TV can accept and display. Common examples are a cable box, satellite box, and off-air tuner. There are also digital and HD-capable versions of each. Some also have a hard drive for recording programs and watching at a later time (time-shifting).

720p-capable 720p refers to an HD signal based on 1280 pixels horizontally by 720 pixels vertically, progressively scanned (the "p"). Some broadcasters use the 720p format, but 1080i (1920x1080 pixels, interlaced) is a more common HD display mode. 720p-capable HD TVs can display images using this type of signal without requiring an external set-top box, such as a digital-cable box or satellite receiver, to convert it to a resolution it can display.

Shareware User-supported software that is copyrighted and typically available on the Internet; the author usually requests a fee (typically $10 to $50) from those who decide to continue using the program after trying it.

Sheet feeder A device attached to some computer scanners that automatically feeds a stack of sheets, one at a time, through it for scanning, thus eliminating the need to hand-feed the pages. Useful for large printed documents.

Shift key A key that changes the function of a character printed by another key when pressed along with that key.

Shortcut An icon on a computer operating system's desktop or program list that launches a program or document when activated; there can be many shortcuts to one program. A shortcut is equivalent to an "alias" in the Apple Macintosh realm.

Shutter range The minimum and maximum shutter speeds available for a digital camera.

Signal-to-noise ratio Abbreviated S/N or SNR, it represents the ratio, expressed in decibels (dB), of an undistorted maximum audio signal and the noise present in the signal. Audio signals typically contain some noise or background from electronic parts. A system's maximum S/N is called the dynamic range. For audio, the higher the number, the cleaner the sound. This number is useful when comparing like products.

Signal type The typical analog type of video signal comes out of older cable boxes, DVD players, camcorders, and VCRs. It can be carried over a composite-video, S-video, or component-video connection. When superimposed on a radio frequency, it can be broadcast over the air and picked up via antenna, or sent via cable to the cable box. If it's digitized first, then superimposed on a radio frequency, it can be delivered over the air as DTV (digital television), by DBS (direct broadcast satellite) to the satellite receiver, or as the digital portion of your cable service. Note: these three delivery methods use different digitizing and usually must be decoded by different tuners.

Simultaneous record/playback For DVD recorders, the ability to watch one program while recording another, or to begin watching a recording from the beginning, pause, reverse, or fast-forward while the recording is still in progress. Only models that record to the DVD-RAM format or include a built-in hard drive offer this function.

Six-channel decoder, DVD players A multichannel (usually six-channel) audio decoder is useful in a DVD player only if you plan to pipe the player's audio signal into a full home-theater system, and the system's digital receiver does not itself have multichannel (usually also known as 5.1 channel) decoding capability. The decoder separates audio into up to six true channels: front left and right, front center (for dialogue), two rear (also called surround) speakers with discrete wide-band signals, and a subwoofer for bass effects. Some DVD soundtracks even have additional channels beyond the expected six.

Sleep timer If you like to fall asleep with the TV on but don't want to leave it on all night, a sleep timer can be set, usually in 15-minute increments, so that the TV will turn off within a specific time. Such timers are included on many sets.

Slideshow capability, MP3 players Allows pictures to be displayed in slideshow fashion, complete with fade-outs and other transitions. Some players let you adjust how long each picture is displayed.

Slim-and-light laptop A laptop PC that contains only the components needed to run installed applications, operate on stored documents and files, and communicate with external devices. Removable-disk drives are connected externally when needed, as the focus of the design is on reducing travel size and weight.

Slot Similar to a port in a computer, but usually used for internal expansions, such as memory, graphics, and so forth, by the addition of boards.

Smart card A plastic card, containing memory and a processor, that communicates with a computer through a reader into which it is inserted. The data on the card may authenticate a user, and/or may provide personal or financial information enabling a transaction. The memory on smart cards can be updated by the system as part of the transaction.

SmartMedia Also known as solid-state floppy disk cards (SSFDC), they are a form of flash memory. They are roughly the size of a large postage stamp and about as thick as a credit card.

SMTP Simple Mail Transfer Protocol, the usual protocol for outgoing Internet e-mail. SMTP is not a secure protocol in that it allows spammers to use it while remaining anonymous.

Software The programs that are run on a computer for various purposes.

Sound, TVs Three different types of sound system are available. Some small TVs have **mono** sound, meaning that all the audio is processed through a single channel. The next step up is **stereo** sound, which splits the audio between two channels for a more lifelike sound. For an "expanded" audio experience, look for a TV equipped with **virtual surround** sound. Using only the TV speakers, this system simulates the "ambient" sound effects of home-theater systems. On most, however, you can turn off the ambience for a given program if you don't like the effect.

Sound board/card A component of multimedia PCs that can realistically reproduce (through attached speakers or headphones) almost any sound, such as music, speech, and sound effects. Sound boards can also connect to other sound equipment.

Sound format, camcorders Camcorders may record with mono, stereo, or PCM stereo formats. Mono records onto only one channel; stereo, onto two channels (left and right). PCM stereo, found on digital camcorders, can either record at SP speed with 16 bits of information on two channels (CD-quality sound, in theory) or divide the audio into four tracks by recording 12 bits on two channels, leaving another pair of tracks free for post-production audio editing and recording.

Sound technology, cordless phones Cordless phones transmit their signals between the base and handset wirelessly using analog (the least expensive), digital, or digital spread-spectrum (DSS) technology.

Spam Besides the trademarked luncheon meat from Hormel Foods, a slang term for unsolicited commercial e-mail—thought to come from a skit by the Monty Python comedy troupe in which the word spam was repeated over and over until it became annoying. Spam is the Internet's equivalent of junk mail and proliferates despite many efforts to reduce it.

Spam filter A feature built into e-mail programs or installed as an add-on that attempts to identify spam messages and remove them from your main inbox. Spam filters on individual PCs have mixed success. Some ISPs also offer a spam-filter option.

Speaker wattage, TVs The audio-output power is expressed in watts, ranging from less than 1 watt to as much as 7 watts. Higher wattage, offered on many sets, may provide a louder sound but will not necessary improve overall audio quality.

Speakerphone A speakerphone feature on a cordless phone offers a hands-free way to converse or wait on hold and lets others chime in. A base speaker lets you answer a call without the handset; a handset speaker lets you chat hands-free conveniently anywhere in the house.

Speech synthesizer A computer output device that simulates human speech using phonetic rules. When used with the appropriate software, a speech synthesizer can "speak" the words that are displayed on the monitor screen.

Spreadsheet A software package, such as Lotus 1-2-3 or Microsoft Excel, that lets the user enter, into "cells," numbers and equations that the program automatically calculates. Spreadsheet software eases the development of financial applications.

Spyware Undesirable software that often rides in on a seemingly useful program, but runs in the background and transmits statistics about your Internet activities to a marketing database for their use and resale. Some spyware is also adware, popping up annoying advertising windows or redirecting a Web browser to undesired sites.

Standard Agreed-upon industry design guidelines for a hardware or software product intended to make it work with the products of different manufacturers. Given the choice, it's usually wiser to choose a standards-based product than a proprietary one.

Standby A computer's power-saving state in which some subsystems are shut off but can resume full-speed operation almost immediately when a key or the pointing device is touched. PCs in standby can also respond to modem-ringing signals or timed events by resuming. It's also called suspend or sleep mode.

Start menu A feature of the Microsoft Windows desktop that provides a single pop-up menu to launch any installed program and access other features of the operating system.

Status bar An onscreen area, usually at the top or bottom of a window, that provides information on the current operation of the software in use.

Still-image file formats, digital cameras The file output, indicated in the image's filename extension, that the camera generates. TIFF and JPEG are the most common.

Still-image resolution settings, digital cameras The number of levels, or modes, of resolution the camera offers.

Storage Any disk (fixed or removable), tape, CD, or online service that stores data.

Storage size (MB) Digital cameras store images as data files, such as those on the hard drive of a computer. The more storage space is available, the more images the camera can store. Most cameras have a few megabytes of internal storage, but many also accept removable memory cards or other media that can store as much as 1 gigabyte (GB).

Streaming Playing an audio or video presentation directly from an Internet Web site without your first having to download it. Streaming requires cooperation between the Web server and a "media player" applet on the user's PC.

Stretch and zoom modes, TVs On widescreen 16:9 sets, such display modes will expand or compress an image to better fill the screen shape. This helps to reduce the dark bands that can appear above, below, or on the sides of the image if you watch content formatted for one screen shape on a TV that has the other shape. The picture, however, may be distorted or cut off a bit in the process of stretching and zooming.

String On a computer, a set of characters treated as a unit.

Subdirectory or subfolder A directory that is contained by another directory, such as C:\windows\system. Usually called a subfolder in a GUI-based OS.

Subwoofer output The ability, found in a few TVs, to output the lower-frequency portion of the audio directly to a powered subwoofer.

SuperVGA See "SVGA."

Surge suppressor or **protector** An electrical device, often built into a power strip, designed to prevent damage to the computer resulting from voltage spikes from the power source.

Surround-sound formats, DVD players Surround sound refers to the ability of your DVD player to play one or more varieties of multichannel audio through your home-entertainment system. Several different surround formats exist, each with distinct advantages and disadvantages. The main format choices are Dolby Pro Logic, Dolby Digital, and DTS.

SVGA SuperVGA, a high-resolution (800x600 pixels) computer-graphics display mode.

S-VHS-C Marketed as a premium variant of VHS-C, it promises a sharper camcorder picture, though performance varies widely. This format uses a cassette that's about the size of a cigarette pack but is more expensive and less widely available than VHS-C.

S-video input, TVs Also known as S-VHS connection or Y/C. An S-video connection splits the video signal into two parts, color and luma. In general, an S-video input will provide better picture quality than either an antenna/cable or composite-video input. These are often used with digital-cable boxes, satellite receivers, and DVD players. Many sets have front-panel S-video input, which lets you make temporary connections to certain camcorders, game systems, and other devices with S-video output.

S-video output, camcorders S-Video is a higher-quality video connection than a standard composite-video hookup. Both of these output types are used to connect the camcorder to a television or VCR to watch and/or record information saved on a camcorder's tape or disc.

S-video output, DVD players An S-video connection from a DVD player's S-video output to the TV provides a picture with more detail and fewer color artifacts than you can get using the TV's composite-video or antenna/cable (RF) connection. S-video output is also used to connect a camcorder to a television or VCR to watch and/or record information saved on a camcorder's tape (or disc).

Swap black for photo ink, printers The photo ink for some printers comes in an extra cartridge. To use these photo inks, you must remove the black-ink cartridge and replace it with the photo-ink cartridge. To go back to printing text or graphics, the photo-ink cartridge must be removed and replaced by the black ink cartridge. This can get tedious. Models that hold all the inks simultaneously minimize the hassle.

SXGA Super XGA, a very high-resolution (1280x1024 pixels) computer-graphics display mode. SXGA+ provides 1400x1050 pixels.

System A single computer, or any group of interconnected computers, and the network itself. Also short for an operating system.

System disk, drive, or volume The currently active data-storage device that contains the critical operating-system files for a running computer.

System software Programs required for the basic operation of the computer and its components. For PCs, this normally consists of the operating system and any associated utilities.

System utilities Programs usually supplied as part of the system software that permit and assist in basic control and maintenance of the computer and its components.

T

Tablet A computer input device often used by designers. Tablets consist of a sensitive membrane, movement (using a stylus or sometimes even a finger) upon which is transferred to corresponding positions on the screen.

Tablet PC Microsoft's name for a pen computer, a portable computer that uses a pressure-sensitive flat-panel screen for control and data input. A tablet PC can convert handwritten notes to electronic text.

Tabletop/console Most TVs are placed on top of or inside a piece of furniture (say, an entertainment center), but some TVs are consoles, meaning they have their own cabinetry and can stand directly on the floor. Rear-projection TVs in particular are often consoles, although newer "microdisplay" models typically require a stand.

Tagline A short quip or quote at the end of an e-mail message.

Tape, computers A magnetic data storage or backup medium on which files are stored in a predetermined and rigid sequence. Updating a tape usually requires making a new copy of the entire tape.

Task Any process currently running on a computer. An application may have several tasks running simultaneously.

Task bar On the Microsoft Windows desktop, a bar with icons and window titles that is used to launch programs, switch between running tasks, and display the status of programs running in the background.

TCP/IP Transmission control protocol/Internet protocol, a shorthand name for the "language" of Internet communication.

Technology, TVs All rear-projection TVs project

their images onto a mirror, which reflects the image onto the screen for you to see. Projection TVs use one of several display technologies to project the image initially onto the mirror. **CRT** or **cathode-ray tube,** is the traditional method, using three 7-inch picture tubes (one each for the red, green, and blue portions of the image). **LCD,** or **liquid-crystal display,** is a newer method that uses three LCD panels, each about an inch in size. **DLP,** or **digital light processing,** is a new technology that uses a microchip containing a microscopic array of pivoting mirrors, and a spinning color wheel. **LCoS** is the newest technology. It uses three microchips, each of which contains a microscopic array of mirror-like LCD elements.

Telecommunications Communications between devices that are not located near each other and must make use of a data communications channel. This occurs when PCs link to a host computer for an exchange of data.

TeleZapper A built-in feature, found in some cordless phones, that reduces the number of computer-aided telemarketing calls you receive.

Template A document guide on a computer, similar to a paper form, that permits the user to simply fill in the blanks to create a new document.

Text display, DVD players A feature that displays text encoded on certain discs, giving you information such as song titles on CDs.

Text file A file that usually contains only ASCII characters, readable by practically any program that uses text.

TFT LCD Thin film transistor liquid-crystal display, an LCD display of the type most commonly used on laptop PC screens, flat-panel desktop displays, and portable products with color displays. Also referred to as an active-matrix LCD.

35mm-equivalent zoom ratio All digital camera manufacturers publish this "35mm-equivalent" focal length simply because people are used to hearing it and knowing what kind of image a 28mm lens produces compared to a 50mm lens.

3:2-pulldown compensation A feature on most digital TVs that can enable things in motion to look less jagged around the edges. It affects only movies converted from film to video—the majority of cinematic movies on DVD. This feature is sometimes referred to as film mode, cinema mode, movie mode, or by brand-specific names such as CineMotion. Progressive-scan DVD players have this feature as well.

Thumbnail A miniature reproduction of an image, usually for display.

THX-certified, DVD players, digital receivers THX is an enhancement to Dolby Digital (DTS) sound processing that further processes the multichannel sound to simulate the acoustics of a movie theater. To hear the benefit, you must use the certified DVD player with a receiver and speakers that are also THX-certified.

Time and date stamp A camcorder feature with which the time and date are displayed in the

viewfinder or on the LCD, and can be set to record on the tape.

Time code An automatic (and accurate) camcorder feature that records the frame reference on the tape in hours, minutes, seconds, and frames. The information, which is recorded separately from the video and audio signals, makes editing easier. The time and date are displayed in the viewfinder or on the LCD, and can be set to record on the tape.

Titling Like the time and date, titling can be programmed to record on a camcorder tape. Most models now have this feature, but its sophistication varies. Some camcorders simply provide a list of premade or built-in titles, such as "Happy Holidays," to choose from. Others let you set and save your own custom titles, such as "Sam's First Birthday Party."

TiVo and ReplayTV Trademarks for two hard-drive recorder brands that use sophisticated onscreen TV program guides to manage the recording of programs.

Toggle A soft switch or control code that turns a setting on and off by repeated action; to turn something on and off by repeating the same action.

Toner A very fine, powdery ink, supplied in a cartridge, that is used in copy machines and laser printers. Toner particles become electrically charged and adhere to the pattern of an image defined by charges on a plate or drum.

Touch-sensitive Any device that responds to light contact with a finger, stylus, or both. Some displays, such as those on a PDA or Tablet PC, use a touch-sensitive screen to input data or control the device.

Tower case A computer case design that employs an upright (stacked) arrangement of drives. Tower cases can sit on a tabletop, but more frequently they are placed on the floor or a low stand adjacent to the work area. The term is often prefixed by full-, mid-, mini-, or micro-, indicating the case's relative size and expansion space.

Trackball A computer pointing device similar to a mouse; it uses a ball mounted on a fixed base to control onscreen cursor movement. You roll the ball with your fingers or thumb in the direction you want the onscreen pointer to go.

Transfer rate An estimate of how quickly an MP3 file can be transferred from a computer to the player. Transfer rate is usually measured in kilobytes or megabytes per second and can vary depending on the player, the interface type, the computer platform, operating system, configuration requirements, file size, and other factors.

Trojan or **Trojan horse** A general class of computer programs that gain system entry by riding in on legitimate-appearing programs or e-mail attachments. The best-known examples are malicious programs that provide hackers remote access to infected systems; however, not all Trojan horses are necessarily destructive.

TV type As digital television has grown, the choice of TV types has expanded. Most models, known as standard or conventional, receive only the tradi-

tional analog TV signal. Digital TVs are available in HDTV (high-definition TV), EDTV (enhanced-definition TV), and SDTV (standard-definition TV) formats. Once the transition to digital TV is complete, SDTV sets are expected to represent the entry level of TVs. **HDTVs** can display exceptional picture quality in a wide-screen (usually 16:9) aspect ratio. **EDTVs** offer a lesser picture quality than HDTV but have a picture that's roughly equivalent to that of progressive-scan DVD players. **SDTVs** may not measure up to the HDTV sound and picture standards, but they're similar to high-quality standard TVs. (For each type, the term "ready," as in "HD-ready," refers to the need to connect an external tuner to decode the incoming digital signals.) Even regular analog TVs can show digital broadcast programs once broadcasters go all digital, if they're connected to an external digital TV tuner/decoder. They won't, however, display the superior quality of digital signals.

Two phone lines, cordless phones A phone that supports two phone lines can receive calls for two phone numbers. Useful if you have two phone lines in the home—say, a business line and a personal line that you'd like to use from a single phone. Some phones have two ringers, each with a distinctive pitch to let you know which phone line is ringing. Also facilitates conferencing two callers in three-way connections. Some have an auxiliary jack data port to plug in a fax, modem, or other phone device.

Two-way intercom, cordless phones For models with a base speakerphone, it allows for conversation between the handset and the base speakerphone. For multiple-handset-capable models, it allows for conversation between one handset and another. Also referred to as two-way paging.

U

UI User interface, the means through which a user controls a computing device.

Ultra DMA or UDMA A further enhancement to the EIDE computer disk-drive interface that can transfer data as fast as 133 MB per second in bursts. A compatible drive is required.

Uninterruptible power supply See "UPS."

Universal remote Controls not only your DVD player, for example, but also other components, such as many different brands of TVs.

Unix A popular but not user-friendly operating system that runs on many platforms from mainframe to microcomputer. It employs cryptic but powerful commands, shells, and pipes, and has TCP/IP protocols built in; good for use in Internet servers.

Update or **upgrade** The process of changing software or hardware to a newer, more powerful, or possibly less-buggy version.

Upgradable A system whose components are designed to be easily upgraded to newer ones, usually by simply unplugging the old one and inserting the new one.

Upgrade path Refers to the means for a computer,

hardware component, or software application to be changed to a more powerful or newer version without adversely affecting the remainder of the system or any pertinent files.

Upload To transfer a copy of a file from one computer, usually a PC, to another computer. In the opposite direction, it's a download.

UPS Uninterruptible power supply, an electrical device that contains a battery pack and will supply adequate power to a computer for a short time in the event of a power failure, permitting it to be shut down in an orderly manner.

URL Uniform resource locator, an Internet/intranet address, such as *http://www.Consumer Reports.org*. Every place on the Web has such an address. Most Web addresses begin with http://, and most Web sites start with "www." Site URLs end with a "top-level domain" (TLD) suffix: Commercial sites end in ".com," organizations in ".org," educational sites in ".edu," and government sites in ".gov." Other TLDs have been established, such as ".info" and ".biz." URLs can also address FTP and other types of sites, along with resources on a LAN.

USB Universal serial bus, a high-speed external interface on newer PCs, used to connect peripheral devices such as printers and digital cameras. An enhancement, USB2, has a much higher speed, with enough bandwidth for digital video and external hard drives. On PDAs, this connection synchronizes data in your PDA to your desktop and transfers it faster than a serial-cable or infrared link.

USB2 Most Windows and Macintosh computers purchased since the fall of 2002 have universal serial bus 2.0 ports (USB2). They can be used with printers that have either USB2 or USB connections. The speed for transmitting data with USB2 can be up to 40 times faster than with USB. Check which connections your computer has before purchasing a printer.

Usenet A large but informal collection of Internet servers that host groups of users known as newsgroups to exchange news and information on specific topics.

User interface Any device, either hardware or software, that provides a bridge between the computer and the user. Examples include the keyboard, mouse, and menu programs.

User-replaceable lamp Rear-projection TVs using LCD, DLP, or LCoS technology, called microdisplay sets (see "Microdisplay"), have a lamp rated to last 2,000 to 6,000 hours. A user-replaceable lamp can be replaced if you're handy with a screwdriver and closely follow the instructions. The bulb costs $200 to $400. A service call, if necessary, typically costs an additional $200.

User-supported software See "shareware."

V

V.90 A standard for 56-kbps modems. A later standard, V.92, alleviates some of the shortcomings of dial-up Internet access, such as lengthy call-setup times, slow upload speed, and phone-line tie-ups.

V-chip A parental-control feature, found in all TVs with screens 13 inches or larger, that can block specific programs based on their content rating. To override the restriction for a given program, you must enter a code.

VCR capability Some hybrid DVD players have a built-in VCR that lets you play and record videotapes as well as play DVDs. Note that such models do not permit the recording of copy-protected DVDs onto videotape.

VCR Plus+ For DVD/VCR combo units, a capability that simplifies time-shift recording by letting you punch in a program's code (from TV listings) rather than the program's date, time, and channel. Gold and Silver versions do most of the setup work for you once you enter your ZIP code.

Version number A number, such as 3.2, indicating an application or driver's place in the history of its development. In general, the higher the version number, the longer the program has been around and under development, and the more revisions it has undergone. Also, the greater the difference between two version numbers, the greater the change in the program.

VGA IBM's Video Graphics Array, a medium-resolution, 640x480-pixel color graphics system. VGA was originally designed for professional applications on top-of-the-line PCs; however, it is now considered to be standard equipment.

VGA/SVGA input, TVs Some sets have VGA or SVGA input, which lets your TV double as a computer monitor.

VHS-C A format for a camcorder using a cassette that's about the size of a cigarette pack—inexpensive and widely available. The tape can be played back in a VHS VCR, using the supplied adapter, or in the camcorder.

Video D/A conversion, DVD players Most standard DVD players use a 10-bit/27-MHz digital-to-analog converter. Progressive-scan models use a 10- or 12-bit/54-MHz digital-to-analog converter.

Video inputs, TVs Video inputs provide a better picture than the antenna/cable input (which combines audio and video), and most TVs are equipped with at least one video input. There are generally three types. **Composite-video inputs,** the most common, provide minor improvement over antenna/cable. **S-video input,** at least one of which is found on most sets 27 inches or larger, is a further improvement. And **component-video input** separates the video signal into three component parts to offer the potential for even finer picture quality; they are useful mostly with a DVD player or other equipment that has component-video output. Digital video inputs—HDMI, DVI or FireWire—are typically found on HD and ED TVs. Front-panel inputs permit easy connection of an external device, such as a camcorder or game system, to the TV.

Video-noise reduction setting May reduce the effects of noise due to poor reception, although this feature may sacrifice some picture detail.

Video out, digital cameras Lets you connect a digital camera directly to a TV or VCR and view your images on the TV screen or record your images onto a videotape.

Video output, DVD players The type of video output you use with your DVD player depends on the type of inputs on your TV or receiver. DVD players come with at least composite and S-video outputs. Both S-video and component-video outputs, however, provide an increase in picture quality.

Videoconferencing Teleconferencing in which video images are exchanged. Although this traditionally involved using video cameras and monitors, routine video conferencing via computer over the Internet has started to become reality.

Virtual reality A computerized simulation of three-dimensional space in which the user can interact and manipulate objects in the virtual world.

Virtual surround sound, TVs Television audio systems by themselves do not offer the true surround sound of a home-theater system but produce a similar effect through special audio processing. Systems offered on some sets include two-speaker surround, Matrix, Matrix/SRS, and SRS.

Virus A typically small, malicious computer program embedded in a legitimate-appearing "host" file, often a downloaded program or e-mail attachment. A computer becomes "infected" with the virus when a user runs the host file. Viruses replicate themselves in an attempt to infect other computers and attach to user files, causing annoyance or damage to the infected system.

Virus signature The unique machine code (binary) pattern of a computer virus program. Most antivirus programs include a search for known virus signatures as a means for quick detection.

Voice-mail indicator A visual indicator on a cordless phone's handset or base that notifies you that you have new messages on your telephone company's message-waiting service.

Voice recognition The ability of a computer to accept input commands or data using the spoken word. Voice-recognition technology has advanced greatly and is likely to become a common alternative to keyboard control and data entry.

Voice recording An MP3 player feature with which the unit has a microphone that's useful for recording interviews, lectures, etc.

Voice synthesizer See "Speech synthesizer."

Voltage spike A sudden jump in electrical power. These can be very dangerous to data and, if large enough, to computer hardware as well.

W

Wall-mountable Some TVs, particularly plasma sets, can be mounted on a wall, although we recommend you hire a professional because of their need for adequate support and ventilation. LCD TVs are also wall-mountable, though mounting makes sense mostly for larger models.

Warm boot To restart a computer from the

keyboard. This method does not always completely clear and re-initialize the system; and a "cold" boot may be required.

Warranty, TVs The length of time the television is covered by its manufacturer for defects or repairs. Most warranty coverage is divided into parts and labor, typically one year for parts and either 90 days or one year for labor.

Water resistance A printer's ability to produce output that will not run or smear if it gets wet. Water-resistance for a printer's ink (or dye, in the case of a dye-sublimation photo printer) may apply to black, color, or both.

WAV Also known as a wave file, this is a file format for storing uncompressed digital audio.

Webcam Web camera, a small camera connected to a computer, for capturing still images or video to send to others over the Internet.

Webmail E-mail account access through a Web-page interface, which allows the mail user to send and receive mail anywhere that an Internet connection is available.

Webmaster The individual responsible for maintaining a Web site's content and links. Usually, the Webmaster operates remotely and does not have (or need) direct control of the computer that serves the Web site.

WEP Wired-Equivalent Privacy. A content-scrambling system for wireless networks that requires each client PC to use a password "key" to access the network. WEP is not secure to a determined hacker and has been supplanted by WPA.

Wi-Fi Nickname for a medium-range (150 feet) wireless connectivity standard, officially known as IEEE 802.11. Wi-Fi enables secure networking of PCs in either a peer-to-peer or a workstation-to-base configuration. 802.11b operates in the 2.4-GHz radio-frequency band and provides data throughput of about 5 Mbps. 802.11a operates above 5 GHz and has about five times the throughput over a somewhat smaller radius. 802.11g, dubbed "Wireless-G," combines the speed of 802.11a with the range of 802.11b so is preferred for most users. 802.11n is the newest version of the standard, scheduled to be ratified in late 2006. It promises increased speed, range, and security.

Wildcard A generic symbol (such as * or ?) that can stand for either a single character or several characters. Wildcards are frequently used in system commands.

Window A portion of a computer screen set aside for a specific display or purpose.

Windows A multitasking, graphical user interface developed by Microsoft for IBM-compatible systems. The program gets its name from using movable and resizable windows in which applications are displayed. Windows supports multimedia, common printer management, TrueType fonts, and copy and paste between Windows applications.

Windows Vista The next-generation family of Microsoft Windows, due in late 2006. It is slated to include visual enhancements, a more-accessible and robust file system, and improvements in stability and security. Vista is expected to be available in several versions to satisfy differing needs.

Windows XP (Home and Professional) The latest family of Windows operating systems. Windows XP replaces prior versions of Windows for personal computers, bringing many of the advantages of the Windows 2000 operating system to the consumer.

Windows XP Media Center Edition An enhanced version of Windows XP Professional that adds a user-friendly, full-screen interface for multimedia features. These include selection and playback of stored digital media files, such as photos, music, and video. Computers with built-in TV and radio receivers can take further advantage of Windows XP Media Center Edition to add TiVolike program-guide and DVR features.

Windows Media Center Extender A set-top-boxlike device that connects a home entertainment system (TV and audio) to an existing home network that includes a PC with Windows XP Media Center Edition. The Extender brings most of the features and content of the Media Center Edition interface into the living room, and can be operated independently of other activities on the networked PC.

Wireless One of any communications links that doesn't use wiring as a transmission medium. Examples are Wi-Fi networking and Bluetooth.

Wireless frequency Cordless phones transmit their signals between the base and handset wirelessly in the 900-MHz, 2.4-GHz, and/or 5.8-GHz frequency bands using analog, digital, or digital spread spectrum (DSS) technology.

Wizard A computer program that takes you one step at a time through a complex process, such as setting up a home network, asking simple questions to set up configuration options.

Word processor A software application, such as Corel WordPerfect or Microsoft Word, that is designed to accept and process normal text (words) as data. Word processors range from simple programs that are little more than screen typewriters to those with complex screen handling, editing, and assistance features. Also

refers to a stand-alone machine dedicated to word processing.

Workgroup A named group of computers connected as a peer-to-peer network.

World Wide Web (WWW or W3) A global, multimedia portion of the Internet featuring text, audio, graphics, and moving image files. The Web is the most popular part of the Internet and is accessed using a program called a browser.

Worm A type of malicious computer program that, once released into a computer, is designed to repeatedly and rapidly reproduce itself without the user's knowledge or consent. One effect is that the system may soon have all available disk, memory, and other resources gobbled up, leading to a system crash. Worms can also spread to other connected systems over a network.

WPA Wireless Protected Access. An improved content-scrambling system for wireless networks that requires each client PC to use a password "key" to access the network. WPA improves on the earlier WEP in that scrambled transmissions do not contain information that can be used by a determined hacker to discover the key.

Write-protected Cannot be written to or changed.

XYZ

X, as in 24X Denotes the rate at which a CD- or DVD drive reads or writes data, in multiples of the speed of the earliest models of that type of drive. For a CD-ROM, 1X is 150 kilobytes per second. For a DVD-ROM, 1X is about the speed of an 8X CD-ROM.

xD-Picture Card Ultra-compact memory media, (20mm x 25mm x 1.7mm in size), developed jointly by Fuji Photo Film and Olympus Optical.

XDS Extended Data Services. Some broadcast signals include additional information about TV programs, such as the channel label, program title, program length, and elapsed time, but the service is not available everywhere. This feature lets the TV display this information when it is transmitted.

XGA IBM's eXtended Graphics Array, a high-resolution, 1024x768-pixel color graphics mode that is very similar to SVGA.

XML Extensible markup language, a "superset" of HTML that allows Web page designers to incorporate new, interactive objects into their pages.

Zip drive A removable-disk drive whose cartridges can hold 100, 250, or 750 MB each.

GLOSSARY

REFERENCE INDEX

Expert • Independent • Nonprofit